Undercover Lives

ACKNOWLEDGEMENTS

I would like to dedicate this book to my parents, Jean and Geoffrey Womack. I would also like to thank my agent Andrew Nurnberg as well as Jill Fairley, Tore Persson, Caroline Brown, Costya Gagarin, the Brazilian Embassy in Moscow and my colleagues at the *Independent*, especially Andrew Marshall.

CONTENTS

ILLUSTRATIONS

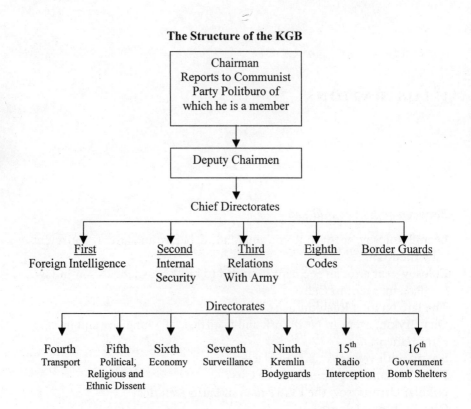

The Structure of the KGB

Chairman
Reports to Communist
Party Politburo of
which he is a member

↓

Deputy Chairmen

↓

Chief Directorates

First	Second	Third	Eighth	Border Guards
Foreign Intelligence	Internal Security	Relations With Army	Codes	

Directorates

Fourth	Fifth	Sixth	Seventh	Ninth	15th	16th
Transport	Political, Religious and Ethnic Dissent	Economy	Surveillance	Kremlin Bodyguards	Radio Interception	Government Bomb Shelters

Departments of the First Chief Directorate

1   The United States and Canada
2   Latin America
3   Britain, Australia, New Zealand and Scandinavia
4   East Germany, West Germany and Austria
5   Benelux countries, France, Spain, Portugal, Switzerland, Greece, Italy, Yugoslavia, Albania and Romania
6   China, Vietnam, Laos, Cambodia and North Korea
7   Thailand, Indonesia, Japan, Malaysia, Singapore and the Philippines
8   Non-Arab countries of the Middle East, Afghanistan, Iran, Israel, Turkey
9   Anglophone Africa
10 Francophone Africa
11 Socialist countries
15 Registry and archives
16 Electronic interception and operations against Western coding systems
17 India, Sri Lanka, Pakistan, Nepal, Bangladesh and Burma
18 Arab countries of the Middle East including Egypt
19 Contacts with Russian emigres abroad
20 Work with developing countries

Directorates were called 'main' if they were large enough to merit their own sub-departments. The numbering of the directorates and departments jumped. Perhaps this was to confuse the enemy but more likely reflected the chaotic development of the organisation, said Vasily Timofeyev, author of the Bangkok and Delhi chapters.

INTRODUCTION

This book was first published in Russian in 1996 under the title *The KGB's Travel Guide to the Cities of the World*. Twelve retired Soviet foreign intelligence officers offered their impressions of cities they had spied in for Russian readers who had had limited opportunities to travel. *Undercover Lives: The KGB Abroad*, based only loosely on the original, is the fruit of my interviews with the agents. Rather than travel tips, I tried to draw from them details of their operations around the globe.

The new freedom in Russia made it possible for the agents to come out into the open and write their memories. Indeed, it is ironical that in the heady days after the collapse of Communism, they were probably more at liberty to reminisce than their counterparts in the CIA and MI5, who fought in the secret war on the side of the 'free world'. Present-day Russian intelligence chiefs did not censor their book because they trusted the retired agents to censor themselves.

Of course, the officers do not reveal any state secrets. Rather, they convey a picture of the lifestyle of Soviet spies, posted to exotic locations beyond the wildest dreams of ordinary Russians, yet doing a job that was by no means always romantic. The details of their day-to-day existence make their stories ring true. Nevertheless, like a packet of cigarettes, this book comes with a health warning. Take everything you read here with a pinch of salt, for the KGB were masters of disinformation.

Most Russians and people in the West remember the KGB as a vast, repressive machine. In Stalin's time, when it was called the NKVD, it was responsible for murdering millions of people and, until as recently as the 1980s, the KGB continued to control what Russians could read and view, prevent them from travelling abroad and punish the few brave dissidents who dared to protest.

Contributors to this book say they had nothing to do with the tyranny inside the Soviet Union; indeed, some condemn the activities of their colleagues at home. Certainly a distinction should be made between the KGB's First Main Directorate, which was the foreign intelligence service, and the other directorates which constrained the Soviet population on behalf of the ruling Communist Party. However, until 1991 when, in the aftermath of the coup attempt against Mikhail Gorbachev the foreign intelligence service was split from the body responsible for internal security and both were made answerable to parliament, political policing and intelligence gathering were conducted by one and the same organisation.

The authors of this book lived in a totalitarian era that is hard for today's young people to imagine. From patriotic and idealistic motives, they served their country in the chilliest days of the Cold War when the Soviet Union, which had still not recovered from the trauma of the Second World War, retained a fortress mentality towards the rest of the world.

Under cover as diplomats, journalists or translators, they went out to combat the 'main adversary', which by the 1950s was no longer Germany but the United States, in all corners of the world. In each foreign country, the KGB had a *rezident* or station chief, usually based at the Soviet embassy, to whom the agents reported.

Western Europe, the US, Asia, Latin America and the Middle East are covered in this book, but that does not mean the KGB neglected the rest of the globe. In Africa, Soviet intelligence worked to undermine US influence and support revolutionary regimes. The KGB also spied in China, Australia, New Zealand and Canada as well as Warsaw Pact states that were supposed to be 'brotherly countries'. In short, the KGB was everywhere, always on the lookout for secrets and potential recruits.

Helen Womack
Moscow, 1998

ROME

Name	Kolosov, Leonid Sergeyevich
Born	25 August 1926
Education	Higher, Masters degree in economics
Special Subject	Foreign Trade
Languages	Italian, French, some Serbian
Military Rank	Lieutenant-Colonel
Worked in	Italy, Spain, France
Marital Status	Married
Sports	Karate
Hobbies	Collecting old locks
Favourite Tipple	'Moskovskaya' vodka
Brand of Cigarettes	Camel

Back to School

My passion for Italy led me into the arms of the KGB. I loved that country so much that when a recruiting officer named Akulov, meaning 'shark', offered to send me back there, I found I could not say no.

From 1953 to 1958 I had worked as an economist at the Soviet trade mission in Rome. During the Cold War, people in the West assumed that any Russian posted abroad must be a KGB agent. But it was not so. I can look you straight in the eye and say that then I was really just an economist.

Those were wonderful years. As a young graduate of Moscow's Institute of Foreign Trade, I fell in love with the Eternal City. I loved the light-hearted Italians, their food, their music. I felt at home there. I was a Latin in my Slav soul.

So when I had to leave, I made sure I threw more than one coin in the Trevi Fountain. 'Arrivederci Roma, goodbye, au revoir ...' I added the Russian words 'do svidania' (until we meet again) to the old song because I could not bear to say 'proshai' (farewell).

Back in Moscow, I went to work at the Ministry of Foreign Trade under Nikolai Patolichev and resigned myself to helping run our trade with Western countries. One summer day, I was called urgently into the office of Sasha Tutushkin, the secretary of the Communist Party cell at the ministry. Sitting with him was a short man with a flat, featureless face which I have great difficulty in visualising now. But I remember his name. It was Akulov. Sasha coughed and said: 'Well, I'll leave you two together then...'

Comrade Akulov motioned me to a seat opposite him, where the light shone directly in my eyes, and began to go over my biography. I was the true son of proletarians (my father Sergei Grigorievich had been an accounts clerk in a factory; my mother Elizaveta Stanislavovna had sewn costumes for the Bolshoi Theatre); I was an active member of the Communist Party and I was a high-flyer in my field of economics. But most positive of all, he said, was the fact that there had not been a single drop of Jewish blood in our family for at least three generations. How would I like to work for the KGB?

I should explain that the Lubyanka, the KGB headquarters, was at that time very short of staff. After Stalin's death in 1953, his henchman Lavrenty Beria had been shot as a British spy. Nikita Khrushchev was unable to trust anyone who had been associated with Beria and so there had been a full-scale clean-out at the KGB. New officers were needed and someone like myself, young but already with some experience and knowledge of foreign languages, was seen as ideal material.

That I was an ethnic Russian, with only a little Polish blood on my mother's side, was also a plus. It was not that the KGB was anti-Semitic exactly. They did employ some Jews for technical work, but they almost never sent them abroad. Nationals from other parts of the Soviet Union, such as the Baltic and Caucasian republics, were treated with the same suspicion. Despite the policy of internationalism, Moscow felt it could rely best on Russians.

Since I fitted the bill, Akulov was offering to send me back to Rome as the number two at the trade mission, but this time my work as an economist would be a cover for my espionage activities.

'Can I have a few days to think about it?' I asked.

'What is there to think about?' he said. 'Patolichev has already signed the papers transferring you to us. Do you have any doubts?'

'No, but...'

Actually, I did have a few doubts. None of my relatives had ever suffered during Stalin's purges and the Communist system had given me a good education, enabling me, a working-class boy, to come from Aktyubinsk in Kazakhstan, where my family was evacuated during the

Second World War, to Moscow to study at the Trade Institute. So I did not think of the KGB as an evil organisation. Rather, having seen state capitalism at work in postwar Italy, I questioned whether Marxism could ever lead us to Utopia. I was writing a dissertation for my old professor at the Institute and had become something of an economic dissident, in favour of a gradual transition to private ownership.

However, my love of Italy proved stronger than that little 'but'. My Estonian wife Eva, who had studied economics with me, also encouraged me. 'If the KGB means a good career, why are you hesitating?' she asked. And so I agreed to join the KGB, which meant I had to go back to school for a special one-year training course. In those days the KGB college was out in the woods at a place called Balashikha in the Moscow region. It has long since been closed down, but I remember it vividly. The complex was surrounded by a high wooden fence on which youths from the village had scrawled in chalk: 'School for Spies'. So our secret was out, at least locally.

We studied in a four-storey brick building and lived in dachas or cottages. We slept three to a room but not in military conditions. We had clubs and drinking parties like at university. One of my room mates was Oleg Lyalin, who years later was to ruin my career through his treachery but then he just seemed to be one of the lads. We were all given a pseudonym when we started school. Mine was Leskov, created from the letters of my real name, Leonid Sergeyevich Kolosov. The instructors had wanted to call me Lesko but thought better of it because it sounded like Madame Lescault, the French literary heroine.

The first lecture was an introduction to the 'family' in which we were told that the nearest person to us was not mother or father but the General Secretary of the Communist Party. I did not admire Khrushchev. He was a *muzhik* (coarse man) rather like Boris Yeltsin. I had to keep my thoughts to myself in class, but many of my fellow students agreed with me, as they were all educated and intelligent men. After lessons we used to tell political jokes among ourselves, for gone were the worst days of Stalin's terror when people were afraid of being sent to a labour camp if they laughed.

We studied a range of academic subjects taught by university professors who were paid a fee for helping the KGB. When we were asked to choose a foreign language, I opted for Italian because I had already studied French at the Trade Institute. Actually, I knew Italian too because in Rome I had had private lessons with an elderly lady called Signorina Piergolini. I should have chosen a completely new language, such as English, which would have been very useful, but I was lazy. As it turned out, my Italian was better than the lecturer's and I ended up teaching the KGB teacher.

As well as languages, we studied Marxism-Leninism but in a more
thought-provoking way than students in civilian schools and colleges.
We were given access to writers critical of the Communist saints such
as Leon Trotsky and the economist Georgy Plekhanov, whose works
were unavailable in ordinary libraries. In our History of Philosophy
course, we read Hegel and Adam Smith and learned about the beliefs of
religious denominations which were suppressed in the Soviet Union,
such as the Uniates (sic) or Ukrainain Catholics who worshipped according to Orthodox rites but owed political allegiance to the Pope in Rome.
The point of these lessons was to make us more sophisticated than the
average Soviet citizen, so that we could hold our own in the debates and
discussions we would inevitably have with our ideological foes abroad.

We also had a course in Comparative Intelligence, in which we studied
the history and techniques of foreign secret services. In the Cold War
years, the CIA was the *glavny protivnik*, or main enemy, but we were
taught to be cautious of the Japanese and the British too, because they
made the most subtle spies. Perhaps there was some truth in our stereo-
types of the different nationalities – the inscrutable Asians, the reserved
and hypocritical Brits.

In Psychology, we read Freud, who was an officially banned author,
and learned how to spot and use people's weaknesses and vices. Hurt
pride could be played on with great success, we were taught, as could a
person's sexuality. Homosexuality was punishable by imprisonment in
the Soviet Union, but what was 'bad' at home was 'good' abroad because
gays were regarded as excellent targets for entrapment. Later, when I was
in the field, I found that blackmail was in fact one of the worst methods
of recruiting because it produced agents motivated by nothing more than
fear of exposure. In espionage, as in most other professions, experience
is worth more than all the hours spent in the classroom.

However, we did have some very good practical training, including
courses in photography and the handling of microfilm, shooting, karate,
car maintenance and fast driving. We even learned parachute jumping,
although James Bond would be amused to know that, since no planes
were available for this activity, we were bussed into Moscow to leap from
towers in Gorky Park. On other occasions, we would travel to the capital
to practise chatting up contacts in cafés and losing counter-intelligence
agents following us on the busy streets. I instinctively knew if I was
being tailed and got good marks for an exercise in which I dodged an
elegant young woman with a blonde bun but tell-tale flat shoes who
chased me from metro to trolley-bus; from trolley-bus to taxi.

Katya, as this trainer was called, was one of a cast of colourful characters who, along with the university professors, were drafted in by the

KGB to teach us the tricks of the trade. One unforgettable member of this group was the ex-convict who had been released from a labour camp to show us how to crack safes. There was also an old aristocrat called Konstantin Alexandrovich, who taught us etiquette and card games, for we working-class lads who barely knew how to hold a knife and fork would have to move in the most elegant circles of Western society. The aristocrat frowned on another class we had in drinking an opponent under the table. The recipe for success was seventy grams of olive oil and an aspirin to line the stomach before starting on the alcohol. If you took another aspirin or an Alka Seltzer afterwards, you would feel fine, while your drinking partner would be in the perfect state to compromise himself.

At the end of the year the KGB bosses offered me the opportunity to become an 'illegal agent', in other words a spy living without diplomatic or journalistic cover under a false identity in a foreign country. The famous, or infamous, Gordon Lonsdale, who was really a Ukrainian called Konon Molody, was one such agent. Using Canadian documents, he lived underground in Britain and revealed to Moscow important secrets about the Underwater Warfare Establishment at Portland. Convicted of spying in 1961, he was swapped at the Berlin border in 1964 for Greville Wynne, the British businessman jailed in the Soviet Union for his contacts with Oleg Penkovsky, whom we regarded as one of our worst traitors and punished with the death penalty.

My Italian was not quite good enough to enable me to pass as an Italian in Italy but I could look convincing as an Italian businessman in, say, Latin America. If I wanted to be like Molody, all I had to do, the KGB said, was let them stage a funeral using the body of someone mangled beyond recognition in a road accident so that my family would believe I was really dead. Then I would be free to start my new life. Keen as I was to serve my country, I balked at this and said I would be happy with the trade mission cover which Akulov had first proposed. I did not lack a spirit of adventure, but you have to be a real addict for danger and excitement to become an 'illegal'.

And so I took my KGB exams, which I passed with flying colours, and started work. But I had to wait a little longer before seeing my beloved Italy again. To begin with, I was sent to push papers for the European Department in a tiny office down one of the long, long corridors of the Lubyanka.

The World's Oldest Professions

The year was 1961. I felt as if I were in prison as I sat in the tenth-floor room, a wood-panelled box identical to dozens of others down the green-carpeted corridor. My job was to analyse agents' reports from Italy which, if they were important enough, would go via the then head of the KGB, Vladimir Semichastny, to the Communist Party Central Committee and the Politburo. My companion in the office was an expert on Belgium. We did not talk much but kept our heads down over our own work, following the principle 'the less you know, the longer you will survive'. Every piece of paper, even the toilet paper it seemed, was top secret and God help you if you lost a document in the atmosphere of fanatical efficiency which prevailed.

All day I longed for the canteen. Although the bosses had a better one, ours was not bad, offering soup, crab meat, bottled fruit, ice cream and coffee, but sadly no vodka. I could afford to eat plenty because my salary had doubled since I left the Ministry of Foreign Trade and I was earning 300 roubles a month. The artificially set exchange rate in those days was eighty kopecks to one US dollar, but it is probably more meaningful to say that my income was twice the average industrial wage.

While I worked at the Lyubanka, I continued to write my economics dissertation, which included reformist ideas. 'If you don't take out the heresy, you'll end up finishing it in a labour camp', warned Nikolai Lyubimov, my kindly professor. So I made it conform, more or less, to the acceptable thinking. On the basis of the dissertation, I then wrote three newspaper articles, one for *Pravda*, one for *Izvestia* and one for the *Journal of Foreign Trade*. I was immediately called in by my KGB boss, Konstantin Petrovich, who began every conversation with the words: 'My dear boy...'

'My dear boy,' he said. 'It turns out that you are not only a talented economist and linguist but also a journalist. Instead of sending you back to the trade mission in Rome, why don't we make you the correspondent for *Izvestia*? Alexei Ivanovich is my good friend. I'm sure he can fix it.' He meant Alexei Ivanovich Adzhubei, the chief editor of *Izvestia*, whose career had not been harmed, I am sure, by the fact that he also happened to be Khrushchev's son-in-law.

The KGB liked to give its agents a journalistic cover because correspondents have such wide access. Unlike diplomats, they can go anywhere from slums to palaces and meet people from all walks of life. But it is a rare journalist who has that added ability so essential for a spy – the capacity to keep secrets. And it is an even rarer spy who can write with enough style to avoid being unmasked and expelled from his host country. You may find this hard to believe, but the majority of Soviet correspondents working abroad really were nothing more than journalists, albeit politically slanted in their craft. In my day, there was only a handful of correspondents around the world who worked for the KGB, most of our agents having diplomatic or commercial cover.

The question was: would I be good enough to satisfy *Izvestia*?

'We read your article,' said Adzhubei, who sported a red shirt and dark glasses to the office. 'Dreadful boring rubbish. When you go to Rome for us, you will have to come up with something a lot more exiting.' The thrill of hearing him say 'when' and not 'if' took the sting out of his criticism. 'Prostitutes,' continued Adzhubei. 'Why don't you write your first article about the prostitutes of Rome? Interview some of the girls. Pay them if necessary. We'll cover your expenses. But only for interviews, mind. Don't even think about the other thing.'

I had got the job. Many bona fide journalists on *Izvestia* were upset because Rome was a plum posting which the KGB had snatched from them.

At the outset, it was important to make Sifar, the Italian counter-intelligence service, believe I was a true correspondent and so for the first three months the KGB excused me all espionage work, freeing me to do straight journalism. In my first article, I described the changes I saw in Italy since I was last there in the 1950s. Then the country was still recovering from the war and it was not uncommon to see poor people walking the streets with sharpened sticks with which they picked up cigarette butts. But by the 1960s Italy was becoming more prosperous. Next I started on the feature Adzhubei wanted about the prostitutes. That may seem a banal subject now but at the time it was a hot topic, as prostitution was officially illegal in Italy and the Soviet Union stuck to the myth that socialist societies had 'no' call girls.

I knew where to find them. As a young economist at the trade mission, I had seen prostitutes around the Coliseum which I had visited, I hasten to add, not because I was looking for sex but because from childhood I had been interested in Spartacus, the gladiator who led an uprising of slaves against the Emperor Nero. Prostitutes were also to be found on the 'Alley of Love', the avenue running down from the more modern Stadio Olympico, built by that great lover of sports and women, Benito Mussolini.

They stood as if they were taking part in a fashion show, girls from all over the world, not only Italian beauties but exotic temptresses from Asia and Africa. I cruised around in the grey Alfa Romeo Giulietta, which *Izvestia* had just bought for me, until after midnight when the police became less active. Then I invited a young woman to sit in the car, paid her the going rate and asked her the story of her life.

Marisa, as she was called, told me a touching tale of how poverty had driven her to prostitution. I scribbled it down with enthusiasm, then snapped my notebook shut and said: 'Where shall I drop you?' 'What?' she said in an offended tone. 'What about our night of love?' 'I have to file to my newspaper,' I said hastily. 'I'll come back for you tomorrow.'

Of course I did not. I was terrified at that time about being followed by Sifar, the Italian counter-intelligence service, and feared a public scandal if they caught me frequenting the red light district. But later I relaxed and did enjoy a little private entertainment on the Alley of Love, about which I saw no reason to inform my bosses at the KGB.

My report on the prostitutes appeared in *Nedelya*, *Izvestia*'s weekend section, causing a sensation among Soviet readers and firmly establishing me in the eyes of the Italians as a real, hard-hitting journalist. I never recruited a prostitute or used one to compromise other people, but you could say the call-girls unwittingly helped the KGB in the sense that they made my press cover look convincing.

I was now able to begin the other work that had brought me to Rome. I still spent every morning news-gathering for *Izvestia* but devoted the rest of the day to the KGB. Of course quite often, when I conducted interviews or attended press conferences, I had the interests of both my masters in mind and my journalism and espionage work overlapped.

I got up regularly at six a.m. and bought all the newspapers at my local kiosk. At nine o'clock *Izvestia* would call me and I would dictate a story about government corruption, industrial unrest or the latest Mafia killing. Not all the news I sent was bad. Adzhubei did not want a wholly black picture of life in the West and I also reported happy events, such as the latest première at Milan's La Scala opera house or the release of a new Claudia Cardinale film. In my first year I produced a respectable 350 articles for the newspaper. And when I left Rome, I received the prestigious Golden Mercury press award from the Italians themselves, who appreciated my broad and fair coverage of their country. So you see I was a model correspondent.

Only after I had fed *Izvestia* did I begin, later in the morning, to meet my agents. I had about fifteen regular informers whom I had inherited from my KGB predecessor and I would see from one to three of them each day. They included Italian politicians, businessmen, cultural figures and two journalists, one from the neo-Fascist newspaper *Tempo* and one from the establishment paper *Il Messagero*. Some of them worked purely for money, but some were sympathetic to the Soviet Union because they were of a generation to have taken part in the anti-Fascist resistance during the Second World War.

I met them in cafés or on the street and noted whatever information they had to tell me. Then I walked around for a bit before going back to the *Izvestia* flat and office on Via Lago di Lesina in order to throw off anyone who might be following me. Walking is an important part of a secret agent's work, which is why we write good travel guides in our retirement. I tried to avoid going too often to the Soviet embassy, where my *rezident*, or boss, was based, because this could arouse the suspicions of Sifar. Instead, I waited for the concierge in my building to tell me a telegram had arrived from *Izvestia*, which was a code to say that the *rezident* was ready to see me. He was, by the way, that same Konstantin Petrovich who had been my boss in Moscow. 'My dear boy ...' he would say as I entered his special secure room, cleaned of bugs, to report the latest information for transmission by telegram to Moscow Centre.

In the evenings I would attend social gatherings, for it was important to mix with the widest possible variety of Italians and foreigners stationed in Rome. I was a member of the prestigious Association of Foreign Correspondents. Membership cost $5,000 a year, a huge sum in those days, but *Izvestia* paid up cheerfully because the contacts there were so useful.

Altogether, I lived very well, far better than the average citizen back in the USSR. I had a spacious apartment, which I shared with Eva and our two daughters, Olga and Irina. It was common practice in the Soviet expatriate community for wives to work as secretaries to their husbands and Eva performed that function for me. It gave her employment and I knew I could trust her. We had an Italian maid whom we believed to be trustworthy, but we turned down the services of a driver because we suspected he was reporting to Sifar.

My combined salaries from *Izvestia* and the KGB came to over $1,000 per month and I also had a generous expense account. The *rezident*, or station chief, even paid my traffic fines when I jumped red lights to throw off cars following me. Some KGB agents complained that they were kept on shoe-string budgets, but they tended to work in the Third World. The Lubyanka was not mean when it came to funding my operations because Italy was regarded as a key country, not as important as America, Britain or France of course, but nevertheless in the top league.

After the war, Italy had benefited from the Marshall Plan and become a member of the new Nato alliance. But it also had a powerful Communist Party, which gave the Soviet Union hope that it could wield considerable influence here. A large part of my job involved monitoring Italy's fiend-ishly complicated internal politics. Whilst I was in Rome, I saw three presidents come and go, but that was nothing compared with the mind-boggling total of thirty governments which had tried to run Italy since the end of the war. As well as struggling to keep abreast of all the party in-fighting, I also followed Italy's relations with the US, the state of the Italian economy and the activities of the Mafia, the neo-Fascists and the left-wing terrorist Red Brigades.

I had my hands full, but Konstantin Petrovich trusted me and gave me more or less *carte blanche* to work as I saw fit. After the frustration of the classroom and the boredom of being desk-bound, it was exhilarating to be operational at last.

The Deal of the Century

One of my first tasks on arrival in Rome was to reactivate 'Fritz', a potentially valuable informer who for some reason had started missing his appointments. Not only was he a rich businessman with his own company, but he also sat in the Italian parliament for the Socialist Party, which was in opposition to the Christian Democratic government of the day. The *rezident* asked me to visit him to find out what the matter was.

Fritz greeted me without ceremony. He was sitting in his kitchen wearing only his vest and trousers rolled up to his knees, soaking his feet in a bowl of hot water. I knew the problem was that we had not stroked and rewarded him well enough, for informers are like women – they need constant, flattering attention. But I adopted a harsh tone because I wanted to frighten him just a little. 'You realise you have already compromised yourself,' I said. 'There is no way back. If you get caught, it will mean big trouble for you and me. So let us work out a regular routine for our meetings.' He was rattled and quickly fell into line. 'I worked badly because I was badly handled,' he said by way of excuse. 'I will look after you better,' I promised.

We agreed that once a week he would come to a prearranged place, say the Olympic Stadium, in his Mercedes Benz, and wait for me, having first of course checked his mirror to see that no one was following him. If there was a problem, then two days later he would turn up at a second place, the Coliseum for example. If it was still not possible for us to meet, then he would ring me, saying he was from the vacuum cleaner servicing company or some such nonsense, letting me know the time when I could come to pick up my 'hoover'.

For emergencies, I told him we would use another system. An old Roman column stood outside his house. If I needed him urgently, I would chalk a cross on it and he should then find a way of meeting me as soon as possible. After this pep talk, I gave him his homework. For our next rendezvous, I said, I wanted a full written report on all the splits and intrigues in his Socialist Party. Fritz looked pale but nodded obediently. Having used the stick, I then offered him a carrot. He could let me have the report when he came to dinner with me at Biblioteka, an expensive restaurant on the Piazza Navona.

My conversation with Fritz produced an immediate improvement in his performance. He came to the restaurant with a thorough report, for which the KGB paid him $500, a generous sum intended as an incentive. And then he decided to teach me a lesson. Being a meat-eating Slav, I had ordered what I thought was a luxurious dinner – turtle soup, Florentine steaks done rare and strawberries with whipped cream. But he said somewhat haughtily: 'My young friend, do you know why the Italians have such a low incidence of heart disease? It is because they prefer seafood.' And then he ordered – oysters with lemon, salmon with black caviar, fish soup, baked fish, pineapple with ice-cream and coffee.

Fish was twice as expensive as meat in Rome and the bill was astronomical. Konstantin Petrovich lost his normally even temper. 'You have a generous budget but it does not run to oysters,' he fumed. 'The next meal with Fritz comes out of your own pocket.' However, the KGB was to get its money's worth from Fritz, for he played a crucial role in helping us to clinch the Deal of the Century, the agreement between Italy and the Soviet Union whereby Fiat helped us to build a giant car factory on the River Volga at a place we called Togliatti after the Italian Communist Party leader, Palmiro Togliatti.

I had the honour of meeting that great man twice. The first time was at a reception in 1962. The *Pravda* correspondent introduced me to him and, very much in awe, I clicked my heels and used the polite form of address in Italian to ask after his health – Com'e sta? But Togliatti, who was a modest man, immediately put me at my ease. 'Comrade Kolosov,' he replied in broken Russian. 'We Communists use "ty" to each other. "Vy" is for waiters and class enemies.'

The next time I saw Togliatti, the atmosphere was altogether more serious as we were together in the presence of Mikhail Suslov, the chief ideologist of the Soviet Communist Party. Suslov, who was like an *eminence grise* to Khrushchev and later Brezhnev, had a reputation for incorruptibility but he did not have much human warmth. In 1963 he came to Rome for a meeting with the Italian comrades, who were split into Euro-Communist and Maoist factions. I managed to get into the meeting, which was held at the Italian party Central Committee headquarters on Via Botteghe Oscure, and sat quietly listening like a fly on the wall. Togliatti was representing the mainstream of the Italian party.

Mario Alicata, a moderate who edited the Communist newspaper *Unita*, was also present. I could hardly believe my ears, but they were discussing whether Italy was ripe for a Communist revolution.

The leftists, led by Enrico Berlinguer, advocated an attempt to seize power in Italy by force. Berlinguer was not actually at the meeting. I suspect Togliatti had not invited him. Suslov was sounding out the rest of the party to see if they would support an armed uprising. Moscow, of course, would have been delighted to see Italy spinning out of the West's orbit. The Soviet Union would provide assistance if Italy really were ready for revolution, Suslov said. But Togliatti declined the offer. The Americans had military bases in Italy, he pointed out. Any uprising would only lead to bloodshed and the Communist Party would end up being banned. It was better for the Italian Communists to take an evolutionary rather than revolutionary path and win power through the ballot box.

Suslov was disappointed, but took Togliatti's advice. I read the coded message which the Kremlin ideologue sent home. 'The talks showed Italy is not ready for decisive action. Comrade Togliatti takes a soft position on the main question,' he wrote. I felt enormous respect for Togliatti. How much better it would be for both the Soviet Union and Italy, I thought privately, if instead of trying to overthrow the system we developed our economic cooperation. And that is what happened.

The idea of building an auto-plant which would provide cheap cars for the Soviet masses came from Alexei Kosygin, our very wise Prime Minister. We had the Zil factory, which produced limousines, and Moskvitch which made a small number of economy cars, but in order to meet growing demand we needed the conveyor belt technology of Western vehicle manufacturers. Germany, France and Britain traded with us on tough conditions, but Italy, which was going through a period of economic crisis and needed new orders to keep its workers in employment, was friendlier. It had two main car factories, Alfa Romeo which belonged to the state, and Fiat which, despite the fact that it was privately owned, was the Soviet government's partner of choice.

In the spring of 1966, together with a famous Soviet journalist called Marietta Shaginyan, I went to make a detailed study of Fiat. Marietta, an Armenian bluestocking with a thick moustache, was a committed Marxist but even she was forced to admit that the Italians provided wonderful conditions for their workers, paying them good wages and pensions, sending the most promising of them to Cambridge for further education and laying on free crèche facilities for their children. 'Can this be capitalism?' she asked, amazed.

Vittorio Valetta, the General Director of Fiat, softened my colleague up even further over a delicious dinner. Marietta had been determined to hate this 'exploiter' who, during the war, had betrayed his country by allowing his factory to be used to make tanks for Hitler. But, over the meal, they got on like a house on fire. They were speaking German, which I did not understand, so I fell asleep. I woke to hear Marietta sobbing and Signor Valetta comforting her. When we left, he presented her with a mink coat and brought on another flood of tears.

'What was all that about?' I asked her in the car afterwards. It turned out that Valetta had told her how he owed his life to a Communist. When the Italian partisans had taken Turin, he had been sentenced to be shot as a traitor. He was standing in a yard waiting for the bullet when Luigi Longo, a resistance leader and friend of Togliatti, intervened to stop the execution. 'It is madness to shoot him,' said Longo. 'Let him work for the good of Italy.' And so Valetta had gone on to build his fortune and, in gratitude to Longo, made contributions to Communist Party funds. 'Imagine that,' said Marietta, starting to wail again, 'a capitalist giving money to the Communists.'

After the visit, Marietta wrote three glowing articles about Fiat, which were published in *Izvestia*, causing me great embarrassment. A general strike had just started in Italy. When Valetta got copies of the articles, he gathered his workers together in Turin and said: 'You idiots, the Soviet press is saying that we have a great future and you are risking it by downing tools.' The Fiat workers immediately returned to their conveyor belts, thus breaking the national strike. The Italian Communist Party was now furious that a Soviet newspaper had made blacklegs out of the Fiat workforce. 'We respect *Izvestia* but why do they keep that idiot Kolosov in Italy?' Gian Carlo Payetta, the Italian chief ideologue, wrote in *Unita*. He did not realise that it was my colleague who had caused all the trouble.

The *Unita* article was a complaint I had to take seriously. *Izvestia*, a government newspaper, reflected the largely economic concerns of the Soviet Cabinet, which was interested in Fiat. But Suslov, the guardian of Communist ideology, was not going to be pleased if relations with the Italian comrades were spoilt. Now I must smooth things over as a matter of urgency, or I might as well pack my bags. I caught Payetta at the airport, about to fly off to Paris. He pretended not to see me. 'It wasn't me; it was that old bag who wrote the articles,' I said. 'You must do something or I will be recalled home from Italy.'

Payetta was mortified when he learned of his mistake. He tore a sheet of paper from my notebook and wrote an apology, saying the Italian Communist Party had no problem with me. I sent this to my editor, Lev Tolkunov, who in turn made sure that Suslov was reassured. The panic was over. And, after a while, the negotiations with Fiat resumed.

In July 1966 a sixteen-man delegation, headed by the Soviet minister for the car industry, Nikolai Tarasov, came out to Rome to discuss details of how Fiat could help us build the factory of our dreams on the River Volga. Valetta led the Italian team in ten days of tough talks, held at the Ministry of Industry, which I covered for *Izvestia*. The Soviet side asked for a credit. The Italians agreed and offered the average European interest rate of eight per cent. But Kosygin had made clear to our negotiators that Moscow could not afford to pay more than six per cent. The talks were deadlocked.

Tarasov called the Soviet team together at our embassy. 'What are we going to do?' he said. 'Kosygin won't budge. We have no room for manoeuvre.' 'What about your friend Fritz?' Konstantin Petrovich asked me. He knew that my informer, while being a member of the opposition, had good contacts in the Italian government. 'Leave it to me,' I said.

I went out that night and made a small chalk cross on the column outside Fritz's house. He responded quickly to my signal. I told him the negotiations with Fiat were going badly and there was a big risk the Soviet Union would conclude a deal with Renault of France instead, thus depriving Italy of a major contract. It was a lie, but he believed it. He asked me to give him a little time and promised to do what he could.

Three days later Fritz brought me a top-secret Italian government document which showed that Rome's bottom line was in fact an interest rate of six-and-a-half per cent. Tarasov cabled Moscow and Kosygin agreed to this figure. It made a huge difference to the Soviet Union, which saved about $40 million on the deal worth a total of $320 million. But the *rezident* said: 'Let them wait another day before we say "yes".' The next day Tarasov returned to the negotiating table, banged his fist on it and told the Italians: 'Six-and-a-half per cent or tomorrow we leave for Paris.' The Italians agreed instantly and that was how the Deal of the Century was concluded.

Togliatti died that same year. He had a heart attack while on holiday in Crimea and the Soviet doctors were unable to save him. So he never saw the little Fiat cars, which we called Zhigulis on the domestic market and Ladas when they went for export, rolling off the conveyor belt at the factory named after him.

Fritz did well out of the deal. The Lubyanka paid him $25,000 for his contribution.

As for myself, I was promoted from the rank of KGB captain to major for, as Moscow Centre put it in a telegram, 'capable handling of an agent which led to considerable benefit for the Soviet state'. As a further reward, I was also given a hand-made hunting rifle, one of a limited edition of

2,000 guns made by the famous Kalashnikov manufactur
Khrushchev to present to visiting dignitaries.

The following summer I went on home leave to Russia and
moose, two deer and six wild boar with the gun during a forest exp
I was with personal friends, not KGB colleagues, on this occasion because
I believed in separating work from pleasure. It was not always possible,
but I tried to do my hunting, courting and drinking independently of my
employers.

Double Standards

For this reason, I would not let the KGB have Baldo. He ran a little
restaurant called the Trattoria da Baldo near my office on Via Lago di
Lesina, where I often used to unwind after work. In contrast to Biblioteka,
it was a modest place with gingham tablecloths and Chianti bottles
hanging from the walls. While you waited, you watched Baldo cooking.
He served up cheap, hearty plates of spaghetti and white wine that came
from his father's farm just outside Rome. The *rezident* urged me to
recruit him but I did not want to complicate our happy relationship.

In gratitude for his hospitality, I used to bring Baldo vodka, which was
a bit exotic in Italy then. Once, after I had been drinking rather a lot, I
also made up a Russian recipe for spaghetti sauce, which I offered to my
host. You needed a suckling pig, Russians' favourite food for special
occasions such as Easter. This you cut up into small pieces and fried.
Then you added onion, garlic, tomatoes and green peas. You poured the
sauce over the spaghetti and sprinkled it with parmesan cheese and black
pepper in the usual way.

Baldo tried it out and was delighted. For some reason, he decided to
call it Spaghetti alla Hitarra (Guitar). It became the most expensive item
on his menu, although it was always free to me. Baldo flourished and
eventually opened a more luxurious restaurant near the Piazza Navona.
I didn't go there much and unfortunately do not remember what he called
his new place. If it is still there, it will be under new management for
Baldo, if he is alive, will be a very old man now. But if you ever come
across spaghetti sauce with suckling pig in Rome, you will know its
Russian origin.

As well as Baldo, my other great friend in Rome was Vladimir –
Volodya – Yermakov, the correspondent of *Pravda*. He was not a KGB
agent but a bona fide journalist. We used to drink together after work
and go on trips outside the capital, for example to the seaside resort of
Frigene. We were together in Genoa, covering the first Soviet trade fair

to break a little of the Cold War ice in Italy. Moscow fashions were a highlight of the exhibition and a team of Russian mannequins had flown out to model the dresses and fur coats. After the première, Volodya and I went backstage to interview the girls. One of them, called Lia, came up to me and said: 'Excuse me, Leonid Sergeyevich, but the leader of our group said it would be all right for me to give you this.' She handed me a parcel, which contained a bottle of vodka, a loaf of black bread and a note from the wife of one of my old friends in Moscow. 'Dear Lyonya,' it said, 'here is a little reminder of home with my best wishes. Please look after my friend Lia and show her Genoa if you can.'

Lia gave me an expectant look with her charming grey eyes. 'When are you free?' I asked. 'Tomorrow morning.' 'OK, I'll pick you up at the hotel at nine. Only are you sure you won't get into trouble for going off with a journalist?' 'Oh no, I'm well in with the group leader. There won't be a problem. Can I bring my friend Rina too?' I should explain here that on the rare occasions when ordinary Russians got out beyond the Iron Curtain, they were shepherded everywhere by minders who reported on their behaviour to the KGB. If they disgraced themselves, they were unlikely to get exit visas to travel again. The Lubyanka was most interested, of course, in any contacts they might have with foreigners, but Lia had felt it necessary to check with the group leader before she even approached me.

'What have you got in your hand?' said Volodya, joining me after he had finished his interviews. 'A loaf of black bread and a bottle of vodka. It's from a friend of a friend who wants to go out with me tomorrow. She's a grey-eyed beauty called Lia. She's got a friend called Rina who's not bad-looking either.' 'Take me with you, Leonardo,' pleaded Volodya. 'I'll lend you Mario. We can go to Portofino.' He meant Mario Moltoni, *Pravda*'s chauffeur, and he was suggesting an outing to a resort on the Ligurian coast for which the only word is divine. 'OK,' I said, 'only don't tell anyone.'

I knew that the Soviet delegation included a representative of the KGB's counter-intelligence service, who had a whole team of minders charged with watching the models. I can't remember his name now, but it was something typically Russian like Vasily Ivanovich. I assumed that he knew who the *Izvestia* correspondent really was. But if he didn't, well, I would be able to square it with him afterwards.

Early the next morning we set off in the silver Fiat-2300 with Mario at the wheel, me in the front passenger seat and Volodya in seventh heaven, squeezed between the two girls in the back. Local legend has it that after God finished making the world, he made Portofino for himself. But then it turned out that one tiny Italian tribe had nowhere to live so God, in his generosity, let them have his own home. It certainly is a stunning place, set against a backdrop of pine-covered hills, overlooking the glittering Mediterranean Sea. The number of yachts in the harbour should have alerted me to the fact that Portofino is also horrendously expensive.

We settled down in a restaurant on the waterfront. Volodya, showing off in front of the girls, ordered: spaghetti alla marinara, grilled prawns, lobster, spigola, which was the dearest fish on the menu, salad, pineapple in lemon sauce, strawberries and ice cream, vintage Verdicchio wine and Napoleon brandy. I felt slightly uneasy, but relaxed when the food came and we had a wonderful leisurely lunch.

At the end, the elegant waiter brought the bill on a silver tray. Volodya blanched. 'Um, Mario,' he coughed, 'you take the girls outside for some sea air and Lyonya and I will join you in a moment.' 'How much cash have you got on you?' he hissed as soon as they had left. 'Thirty thousand,' I said. 'I've got thirty as well. And you know how much the bill is? Seventy-five. What are we going to do?' I let him sweat for a minute, then saved him from doing the restaurant's washing-up by producing my cheque book. 'Thank the Almighty,' said Volodya, 'I'll pay you back when we get to Rome.'

The mixture of relief and wine made us merry in the car on the way home. This time Volodya and Rina were together in the back while Lia sat on my knee in the front. 'Only you ...' crooned a voice on the radio. Poor Mario did his best to keep his eye on the winding road out of Portofino.

Traffic jams had built up on the autostrada going into Genoa and the next fashion show had already started by the time we got back. We made feeble excuses about having been stuck in city traffic, but the organisers had to rearrange the running order of the show so that Lia and Rina could come on at the end.

Afterwards we sat up all night with the girls, talking and drinking in their hotel room. At dawn, when they finally retired to bed, Volodya and I went out to an early-morning street market and bought white roses, which we took back and laid at the feet of each sleeping girl. It was a gesture of gratitude for the flirtatious but essentially innocent time we had spent together. But again I felt uneasy.

Our little adventure had not gone unnoticed, of course. 'I know you went gadding off to Portofino,' Vasily Ivanovich said to me with a leer. And then he asked a favour. The man from counter-intelligence had come abroad with limited spending money and a long shopping list of presents to buy for his relatives back home in Moscow. Would I help him? Dutifully, I escorted him around the department stores in search of the cheapest souvenirs. When we came to number 36 on the list – his mother-in-law – his money had run out, so I gave him a few more lire to buy a gift for her too. He was effusive in his thanks. And as things turned out, it was the best day's shopping I ever did.

From Genoa, I travelled on to Venice to meet one of my neo-Fascist contacts and thought nothing more about our little adventure with Lia and Rina. But back in Moscow on home leave a few months later, I went into the Lubyanka to receive a surprisingly dry welcome from the head of the European Department. 'Leonid Sergeyevich, the party committee wants to see you at 11.15 tomorrow morning,' he said. 'What for?' I asked naively. 'You'll find out.'

There was a cell of the Communist Party in those days in every college, factory and ministry in the Soviet Union to oversee the ideological and moral guidance of the students or workers. Even the powerful KGB was no exception.

'What does the party want me for?' I asked Valya Kovanov, a colleague who used to work in Italy before his cover was blown and the bosses recalled him. Now he represented our department on the committee. 'I was going to ask you that,' he said. 'The agenda says: "Concerning the amoral behaviour of comrades Kolosov and Yermakov at the trade fair in Genoa." What did you do with the girls?' 'We just sat and talked,' I said. 'Sat or lay?' he laughed. 'You'd better tell the truth because they've got a huge file on you.'

The next morning I appeared before the kangaroo court. The committee secretary looked at me stonily. 'Leonid Sergeyevich, we are told that you are an excellent agent, a family man with a loyal wife and two lovely daughters. So what the hell do you think you were doing with those girls in Genoa?' I tried to lighten the atmosphere. 'Well, I prefer women to men . . .' But the joke sank like a lead balloon.

'Comrade Kolosov,' barked the secretary, 'no one is suggesting you are a homosexual. But womaniser would seem to be not far off the mark. The models talked to their friends. And we have our ears. We know that you went to Portofino, that you spent the night with the girls and that you gave them expensive presents. We also know that the *Pravda* correspondent egged you on . . .'

When I realised that dear old Volodya had tried to take all the blame himself, I interrupted: 'Comrades, you can think what you like about me but Vladimir Yermakov is innocent. It was I who invited him to meet the girls. And by the way, one of them was an old friend I used to know in Moscow.'

'Ah, so he was whoring in Moscow,' interjected a member of the committee. For moral guardians, these party people used some vulgar language. 'No, I was not,' I said, 'and neither did I misbehave in Genoa.

We were just being hospitable, showing the girls around and sitting with them in the hotel.'

'You can do it in a chair ...' said the same member to sniggers from the rest of the committee. 'That's enough,' said the secretary, 'this is a serious matter. So, Comrade, do you deny that you had sexual intercourse?' 'Absolutely.' 'Then why did you give the girls roses?' 'It was just a friendly gesture.'

'You see, Comrades,' said the secretary, 'how insincere Leonid Sergeyevich is? He can't just admit that he had a bit on the side. He insists on telling us about "friendly gestures". What are we going to do with him? There is a suggestion that we should give him a strict reprimand, enter it on his party card and ask the leadership to consider withdrawing him from Rome.'

Valya Kovanov stood up to defend me, saying that good agents were hard to come by and KGB operations would suffer if I were recalled. A reprimand would be sufficient, he said. The court retired to consider its verdict.

In the end, I escaped without even a black mark on my party card, which would have been a blot on my career. For this, I believe I have to thank not only Valya but Vasily Ivanovich. Remembering how I had saved him from the wrath of his mother-in-law, the counter-intelligence officer evidently put in a good word for me in my hour of need.

As soon as I was off the hook, I went away to relax with Eva and the girls at a KGB sanatorium at Kislovodsk in the northern Caucasus. Of course, I did not tell my wife what had happened. But Volodya and I often laughed about it afterwards. Indeed years later, just before he died of emphysema in Moscow at the tragically young age of fifty-three, he said to me: 'Hey Casanova, do you remember Lia and Rina?' The party committee had made sure that I would never forget them.

Considering the fuss that was made over those two girls, I was puzzled, to say the least, by the KGB's attitude to another woman who was not my wife, an American called Helen Smiles. I met her a few months after my grilling at the Lubyanka at a cocktail party laid on by our embassy in Rome to mark 7 November, the anniversary of the Bolshevik Revolution. She was with an older woman whom she introduced as Militsa Sergeyevna.

'You are the correspondent of *Izvestia*?' she said in fluent Russian with only a trace of an accent. 'Oh, how interesting. You journalists are progressive people, I know, so I'm not afraid to be seen talking to you, even though I am the daughter of a former Tsarist general and my aunt here is his sister. That does not embarrass you?' 'Not at all, mademoiselle,' I said. 'Madame,' she corrected, 'I'm a divorcee.' 'And what

brought you to Rome?' I asked pleasantly. 'An aeroplane,' she quipped.
'No, actually I am working at the US embassy. I'm the secretary to the
naval attaché.' My heart missed a beat.

'My dear boy,' said Konstantin Petrovich, the *rezident*, when I told
him of my new acquaintance. 'The Lord God Himself has forgiven you
all your sins. We'll check with Moscow Centre to make sure she's not a
plant. If she's not, then she's a treasure.' A few days later the bosses at
headquarters confirmed that Helen Smiles or 'Lada', as they code-named
her, was not on any list of known CIA agents. 'Develop the relationship,'
ordered the *rezident*. 'Spend as much money as necessary.'

My wife, who was a great asset to me when it came to entertaining,
and I began taking Helen and her aunt out – for trips to the theatre,
picnics in the country, then whole weekends outside Rome. 'I feel as if
we have a new family,' twittered the old lady. Once, Helen did ask me a
little suspiciously if I had any interest in her work. 'Good Lord, no,' I
said. 'I'm just a journalist, not a spy.' 'That's all right then,' she said,
'because I was starting to think your interest might be professional.'
'Helen, how could you? I'm interested in you as a woman, of course. I
find you very attractive.' Which was not entirely a lie, for she was a
striking brunette, although on the wrong side of forty.

'I think she's in love with you,' said Konstantin Petrovich when I next
reported to him. 'Right,' he said, adopting a decisive tone. 'Pack your
wife and the kids off to Moscow for the winter holidays and start an
affair with her. A woman of her age will be eager enough. As soon as
you've got her into bed, make sure she starts bringing the secret documents.'

I was flabbergasted. 'For an innocent flirtation with two models in
Genoa,' I said, 'I was hauled over the coals. And now I'm being ordered
to commit adultery. What if . . .' 'Don't worry,' said the boss, 'if there are
any problems with Eva, we'll have a talk with her and explain that the
interests of the Motherland come first. And really, my dear boy, it's
time you learnt to distinguish between f***ing around and operational
requirements.'

So you see, in its own peculiar way, the KGB also separated work from
pleasure.

I followed the boss's instructions and sent Eva home. I took Helen out
to a very expensive restaurant called Est, Est, Est. And I even went back
to her place for coffee. But the affair went no further because she suddenly
left for the United States. On the day of the flight she rang me, saying:
'Lyona, I'm sorry, but I have to go home urgently. My aunt is dying n
Washington.' I assumed the Americans had found out what was going on
and were pulling her back in the interests of national security and her

own safety. But I pretended to believe her story. 'I'm so sorry, my dear. I'll come and see you off.'

I took roses to the airport. There were tears in her eyes as she said goodbye. 'Forgive me,' I said. And at that moment I was absolutely sincere. There are times in an agent's life when he should be honest. Within reason, of course.

Dark Forces

Italy is a sunny country of gondolas and ice cream and grand opera and its people are known the world over for their gaiety and expressiveness. But dark forces also lurk there which, as a KGB agent, I not only encountered but actively sought out for it was my duty to be fully informed and warn Moscow of any tendencies which could threaten Soviet interests.

Shortly after arriving in Rome, therefore, I made contact with the neo-Fascists. I had an informer on matters concerning the extreme right, a young freelance journalist with Fascist sympathies called Sylvester. I met him at a reception at the American embassy. At first he was very hostile to me as a representative of the Soviet press. But after I told him that I did not especially love Marx and Lenin myself, he was happy to chat and accept my business card.

A few weeks later he turned up at my office, very upset because he had crashed his car and had no money to pay for the repairs. I opened one of the bottles of vodka I always kept ready in my freezer and tried to console him. 'How would you like to earn some money by writing an article for me about the MSI?' I asked, referring to the Movimento Sociale Italiano, as the neo-Facist Party was called. 'It won't be for publication, just to help me orient myself on the Italian political scene, because as you know I have not been here very long.' Sylvester agreed and a few days later brought me a very useful report, for which I gave him $500. 'You are so rich?' he asked, not yet suspecting who his real paymasters were.

I continued to court Sylvester. He was the neo-Fascist I went to meet in Venice after my ill-fated trip to Portofino. What I really wanted from him was an introduction to the leader of the MSI, Georgio Almirante. Eventually Sylvester managed to arrange an interview for me. It took place at the party headquarters in Rome. Two bodyguards met me and escorted me into the presence of Almirante, a thin, grey-haired man with a nervous twitch. He was dressed not in uniform or leather but a boring black suit, white shirt and dark tie like any other politician. Her offered me tea.

Almirante rejected the label 'Fascist' for his party, but proudly declared that he saw himself as the heir to Mussolini. 'Il Duce' had built the autostrade and wiped out unemployment, he said. Italy needed such order again. He could not see why the Soviet Union should object to that since it kept its own people under even tighter control. 'Hitler had concentration camps and so did Stalin,' he said. 'What was the difference?' He asked me why I was so interested in the MSI. 'I just want to understand the Italian political landscape for my paper,' I said.

The MSI was, at that time, improving its standing with each new election. At first only two or three per cent of the electorate had supported it but at the height of its popularity in the mid-1960s, it was polling seventeen or eighteen per cent of the vote. I briefed the Italian Communists after my meeting with Almirante as well as sending a report to Moscow in which I assessed the neo-Fascists as a threat to be taken seriously. They could, for example, be involved in a coup attempt.

Moscow Centre ordered me to do all I could to discredit them. The scathing article I wrote for *Izvestia*, headlined 'The Little Duce', was reprinted in *Unita* and therefore seen all over Italy. Afterwards I got an anonymous letter which read: 'You bastard, if you sully the honour of our party again, yours will not be the only life in danger.' I sent Eva and the children out of the country for a few months after that, but nothing happened. Eventually, the neo-Fascists started to decline in importance and were replaced by a new threat, the terrorist Red Brigades.

If you go far enough to the extreme right, you meet the extreme left coming the other way. Some of the neo-Fascists actually went over to the Red Brigades, ultra-leftists even more hardline than Enrico Berlinguer on the left of the Italian Communist Party. They were Maoists and, for a period in the 1970s, received funding from China, which of course the Soviet Union did not like. The Red Brigades were most notorious for kidnapping and murdering the former Italian Prime Minister, Aldo Moro, in 1978.

I had no success in penetrating them, although I knew their financial manager, Giuseppe Alessandrini, because years before he had been a small businessman and visited me at the Soviet trade mission. Once, when I was back at KGB headquarters, I got a tip-off that he had come on a visit to Moscow. I rang him at his hotel and arranged to meet him the next day. But he did not turn up. Later, I was told, he stole the Red Brigades' money and was found murdered in Shanghai.

That was the extent of my contact with the terrorists. The KGB did not itself engage in terrorism in Italy or use organisations such as the Red Brigades to commit violence on its behalf. Moral considerations aside, there was simply no point in doing so because we were able to wield far more influence by working through the Communist Party. But the Lubyanka is convinced that the CIA did hire terrorist killers, as a different operation suggested.

The Red Brigades were a passing phenomenon. Far more enduring as a dark force in Italy is the Sicilian Mafia, which still challenges the rule of law today. The KGB *rezident* was both eager for and fearful of contact with the godfathers.

I had a good friend in the Italian press corps called Felice Chilante. A talented writer, he was the author of several children's books as well as a regular contributor to *Paese Sera* and *Unita*. The activities of the Mafia were among the subjects he covered. One day in early 1964, he came to me in a terrible state. He had just received a visit from an old gentleman accompanied by two thugs.

'I am Nicola Gentile, the blood brother of Al Capone,' the old man had said to Felice. 'I want to publish my memoirs.' 'What's stopping you?' my friend had replied. 'Nothing stops me. But I cannot write myself. I have seen your articles on the Mafia. They are rubbish but you write with style. I want you for my ghost writer.' 'And what if I refuse?' 'I do not advise it.' With that, the three Mafiosi had left.

'What am I going to do?' asked Felice, nearly hysterical. 'Take me with you,' I said. 'Ring the Godfather and ask if he is prepared to receive a Soviet journalist as well. I will interview him for *Izvestia*.' 'I know nothing about this,' said Konstantin Petrovich, when I told him of my plans. 'If you get into trouble, on your own head be it. But if you get any information, *Izvestia* and the KGB will share it 50–50.' And so Felice and I flew down to Palermo together at Nicola Gentile's expense.

We were picked up at the airport by a white Mercedes Benz, which took us to a villa by the sea. Felice said the guards who opened the iron gates were the same gorillas who had come with the Godfather to his flat in Rome. We were treated like kings for three days. We went out on a fishing trip, catching tuna. The food, of course, was marvellous. And the bodyguards offered me a choice of girls – Italian, African or Chinese. 'No thanks,' I said, 'we Russians only sleep with our wives.' For I really could not afford to compromise myself in that already dangerous situation.

I was nervous when I began the interview. 'Commendatore,' I said, 'you know I cannot write well of you because I represent a government newspaper.' 'My son,' he replied, 'write as God dictates to you.' 'And you will not kill me afterwards?' Gentile laughed. In fact he was keen to give the interview because nothing was known about the Mafia in the Soviet Union and he welcomed any publicity, even if it was negative.

He told me the history of the Mafia, which dates back to the thirteenth century when the Sicilians were defending themselves against French invaders. Indeed the word Mafia is made up of the first letters of the words of the battle cry: 'Morte Ai Francesi, Invasori, Assassini'. He also showed me two ancient documents on yellowing parchment. He forbade me to photograph them, but I have a trained memory.

One was the Mafia's ten commandments of which two were: help each other in avenging insults to any member of the Brotherhood; and fairly share all legal and illegal gains. The other was the oath of loyalty made when an initiate cuts his right hand with a knife and burns a paper with a drawing of a crossbones on it in the flame of a candle. 'I swear to be loyal to the Brotherhood as the Brotherhood will be loyal to me. As this image turns to ash and mixes with the drops of my blood, so I will be obliged to give all my blood to the Brotherhood. As ash can never again become paper, so I can never leave the ranks of the Brotherhood.'

Then Gentile told me his own personal history. As a young man, he had emigrated to the United States, where he had run the drugs business for the legendary Al Capone, 'king' of Chicago. Al Capone had ordered the execution of over 200 traitors to the clan, although he himself could not stand the sight of blood and used to faint when his nurse gave him injections. Gentile could not match the record of his boss, but he had the murder of at least seventeen people on his conscience. Criminal charges could never be pinned on him, but in the end he was expelled from America and retired to his native Sicily. He was a charming old buffer of about seventy at the time I met him. Privately, I called him 'Ded', which means 'Grandad' in Russian.

I published my article in *Izvestia* under the headline 'The Knights of the Lupara', this being a reference to a special hunting gun for killing wolves which the Mafia also used for shooting its victims in the face. On my next visit to Palermo, I gave 'Ded' a copy, which pleased him, as well as an old Russian icon, which I think delighted him even more. He was now favourably inclined toward me and I saw him several more times that year. I cannot say that he became a KGB informer for, of course, he had the power to put me in metal box at the bottom of the sea. But he was the source of one vital piece of information.

We were sitting on a summer's day on the terrace of his villa when he suddenly said to me: 'My son, do you really only work for your newspaper?' I looked him straight in the eye, as we were taught at KGB school, and lied. 'Yes, I do not have time for any other work.' 'That's a pity,' he said, 'but perhaps you can pass this on.'

He began in a roundabout way, asking me why I thought Italy had so many coalition governments. It was because instability suited the real masters of the country, the freemasons of the Panorama-2 lodge, he said.

I was very dubious, but the scandals surrounding P-2 years later were to prove he had a point. And then he said something very specific: in the next few days, an Italian paratroop colonel called Roberto Podesta would walk into the office of Prime Minister Aldo Moro, a left-centrist who was not unfriendly to the Soviet Union, and shoot to injure him. Podesta would be arrested and under interrogation say the Communists had ordered him to assassinate Moro. Podesta's 'confession' would be used as a pretext to round up all the Communists and Socialists in Italy. Prison camps used by Mussolini had already been reopened and prepared to receive them. Antonio Segni, already President, would then take more power for himself. But other coup plotters, General de Lorenzo, the former head of Sifar and now commander of Italian ground forces, the neo-Fascist leader Georgio Almirante and Licio Gelli, the head of P-2, would push him aside and Gelli would become the new Mussolini. The CIA was also behind the plot, said Gentile.

I was stunned. 'Why are you telling me this?' I asked. 'Because I hate the Americans for ruining my narco-business,' said the Godfather. Back in Rome, the *rezident* said such a sensational claim would have to be checked out very carefully. It was true that Volodya Yermakov and I had seen tanks moving on the outskirts of the city, but they could just have been carrying out routine manoeuvres. I asked Fritz to find out what he could and he came back with papers confirming that there had indeed been a series of secret meetings between the figures Gentile had mentioned.

In the end no coup took place. After yet another government crisis, Italy got a new coalition in which the centre and the right were more strongly represented and perhaps the far right and the CIA concluded that it would be better to work with this team than risk a *putsch*. The fuss which, on Moscow's instructions, I raised in the Italian press may also have made them think twice.

I passed all the information I had on to two muck-raking journalists from *Espresso* called Scalfari and Januzzi. They published long articles about the alleged coup plot in which they revealed state secrets about the structure of Sifar, the Italian counter-intelligence service. General de Lorenzo sued them for libel, which turned out to be a big mistake on his part because the Prosecutor General, Vittorio Occorsio, demanded to see all the documents in the case and ended up concluding that in July 1964 there really had been a right-wing conspiracy, code-named Piano Solo, to seize power in Italy.

General de Lorenzo obtained immunity from prosecution by entering the Italian parliament as a deputy for the neo-Fascists. President Segni retired and not long afterwards died of a heart attack. Gelli fled to

Switzerland. As for the journalists, they were in danger of going to jail for eighteen months for revealing state secrets, but the tiny Republican Party stepped in and offered them seats in parliament too.

In the months and years afterwards, anyone who knew anything about Piano Solo ended up dying an unnatural death. To begin with, minor figures were found shot or were involved in suspicious car accidents. Occorsio, the prosecutor, was murdered by the neo-Fascists in 1976. And in 1978 Aldo Moro himself was killed by the Red Brigades. The CIA will hotly dispute this, but it is the considered opinion of the Lubyanka that the Americans were behind his execution.

As for Nicola Gentile, he did not live long after he tipped me off about the coup. Like Don Corleone at the end of the film *The Godfather*, he collapsed while pottering about in his garden in Sicily and died in December 1964, evidently of a heart attack.

A Little Warning

When Gentile died, I lost his protection and it became much more dangerous for me to visit Palermo. I met some of the 'New Mafia', the young men who took over after the Godfather died, but they were not exactly friendly. Once, when I was covering a visit by a Soviet trade delegation, I met an attractive Sicilian girl called Valeria. I even got as far as kissing her. But she warned me that if I wanted to stay alive, I had better leave her alone because she was the moll of one of the new gangsters. I quickly backed off. I had genuinely not known she was someone else's girlfriend. But even when I was not treading on anyone's toes, it was clear to me I could no longer count on the warm welcome and protection I had enjoyed from 'Ded'. This was a pity, because I had unfinished business in Sicily, which was to unravel the mystery which still surrounded the death in October 1962 of Enrico Mattei, the President of the national oil company Ente Nazionale Idrocarburi (ENI).

At the beginning of the 1960s, an American-led cartel called the Seven Sisters dictated the terms on which oil was produced and traded around the world. Countries which benefited from the Marshall Plan were forbidden to supply 'strategic goods' to the Soviet Union, which included drilling equipment for oil and gas and pipes to carry fuel. Mattei, who had fought in the anti-Fascist resistance and sympathised with the Soviet Union without being a Communist, flagrantly broke this rule by supplying us with pipes in exchange for which Italy received Soviet gas. He further enraged the Seven Sister nations, which used to take seventy-five per cent of all profits for themselves, paying only twenty-five per cent to the producing countries, by giving the Soviet Union a 50–50 deal. He had plans to supply us with more equipment in exchange for Soviet oil.

Shortly after I arrived in Rome in July 1962, I received a tip from one of my informers that a killer called 'Carlos' was preparing to assassinate Mattei. I immediately flew to Milan to warn the tycoon, whom I had known since my days as an economist at the trade mission. He received me in the ENI office, where we drank an aperitif. I told him what I had heard. 'Who asked you to tell me?' he said. 'My ambassador,' I replied, because I did not want to reveal that I was now working for the KGB. In retrospect, perhaps I should have done so because then he might have taken me more seriously. As it was, he thought I was just a sensation-mongering journalist. 'Don't worry,' he laughed, 'I'm better guarded than your Politburo.'

I returned to Rome and he flew off to Sicily, where ENI was prospecting for oil and kept another office. Mattei had presidential ambitions and while he was in Palermo he gave a speech to local workers on what he would do about unemployment. Then he prepared to return to Milan in his private jet.

His personal pilot, a comrade in the resistance called Bertuzzi, was in the cockpit, getting the plane ready for take-off. Suddenly the barman from the airport café ran out and said Bertuzzi's sister wanted him urgently on the telephone. The pilot went to take the call. 'Pronto,' he said, but heard nothing but the pips. He went back to the plane and continued his countdown. The jet took off normally but in midair between Palermo and Milan it exploded. 'Carlos' had planted a time bomb on board in the five minutes the plane had stood unattended on the tarmac. The body of the barman who had called Bertuzzi to the phone was found some days later in a ditch.

Of Enrico Mattei, all that was found after the blast was his arm with his Omega watch still ticking despite the enormous impact. The Swiss manufacturers shocked me greatly by producing an advert, cynical by the worst standards of capitalism, in which they said that an Omega would keep on working even after a midair explosion. *Izvestia* marked the death of Mattei in a more dignified way. Our obituary, entitled 'Enrico did not come back', was the first appreciation of the life of a capitalist ever to appear in the Soviet press.

I mourned Mattei and then more or less forget about him until I went to Sicily to cover the earthquake that hit Palermo in 1967. There I happened to meet Mauro de Mauro, a journalist from the local paper Ora, who was investigating the murder of the Italian 'king of oil'. I kept in touch with him and from time to time he gave me an update on what he had found out. 'Carlos' had been a hit man from Cosa Nostra, the US branch of the Mafia, but it looked as if the assassination had been ordered by the CIA because of American displeasure at the flouting of Seven Sister rules.

In 1970, Mauro asked me to meet him in a café in Palermo because he had some new information for me. I arrived at the appointed time, but he did not show up. On 18 September, a small item appeared in the local paper, saying he had disappeared. I waited a while and then returned to Rome. Two or three months later, one of my informers in Sicily told me that Mauro's wife had heard him talking quietly to someone he evidently knew on the steps of his home. Unsuspectingly, he got in a car with this person and they drove away. Mauro was taken to a villa, where torturers tried to extract from him what he knew about Mattei's murder. Then the journalist was injected with a tranquilliser. Unconscious, he was put into a metal box loaded down with stones and dumped over the side of a schooner into the sea. The source of this information was a Sicilian priest to whom one of Mauro's executioners later confessed.

You can imagine my feelings. I could only hope that my poor friend had not woken up in his metal coffin before death took him.

In view of what had happened to Mauro, I came to take a lighter view of problems I myself had had on the road out of Palermo. I was driving north to Rome in my green Citroën when I noticed that a dark blue Fiat-230, its number plate obscured by dirt, was following me. Something was rattling in my engine so I pulled over to have a look under the bonnet. It was nothing serious, just a screwdriver I had left in there. As I bent over, I studiously avoided turning my head but hoped the car that had been sitting so insistently on my tail would now drive past. Suddenly I heard a 'pukh' and felt a sharp pain in my leg. Then the Fiat roared off into the distance. Meanwhile blood was flowing from a bullet wound in the soft flesh just above my ankle.

I returned to Palermo and went to stay with a Communist friend called Aldo. I didn't want any fuss. An offended diplomat may cause an international incident but a KGB officer should never draw undue attention to himself. So I did not go to a hospital, but asked Aldo to find a doctor who would tend me at home. The doctor removed from the wound a 7.62 calibre bullet, the kind that comes from a pistol.

'What does this mean?' I asked Aldo. 'They don't shoot like that in Sicily,' he replied. 'It means you have been lucky and got off with a warning. Don't come here any more.' I heeded it to some extent, although I did not stop travelling to Palermo altogether. I just did not go on my own any more, but stayed in the safety of press groups and official delegations.

The Red Pope

As the Kremlin awes Westerners not only with its red walls and star-topped towers but also with its political overtones, so St Peter's in Rome held a fascination for me that went beyond architecture. To Homo Sovieticus it was the centre of a hostile empire.

This view of the Vatican predated the Bolshevik Revolution. Even in Tsarist times, the Church of Rome was seen as the headquarters of the enemy, probably because Orthodox Russia had so often in its history been in conflict with Catholic Poland. But attitudes hardened even more when the Communists came to power. Partly it was a question of dogma. Marx condemned religion as the 'opium of the people', but really it was a matter of Russian nationalism.

In 1962 Nikita Khrushchev, who had already denounced the abuses of Stalin and brought about a political and cultural thaw, decided it was time to improve the atheist Soviet state's relations with the Church. He had ulterior motives. The economy was doing badly, his own political position was weakening and he needed to attract popular support, which meant looking beyond the Communist rank and file to the mass of dissatisfied religious believers. Mostly they were faithful to the Russian Orthodox Church, of course. But Khrushchev, being a Ukrainian, knew that in his home republic there were also the Uniates, who observed eastern rites but owed political allegiance to Rome. In addition, on the border with Poland and in the Baltic republics there was a significant Roman Catholic population.

Warsaw Pact countries such as Poland, Catholic for centuries, had just opened official relations on a state level with the Vatican. The Soviet Union should do the same, thought Khrushchev.

His sudden goodwill to the Church coincided with the accession of a new Pope, John XXIII, who also changed Rome's tone towards the Soviet Union. The Vatican newspaper *Osservatore Romano* softened its propaganda against Moscow and the Pope ordered the closure of Russicum, a secret school that had trained priests to work in Warsaw Pact countries as anti-Communist agents. The KGB was very interested in this new pope and instructed me to gather information on him.

Some time later Alexei Adzhubei, my chief editor and also, you will remember, Khrushchev's son-in-law, asked me to arrange for him to visit Rome under the auspices of the Italian–Soviet Friendship Society. He came out in March 1963 and spent his first day drinking in the hotel with a group of journalists. When they got up to leave, he asked me to stay behind. 'I want to speak to you about something secret,' he said. 'Let's go out on the street then,' I replied. There he told me, 'Khrushchev wants you to fix me a meeting with the Pope.'

It was a tall order, but I had my contacts. I spoke to the head of public relations at the Vatican, a Dutch Jesuit called Willy Brandt, who agreed to come and meet Adzhubei at the *Izvestia* flat. 'We must lay on a real homely Russian welcome for him,' said Adzhubei. So his wife Rada, who was also the Kremlin leader's daughter, and my wife Eva slaved to produce a huge traditional meal consisting of caviar, borscht, cutlets and cranberry jelly. Salted cucumbers were laid out to go with the vodka. And then the women were dismissed to a back room.

Our other preparations had included checking for bugs which might have been planted by Sifar. A technical team from the embassy came in to do this, for we did not want anyone to overhear our conversation.

Willy Brandt arrived in a black overcoat under which he wore a black suit with a dog collar. He was very dry and reserved. At first he refused the vodka. But Adzhubei, who had an amazing talent for breaking the ice at parties, could make even a dead man drink. Soon the spirit was flowing and the pale-faced Jesuit became flushed. Eventually he relaxed to the point of agreeing to help us. Adzhubei should go the next day to the Vatican library as a 'tourist', he said. Rada and I could accompany him. The Pope would come in and 'bump into us' as if by coincidence. He would then invite us into his office for talks. And that is exactly what happened.

The Pope indeed bumped into us and so began a historic dialogue between the Vatican and the Soviet Union. During the talks, the Pontiff was flanked by a monk in black robes who was introduced as Padre Kulik. Judging from his surname, he was a Ukrainian and he must have been briefing the Pope on conditions for Catholics in his native land. After the initial pleasantries, Adzhubei came to the point by handing the Pope a message from Khrushchev, written in Russian, which said that Moscow appreciated John XXIII's peaceful policies and thought the time might have come to establish official relations between the Soviet and Vatican states. As Khrushchev's son-in-law, Adzhubei said, he had authority to negotiate.

The Pope replied by handing Adzhubei a letter, also written in Russian. The Vatican appreciated Khrushchev's peaceful policies and trusted they would continue, it said. Verbally, the Pope added that he thought the idea of official inter-state relations a good one. But the Vatican had two conditions before further talks on this subject could take place. First, priests jailed in the Ukraine must be freed and the Soviet authorities must stop persecuting Uniate believers; and second, the Russian Orthodox Church itself should be given more freedom.

Communism had lasted for only fifty years while the Church had existed for nearly 2,000 years, the Pope said. 'I do not know what will happen to Communism but the Church will remain and therefore it is in your interests to extend religious freedom in your country.' And with those words of advice, he brought the meeting to an end.

We had an agreement not to brief the press, who had somehow heard about the meeting – journalists can smell news on the air. And so when we were mobbed by reporters as we emerged from the Vatican, we denied we had met the Pope. 'Oh come on, Lyonya,' said one of my close friends, Ugo Mannoni of *Paese Sera*, 'surely you can tell me. Was there a meeting?' I looked him in the eye and said: 'No.' But the Vatican broke its promise and published a small announcement about the talks. The next day Ugo rang me. 'Lyonya,' he said, 'what's the Russian for *putana*?' 'Well, we have two words, one is *prostitutka* and the other is *blyad* [whore].' 'What's the difference?' 'Prostitute is a profession, whore is more a question of character.' 'In that case you are a whore,' he said and rang off.

As a result of the Vatican leak, the Italian press began writing about the possibility of warmer Church relations with the Soviet state. Right-wing newspapers were highly critical of the idea and dubbed John XXIII the 'Red Pope'. The Americans were none too pleased, either. And in Moscow there must have been some Communist Party hardliners for whom the prospect of detente with Catholics was distasteful. In short, we had our enemies.

Adzhubei returned to Moscow in April and reported to Khrushchev. The Pope waited to see if the Kremlin leader would make a move towards meeting his conditions. And in fact he did. Some Uniate believers were released from a labour camp and Khrushchev also set up the State Committee for Religious Affairs, a body which was to supervise growing Church activity in the Soviet Union. Lenin and Stalin had demolished churches and sent priests to the gulag archipelago. The new rule was that believers could worship freely provided they did not spread religion further by teaching or engaging in charity. Education and welfare remained the prerogatives of the state.

But then in June 1963 John XXIII died and the peace process lost momentum. Indeed years were to pass – years in which Leonid Brezhnev presided over stagnation in the Soviet Union and the Polish Pope, John Paul II, took up strong anti-Communist positions once more – before there was a diplomatic breakthrough during Mikhail Gorbachev's era of glasnost and perestroika.

In December 1963 Adzhubei came back to Rome, not with any hope of meeting the new Pope, Paul XI, but just to feel the pulse in the Eternal City. Shortly before he arrived on a flight via Singapore, my neo-Fascist contact Sylvester warned me to be careful as 'something unpleasant' was being planned for my guest. But the visit passed off without incident.

Adzhubei was due to fly back to Moscow on 5 December. The embassy had offered him a limousine, but he told me he would prefer it if I just drove him out to the airport in the *Izvestia* Giulietta. 'Bring her over to the hotel now and park her ready for next morning,' he said on the eve of his departure. I suppose he was thinking that we would drink a lot that evening, which is of course what happened.

And so the car stood overnight outside the hotel. Adzhubei's parking instructions had been made over the telephone. Alarm bells should have rung in my mind, but I was careless.

The next morning the ambassador, Semyon Kozyrev, turned up at the hotel with a Mercedes Benz flying the red Soviet flag. Despite Adzhubei's desire to go quietly, he was a VIP and protocol dictated that he should be seen off properly. 'Look, I'll only offend the ambassador if I do not ride with him,' said Adzhubei. 'You follow behind in the Giulietta.' We reached the airport and our guest flew off to Moscow.

But as I was driving back to town at 140kph, disaster struck. Suddenly there was a bang and I lost control of the car. It veered into the left lane but fortunately there was no oncoming traffic. I was not wearing a seat belt and managed to fling myself through the door before the car hit a tree and bounced back into the middle of the road. One minute I was listening to the new hit 'Hey, Hey Paula' on the radio. And the next thing I knew I was hanging encased in plaster, staring up into the face of Professor Dario Spallone, Togliatti's personal doctor, who was treating me in hospital for two broken legs, a broken shoulder, a cracked vertebra, a fractured skull and a face injury.

Specialists from the GRU, or Soviet military intelligence service, who examined my smashed vehicle on the Via del Mare, found that a piece of sharpened metal had been carefully inserted into one of my wheels to penetrate the inner tube gradually and make the tyre burst when the car reached a high speed. The perpetrators had reckoned that the Giulietta would be carrying the weight of two people, myself and Adzhubei. But since I was alone and the car was lighter, the effect was delayed and the accident happened on the way back from the airport.

Who was responsible? I am sure it was some combination of dark forces on the extreme right, possibly in Sifar and the CIA. True, Khrushchev did not have much political life left then and was soon to be ousted by Brezhnev. But if hardliners in Moscow had been involved, that would eventually have emerged and I would have found out. On the contrary, everyone at home was very distressed.

Immediately after the accident, the *rezident* cabled Moscow to say I had 'crashed myself', the literal translation of the verb *razbitsa* which he used. In Moscow, this was taken to mean that I had been killed. Adzhubei received the telegram when he landed at Sheremetyevo Airport and cried on the tarmac. He ordered an obituary to appear in *Izvestia*, over which I chuckled some months later, remembering Mark Twain's comment when the same thing happened to him – 'Reports of my death have been exaggerated.'

After the crash, the *rezident* wanted me to leave Rome, not for my own welfare, but because a lot of publicity had surrounded the accident, which of course the secretive KGB did not like. But Adzhubei convinced Khrushchev that he had been the intended victim and I was not to blame. At that, the Kremlin leader told the KGB to keep me on and get me the best medical treatment money could buy. Two months later, I was back at work, walking with the aid of a stick.

How glad I am that the KGB did not withdraw me then, for in 1964 many adventures, some scandals and a few triumphs still lay ahead of me. Now I am retired, with thirty books and two film scripts to my name, I often think back to my early days as a wartime evacuee in Atktyubinsk. I was a wild teenager and used to hang out with the local gangs. They called me 'the intellectual' because I had seven years of education up to the age of 14. Once we got drunk and went to have our fortunes told by an old gypsy woman. She predicted for me a future in which I would travel, have money, live dangerously and be betrayed. 'Rubbish,' I thought and laughed about it with the lads. But now I can only conclude that the gypsy must have had access to my personal file.

BANGKOK

Name Timofeyev, Vasily Ivanovich	
Born 10 June 1945	
Education Higher, masters degree in history	
Special Subject History	
Languages English	
Military Rank Colonel	
Worked in Thailand, India	
Marital Status Married	
Sports Football	
Hobbies Photography	
Favourite Tipple Beer	
Brand of Cigarettes Java	

Tricks of the Trade

Vasily Timofeyev is not my real name. I cannot reveal that or show you my face because I am still active in the Russian foreign intelligence service. I was never a Communist fanatic, but a patriot serving my country. I believe my work continues to be useful and it is too early for me to retire while I still have something to give to the new generation of Russian secret agents.

My KGB career began when I went under journalistic cover to Bangkok in 1975 but I cannot say for which news organisation I worked. My first task when I arrived in Bangkok was to study the city thoroughly. Naturally, before I set off, I read all the books I could find about Thailand in our limited Soviet libraries. But I could only get to grips with Bangkok in the way the KGB wanted by being there, exploring it inch by inch.

The city that a tourist sees is very different from the city as seen through the eyes of a secret agent. To holiday-makers, Bangkok is the 'Venice of the East', an exotic place of canals and temples, bazaars and boutiques, hotels and girly bars. To me, initially, it was just a grid of

streets which I must get to know like the palm of my own hand in order
to keep ahead of the 'Special Branch' or Thai counter-intelligence service,
which was likely to be following me wherever I went in my salad-green
Datsun-2000.

Every evening and weekend I went out in the car, learning new routes.
My wife Svetlana, who worked at the Soviet embassy as a filing clerk,
helped me by doing the map reading. We started with a small square in
the centre of the city and worked our way, square by square, to the
outskirts, where modern buildings gave way to slums. Out on the edge
of town, there were few signs to tell the visitor where he was going.

Still, I got to know every highway and back alley in Bangkok. When I
returned for a visit in 1993 after an absence of thirteen years, I did not
recognise the place, so much urban development had there been since
my day. But in the 1970s, I could have earned my living as a taxi driver
there. If the Special Branch was on my tail, I knew where to make a quick
turn to throw them off, although it was sometimes tricky when we were
bumper to bumper in the city's prodigious traffic jams.

As well as studying the road network, I also inspected the restaurants,
not from the point of view of a gourmet but applying the KGB's peculiar
system of awarding stars. Somewhere I had read or heard that there were
10,000 restaurants and cafés in Bangkok but of those, I knew only about
five per cent were likely to be suitable for intelligence work. For clandestine meetings with agents or prospective informers, you need a restaurant which is not too crowded, otherwise diners at the next table
might overhear your conversation. On the other hand, if the restaurant
is nearly empty, you will stand out and draw excessive attention from
the waiters. The lighting should be subtle and the decibel level of music
just right, neither too low so that others can hear what you are saying
nor too loud so that you have to shout to make yourselves heard.

I tested restaurant after restaurant, looking for the perfect combination
of features. I would go in and order something cheap, often just a soft
drink, and assess whether it was worth returning to the establishment
on KGB business. Eventually, I picked twelve or fifteen places for my
entertaining, ranging from inexpensive to pricey. For it is no good overwhelming a modest guest with too much luxury while an important or
self-important person will be insulted if you do not wine and dine him
in the style to which he is accustomed. Best of all, I liked to take my
sources to the hotels where the Western tour groups stayed, for here the
food and service were reasonable and we could merge with the crowd of
temporary visitors.

To be avoided at all cost are restaurants in the city centre. A place like
Charlie's, run by an émigré from Switzerland who insisted on the highest

standards from his Thai staff, would no doubt have earned five stars in a good food guide. It was popular with foreigners, who sometimes tired of spicy Thai cuisine. I used to bring Svetlana here for her birthday. But for operational purposes, it was absolutely useless as the entire diplomatic and press corps lunched and dined at Charlie's and if I brought a secret source here, I could be sure we would be recognised by a dozen people.

It took me a while to learn this elementary lesson. When I first arrived in Bangkok, I took a Japanese diplomat out to lunch in the restaurant of the central Hotel Dusit Tani, hoping to woo him over the shrimps and chicken into cooperating with the KGB. But while we ate, several of his colleagues from the Japanese embassy passed our table, smiling politely. There was no point in courting him any further as we had been seen together, spotlit as if we were on a stage.

However, even knowing an obscure restaurant on the edge of town is no guarantee of success as my colleague Sergei, an experienced diplomat at the Soviet embassy, found out. He was developing a relationship with a Western diplomat, who happened to live in the same building as he did. Convenient though it would have been, he could not invite his contact to his flat as it was almost certainly bugged by the Special Branch. Instead, he had started inviting him to Savatdi, a seafood restaurant in the suburbs which was a five-star establishment according to the KGB's criteria. The food was good, too.

'Wonderful restaurant,' said the Western diplomat after another of their dinners, 'but it's awfully difficult to get to, right out in the sticks. We live in the same building. Why don't you give me a lift next time we go out there?'

The last thing Sergei wanted was for the Special Branch to spot him together with his contact in the same car. So he told the diplomat he was sorry but he always travelled to the restaurant straight from work and he should continue to make his own way to their meetings.

The next time they were due to dine, Sergei slipped home to change his shirt. When he went out to his car, it would not start immediately and he made quite a lot of noise revving up the engine in the courtyard. 'Hey, wait for me,' shouted the Western diplomat from his balcony. 'What a stroke of luck that you're home this time. You can take me with you.' 'Get in,' said Sergei through gritted teeth.

A secret agent never goes directly to a meeting place. First he must drive around for a bit to make sure nobody is following him. He must have an excuse for his detours, which will seem plausible to anyone on his tail, the need to go to the post office, for example, or to visit a shop.

With the Western diplomat in his car, Sergei now had to justify his circuitous route to the restaurant. He popped into a couple of shops selling auto parts to make it seem natural that he was taking such a long time to get to their destination. The Special Branch was nowhere in sight. But Sergei had another problem.

It is not the done thing for secret agents to park their cars outside the place where they are meeting a contact. We always leave our vehicles some distance from the rendezvous – the street outside a cinema does nicely because anyone seeing the car assumes we are inside a watching a film. Sergei knew a cinema a few blocks from the restaurant, but how could he explain to the diplomat why he was parking here?

He got out of this awkward situation by pretending his car had broken down. He had an anti-theft device in his Toyota which blocked the engine if someone tried to steal it. Surreptitiously, he switched it on and the car ground to a halt, right outside the cinema. 'I don't know about you but I'm ravenous,' said Sergei to his guest. 'I can't be bothered fixing the car now. Let's walk to the restaurant, eat something and I'll take a look at the engine later.'

After the meal, Sergei fiddled about under the bonnet and 'miraculously' got the car going again. The Western diplomat never suspected anything and continued to meet my colleague, who was careful from then on to avoid situations where he would have to give him a lift.

Postal Games

When a KGB agent knows his roads and restaurants, his work is only half done. Preparing to spy in a city, he must also build up a collection of places suitable for setting dead letter boxes. This term, as you probably know, refers to the containers in which secret documents, microfilm or messages are left for collection when agent and informer are unable to meet each other face to face. The social and natural conditions in Asia call for a particular application of the spy's postal system.

Personally, I did not use dead letter boxes very much. Although I made a mental note of potential sites in case I needed to post or receive a message, I tended to see my contacts in person. It was the agents working under diplomatic cover who used the dead letter boxes. Dropping off or retrieving a container, you are exposing yourself to considerable risk and it is better if you are armed with diplomatic immunity to meet the counter-intelligence officer who may be waiting to pounce on you from behind a bush. The better-protected diplomats dealt with informers in sensitive positions, often offering the most valuable classified information, who preferred the anonymity of a dead letter box.

Agents like me, who posed as journalists and were not above the law, were assigned to meet sources who were prepared to show their faces to the KGB. Whatever the means for gathering data, we pooled our material because, whether we acted the part of diplomats or correspondents, we all reported to our boss, the *rezident*, and worked as a single team for the KGB.

My colleagues spent hours hunting for ideal places for dead letter boxes in Bangkok. Residential areas were no good because white men – *farangs* the Thais called us, a corruption of the word foreigner – stood out in the crowd. If the district were wealthy, some guard would be sure to notice an outsider behaving suspiciously. If it was poor, the slum-dwellers would be equally alert to the appearance of a European in their midst. But there were few open spaces either. Beautiful though Bangkok is, with its canals and temples, it can hardly be called a green city. It has only one park, the Lumpini, and the zoological gardens, both of which are crowded during the day. Walking after dark in Lumpini Park is not advisable as criminals, drug addicts and homosexuals gather under the trees, creating a no-go area for decent people and spies.

In the West, a dead letter box can be an empty cigarette packet or a beer can, casually left under a park bench or at the foot of a tree, for microfilm to be secreted inside. But that will not do in Thailand, where the people are so poor they will pick up a cigarette box in the hope of finding a cigarette left in it or take an empty beer can home to use as an ashtray. A hollowed-out piece of wood makes a better container in Asia.

Tossing it into a grass verge is not a good idea, however, as poisonous snakes, lizards and scorpions lurk in the tropical vegetation on the roadside. Scrabbling about in the dark and plunging your hand into undergrowth is more unpleasant than you might think and many of our boys wore rubber gloves when they did this work.

One colleague in particular had a stressful experience on a grass verge on the outskirts of Bangkok. Earlier in the day, his contact had gone past in a car and tossed from the window an oil canister containing important documents. Oleg, for that was his name, had the job of picking it up.

Everything went smoothly at first. He found the spot, groped in the grass and got the canister. But just as he was about to return to his car, he spotted a police patrol approaching with its blue light flashing. His first thought was that his informer had been arrested and spilt the beans but, being an experienced agent, he did not give way to panic. He tossed the container some distance away and delved again into the grass.

'Looking for something, sir?' asked the policeman. 'Yes,' said Oleg, 'I've lost my poodle.' The policeman began shining his torch. 'Don't do that,' said Oleg. 'You'll only frighten her. I'm sure she'll come back to me soon. Here Fifi, Fifi, Fifi . . .' The policeman smiled, got back into his patrol car and drove off leaving Oleg to recover the can.

My own tip for anyone wanting to use a dead letter box is this: find a multistorey administrative building where the clerks and managers all go up and down in the lifts. You can be sure that hardly anyone will use the stairs. The landing between floors is the perfect place to leave an object for retrieval because it is a 'dead zone', visible neither from the floor below nor the floor above. If someone is coming up or down the stairs, you will hear them before they see you and be able to hide the container in time. Ideally, the message should be picked up within half an hour of it being deposited.

But if you want my opinion, I think dead letter boxes are overrated. They are needed occasionally, when a direct meeting is really risky. Often, though, it seems to me that agents use them because, like little boys, they enjoy playing spies' games or because the theorists at Moscow Centre expect to see their techniques being applied.

The same is true of equipment, not that we use anything fancy, shooting pens and suchlike being the creation of Ian Fleming. In my day, we were provided with nothing more than bulky 'mini' tape recorders. But I always preferred to switch on my brain rather than rely on a machine. I do not believe in technology for technology's sake. In espionage, the most important thing is being able to work with human beings.

Problems of National Character

Some human beings are easier than others. I must admit I found it difficult to recruit Thais and not only because I did not speak the Thai language, leaving that to specialists in our embassy and relying on English as the lingua franca. The problem was the Thai national character, which did not lend itself to intelligence work.

The psychology of a people is always a major factor for a spy hoping to find someone ready to betray his country. Citizens of democratic states rarely cooperate with foreign intelligence services because if they are disgruntled with their governments, they only have to wait until the next election to register a protest. Subjects of monarchies are, for some reason, particularly loyal.

Quite good, in my opinion, are Africans and Arabs because they have more of a tribal awareness than a sense of nationhood. Those who have been under colonial yoke will sometimes be ready to change masters. Americans and other Westerners may sell their souls if they have been living abroad for a long time and especially if they are short of money.

The Thais fall into the category of the almost incorruptible. They are very independent-minded, never having been colonised like other peoples in Asia, and fiercely loyal to their monarchy. Whilst I was in Bangkok, prime ministers in civilian suits and generals' uniforms came and went but King Bumipon Aduliadet and Queen Sirikit remained constant like the sun and moon.

Prerevolutionary Russia had had good relations with Siam, as Thailand was called in those days, but the Thais were extremely offended when the Bolsheviks executed Tsar Nicholas II. When China went Communist in 1949, Thailand tensed up even more, fearing that a red wave would sweep away its ancient traditions. In the 1950s, Thais faced imprisonment under a law that made it a crime even to meet a Communist, a label which by definition included every Soviet citizen posted abroad. Not every citizen was a party member, but anyone abroad had to be.

That law had been abrogated by the time I arrived in Bangkok, but some Thais were still nervous about meeting me. Ordinary Thais were simply ignorant about my homeland. 'Where is your Russia?' a prostitute in a girly bar asked me. 'Between Finland and Japan,' I told her because she had met Finns and Japanese in the course of her work but never any Russians. Educated Thais were cautious. Government officials, for example, would always come in twos to meet me, knowing that I could hardly proposition one in the presence of a chaperon.

But the anti-Communism of the Thais was only part of the problem, which really went much deeper, into the roots of their culture.

When I first arrived in Bangkok, it seemed I could never get hold of any Thais because they were forever celebrating festivals. As well as Songkran or New Year, which they mark in April by throwing water over each other and releasing lucky fish into the streams, the Buddhist Thais also have an important festival in May to pray for a good harvest and a beautiful holiday called Loi Kratong or the Feast of the Floating Lotus. This takes place in November, when they launch 'boats of hope', little homemade ships with candles which flicker on the water while the people feast in the canal-side restaurants.

Meanwhile the large Chinese community in Thailand has its range of festivals, all at different times from the Thais.

After several times making the mistake of arranging a meeting on a red letter day and being disappointed when my contact did not show up, I started carrying a little calendar with me to make sure all my business was planned for working days. You may ask why the Thais had not just said they could not meet me because it was a holiday. The reason is they think it impolite to give a refusal, preferring to smile and make an arrangement in the full knowledge they are going to let you down.

Even on working days, I was always coming up against this Asian trait which to straightforward Europeans – and in this regard Russians are European – seems like insincerity. 'I'll have to think about that proposal,' a Thai will say to you when in fact he has no intention of ever seeing you again. 'That's very interesting, we'll talk about it later.' 'I'm sorry I can't meet you today, maybe next week?'

In just such a way, an official from the Thai Foreign Ministry gave me the brush-off when I had just arrived in Bangkok, although I was too naive then to see it. I met him at a reception, we exchanged cards and had quite a friendly chat. Time to make the next move, I thought. 'It would be nice to meet in a restaurant sometime,' I ventured. 'Certainly Mr Timofeyev,' he replied. 'We must definitely get together in a more intimate atmosphere. Give me a ring at the ministry in a couple of days.'

That to me seemed like a green light. But when I phoned him and suggested a concrete date, he said he was sorry but could not make it on that day. Would I ring again? I did and offered a different date. Again it did not suit him. So I asked if he would like to suggest a time that would be convenient. He said he would get back to me but I waited in vain for his call.

'The usual story,' said Nikolai Petrovich, who was a very wise old *rezident*.

Slippery though the Thais are, I did eventually manage to hook a local informer, a lawyer who was hired by a Thai general to represent him in a property dispute with the Soviet embassy and who ended up passing political gossip to me. But 'Lotus', as the KGB called him, had another infuriating Thai characteristic.

'Mai pen rai,' the Thais say all the time, 'it is of no significance.' Being Buddhists, they understand that the affairs of this world are all transitory and insignificant compared with the universe and eternity. You lose your wallet, 'mai pen rai', your mother dies, 'mai pen rai'. Nothing, not even the greatest tragedy, is to be taken too seriously and certainly not the KGB with its ludicrous secrets.

This was brought home to me on one occasion when I was having lunch with Lotus. Filling me in on what this government minister had done and that civil servant had said, he kept glancing at his watch and I realised to my horror that he was expecting someone else to join us at the restaurant, where as far as I was concerned we were having a top secret *tête-à-tête*. 'Ah, Virat,' he cried, when another Thai gentleman walked into the restaurant, 'I'll be with you in a moment when I've finished talking to my friend here.' From Virat's smile, I saw that he knew perfectly well who I was.

I was furious with Lotus. 'You told him about me? And you deliberately invited him here when you knew we had a meeting?' 'Why not? He's a friend. He just wanted to see me on some legal business,' said my informer who thought he could kill two birds with one stone.

I gave Lotus, who was after all taking money from the KGB, a long lecture about the importance of the cloak if not the dagger. I instructed him to tell Virat he had only been giving me a consultation about what documents I needed to export a Japanese car from Bangkok to Moscow. And then I told him to lie low for six months.

But it was useless to try and instil a sense of conspiracy in the Thais. 'Mai pen rai.' Perhaps they were right. We Russians were ridiculously secretive. I think it was the result of Stalinism. There is a joke on the subject about a Russian who rings his friend up and says: 'Hey, Ivan, have you read the latest news in *Pravda*?' 'Not now,' says Ivan in a stage whisper, 'this is not topic to discuss over the phone.'

Bar Flies

'Wherever you find yourself – in shops, at the petrol station, on the beach – always be alert to the possibility of meeting a foreigner. The kind of people we are interested in – American soldiers, embassy technical staff – do not necessarily come to diplomatic cocktail parties. So be more imaginative. Look for them in bars or by the sea. There is always a chance they will be ready to cooperate with Soviet intelligence.'

This was one of the recommendations that Nikolai Petrovich made in a little guide for beginners which he gave to me when I started work in Bangkok. Reading it, I understood that in the KGB there was never any rest for the wicked. Even at leisure, we agents had to keep our eyes open for potential recruits.

I took the *rezident*'s advice and looked for likely traitors in all kinds of places. I sought them at Pattay, the resort on the Bay of Siam which, already in the 1970s, was beginning to attract the tourists that now provide Thailand with one of its main sources of revenue. On one occasion, having received a tip-off that a deserter from the US army had taken refuge in a Buddhist monastery, I spent a day posing as a feature writer among the saffron-robed monks in the hope, vain as it turned out, that they would introduce their new brother to me.

Most of my hunting, however, was conducted from the vantage point of a bar stool. I sat in Butterfly and Club 19, pretending to ogle the bikini-clad beauties who drank with the clients and went further if required, but really taking an interest in the lonely men who bought their services. What did I care if some of the ladies, seeing that I never accepted their invitations, concluded I was gay?

I drank in the ordinary pubs as well as the girly bars, for not every potential traitor uses prostitutes. Perhaps he just likes a quiet whisky and a game of darts. In one such pub, I did not even have to make an effort as Roger just fell into my hands.

I was in the company of a Swede when Roger joined us. We were both speaking slightly accented English and Roger was pretty drunk and it never occurred to him that I was anything but another Swede. I did not disabuse him after my Scandinavian friend left, just let him go on thinking that I was Swedish too.

It was a bit risky, but I was confident I could pull off the act. I told Roger I worked for an international electronics firm. I learnt that he was on the technical staff at the American embassy. It seemed he worked with the electronic equipment for coding and decoding. This was very interesting. The *rezident* gave me permission to continue the operation under the 'Swedish flag'.

Roger and I began to drink regularly together like two bar flies. 'I'll get this round,' he said expansively, but when he opened his wallet he found it was nearly empty. 'Sorry mate, the next one will be on me.' It emerged that he was turning forty, with a mortgage, a demanding wife and four kids at fee-paying schools in California. He was short of a few dollars even for a little relaxation in the pub.

'Perhaps I could help you,' I said. 'You're in electronics. I'm in electronics. My firm is always looking for talented people like you. We'll talk about it next time.'

Of course I did not recruit him in our usual pub, where we were by now well known, but took him to a quiet place down a back street to make my offer. He said he was ready to provide any kind of information as long as the salary was attractive.

Over the next few months, he supplied the KGB with valuable technical intelligence in exchange for cash payments. When he was due to leave Bangkok, I said the 'firm' would be glad to renew his contract in the United States.

To which he replied: 'I don't doubt that the KGB reaches all over the globe but I don't want to run any more risks, thanks pal.'

'You mean you knew it was the KGB all the time?'

'Sure. You were asking for things that went way beyond the interests of a "large international firm". But I didn't let on. Somehow I found it easier to work for a Swede.'

And that was the last I saw of him. As far as I know, he got away with his little treacherous fling. I was left with happy memories. It had been good while it lasted.

Misapprehensions of a Layman

When I went to work in Bangkok, the Vietnam War had just come to an end. The Americans, who had flown on bombing raids from airstrips in Thailand and used the girly bars of the capital for their R and R, retained some military bases on Thai territory after the conflict, in which Moscow had supported Hanoi. Naturally, the KGB was very interested in these bases.

One morning, the Soviet ambassador emerged from his residence to find that someone had left a gift for him on the steps, a beautiful basket of Thai orchids. It was not his birthday or the anniversary of the Bolshevik Revolution, so he handed it to our lads in the technical department to make sure it was not a terrorist bomb.

After carefully unwrapping the cellophane and gingerly taking out the flowers, the KGB security specialists detected a small, hard object in an envelope at the bottom of the basket. Not a bomb but a key. There was a short accompanying note.

The anonymous author invited us to go to the Central Post Office and use the key to open a poste restante box in which we would find what he called 'important documents'. If we put $500 in the box, we could receive another instalment of classified information.

We gathered in the KGB *rezident*'s office to discuss the offer. The phantom mole had shown a degree of skill in approaching us. Evidently he had read a lot of spy novels. The basket of orchids, delivered by a florist, was an inspired idea because it saved him the necessity of coming in person to the embassy, where he risked falling under Special Branch surveillance. But his proposed method of continuing the relationship exposed him as an amateur and did not suit us at all.

After markets and railway stations, post offices must be among the busiest places in any city. Crowds of people are always in there, buying stamps, having their parcels weighed, sending telegrams. There was an enormous risk that our would-be agent or one of our own men would be observed at the box, which was far from ideal as a dead letter box.

Still, the offer of the documents was tempting. Clearly, Nikolai Petrovich was not going to send me to pick them up for my job, working under journalistic cover, was not really to handle secrets so much as to meet the kind of sources, Western journalists for example, who could analyse publicly available information, also of interest to the KGB. A diplomat with his immunity from prosecution would have to go to the post office. But not any diplomat. Only Vladislav fitted the bill.

He was in his late fifties, with only a few weeks to go before the end of the last foreign posting of his career. If he got caught red-handed with the documents and declared persona non grata, it would not really matter. On his return to the Soviet Union he would be rewarded with a medal for having spared his younger colleagues from the danger of expulsion.

Straight after our meeting, Vladislav went to the Central Post Office, a gloomy, grey 1930s building on New Road. Later he described how uncomfortable he had felt as he carried out his mission for, if he had been challenged, it really would have been very difficult for him to explain how he came to have a key to someone else's box. But the operation went smoothly and he returned to the embassy with a packet of secret papers from the Pentagon.

Nikolai Petrovich was excited by the material but remained unhappy about the manner in which were operating. Going to the post office in this way was like driving a car blindfolded. Sooner or later we were going to hit a problem. We could not afford to let a layman dictate the rules of the game.

Thus, when Vladislav returned to the box with the $500, he also deposited a copy of the *National Geographic* and an invitation to the mole to meet him in a restaurant. 'Carry the magazine with you,' said his brief note of instruction.

Vladislav waited in vain for the dilettante spy to appear at the Gay Lord Indian restaurant on Siamese Square. In the end there was nothing for it but to risk another visit to the post box where, sure enough, he found another Pentagon document with a message in red capital letters printed across the top: 'I CANNOT MEET YOU.'

Now the *rezident* had a dilemma. The documents we had received so far, mostly papers describing the administration of the US military bases in Thailand, were indeed informative and we were in the market for some more. But there were no really valuable secrets, about American strategic plans for example, which could justify the taking of undue risks.

From the nature of his documents and the fact that he could visit the post office, it was clear the mole did not belong to that category of US military personnel – those working with codes mainly – who were not allowed to go into town unaccompanied. The amateur, who risked a US court martial if he were caught, just thought he was protecting himself by avoiding a direct encounter but in that he was labouring under a misapprehension.

The professional thing to do, safer for all concerned, is to meet openly. A quick drink in a bar or a snack in a café can be made to look like a 'coincidental meeting' and nothing could be easier than slipping secrets or money into the menu and passing them to your partner at a convenient moment. The more natural an act looks, the better, while paranoia can invite trouble.

In the case of our mole, we only needed to meet him once, to find out exactly where he was obtaining his documents, how he was storing them, whether anybody else was helping him and what more he had to offer and then he could use a dead letter box if that was what he wanted. Only it should be a proper dead letter box.

Vladislav went to the post office for the last time. He told the American traitor he would wait for him for three evenings running at the Gay Lord. If he did not come, then the pen friendship was over. The KGB would not use the post box again.

This had the effect of forcing the mole to surface. He turned out to be a young American soldier called Martin. His base was closing, as the Americans were scaling down their presence now there was peace with Vietnam, and his commanding officer had ordered him to shred some documents before they departed. Martin had decided to earn some money by selling the waste paper to the KGB instead.

We bought the rest of the documents from him in a job lot for $5,000, which no doubt set him up nicely when he returned to civvy street in the United States. We tried to keep in touch with him there, but he had given us a non-existent address and telephone number. The Americans often did that. They were happy enough to cooperate with the KGB abroad, but were afraid to do it when they got back home.

You might ask what use Martin, who probably went on to be a garage mechanic or factory worker when he got out of the US army, could be to Soviet intelligence. The answer is that Moscow always took the long view. He might marry somebody whose first husband was second cousin to someone else who worked in the State Department and had a gambling problem. A secret agent should always keep his options open. You never know ...

A Nose for the Inedible

As dangerous as the sincere amateur is the professional with underhand intentions. If a spy is to survive long enough to collect his pension, he must learn to distinguish between people making genuinely interesting offers and counter-intelligence *agents provocateurs*. Like edible and poisonous mushrooms, they are often very difficult to tell apart. The ability to discriminate grows with experience.

I had not been in Bangkok long when I had to put my nose to the test. I received a telephone call from Utai, a Thai journalist I knew quite well, who asked if he could drop in to see me at home. I assumed he was going to ask for some small favour, so I did not bother to inform the *rezident* that I had invited him over for morning tea.

The next day I looked out of the window to see three Thais getting out of a dark blue jeep in the driveway to my house. I invited them onto the veranda as it was still quite early and the sun was not yet unbearably hot. Together with Utai was a dark-skinned man in his thirties who introduced himself as Kasem. I guessed he was a native of Yala, the Muslim province which borders Malaysia. The third man looked a bit Chinese. He did not give his name and was a silent presence during the conversation.

'Are you in a position to pass the information I am about to give you to the Soviet leadership?' Kasem began, dispensing with any polite preamble.

I was not prepared for this. 'Well, first you had better tell me who you are,' I said rather uncertainly. 'I am the leader of the pro-Moscow wing of the Thai Communist Party,' answered Kasem. Now I was really knocked off-balance. Playing for time, I handed round a packet of cigarettes but only the 'Chinese', who must have been Kasem's bodyguard, took one.

The Thai Communist Party was an illegal organisation and the least contact with it on my part could lead to me being expelled from Bangkok. My first instinct was to tell my visitors that I did not interfere in the internal affairs of my host country and politely ask them to leave. But I was also tempted. That there was a pro-Moscow wing of the party was news to me and would likely be news to Moscow too.

The Thai Communists had always been supported by China. However, Peking and Bangkok had just opened diplomatic relations and, for what it was worth, China had given its word it would no longer back the underground Communists. I guessed there must have been a split in the party, with some comrades arguing that Peking could be trusted to continue giving covert aid and others advocating a realignment with the Soviet Union.

If this were the case, then the KGB would be very interested. I decided to continue the conversation, reckoning the risk of us being overheard by the Special Branch was small as we were out on the veranda, beyond the range of the bugs I assumed were in the house.

'Tell me more,' I said, drawing on my cigarette. 'You have not answered my question,' said Kasem. 'Whatever you tell me, I am obliged to pass on to my seniors at the embassy. They decide whether it is worth informing Moscow. I am just a messenger.'

At that, Kasem began to tell his story. My hunch was right. There had indeed been a split in the Thai party. The true Marxist–Leninists had decided to abandon the Maoist path and seek links with Moscow. What did he mean by links? The comrades needed money to buy weapons, he said, wiping his brow with a handkerchief. Evidently he was as nervous as I was. He added that the pro-Moscow wing could count on 3,000 fighters ready to take up the armed struggle against the regime in Bangkok.

This figure put me on my guard a bit. As far as the KGB knew, the entire Thai Communist Party had no more than 4,000 members, but perhaps our statistics were out of date. I asked Kasem to identify others in the leadership of the new pro-Moscow faction. It was not easy for me to spell the Thai names so he wrote them down for me in my notebook. Then I showed the guests out, having agreed to keep in touch through our mutual friend Utai.

After they had gone, I sat in a chair and collected my thoughts. Was this a provocation or a genuine appeal to Moscow? A junior like me could not make such an assessment alone. The bosses would have to decide. All I had to do was make sure I did not make any elementary mistakes.

My notebook was lying on the table with Kasem's list, which would compromise me if it was found on my person. And if the Special Branch were trying to set me up, they would stop me and look for precisely this evidence. I tore the top sheet off the notepad and the one underneath where the imprint from the writing was legible. How was I to deliver this to the embassy?

I got into my car, stuffed the paper into the ashtray and put a lighter at the ready next to it. If I was stopped, I would have time to set fire to the note and the Special Branch would find only the ash. However, these precautions proved unnecessary and I reached the embassy safely.

Nikolai Petrovich listened to my account of Kasem's visit without enthusiasm. Evidently he smelt a rat but he, too, was unable to take any decision on his own. We sent a telegram to Moscow Centre, which reported to the KGB chairman, Yuri Andropov, himself. The Asia specialists at headquarters were puzzled that among the names Kasem had given me were Thai Communists they had thought to be dead or in exile.

Nevertheless, Moscow Centre instructed me to continue meeting the Thais with the aim of extracting more information. This was only to be done verbally. I was not, under any circumstances, to accept any documents from them. Neither was I to make them any promises. 'No more meetings at home,' the *rezident* said, adding his word of advice. So the next day, I phoned Utai from a public call box and told him I would meet his friends in the café of the Metro cinema.

Kasem was visibly displeased when I told him that before Moscow could decide whether to finance his organisation it needed some more facts, but he quickly recovered his Thai politeness and forced a smile to his face. He told me the KGB had been hasty to write the obituaries of

Communist leaders on his list. They were far from being dead souls. As for the others we thought were in exile, it was true they had been abroad but now they had returned to Thailand. He ended our meeting with another passionate appeal for money, $100,000 to be exact. 'If you do not help us, the Fascist regime of Kukrit Pramot (the then prime minister) will wipe us out,' he said.

Again I reported to the bosses, who gave the go-ahead for a third, cautious meeting with Kasem. But I did not have time to arrange it before Utai seized the initiative by turning up uninvited at my house one evening. I switched my stereo up to full volume to drown out our conversation. 'Kasem wants to see you urgently. He is waiting for you at his house now,' Utai wrote in my notebook. 'It is not convenient,' I wrote back. 'I will see him tomorrow at one in the café of the Hotel Victoria.'

Nikolai Petrovich did not like this at all. He thought long and hard before deciding whether to send me to the rendezvous. In the end, he said: 'You had better go and find out what they want, but be extremely careful. Do not fall for any provocations.'

Kasem was already having coffee when I walked into the café. I noticed he had a manila file on the table in front of him. He asked if there were any progress on the question of financial support for his party. I said he should not raise his hopes in this regard. But he did not seem to be in the least put off by my answer. Leaning forward, he whispered to me: 'In this file is a full list of all our activists, details of our operations and a letter to your government with our proposals for cooperation.'

I knew I must not touch the file. Instead, I leant back in my chair and looked round the café. At a table nearby, I noticed the 'Chinese' with several other thick-set men, almost certainly waiting to arrest me as soon as the compromising material was in my hands.

'You recognise Chavalit?' asked Kasem. 'He's in charge of our security.'

'I'm afraid Chavalit will not be of much help to you if someone in your party has given the police a tip-off that you are intending to pass important documents to a representative of the Soviet Union,' I said.

'We do not have any traitors,' replied Kasem, a little flustered.

'I hope so. But for your sake, I cannot allow you to take the risk,' I said.

'There is no risk. Take the file. Take the file. Go on, take it,' he cried, getting desperate.

'No. You bring it to the embassy,' I said and walked out. In this way, I turned the tables on Kasem.

'One hundred per cent provocation,' concluded Nikolai Petrovich, when I reported back to him. And sure enough, we never heard any more from the 'underground Communists', who may simply have been trying to defraud the Soviet embassy out of $100,000 but who were, more likely, *agents provocateurs* from Thai counter-intelligence.

Double Agent in a Nest of Spies

Now that I have explained some of the difficulties of intelligence work, it will be no surprise to learn that, during my five years in Bangkok, I only managed to recruit a handful of informers one could call agents, in other words people who worked for the KGB consciously, on a regular basis and for money. But I had many more unpaid sources who, without intending to betray their countries, helped me greatly.

Many were Western journalists who risked nothing by talking to their Russian 'colleagues' about subjects which, far from being secret, were on the front pages of newspapers and TV screens all over the world. I valued them, however, because they had sources I could not tap and 'angles' which differed from the Soviet point of view.

I drank with them at the Foreign Correspondents' Association, which in those days was based in the old Oriental Hotel on the banks of the River Chao-Prai. A German photographer called Hans Wenzel, who was the clown of the club, never tired of calling it the 'nest of spies'. He used to come up to me and say things like: 'Watch that guy over there, he's from the CIA.' I expect he made the same kind of silly jokes behind my back. Many a truth is spoken in jest. I think it was unlikely I was the only secret agent among the foreign correspondents there.

Loud-mouths and charlatans were often to be heard at the bar of the press club, which admitted non-journalists as associate members. I remember being impressed by a pudgy Indian called Prem Shukla, who used to brag he was a close personal friend of Indira Gandhi, until I discovered he was nothing more than a tailor in a workshop in one of the back streets of Bangkok. I was also nearly taken for a ride by a bankrupt Taiwanese trader called Wong, who offered me military secrets from Red China but was really planning to sell me blank microfilm before disappearing to Hong Kong.

Some of my best informers came from the club, however. Here I met Richard, a penurious American journalist who went further than his colleagues and, first for gifts, later for money, provided written reports on political subjects for a 'small-circulation Soviet government publication'. I think he guessed it was the KGB. Here, too, I met an elderly Frenchman called Marc, whose information was so valuable that it helped to change Soviet policy towards the Khmer Rouge.

Cambodia was a blank spot on the map for the KGB, which had no agents of its own in Phnom Penh. Blindly the Soviet Union accepted the reports of its ally, Hanoi, and supported the dictator Pol Pot just because he was a Communist. When I first arrived in Bangkok in 1975, Western journalists were always going to the border with Cambodia to interview the latest refugees from the genocide being carried out by the Khmer Rouge. But Moscow did not want its ideological preconceptions challenged with talk of the killing fields. When I passed on what Western sources said about the massacres, I was reprimanded by Moscow Centre for swallowing CIA disinformation.

As time passed, however, and more and more people spoke of the piles of skeletons in the Cambodian paddy fields, Moscow could no longer bury its head in the sand. Sheepishly, the bosses who had criticised me asked if I could not, after all, get them something on Cambodia. Luckily for me, just at that moment, Marc walked into the Foreign Correspondents' Association.

He was stringing for the French new agency AFP because he was desperate for money, having been forced to leave Cambodia, which had been his adopted home for twenty years. He had gone to Indo-China as a French soldier in the 1950s, married a Cambodian woman and had children there. He had worked as a press officer in a government ministry and even been an adviser to Prince Norodom Sihanouk.

But when the Khmer Rouge entered Phnom Penh, he had lost everything. He had been arrested, beaten up and deported with other foreigners. A far worse fate had almost certainly befallen his Cambodian family, which was middle-class and therefore open to accusations of being 'bourgeois'. His wife and children could hardly have survived the genocide.

Now here he was, washed up on the friendly shore of Thailand but struggling to start a new life from scratch. He really wanted to return to Paris, where his sister had a house, but his documents had been lost and he was embroiled in a wrangle with French bureaucracy over his rights to draw a pension in France. He gladly accepted an offer to 'string' for the KGB as well as AFP.

Marc, who spoke the Cambodian language fluently, not only monitored and interpreted the reports of Khmer Rouge radio for us but also interviewed the refugees in the border camps. His dispatches were presented in such a professional way and he conducted himself so discreetly that we began to suspect he must have experience as a secret agent. Perhaps he had been involved in military intelligence when he had served in the French army. Perhaps he was still reporting to the French secret service.

'There is a way of checking if he is a double agent,' said the *rezident* when I expressed my concern. 'It's not easy but it can be done.'

Our plan was to give Marc a parcel and ask him to pass it urgently to a Soviet seaman who would meet him down at the docks. The seaman would not turn up and Marc would be left with the package which, unbeknown to him, would contain a hidden microphone. If he was honest, he would bring the parcel straight back to us and admit the failure of the mission. If he was working for two masters, he would let us think the delivery had gone ahead and hand the parcel over to his other employers. We would hear them ripping open the paper and find out who they were.

But Marc never let us make this experiment. His pension problems were sorted out and he left for France before we had time to test his loyalty. To this day I do not know if my best agent was a double, but I have come to the conclusion that it does not matter. He provided facts that lightened our darkness. Thanks to him, the truth about Cambodia slowly dawned. His information did not belong to any one country. It was part of the grim history of the twentieth century.

CAIRO

Name Bausin, Lev Alexeyevich	
Born 22 May 1928	
Education Higher	
Special Subject Metallurgy	
Languages Arabic	
Military Rank Colonel	
Worked in Egypt, Lebanon	
Marital Status Married	
Sports Tourism	
Hobbies Numismatics, poetry of the silver age	
Favourite Tipple Martel	
Brand of Cigarettes Romance	

Sunrise over the Pyramids

'Cairo is a big, murky pond. You'll find everyone's trying to fish here. But just be patient and discerning and you'll make some successful catches.'

Nikolai Fyodorovich, the KGB *rezident* at the Soviet Embassy in Cairo, was briefing me at the start of my first foreign posting in 1960. As an inexperienced thirty-two-year-old, with the cover of attaché, I was in awe of this veteran agent with his cunning, bear-like eyes. Later I discovered that the staff, while respecting him as a fair boss, nicknamed him 'The Angler' because of his fondness for fishing metaphors.

'Egypt is very important to the Soviet Union,' continued the *rezident*. 'You must not do anything to offend the Egyptians. When you meet them, make sure you never say anything critical of President Nasser. The Arabs are like women; they can't take criticism.

'And another thing ... Never, ever trust anyone completely. Not even yourself.

'Well, that's enough advice for now. You must be tired after your flight.

Go to the common room and get some coffee. Take three days off to sort yourself out. You won't have a car for the first few months but that's all to the good. Get to learn the city on foot.'

Actually, I wasn't tired at all but feeling an incredible buzz after coming from the dreary Moscow winter into the bright, hot climate of Egypt. Neither did I need any time to make my domestic arrangements, as my wife was joining me later and, until I got a rented flat, I would be living in our embassy on Zamalek Island. But I did need coffee. I went to the staff lounge where I found Valentin, an old friend also working as an attaché, hovering over the coffee pots. He had become an expert at making the strong, dark, spiced coffee, the drinking of which is virtually a religion in Egypt.

After several cups, Valentin made a suggestion: 'If you've got three days off, why don't we go and see the sunrise over the pyramids?' I leapt at the chance. Every foreigner should see the pyramids, regardless of the work that brings him to Egypt.

We set off early the next morning when it was still dark. After we had driven for about half an hour, the asphalt road suddenly rose steeply and we found ourselves at the foot of a huge stone edifice – the biggest of the three famous Pyramids of Giza. In the first shafts of light from the rising sun, the pyramid took on an ochre colour, perfectly harmonising with the sandy landscape around. I was stunned into silence.

During his time in Egypt, Valentin had become very knowledgeable about the pyramids. 'This is the Pyramid of King Cheops, build in 2690 BC,' he said. 'It took two million blocks to build it. Just imagine the work for the slaves. Let's climb to the top before the crowds of tourists and souvenir sellers arrive. And we must watch out for the police.'

'Why the police?' I asked. 'We're not planning to steal a brick are we?'

'No,' laughed Valentin, 'it's just that you're not supposed to climb to the top. There have been lots of accidents, people have lost their balance and fallen to their deaths. But this is Egypt. You can easily give the police a little bribe and promise you will take responsibility for your own safety. Come on, you're not scared, are you?'

'Of course not,' I said. 'I've done mountaineering in the Caucasus.'

'Then onwards and upwards.'

On the flat top of the pyramid, we caught our breath and looked out at the panorama of the desert, the palm groves and Cairo with its minarets glinting in the distance. I was filled with wonder and a feeling of peace.

Valentin was careful not to overwhelm me with information on my first day but advised me to visit the Cairo Museum if I wanted to know more. At the bottom of the pyramid again, we had a cold beer. There was just time to see one more famous sight – the Sphinx. It was still early but already crowds of tourists were clicking their cameras and taking camel rides.

The Sphinx has the body of a lion and the head of a man. It is generally believed the face is a portrait of the Pharaoh Chephren, although some archeologists say the Sphinx is much older than the pyramids and the likeness to the king is purely coincidental. The Sphinx seems to symbolise wisdom and the divine power of the pharaohs. But it has been standing guard over the desert for six thousand years, laughing at time, and no experts – not even Valentin – have fully unravelled its mystery.

Apart from my young friend, an elderly, half-blind sheikh called Mahmud was an important guide to me in my early days in Cairo. He taught me Arabic on a three-month intensive course at the Al-Ahzer Islamic University. At first I was afraid he might be an agent of the Mabahis or Egyptian counter-intelligence service. But he was very tactful, never talking about politics or asking any sensitive questions. He just helped me to understand Egyptian history and society. In that way, you could say he helped the KGB, although he was never an agent.

We call Rome the Eternal City. But the old sheikh thought Cairo better deserved the title. 'When you walk through Cairo, your shoes are covered in the dust of 4,000 years,' he used to say.

Although the old man believed Allah was almighty, he never tried to convert me to Islam. But he did show me some of the city's 1,500 mosques, including the famous mosque at the university, which dates back to the ninth century. For a small fee, you can climb the minaret and get a bird's eye view of the city – labyrinthine streets, grey roofs and other minarets. From the point of view of a KGB agent, minarets are not much use. They make poor meeting places or sites for dead letter boxes because tourists are always tramping up and down their dusty stairs. But they can be useful landmarks if you lose yourself in the winding streets.

At the risk of sounding trite, Cairo is a city of contrasts – the bright centre and the grubby backstreets, the scent of French perfume at official receptions and the stink of the street markets, the complacent rich and the desperately poor. Cairo in the 1960s was a little like present-day Russia in its painful transition to capitalism. Of course, I am more shocked at the sight of pensioners begging in Moscow today than I was by the poverty in Cairo then, for Egypt was after all a developing country.

It is a wonderful, colourful country, a magnet for tourists, who arrive by the bus-load. The streets of Cairo buzz with the voices of guides conducting tours in dozens of languages. You can learn many interesting things from them. Eventually I was to become something of an expert myself and I acted as a guide to a variety of people who visited from the

Soviet Union. But I had not come to Cairo to see the sights. I was here
to work for the KGB.

Turns of Fate

My job was to gather political intelligence for the KGB's First Main
Directorate, the division which sent spies abroad. That meant I had to
monitor the press, attend diplomatic cocktail parties, meet informants,
try to recruit new ones and generally keep my finger on the pulse of
Egyptian politics.

The *rezident* had already made clear to me how seriously Moscow
regarded the relationship with Cairo. Egypt was the gateway not only to
the Middle East but also to Africa. Under Anwar Sadat and Hosni
Mubarak, it was to move closer to the West but in my day, when Gamel
Abdel Nasser was still in power, it was a strategic partner of the Soviet
Union. The drunken, womanising King Farouk had been overthrown
in 1952 and Nasser was leading Egypt, a member of the Non-Aligned
Movement, on its own particular path to Socialism. You could never
stifle the bazaar in Egypt as we nearly killed the free market in Russia.
But the Suez Canal, heavy industry and the banks were nationalised. The
Soviet Union was keen to help the Egyptians. For example, we built them
the Aswan Dam. It cost three times as much as the famous Bratsk
Hydroelectric Power Station and was designed to withstand an atomic
hit.

After the course with the sheikh, my Arabic was quite good, although
it would always be obvious I was a foreigner. Arabic is a difficult language
and the KGB never had an 'illegal', in other words an agent without the
usual cover of diplomat or journalist, fluent enough to pass himself off
as an Egyptian. I think one of the reasons the KGB chose me to work in
the Arab world was that I have rather dark skin, the result of some gypsy
blood way back in the family. Clearly I was not an Arab, but neither was
I the stereotypical Slav and the Egyptians sometimes took me for a Greek.

In fact, both my parents were Russian. I was born in 1928 in a village
near Yaroslavl. My mother, Yevgenia Vasilievna, looked after me, the
only child, while my father, Alexei Fyodorovich, had a high-flying career
in Stalin's government. He was a People's Commissar for the fuel industry
in the Russian Federation. Obviously he was a member of the Communist
Party. You could not be anything else in his position at that time.

I followed in his footsteps, opting for a technical training at the Stalin
Institute of Steel from 1945 to 1951. One day two bald, avuncular types
came and offered me some further education. I thought it was perhaps

linked with atomic work, but it turned out to be cryptography, which I studied for two years at a special school in Moscow. We did higher maths and the theory of probability, all necessary for code-breaking. I was naive, I suppose, but I did not realise immediately that the uncles were from the KGB. By the time I was involved, it was too late to back out. But I just took it as my duty. We all thought in terms of duty in those days.

Arabic studies came later when I went to the Military-Diplomatic Academy in 1956. I can't say it was ever my ambition to learn this language. I was not very linguistically inclined. The only language I had was German, just enough to read the technical journal *Stahl und Eisen*. I did not apply to study Arabic. If I had done so, the KGB would have been suspicious of my enthusiasm and given me some other work. No, the suggestion came from the bosses. Of course, the Arabs would see the hand of fate in the development of my career.

During my KGB training, I also studied photography, an important skill for all agents. In a competition for photographs of Moscow, I won a Soviet-made Zorki camera with a wide-angle lens for taking panoramic pictures. After that, I was inspired and photography became not just a work requirement but one of my favourite hobbies.

I was up at a viewing point, taking some photos of the Cairo skyline, when I made one of my first contacts in the city. A young European, also carrying a camera, came up to me and said, 'What exposure do you advise?'

'Depends on the film,' I said.

'Kodak colour, 18 din,' he replied.

'Well, try a size-8 diaphragm with a speed of 1.125 seconds.'

The young man took a few shots, then decided to make my acquaintance.

'You're not local,' he said.

'Just arrived from Moscow. I'm an attaché at the embassy.'

'Oh, I work in an embassy too, but I'm not a diplomat. I do administrative work. There's plenty to keep me busy.'

My new friend took a few more photographs, then ran out of film.

'Here, take mine. It's also Kodak.'

'Thanks, how much do I owe you?'

'Nothing. Consider it a gift from an amateur to a real professional.'

In the Middle East, it pays to flatter and be generous. Everywhere, that is, except at the bazaar, where you will be taken for a fool unless you theatrically insult the trader and his goods until you get a good bargain.

'Do you like pigeons?' my new friend suddenly asked.

'Yes, beautiful birds, the symbol of peace,' I said, somewhat puzzled.

'No, I mean to eat.'

'To eat? I've never tried them.'

'Well then, if you've got time, I propose we try some, roasted on a spit.'

It would have been churlish to refuse. The young man was hardly going to set me up. 'Let's go,' I said. We walked down from the citadel, drove through the city-centre traffic jams, took the road out along the right bank of the Nile and stopped on the outskirts of the city at a rough-looking, open-air casino advertising 'Pigeons'. Beside the restaurant-casino were several clay dovecotes form which whitish-grey birds, slightly different from usual pigeons, flew back and forth.

'This is the best breed for roasting,' explained my friend, who in my thoughts I later nicknamed 'Grand' in honour of our frequent lunches together at the Grand Hotel. The birds were small but very tasty, more tender than chicken. They literally melted in the mouth. A cool breeze blew from the Nile. Stray cats and dogs gathered around our table. Grand chucked them some scraps and they began to fight over them. 'The politics of imperialism,' I joked. 'Set the hungry against each other and then rule.' Grand seemed to appreciate my humour. 'The United States does exactly that in the Middle East,' he said.

My friendship with Grand deepened, based on our mutual love of photography. Once he rang up and asked if I would like to meet President Nasser's personal photographer. 'You know him? Of course I would like to meet him,' I said. I spent a happy day with the official photographer, talking about pictures and showing him the wide-angle lens I had won as a KGB trainee in Moscow. But I quickly realised that, although the photographer was very close to Nasser, the KGB could get little out of him. He was at the top of his profession, but had not the slightest interest in politics. Also, he was very busy and it was never possible to coax him out to a neutral place where we could talk in private.

Of course I reported to my boss, The Angler, on my relationship with Grand, but he was not enthusiastic. 'Just a minnow,' he said. 'His country is of no great value to us. We're more interested in the US, Britain, France.' I stayed friends with the young European but the KGB did nothing more than make a note of him, just in case he turned out to be useful in future.

However, after I left Cairo five years later, another of our agents to whom I passed on my contacts did make use of him. Grand happened to mention that his ambassador had an antique clock decorated with por-celain figurines. Amour or dancing shepherds or something of the sort. Grand was persuaded to bring the clock over to us for a couple of hours one night. Our specialists fitted a bug before handing it back and from then on the clock told the ambassador the time and the KGB everything that went on in his room. He was a busy man, meeting many other diplomats and Egyptian government ministers. Often their conversations were transmitted to Moscow Centre by telegram, sometimes marked 'urgent'.

Even now, although more than thirty years have passed and I have retired on a KGB pension, respect for Russian state secrecy prevents me from revealing which country Grand and his ambassador represented.

On Wheels

The thirty years seem as yesterday. I remember Cairo so vividly, the chaotic streets with the gallant traffic policemen, the donkeys that knew they should stop at red lights. I myself tramped the streets for many months until finally I was given the use of an embassy car, a new Opel Record which we imported from Lebanon where cars were cheaper. At last I could brush the 'dust of 4,000 years' from my shoes. I could also ride out into the countryside, which was important because Cairo, like any other capital city, was not really representative of the country as a whole.

After I had clocked up several thousand kilometres, I put the car into a local garage for a service. I broke the embassy rules by leaving it there overnight. The next day it was delivered to the embassy, beautifully cleaned. But a red light came on in the *rezident*'s mind and he reminded me of his golden rule: 'Never, ever trust anyone completely.' And indeed, when one of our chauffeurs examined the car, it turned out that a small bug had been planted inside.

It was impossible to tell whose bug this was. It could have been installed by the Egyptian counter-intelligence service or perhaps by a CIA agent working at the garage. What were we to do? We could rip it out, of course, but then they would know that we knew. Or we could play a little radio game. After seeking advice from Moscow Centre, we decided to leave the bug in place and use the Opel to tell the other side what we wanted them to know. To start with, I could only have neutral conversations with my passengers. Believe me, it is very difficult to censor your speech as you are driving around.

Eventually, however, the Opel was to play its own small role in a worldwide KGB effort to stop a plot by the CIA to murder Third World leaders. The *rezident* found out about the plot in a telegram from Moscow Centre.

'We have reliable information that the CIA is planning a secret operation to liquidate the leaders of Third World countries and national liberation movements whose politics clash with Washington's interests.

Scientists in America are developing chemical preparations and local citizens are to be recruited as agents to carry out the plot. One of the targets is President Nasser, whose domestic and foreign policies are viewed very negatively in Washington. In view of the close relations between Egypt and the Soviet Union and the particular role of Nasser in the national liberation movements of the Middle East and Africa, we believe special methods should be used to inform the Egyptian leadership of this matter.'

There was indeed such a plot. Remember, this was at the height of the Cold War, when the world was very tense over the Cuban Missile Crisis in 1962. A US Senate report confirmed in 1975 that there were attempts on the life of President Fidel Castro. And during the civil war in the Congo, the former Prime Minister, Patrice Lumumba, was murdered by agents of President Tshombe's government with the involvement of the CIA.

'Outrageous,' fumed the *rezident* when he had read the telegram. 'Do they think the Third World is a chess board and its leaders mere pawns to be taken out of the game?' he demanded, avoiding for once the fishing lexicon. 'We cannot allow a repeat of the tragedy with Patrice Lumumba. Time to activate your bug, I think, Comrade Bausin. I give you permission to take anyone you like in the car and speak freely about this CIA plot.'

The idea was that if the Egyptians were listening, then they would be warned and could tighten security around President Nasser. But what if the bug were planted by the Americans, not the local secret service? 'So much the better,' said the *rezident*. 'Let them know that we know about their plan and do not intend to keep silent about it. Maybe we will embarrass them out of committing terrorism.'

Nasser, of course, was not assassinated by the CIA but lived on until 1970. Perhaps he had my Opel to thank for that. The KGB also published a great deal all over the world about American dirty tricks with the aim of forcing the CIA to change its behaviour.

As for my car, it continued to give good service. Eventually we took the bug out and in its place I was given a state-of-the-art alarm system which tipped me off if I was driving into a trap. For example, once I was heading for a meeting with a secretary from an Asian embassy, which must remain nameless, to receive a top secret document he had promised me on his country's relations with the US. On the way, the alarm went off and I returned to the embassy where our radio team informed me they had been picking up signals suggesting the counter-intelligence service was waiting to catch me red-handed with the document. Evidently the Asian embassy man was a *provocateur*, but I got away and lived to fight another day for Soviet foreign intelligence.

A Weakness for Stamps

Since retirement, I have been interviewed several times by the Russian press, which jokingly calls me the 'Russian Lawrence of Arabia'. It is true that my career took me all over the Arab world, to Iraq (1967–8), to South Yemen (1968–71) and to Lebanon (1976–8). Beirut was to the Middle East what Vienna was to Europe – a real 'nest of spies'. It was very easy to work in Lebanon because the country was so anarchic and the local counter-intelligence services were weak. Lebanon had an official Communist party and the Soviet embassy there was free to publish a newspaper giving the view from Moscow.

Cairo was much tougher for a KGB agent because there was strict political and social control from the presidential palace and the Mabahis was active. Nevertheless, information could be discovered there and a good place to look for it was in the community of political exiles who lived in Egypt.

Once, as I was walking along one of the broad, bank-lined streets which radiate out from the central Al-Tahrir (Liberation) Square, I spotted a little philatelist's shop and went in. A dark-haired man in spectacles sat behind the counter, sorting through envelopes and catalogues. 'Come in, what can I do for you?' he said. 'Well, I was interested in the stamps in the window. I've been a keen stamp collector since childhood.' That much was true. As a child, I often used to buy animal stamps on Kuznetsky Most, the famous street of book and antique shops in central Moscow. 'The habits of childhood come back to us in our mature years,' said the owner.

'Do you have any stamps of French African colonies?' I asked, hastily calculating whether I had enough money on me to buy some. For I had to make my visit look natural. The owner invited me to sit in the shop, which smelt of sandalwood, and ordered a boy to bring coffee. There were no other customers and we began to chat.

It turned out that the owner was a Palestinian who had come to Cairo after the first Arab–Israeli war in 1948. His name was Ali. He had contacts with philatelists all over the world, although he found it difficult to obtain stamps from the Soviet Union. He also knew all the philatelists in Cairo who, he said, met once a month in a nearby café to swap stamps and talk politics.

'Politics?' My ears pricked up. 'Yes, of course, the stamp collectors are all men and they are hardly going to talk about women's fashion, are they?' 'Can I come to one of your meetings?' 'You're welcome. I'll introduce you. There are some interesting people with rare collections.'

That was enough for a first visit. I did not want to seem too pushy. I bought a set of prerevolutionary Egyptian stamps with the head of King Farouk. The French colonial stamps turned out to be too expensive. 'Next time I'll bring you some Soviet stamps,' I promised. 'I will await your gift. May Allah keep you.'

I became both a regular customer at Ali's shop and a member of the café circle, which included Egyptian civil servants, bankers, students and a few diplomats from Third World countries. One of them, an African who looked like Don Quixote in Paul Gustave Doré's illustration of the famous novel by Cervantes, was fanatical about ship stamps and would pay anything to get new additions to his collection.

The *rezident* was sceptical about my stamp circle. 'A quiet pool,' he said. 'There won't be any big fish in there. But carry on. Only any money you spend on stamps comes out of your own pocket.' That was tough, as my monthly salary was only 80 Egyptian pounds or about $200 according to the exchange rate of the day, which gave me a better standard of living than the average worker back in the USSR but not a luxurious lifestyle by any means. But the KGB did not pay expenses unless an operation brought results. It justified this stinginess by saying we should not waste 'the people's money'.

And then I hooked a fish. At the next meeting of the café circle, we were having a little auction and the diplomat asked if he could borrow some money from me to buy a ship stamp. 'If I don't give him any, he'll get offended but if I do, will he give it back? I can hardly ask him for a receipt,' I thought to myself. Nevertheless, I took out my wallet and, in a dark corner of the café, gave him half my month's salary. He gushed with gratitude.

Time passed and Don Quixote did not repay his debt. Then one day he came up to me and announced that he was temporarily in charge of the telegrams at his embassy and could, if I wanted, repay me with a coded text and a translation of it.

I had to think fast. If I accepted his offer immediately, I would blow my cover and give myself away as a KGB agent. (In our embassy, as in Soviet embassies around the world, a third of the staff, including the ambassador of course, were bona fide diplomats, a third served the KGB and a third worked for the GRU or military intelligence.) On the other hand, if I refused, I might lose not only my money but also an opportunity of the kind that does not crop up every day.

'Well,' I said, 'personally I'm more interested in stamps than coded telegrams. Codes are not really my hobby. But I can ask a colleague. Maybe he will be interested.' Don Quixote's face fell. He was obviously hoping for a quick deal and some more money. Eventually Moscow Centre did give the go-ahead and we accepted the telegrams. But then it mishandled the situation. When the texts were received the desk men in Moscow were dismissive, saying they already knew the codes of this African embassy, which again I am afraid I cannot identify. 'Short-sighted idiots,' bellowed my *rezident*. 'They want the codes of the American embassy immediately, on a plate. Don't they realise that your Don Quixote might one day become his country's foreign minister and go and work in Western Europe?'

Actually the *rezident*, who was strict with his staff but always defended them to the bosses in Moscow, like an old-fashioned officer, turned out to be not far off the mark. Don Quixote went on to become the deputy head of mission at his country's embassy in Paris, quite a big fish that got away.

With Ali, the Palestinian shop owner, on the other hand, I developed a fruitful, long-standing relationship. After checking his honesty, the KGB used him as a post office. We needed to communicate with our illegal agents in other Arab states and Africa. Letters sent from abroad would be noticed but, through the Palestinian diaspora, Ali arranged for our letters to be carried to and posted within the countries concerned. The texts were innocent on the surface, but had coded messages for our agents.

Once Ali asked for a favour in return. He wanted arms for the Palestinian Liberation Organisation. But we said no to that. The KGB did not trade in arms. That was the prerogative of the Soviet Ministry of Defence. The KGB never supported international terrorism. The United Nations recognises the right to armed struggle for national liberation. Fighting the Israeli army was one thing. Killing civilians was quite another. We argued with the Palestinians, as with other national liberation movements, that terrorism discredited them. Moscow never supported those Palestinian extremists who wanted to wipe out Israel.

The Strains and Uses of Conspiracy

The real life of a spy is rarely as exciting as the action films suggest. More often it is hard and nerve-racking. One of the best covers for an agent is that of foreign correspondent because there is a fine line between journalism and espionage. Both reporters and spies are gathering information, which is laborious work only occasionally crowned with a triumph. But spies have the added mental burden of always having to act out a part. This is difficult if, like me, you are by nature a sincere person. Many of us got stomach ulcers or other stress-related symptoms. Look at me, I still smoke all the time and drink far too much coffee. It is the legacy of a career in which I could never be myself, not even at home.

It must have been hard for my wife Marina, too. We lived in a nice apartment, not the height of luxury but smart enough for the entertaining an attaché has to do. We were able to save money so that when we returned to Moscow we could buy a private car, an unattainable dream for most Soviet citizens. And Marina was not so restricted as women in other Arab countries. She could go anywhere in Cairo except into the mosques and there was no ban on alcohol. Yet she could never forget she was married not only to Lev Bausin but also to the KGB.

Before wives went abroad with their husbands, they were given a little talk at the Lubyanka about how they should behave themselves. They were told that if their husbands returned home late at night with lipstick on their collars, there were to be no jealous scenes. It was all part of the job. My wife was not a KGB agent herself. For that, she would have needed years of special training. There were some KGB couples, but we were not among them.

Despite the stresses, we managed to relax. We enjoyed Egyptian cuisine, which has hardly changed since the time of the pharaohs and is based on beans and pulses enlivened with fresh herbs, olives, lemons and garlic. We had days off at Hurghada, a Red sea resort unspoilt in those days by the subsequent tourist boom, and I swam in mask and flippers among the corals and shoals of rainbow-coloured fish. And I loved going to the cinema to laugh at horror movies and Tom and Jerry cartoons and lose myself in longer films such as *The Life of Christ*, none of which could be seen in Moscow at that time.

I remember once a Bedouin came into the cinema and tied his camel to the arm of his front-row seat. When the manager came to object, he coolly showed two tickets, one for himself and one for the camel. He could not leave the beast outside, he said, because it might be stolen. To the slow handclapping and whistling of the audience, the manager tried to push the camel out. But it was useless. Two strong young policemen had to be called to remove the stubborn creature and restore order.

I also broke the routine of work when visitors came out to Cairo from the Soviet Union. The most important visitor was Nikita Khrushchev who arrived in Cairo for a two week visit in May 1964. After docking at Alexandria, he travelled with President Nasser by train to Cairo. The entire route was lined with crowds of waving Egyptians, encouraged by the authorities to give the Kremlin leader a warm welcome. The *rezident* was very irritated by the visit because all spying operations had to be suspended to avoid the risk of a scandal while Krushchev was in town and we spent most of the time stuck in the office. However, I did attend a ceremony at the Cairo Officers' Club at which Khrushchev announced he was waiving half of Egypt's debt for tanks, planes and anti-aircraft defences bought from Moscow and also made Nasser a Hero of the Soviet Union, our highest award.

Like me on arrival in Cairo, Khrushchev followed tradition and visited the pyramids. He didn't climb up himself – his belly was too big for that – but he watched while an elderly Egyptian who said he was devoted to the Soviet Union attempted to break the record for running to the top. Much impressed, Khrushchev presented him with his own watch when he descended. The Soviet leader also officially opened the Aswan Dam, went fishing in the Red Sea and, together with Nasser, toured an irrigation project on the Nile. Despite his bulk, Krushchev had more stamina than Nasser, who couldn't keep up with his pace in the heat and had to return early to town. A pleasant interlude for me was escorting Krushchev's modest wife Nina around the bazaar.

Another visitor to Cairo was the cosmonaut, Yuri Gagarin. Again the KGB got very little out of this event, as he was shepherded around by the military attaché and we were excluded from meetings with Egyptian officials which could have been interesting. All I have to remember the visit by are some photographs which I took at the embassy reception, where all the women, both married and unmarried, went crazy and just had to kiss the first man in space.

On another occasion, the ambassador summoned me to his office and called my bluff as an expert on ancient Egypt. 'What do you know about Thebes?' he asked. 'Um, one of the most important political and cultural centres of the ancient world,' I waffled. 'The residence of the pharaohs, the capital of Egypt in the middle dynasty.' 'What else?' 'Well, and that's where they found the tomb of Tutankhamun, isn't it?' 'Correct,' said the ambassador, 'but not good enough if you are going to accompany the Culture Minister of Adzharia to Luxor. You had better read up on the subject.'

This was in the days before Islamic terrorists made Luxor a dangerous place and I was excited at the chance of a free trip to see some of the greatest monuments of ancient civilisation. On the other hand, how was I going to cram a whole history of art course into my head in a couple of days? I did not want to look foolish in front of the VIP from Adzharia, which was part of the Soviet republic of Georgia. All worked out well, however. When we reached Luxor, 550 kilometres from Cairo, I hired an extremely knowledgeable local guide called Abdul Hamid Bihi. As for the minister, he could not have been more appreciative. Visiting Luxor, I was inspired to start building up my own library on ancient Egypt. But the KGB kept me very busy and I have only got round to reading all the books properly since I retired.

I knew enough then, however, to show a young woman a good time at the pyramids. Her name was Larisa and she was an Aeroflot stewardess. I had met her on the plane when I first flew out to Egypt but our little flirtation went nowhere because she was engaged to be married. But then she turned up again in the crew which flew the stars of the Bolshoi Ballet out to perform *Swan Lake* at the famous old Cairo theatre where Verdi's *Aida* was premiered. Sadly, the theatre is no more as it burnt to the ground some time after I left Egypt.

Larisa, of course, had tickets for the ballet but I said to her: 'Surely a girl from Moscow does not want to go to the Bolshoi when she is abroad. Let's give the tickets away to some Egyptian who would appreciate them. And I will show you one of the wonders of the world.' 'The Hanging Gardens of Babylon?' laughed Larisa. 'No, the Pyramid of Zoser. It's not the biggest but it is very charming.' 'How can I refuse?'

We set off towards Giza as it was growing dark. Larisa was quiet. She did not ask me any questions about my work or family but just smiled when she caught my eye. I noticed there was no wedding ring on her finger. As if by telepathy, she suddenly said: 'I didn't get married. My so-called girl friend stole him while I was away flying.' 'The will of Allah, as they say in the East,' I said, 'or as we Russians put it, all that you do is for the best.'

I stopped the car at the pyramid and we climbed the steps to the top. The Pyramid of Zoser was the first stone building in the world but I did not want to bore Larisa with a lecture. We stood close together, looking out over the moonlit dunes. The delicate scent of desert grasses floated on the air. Or perhaps it was her perfume. Our thoughts and feelings emerged, our hearts beat to a single rhythm. How rarely this happens in life. We drove back to Cairo in companionable silence. At the hotel, she kissed me and said: 'Thank you for this gift from you and from Fate. I will never forget this evening.'

Fortunately, Mrs Bausin never found out about this little affair. Constantly living a lie for the KGB may have been a strain, but for a young man, there were occasions when conspiracy had its uses.

The story did not quite end there. I saw Larisa once more at the airport as she was preparing to leave. I suppose she must have guessed that I was a KGB agent, for she told me that among her passengers were some political exiles whom she had overheard discussing the overthrow of a certain African government supported by Britain. I thanked her for the tip-off and waved her goodbye. Sadly, I never met Larisa again. I looked out for her each time I flew Aeroflot. But ever afterwards, the stewardesses who brought me my cold chicken and peas were always fat and middle-aged.

Theory and Practice

In Stalin's time, the secret police repressed millions of innocent people but I had no qualms about working abroad for the KGB in the 1960s and 1970s, when it was a totally different organisation, defending the interests of the Soviet Union, by means of asserting influence.

Working as we did with people, we agents had to be good psychologists. Either we influenced others or they influenced us. At the start of my posting to Cairo, I was courted by a Kuwaiti diplomat, who took me out to bars where we watched displays of belly-dancing. He had an axe to grind. He wanted the Soviet Union to support Kuwait's application to join the United Nations. As soon as his country was admitted to the world body, with the blessing of the Soviet Union as well as the other permanent members of the UN Security Council, he lost interest in me and ended our meetings, which had been a complete waste of time from the KGB's point of view. Usually, however, it was the other way round. I was wooing people who could be useful to Moscow.

I did it gently. Maintaining a relationship with an informer is, indeed, like dating a woman. He or she needs attention and affection. I never recruited anyone by means of blackmail. That crude method, which the KGB did use inside the Soviet Union, produces poor agents who work only out of fear. All my recruits were volunteers. Either they helped the KGB out of a sincere love for the Soviet Union, or they were paid. No agent of mine was ever jailed. I can lay my hand on my heart and say I never hurt anyone.

But the KGB was not only trying to influence individuals to work on its behalf. It also aimed to move whole societies in directions which suited Moscow. To this end, it used what the intelligence theorists called 'active measures'. Indeed, until it was closed down in the wake of the abortive hardline coup in Moscow in August 1991, there was a whole KGB department called 'A' branch, devoted to these measures.

When the snake tempted Eve to eat the forbidden fruit in the Garden of Eden, that was a classic example of active measures being used. Active measures included planting disinformation in the press or raising provocative questions in parliament, in fact anything short of violence which would arouse a people or a government into taking the kind of action the Soviet Union wanted to see.

The Lubyanka must have thought that its agents in Cairo were being lazy for, on one occasion, an officer from 'A' Branch came out to give us a lecture on the importance of active measures. We took him for a meal in one of the restaurants on the bank of the Suez Canal. 'With the aid of active measures, you should expose the imperialist policies of Western

countries and discredit them in the eyes of the leaders and peoples of the
Middle East and Africa,' he droned. 'But that's enough theory for now.
Someone take me to the other side of the canal. When I return to Moscow,
I want to boast how I crossed from Africa to Asia in fifteen minutes.' I
had to accompany this fellow, who was obviously on a freebie, because
he did not know the ferry timetables and could have got stuck on the
other side. And of course when he left, the job of increasing Cairo's
output of 'active measures' fell to me.

It was not easy. Of the two main Egyptian daily newspapers, one was
overtly pro-American and therefore unassailable. The other semi-official
publication was loyal to Nasser and there was little chance of a lowly
Soviet attaché having much influence on its chief editor. I did my best,
however.

One day an invitation to a new play arrived at the embassy and, since
no one else wanted to go, I went. It turned out that the playwright, to
whom I gave a bouquet of flowers, was also the drama critic of the
newspaper. Through him, I got a foot in the door. But when I tried to
offer him an article about China for publication, he said steadfastly: 'You
know that our country takes a strictly neutral position towards all the
great powers. If you have got anything on the Bolshoi Theatre, we could
run that.'

'A fat carp,' declared my *rezident* when I briefed him afterwards. 'You
can't catch him with a rod and line. You need a net but we haven't got
one big enough. Still, Moscow's orders must be carried out. Keep fishing.'

I was close to despair when I came across a little private weekly
newspaper called *Something for Everyone*. It really did have a wide range
of articles, from commentaries on global politics to advice on how to get
rid of cockroaches. There was a column of curious items called 'Secrets'.
'I must visit the editor of this intriguing publication,' I thought to myself.
I found him in a small office with a whirring air conditioner.

'At last I receive a visit from a Russian,' laughed the editor as he
welcomed me. 'I'm very pleased that you are interested in my "Secrets"
column. But have you noticed we don't have much on the Soviet view of
things? Do you know why? Because Tass and Novosti are so boring. You
have to admit that Reuters and the Associated Press provide more lively
stories.'

Although I was a little shocked by his directness, I had to agree with
his assessment of the official Soviet news agencies. I decided to be direct
in return. 'Do you like America?' I asked straight out. 'What is there to
like about it?' he replied. 'They give us a little wheat and then twist our
arms, choosing our friends and enemies for us.'

'Well then,' I said, 'I have an anti-American article for you. Will you publish it?' 'I certainly will, you can be sure of that.' 'Write this down then: "According to certain sources, American planes based in Libya are carrying out reconnaissance flights over the Suez Canal and the territory of some African countries." ' 'Is that all?' 'For now, yes.' 'We could add,' said the editor, 'that King Idris of Libya knows about this but is doing nothing.' 'Is that true?' 'Well, it's no secret that the king is weak and the Libyan monarchy will soon crumble. Now, if I publish this, I trust you will take me out to lunch at the Hilton Hotel.' 'Agreed, on the day of publication I will call for you.'

Not wanting to hear the *rezident*'s inevitable comments, I delayed telling him about this publishing venture until the article came out, when I proudly presented it to him as a birthday gift. 'Thank you,' he said, 'but do you know the first thing about this journalist? As for the Hilton Hotel, it is a notorious nest of spies. But go to the meeting anyway. Get some more background information on the editor. We will cover you in case of a provocation.'

The glass doors of the five-star hotel opened automatically for us and the editor led me to a quiet corner of the restaurant. 'We'll start with two double whiskies and then have lobster and steak, unless you have any objection,' he said. 'Of course not, by my guest.' 'Well, how did you like the article? You know the Libyan embassy called up immediately to deny it, but let them prove us wrong.'

The editor was happy to talk about himself. His name was Ibrahim but I gave him the pseudonym 'Nalim' which in Russian means 'eel'. 'That should please the *rezident*,' I thought. But the *rezident* was not going to like the bill for the meal, which was so large that my shock must have shown on my face. 'Don't be surprised,' said Nalim. 'This is the best hotel in the city.' 'Oh no,' I said hastily, 'your help is worth two such meals.' 'Same again next week then,' he said, and I ended up having to repeat the whole exercise. Only at our second lunch of lobster, steak and whisky did he drop the bombshell: that his uncle headed one of the branches of local counter-intelligence.

When the *rezident*, who by the way only let me put one of the two meals on expenses, learnt this piquant little detail, he cabled Moscow Centre urgently for advice. The answer came back that we should continue to feed Nalim articles, but treat him with caution. We tried to find out as much as we could about this journalist, who had become friendly suspiciously quickly and seemed to offer access to Egyptian secrets beyond our wildest dreams.

Eventually, I myself brought the drama with Nalim to a climax. At one of our meetings, I put on a worried look and told him I had been given the difficult task of writing an analysis of American policy in Egypt.

'I don't know where to begin,' I said. 'I can hardly quote the ra-ra articles of the pro-American press and the other papers only report briefly on which US officials are travelling where.' 'That's tough,' said Nalim. 'But maybe I can help. My uncle has a dossier on the activities of all the American diplomats in Cairo. I'm sure he won't mind giving it to his beloved nephew.'

My heart nearly missed a beat. I tried not to sound too enthusiastic. 'It would certainly be a start,' I said.

Next time I visited Nalim's office, he locked the door, opened the safe and gave me an envelope, adding with a wink that it would soon be his uncle's birthday and he would like to give him a present. I got safely back to the embassy with the envelope. This was no provocation. The *rezident* was delighted with the contents – a list of names of CIA operatives and informers, including one man we had thought was working for us. 'If the Egyptians know who the CIA agents are, why don't they move against them?' I asked. 'Ah,' said the *rezident*, 'it's easier to control the situation when you know who is who.'

Nalim was paid 50 Egyptian pounds for this valuable information about the 'main enemy', as the KGB called the CIA. His motives were purely mercenary, but that did not worry us. He became a regular informer and served Moscow's interests for several years after I left Cairo.

'Oh Fate, Take Me Back to Cairo'

My time in Egypt was coming to an end. The KGB did not like to keep its agents in any one posting for more than five years, lest habit started to dull their alertness and they began to go native. As it happened, I was homesick for Russia. I had a good life in Cairo, but there was something alien and temporary about it. I missed the Russian countryside and having friends I could choose instead of the narrow circle of embassy colleagues I was obliged to tolerate.

But before I could leave, a few loose ends had to be tied up. For one thing, we had decided to bring out a book called *The True Face of the CIA*, using in part the material Nalim had supplied. We could not expect Nalim to publish this himself for, as we say in Russian, you cannot take meat and milk from the same cow. So I approached the owner of a small private newspaper called *Facts*, who sometimes ran the pro-Soviet feature articles put out by Novosti. His name was Avgur and he lived very poorly in a working-class suburb. Partly for money but partly, I think, because he genuinely admired the Soviet Union, he took on the project and some months later I was proud to see, along with *Time* and *Newsweek*, our book in the city's new kiosks.

Some years before, Avgur had worked in Saudi Arabia as, he claimed, the public relations advisor to King Saud. In addition to producing the book for us, he also gave me a written analysis of the political intrigues at the royal court in Riyadh. This was sensational material as Saudi Arabia was then a complete blank spot for the KGB. We had no agents there and all we knew about the country was the little we could extract from the Muslims of Soviet Central Asia who were allowed to go on pilgrimage to Mecca. Unfortunately, the KGB was not able to make use of Avgur's analysis because we only had his word for it that he had worked for the king and no second source to confirm what he was saying.

My last job in Cairo was to recruit an Egyptian counter-intelligence agent who was working at a West European embassy in which we had a strong interest. The problem was to get him on one side for long enough to make him a proposal. Colleagues suggested different ideas, including following him home from work and approaching him in the street. But since I was about to leave and had nothing to lose, I had the bold idea of going directly to visit him at his apartment. The *rezident* approved, for it was a practice of the KGB to use outgoing agents for slightly more risky jobs. If a scandal broke, they would soon be safely in Moscow anyway.

The man's name was Muhammed and he welcomed me when I called at his flat without an appointment. While his wife served coffee, we chatted about this and that. And then Muhammed himself opened the negotiations which led to him working not only for the Egyptians and his European employers but also for the KGB. Evidently he was attracted by the prospect of three salaries.

The fish was hooked, but I had to pass him on to those who came after me in Cairo. Mother Russia beckoned. On the plane home, I remembered the words from the old song: 'Oh Fate, take me back to Cairo.' But after two years on the desk in Moscow Centre, I was sent out to Iraq. I only ever saw Egypt again as I passed through in transit to other destinations in the Arab world.

BERLIN

Name	Kevorkov, Vyacheslav Erwandovich
Born	21 July 1923
Education	Higher
Special Subject	Officer training
Languages	German, English
Military Rank	Major-General
Worked in	Germany, Belgium
Marital Status	Married
Sports	Rowing
Hobbies	Collecting the wise thoughts of my friends
Favourite Tipple	Tomato juice
Brand of Cigarettes	Chocolate ones

Among the Ruins

Four admirals, representing the US, Britain, France and the Soviet Union, are sitting round a table, drawing lots from a vase. Admiral Melnikov of the Soviet fleet plunges his hand into the pot and pulls out a slip of paper. '*Graf Zeppelin*,' he cried. 'Germany's first aircraft carrier. That's ours now.'

I witnessed this surreal scene as a humble naval translator attached to the Red Army when it entered Berlin in 1945. Like many Russians of my generation, I first visited Germany not as a tourist but as a serviceman. I interpreted in many situations as I worked for SVAG, the Soviet Military administration in Germany. On one occasion, I even translated for Marshal Zhukov. But after all these years the admirals, sitting like guests at Alice in Wonderland's tea party, stick in my mind.

They were meeting in a villa outside Berlin to carve up the Nazi German fleet. The atmosphere at the lottery was very convivial. The drink flowed and, after all the ships had been shared out, a huge banquet was held. Winston Churchill was yet to stand up in Fulton, Missouri, and make his famous speech about Stalin lowering an 'iron curtain from

Stettin to Trieste', which for Moscow signalled the start of the Cold War, and the Allies were still on friendly terms.

I can't remember now exactly how Hitler's fleet was split up, but the Soviet Union did not do particularly well out of the lottery. The *Graf Zeppelin* may have been a fine vessel but she was lying at the bottom of the Baltic Sea, having been scuttled by the Germans. What the Soviet Union had won was the right to salvage her. In addition, we got several smaller ships. Admiral Melnikov was disappointed.

I can only guess at the admirals' more private thoughts as they divided up the spoils of victory. Personally, I felt no bitterness towards the Germans who had invaded my country, no sense of triumph over them now that their war machine was crushed, just a deep sense of their national tragedy.

Outside on the streets, Berliners were working round the clock to rebuild their shattered city. On Unter den Linden avenue, a tattered Nazi propaganda banner, quoting Hitler's prewar promise 'Give me ten years and you will not recognise Germany', took on a whole new meaning against the backdrop of destruction. But the Germans were determined to forget the nightmare as quickly as possible. They were also incredibly well organised. Lacking bulldozers, they shifted rubble by hand. I was especially impressed by the women, bright scarves knotted round their heads, lifting stones, moving timbers, still coming across corpses in the ruins. They refused to feel sorry for themselves but worked doggedly, by lamplight when the daylight faded. 'The sooner we rebuild our factories, the sooner we will eat,' they said. I respect them for that. Actually, I always had admired the Germans.

The German military attaché was a neighbour of ours when I was growing up on Rileyeva Street in Moscow in the 1930s and as a boy I played with his children. Later, when war broke out, I studied German at the Military Institute for Foreign Languages. I was being prepared, of course, to translate during the interrogation of enemy prisoners of war. But German was also a language I enjoyed, probably because I had heard it in childhood.

The prisoners were held in various camps, including one near Tula, south of Moscow, where local coal mines and forests provided work for them. I assisted at the interrogation of German soldiers taken in various battles on Soviet territory. They were painfully young, only eighteen or nineteen years old. I never met the hardened killers from the SS.

I particularly remember one POW, a lad called Heinz from Bavaria. When we began questioning him in the barracks, he broke down and cried. Then he pulled out a pack of photographs – the Germans always carried lots of photos on them – and showed us a picture of his new bride on skis in the Alps. 'Do you have a girlfriend?' he asked me, and when I said yes he promised to make a gift for her. Later Heinz, who was a cobbler by trade, gave me a pair of shoes he had sewn from black leather. 'I hope they fit her,' he said.

We interrogated in teams of three, including the translator. A military officer would try to extract from the POW details of his unit and where it was positioned. Then a 'political officer', the equivalent of the chaplain in our atheist Red Army, would try to make the prisoner see the error of his ways and convert him to our Communist faith. Occasionally, a German would be 'turned' and sent back to the front to spy for us. But most of the lads were to stay in the camps for the duration of the war – and longer.

Although few of them went so far as to become Communists, the Germans quickly realised that Hitler had betrayed them with his promise to make them the master race. I remember how one German officer, told that if he did not cooperate he would find himself on trial together with Hitler, declared that it would be an honour for him to be judged alongside his Führer. He still saw the dictator as a hero. But very soon afterwards, the atmosphere in his barracks had changed and he was joining in as the prisoners told jokes about the Nazi leadership. For example: 'Goering goes to see Hitler. He is pulling an ugly, knobbly creature on a lead. "Why have you brought your tortoise?" asks Hitler. "That's not a tortoise," says Goering. "That's Goebbels." '

Former prisoners have themselves told me that they also came to appreciate the way they were treated in the Soviet Union. Although this was not always popular with ordinary Russians, many of whom were starving, Stalin insisted on abiding by the Geneva Convention, which meant that prisoners should be fed and otherwise kept in the same conditions they had enjoyed in the army. 'We came to kill you and you treated us like human beings,' one ex-prisoner said to me years afterwards.

The prisoners were not released immediately after the war, however, but held here until the early 1950s as a punishment for the devastation Hitler had wrought. Kept separately from our own criminals and political prisoners in the gulag archipelago, they were sent out to work in construction brigades. The skill of the Germans can still be seen today in the solid buildings they erected in Moscow, including the Peking Hotel and the block on Sadovaya Samotechnaya Ring, which houses foreign correspondents.

You would have thought that the POWs, when finally freed, would have joyfully returned to Germany and never thought of the Soviet Union again. Of course, most of them did settle happily at home. But quite a number of them chose within a short time to return to Moscow to work as journalists. They had picked up the Russian language and an understanding of the country. In a few cases, they put this to use on behalf of the Bundesnachrichtendienst, the West German intelligence service. But mostly they were bona fide correspondents with a genuine interest in Soviet affairs.

In particular, I remember two – the late Heinz Late of Ruhrnachrichten, a grouping of small local newspapers in the Ruhr region, and Hermann Pörzgen of *Frankfurter Allgemeine Zeitung*. He achieved his ambition of living and dying in his adopted Russia.

Pörzgen had been a correspondent in Moscow before the war and had accompanied the German military attaché on a trip to the Baku oil fields. Because of this, after Germany invaded the Soviet Union in 1941, he was treated not as a mere POW but as a spy and sentenced to ten years in the notoriously tough Vladimir prison. On his release, he immediately applied to return to Moscow. Why? 'Because I got to know the Russian people,' he told me. 'Even my guards in jail took risks to help me. I understood that the Russian spirit was a mixture of cruelty and warm-heartedness. I was fascinated.'

Late was another Russophile who wanted to interpret the Soviet Union for his fellow Germans. Sometimes oppressed by the atmosphere in the enormous correspondents' ghetto on Kutuzovsky Prospekt, he would take his typewriter out into the woods and sit under the trees, tapping out his articles about Soviet life.

But Late also believed the Russians should know more about the German people. He was a man with a mission to promote mutual understanding. My future career with the KGB was to be devoted to a delicate process of rebuilding trust and friendship after a terrible war which had left more than buildings in ruins. I could not have operated without vital help from the enlightened Heinz Late.

But all that was to come later, in the 1970s, when Chancellor Willy Brandt was pursuing his Ostpolitik. Before that, the Berlin Wall was thrown up and almost overnight Europe was divided. As for me, I left the services and went to work in the Lubyanka, the formidable granite headquarters of the Committee for State Security.

Massaging the Media

At the end of the war, I had stayed on in Berlin as a junior officer, helping to demilitarise Germany. We used to go into beer cellars, looking for radio equipment which the Wehrmacht typically hid in sealed chambers behind the huge barrels. I was still in Germany in 1949 when it split into two states and remember the Western powers' airlift of supplies to Berlin, now an island surrounded by Soviet-controlled territory. This was a tense time, when it seemed a new war could break out. But then I returned home to study at the Military Academy in Moscow.

I was hoping to become a military attaché, like our old German neighbour whose children had been my boyhood friends. I was good at languages, perhaps because I was the child of a mixed marriage. My mother Maria was Russian while my father Erwand was an Armenian who, having escaped massacre at the hands of the Turks in 1915, went on to become a tailor and lived to the ripe old age of 105. At the Military Academy, I not only improved my German but also studied Turkish and English. In addition I learnt to dance, an essential skill for a would-be diplomat.

But it was not to be. Instead I was forced to join the KGB in a large intake of fresh staff after the death of Stalin and the execution of his secret policeman Lavrenty Beria, whose appointees the new Kremlin chief, Nikita Krushchev, did not trust.

Just as officers from the regular German army hated the SS, so men of military honour in the Soviet Union despised the KGB. I had very negative feelings about this organisation, whose atrocities were already known thanks to Krushchev's famous speech to the Twentieth Congress of the Communist Party in 1956. Thus, when the KGB called me to work for them, I asked my senior officers at the academy to save me. 'We cannot go against the KGB,' they said, 'but if you manage to get out of this situation yourself, we will take you back.'

Although I was a good student, I deliberately did as badly as I could during my initial training with the KGB. Then I returned to the military, proudly showing them my poor references and assuming they would welcome me with open arms. Instead they rejected me as a failure and I had no choice but to go crawling to the Lubyanka again.

By now the door was closed to the elite First Main Directorate, responsible for intelligence-gathering abroad, and I had to be satisfied with the Second Main Directorate, which did the duller job of monitoring the activities of foreigners inside the Soviet Union. I say I had no choice. Of course, I could have refused point blank to work for the KGB. Then I would have been expelled from the Communist Party and become an ordinary Soviet worker. But that was hardly a choice.

I started my new job in 1960 and it was very boring indeed, although at least I was not reduced to following tourists. Guides from the state tourist agency, Intourist, took care of that. It was a Western myth, however, that all the rooms in Soviet hotels were bugged. Frankly, the

KGB simply could not afford such a blanket eavesdropping operation. So it concentrated only on those visitors about whom it had suspicions. They were offered special rooms, where there were of course hidden listening devices.

I was one step up, working with resident journalists, who were paranoid and saw the KGB everywhere. But not all their drivers and secretaries reported to the 'organs', as they called us. And again we only followed them and bugged their flats and offices on a selective basis.

This really was the low point of my career, but gradually my work became more interesting as I began to specialise in dealing with the German press corps. Bonn had a law banning the use of journalists as spies, but there were cases of West German correspondents who admitted to us that they were earning extra money by gathering intelligence for the Bundesnachrichtendienst. Obviously I cannot name names. In addition to these men who had laid themselves open to blackmail, there were journalists who sympathised with the Soviet Union and were critical of their own government.

But KGB head Yuri Andropov, who despite his severe image was actually a man far ahead of his time, was not interested in hooking journalists like these to work as secret agents. Rather he wanted to exert political influence over them and also understand more about their countries. For it was the tragedy of our Soviet leaders – and Andropov was no exception – that they rarely travelled abroad and knew little of the world outside. Much of the KGB chairman's knowledge came from watching foreign films in the special closed cinema at the Lubyanka.

And so, presenting myself as a journalist, writing in the Soviet media under the Georgian-sounding pseudonym of Tschitashvili, I kept up regular contacts with various correspondents. We used to meet for lunch in the restaurant of the Hotel Ukraina, one of the seven 'wedding cake' skyscrapers which were Stalin's legacy to Moscow, and situated conveniently close to the complex on Kutuzovsky Prospekt where most of the foreign journalists lived.

I was to the German press what Viktor Louis was to Fleet Street – the source who leaked the information the Kremlin wanted the world to know. Over these lunches, the journalists also briefed us – and thus the KGB and the Politburo – on their countries' internal politics, which was very useful, sometimes helping Moscow to prepare its negotiating positions. It was as if the Soviet Union had a second tier of diplomats, interpreting the world for it.

The journalists, and even their editors back home, mostly knew they were dealing with the KGB, although we did not spell it out to them. But they were happy enough to play the game, because we gave them good information which they could attribute to 'informed sources'.

I never knowingly gave my correspondents disinformation, although I did massage the truth into forms acceptable to the Kremlin. The correspondents rewrote what I gave them anyway in the style that suited their papers. An example of the help I gave my privileged journalists was telling them unattributably that Leonid Brezhnev had had a heart attack, when the press corps as a whole was being told officially he had nothing worse than a cold.

In these pre-glasnost days, we all had to work within the framework set by the Soviet authorities. I tried to be as open as I could, while the journalists learnt to read between the lines. Andropov actually favoured widening the limits of the possible, but he had to fight his corner in a predominantly conservative Politburo. He planted the seeds of glasnost. But it was not until the Old Guard died and Mikhail Gorbachev came to power in 1985 that the flowers of freedom blossomed.

An Olive Branch at Christmas

Although I had made an inauspicious start at the KGB, my bosses came to trust me and I was given a chance to see Germany again. At first I travelled only to the GDR to liaise on the Lubyanka's behalf with the East Germans.

I was in Berlin in 1961, just days after the Wall went up. I knew it was going to happen – the East German Communist leader, Walter Ulbricht, had complained to Krushchev that West Berliners were flooding into the East to buy up the subsidised goods there and the Kremlin leader had advised him to isolate his young Communist state – but it was still a shock. The Wall really did materialise almost overnight. One day there was a trail of barbed wire and the next there was a gigantic concrete barrier between the two Germanys, cutting through people's lives. There was no panic. Germans do not panic. But I remember the distress of a young man called Heinz Reichenbach, who played the accordion in a café in East Berlin. Like the good German son that he was, he used to visit his mother in West Berlin regularly and telephone her every morning. Suddenly he lost all contact with her. The escape attempts and the shootings at the Wall had not yet started but immediately, seeing the suffering of Heinz and others like him, I felt a deep unease. Someday this absurd division of East and West would have to end, I knew.

A few years later, I was fortunate to join a small team working to undermine the divisive effect of the Wall, starting the process which would finally bring down this ugly symbol of the Cold War. I continued to assist the press in Moscow, but this work became a cover for a secret, extended mission which took me to Berlin over 700 times. Although I did not actually live in the city, travelling back and forth so often, I got to know it very well.

The year was 1969. Andropov was worrying that the Soviet Union was becoming cut off from the rest of the world. Foreign Minister Andrei Gromyko, known as 'Mr Nyet' in the West because of the hard line he always took in negotiations, was obsessed with the idea that, if there were to be East-West detente, only friendship with the USA was good enough for a super power like the USSR.

But Andropov understood that this relationship could not be an equal one, as America had far more economic power than the Soviet Union. Instead, he thought we should look to Europe for new friends, especially to Germany, with which Russia had centuries-old ties broken by the aberration of the Second World War. For this, we needed a dialogue not only with our East German allies but also with the leaders of West Germany, bound up in Nato. Andropov entrusted me with the task of making contact. 'Only do it discreetly,' he said.

Working with me from the outset was another Russian specialist on Germany, Valery Lednev. Unlike me, he did not serve the KGB but was a bona fide journalist writing for the newspapers *Izvestia* and *Sovietskaya Cultura*. How were we to get an introduction to senior West German politicians?

We tried the obvious thing and took the West German press attaché, a man called Reinhelt, out to lunch. The venue was, as usual, the restaurant of the Hotel Ukraina. Without revealing why we sought a contact, we asked him if he could put us in touch with someone at the top in Bonn. 'Well, I'll have to ask my wife about that,' he said, and we understood at once that he was giving us the diplomatic brush-off.

Then we tried Hermann Pörzgen, the veteran correspondent of *Frankfurter Allgemeine Zeitung*. With him, we were a little franker. 'Andropov is interested in making friends with West Germany,' we said. 'Oh,' he said, 'can I mention this in the book I'm writing?' Obviously, cooperation with the too-talkative Pörzgen was out of the question.

We were beginning to despair when we ran into Heinz Late, the correspondent of the Ruhr regional news network, at a cocktail party given to mark Press Day on 5 May in the House of Journalists, one of the pretty old mansions on Moscow's inner Boulevard Ring. He was waving a copy of *Mezhdunarodny Zhizn* (*International Life*), one of the grimmer Soviet newspapers, and he already had a few drinks inside him. 'Why do you write this nonsense about Fascists in my country?' he complained. 'You know nothing about the real democratic, modern Germany. If I want to speak to politicians in my country, all I have to do is pick up the phone. But you can't talk to your leaders. Your system is still so closed.'

A light went on in my head. 'He can talk to his political leaders on the phone.' Valery and I drank some more with him, calmed him down and we ended up going back to his flat on Kutuzovsky Prospekt for an all-night session with a bottle of vodka.

In this relaxed atmosphere, we explained to Heinz what we needed. 'Can you find us a solid contact in Bonn?' 'I'll ask Schmelzer, my chief editor,' he said. 'He knows everyone.' 'But it must be done discreetly,' we said. Heinz could be trusted. The next day he flew to Germany and two days later he came back, saying: 'Schmelzer can fix it. Who do you want to meet?'

Andropov reported to Brezhnev, who said only a contact at the highest level would do. That meant Kurt-Georg Kissinger, the Christian Democratic Chancellor. But Schmelzer suggested we wait a little. Elections were due in West Germany that autumn. The Social Democrat Willy Brandt was almost certain to win. It would make more sense to start a new relationship with him.

And that is what happened. Brandt was elected in October 1969 and shortly afterwards Schmelzer advised us that the man with whom we should deal was Egon Bahr, a journalist who had been close to the new Chancellor when he was still Mayor of West Berlin and who had now come to Bonn to work as his state secretary.

Andropov, Lednev and I met at a secret KGB flat near my childhood home on Rileyeva Street and decided that Valery, as the clean journalist, would travel to Bonn to 'interview' Bahr while I, as the KGB staff officer, would control the operation from Moscow. During the meeting, if a suitable moment arose, Valery would put forward the idea of starting a Soviet-West German dialogue. But the problem was how to convince Bahr that a simple Soviet journalist could be speaking on behalf of the Politburo.

Andropov had an idea. Some months earlier Brandt, the author of Ostpolitik or the policy of pursuing detente with the East, had written a letter to the Soviet Prime Minister, Alexei Kosygin. 'We need a direct link with which no one will interfere,' he had said. He had expressed our very idea. No one knew of the existence of this letter except Brandt and the top Soviet leadership. If Valery carried it and showed it to Bahr, there could be no doubt that he had the highest authorisation to discuss the opening of a channel of communication. The channel would have to be secret because our East German allies on the one hand and Bonn's Nato partners on the other would be unlikely to approve of it.

Valery flew to Bonn on Christmas Eve, hardly a good time to be doing business in a punctual country like Germany, but Schmelzer managed to arrange an interview for him with Bahr. It was five o'clock in the afternoon. Bahr's secretary was packing up to go home for the holiday. 'I'll be going home myself soon,' Bahr said pointedly to the Soviet journalist.

But in a master stroke, Valery took from his pocket a little plastic Christmas tree which he had bought in Moscow. Bahr was touched by this cheap souvenir, which served as an olive branch in the season of goodwill. Then Valery showed him the letter. Bahr said afterwards he went cold when he saw it. He immediately understood its meaning. 'Behind you stand those with the power to decide our relations?' he asked. 'The man at the very top,' Valery said, meaning Brezhnev. 'OK, I'll tell Brandt. Come back tomorrow.'

The next day, Christmas Day 1969, it was decided to open the secret channel with Bahr on the German side and Lednev and myself on the Soviet side acting as go-betweens for Brandt and Brezhnev. In the New Year, Bahr flew out to Moscow. Despite the bitter cold, he came without a hat. Valery lent him his fur *shapka* when he met him at Sheremetyevo airport. Bahr was received by Gromyko at the Foreign Ministry, another of the 'wedding cake' skyscrapers. Then Valery took him home to meet his wife, who cooked a wonderful supper, and me. Valery introduced me as his boss. He did not say that I was from the KGB. But Bahr said years afterwards that, even if he had known, it would not have changed anything. 'All that mattered was that Slava [the diminutive form of my name] had influence,' he said.

We agreed that we would meet regularly at Bahr's residence, 14 Pückler-strasse, West Berlin. We would never meet in the GDR because we did not want the hardline Erich Honecker to know what was going on. Neither would we use the phone or write anything down. All our arrangements would be verbal so that the West German Foreign Ministry did not find anything out. It was harder for the Germans than for us to keep secrets because they had a democracy and everything leaked out. But at this stage, we did not see why our fledgling friendship should become the business of the Americans, the British and the French.

Of course the Soviet Union's war-time allies quickly realised that meetings were taking place. When Valery and I visited West Berlin, we were followed, first by clodhopping CIA operatives who made no attempt to hide the fact they were tailing us, then by the British who were hardly more subtle. We used to stay at the Hotel Am Zoo. Thinking we might be homosexuals, the British sent two pretty boys to linger in the corridors and try to pick us up in the bar. 'I'll deal with this,' said Valery, who had strong feelings about homosexuality.

Later, I went into his room to find him sitting on the floor with the two British agents. He had laid out a train set which he had bought for his son back in Moscow and was making his guests, whom he had already got terribly drunk on vodka, dizzy as the little wagons raced round the track. 'Drink more, drink more,' he cried. 'It is the only cure for sexual deviance.' The British got the message and started sending leggy young women to follow us instead. But neither they nor the Americans found out what we were discussing in our meetings with Bahr.

East Germany we also managed to fool. Erich Mielke, the head of the Stasi secret police, soon spotted that we were going back and forth to West Berlin with suspicious regularity and demanded an explanation. Andropov sent me to reassure him that the Soviet Union was not doing anything behind the back of its loyal Communist ally, but that it simply wanted to improve relations with West Germany. 'I know what you're up to,' said Mielke. But from his questions, it was clear that he didn't. He thought we were talking about economic matters and I did not disabuse him. 'I read in *Der Spiegel* that someone had given Brandt three kilograms of caviar for his fiftieth birthday,' Mielke persisted. 'Was it you?' 'Oh, all right, yes,' I said, feigning petulance. 'Now our secret's out.'

Having extracted this from me, he calmed down. And he never found out about the weighty political issues which were really the subject of our discussions in the secret channel between Bonn and Moscow.

Confessions of a Go-Between

We used the channel for twelve years, from 1969 to 1982. In this time, we discussed all manner of subjects which were of mutual interest to West Germany and the Soviet Union. Afterwards, they would be discussed more widely in the Bundestag and the Politburo and some information would eventually reach the general public.

One of our biggest achievements at the start of the dialogue was the writing of a Friendship Treaty between West Germany and the Soviet Union. Signed in 1970, it committed each side to respecting the other's territorial inviolability. This may sound like diplomatese, but it brought tangible benefits for West Berliners, who felt stranded and insecure, cut off as they were from West Germany proper by a stretch of East German territory. The people of the divided city would have to wait until reunification in 1990 to get full German citizenship, but the agreement at least gave them the confidence of close links between West Berlin and West Germany, which were now guaranteed by an international treaty.

Once friendship had broken out, Brandt and Brezhnev, who were both expansive characters and lovers of the good life, wanted to meet each other. Brezhnev took Brandt yachting off the Crimean coast in 1971. And Brandt also invited his new Soviet friend to Bonn.

We tend to remember Leonid Ilyich now as a feeble old man, falling down stairs under the influence of alcohol and slurring his speeches to the Communist Party faithful, but in his younger days he was charming and elegant, although flawed already by the self-love that allowed him to hang blown-up photographs of himself all round his flat and award himself medals. He was also naive and anxious to do the right thing.

In Bonn, of course, he would be meeting Brandt and his Norwegian wife Ruth, but he was also keen to have talks with the Bavarian leader, Franz Joseph Strauss, whom we regarded as West German's most reactionary politician and therefore a figure of particular fascination. Would Brandt mind if he did this? I was ordered to use the secret channel to find out. Brandt, of course, was completely relaxed about it. West Germany was a democracy. During his visit, Brezhnev would naturally be free to meet opposition as well as government figures. But this was a novel idea for the Kremlin leader, who would not have dreamt of letting a top guest to the Soviet Union meet any of our dissidents.

The visit went ahead. Brezhnev prepared carefully for it. He packed a smart new blue suit and gallons of eau-de-cologne. I once saw the inside of his Moscow flat at 26, Kutuzovsky Prospekt and his bathroom was full of bottles of aftershave lotion. He must have taken the whole collection with him to smell sweet in West Germany.

The talks with Brandt went very well, but were routine compared with the meeting with Strauss, which took place at the villa outside Bonn allotted to Brezhnev for the duration of his stay. Strauss and Brezhnev, who both loved beer, eating and women, got on like a house on fire and quickly found a common language despite their ideological differences.

'You probably think I am a second-rate politician because I have never been Chancellor,' Strauss said to his new friend, 'but I am a good historian. And I know that whenever Germany and Russia were together, there was order in Europe. When they fought, Europe was in chaos. It was always thus and will always be so.'

Brezhnev was an uneducated man who knew little history, but he was deeply impressed by these words. 'This channel of yours is a wonderful idea,' he told Andropov when he returned to Moscow. Thus Andropov's position in the Politburo, and especially *vis-à-vis* the US-oriented Gromyko, was strengthened. And the future of our dialogue with the West Germans was secure.

As time went on, Brezhnev and Brandt became such good friends that opposition Christian Democrat politicians in the Bundestag began saying the Chancellor was virtually a Communist. 'Can we do something about this?' Bahr asked at one of the regular meetings with Valery and me in West Berlin. We passed the message on to Moscow and it was arranged that Brezhnev would make a speech attacking Brandt at the next Soviet Communist Party Congress. This he did. The CPSU and the SPD were linked only by a common desire for peace in Europe, he said. Communists and Social Democrats remained ideological enemies. And that satisfied everybody.

Brandt also took an interest in Brezhnev's health, which began failing in the 1970s although he clung on to power until 1982. On one occasion, the Chancellor, thinking he was being sympathetic, prepared a telegram to Brezhnev, wishing him a 'speedy recovery after his heart attack'. This time Valery and I asked for Bahr's understanding. 'If Willy sends that,' we said, 'you might as well start arranging our funerals as well.' For the German and Soviet mentalities were very different. Kremlin leaders did not appreciate interest, even of a well-meaning nature, in their health. It is only now that President Boris Yeltsin tolerates comment about his internal organs.

Our fruitful relationship with Brandt came to a sad end, however, as scandal finished off his political career. Moscow knew that Erich Honecker had been jealous of the West German Chancellor since ecstatic crowds chanted 'Willy, Willy,' when he visited Erfurt, East Germany, in 1970. But the unmasking in 1974 of Brandt's aide, Gunther Guillaume, as an East German spy, came as a complete shock to us. The West always assumed that we knew everything our Warsaw Pact allies were up to, but it was not quite so. Guillaume was new to the KGB and for a while we worried that the secrets of the channel had become known to the Stasi. But we were saved by the fact that we never wrote anything down.

At about the same time as the spy scandal, Brandt was also hit with a sex scandal. Critics inside his own Social Democratic party claimed to have photographs of him naked with a woman journalist in a train compartment. If Brandt did not resign over Guillaume, they said, the compromising pictures would be published instead to force him out of office.

Brezhnev could not understand this at all. 'Ha,' he said, 'so what? So Brandt's had a woman. Imagine if I was to resign every time I had a woman.' And he wrote a letter to the Chancellor, telling him not to be afraid, the Soviet Union would stand by him. Brandt replied that he intended to hold on. But then, as we were travelling by taxi through West Berlin, Valery and I heard a news flash on the radio: Brandt had resigned and the post of Chancellor had passed automatically to his deputy, Helmut Schmidt.

Brezhnev was very upset. He got used to people. He had come to like

Brandt. And now he would have to get to know his successor. Schmidt was not Brezhnev's type at all. A drier character than Brandt, he was also more pro-Nato. Nevertheless, the Kremlin leader wrote to him, saying the secret channel of communication had paid political dividends and he hoped it would continue.

Valery and I made it clear we wanted to go on working with Bahr, whom Schmidt did not entirely trust because he had been so close to Brandt. The new Chancellor yielded to our request and Bahr continued to speak to us on Bonn's behalf. But he lost his post as state secretary and became a more lowly SPD faction leader in the Bundestag.

For a while the channel worked as before. But we felt Schmidt spoilt the West German-Soviet friendship when he stood up at the Institute of Strategic Studies in London and gave a speech complaining about the Soviet Union's deployment of SS-20 long-range missiles on the territory of the republic of Belorussia. The rockets were not targeted on Germany, but rather intended to fly over and hit the United States if the need unfortunately were to arise. But Schmidt said they disturbed the balance of forces in Europe. As a result of the fuss he made, the US began deploying Pershing missiles on German soil, which provoked a wave of peace demonstrations in Germany at the end of the 1970s.

Relations between Bonn and Moscow were now at a very low point. Brezhnev was due to visit Germany, but he said he had no appetite for the trip. Schmidt said that if he did not come, relations would deteriorate even further. Brezhnev allowed himself to be persuaded and, in the end, he had not too bad a meeting with Schmidt, who honoured the Soviet leader by inviting him to his home in Hamburg in 1978.

During the Second World War, Schmidt had served in an anti-aircraft unit which penetrated Russia as far as Zavidovo, the place where Brezhnev was later to have his hunting lodge. As a young man, Brezhnev had fought the Nazi invaders, although further south, where he would not have run into Schmidt's units. Nevertheless, Schmidt said rhetorically to Brezhnev: 'I could have shot you. And you could have killed me. Our countries must never fight again.' At this, Brezhnev's chin trembled and he nearly cried. He was by now a sentimental old man. And although the warmth of the Brandt era could not be rekindled, at least the damage to the West German-Soviet relationship was limited.

In December 1979, the channel was again under threat, this time because of our behaviour. The Soviet Union was planning to invade Afghanistan. Andropov told me privately he was against the adventure. He said, with foresight, that Afghanistan would become our Vietnam. But the Politburo ordered it. The question was whether we should give our friends in Bonn an advance tip-off.

'If Schmidt wakes up and finds out from the newspapers that we have gone into Afghanistan, then the special channel will be dead,' said Andropov. 'But can we trust him not to leak the information to the Americans?' 'I don't know,' I said. 'We can talk to Bahr. But there's no guarantee. Schmidt is very close to the White House.' 'Well,' said Andropov, 'we'll put it to the test. Is Helmut Schmidt a gentleman?'

Together with me this time, Valery set off on another of his badly timed Christmas visits to Germany. From West Berlin, we rang Bahr, who was in Bonn, and requested an urgent meeting. 'I can't possibly get away,' said Bahr. 'Send Valery to me in Bonn.'

I accompanied my colleague to West Berlin's Tempelhof airport. I was getting ready to wave him goodbye when the border guard said he could not travel because he did not have a visa for West Germany. 'But West Berlin is part of West Germany,' we said. 'Unfortunately your government does not recognise that fact,' said the border guard with obvious pleasure. It was hopeless to argue with him. Instead, we rang Bahr again, who had to send out his assistant to pick up Valery's passport. Then he returned again with the visa. The whole process took a frustrating twenty-four hours, during which we kicked our heels at our beloved Hotel Am Zoo.

By this time, the sacred German Christmas holiday had already started and Bahr had left Bonn for his home in Flensburg on the border with Denmark. Valery travelled there to meet him and Bahr picked him up in his car. They had a lucky escape as the speeding vehicle hit a moose in the road, which only added to Valery's already nervous mood. Throughout the journey, he kept twiddling the knobs of the car radio, terrified that the invasion of Afghanistan would be announced before he could complete his mission.

But during a walk by the sea, Valery managed to give Bahr advance notice that Soviet troops were poised to storm Kabul. 'Have you gone mad?' said Bahr. 'It will be the end for all of us.' Schmidt was informed by telephone and, because of the urgency of the situation, he received Valery at the place where he was spending his Christmas holidays. The Chancellor was calm. 'When will it happen?' was all he asked. 'In the next few days,' said Valery. 'Brezhnev asks you to keep this strictly between ourselves.' Schmidt said neither yes or no.

But the Chancellor did indeed turn out to be a gentleman. Bahr told us later Schmidt said to him: 'I'll be interested to know when the Americans inform us. They have satellites. They must know now.' But they kept silent right up to the last minute. Immediately after the invasion, Bahr went to Washington and asked why the Americans had not shared their intelligence with their German allies. He never received a satisfactory answer from the Carter administration.

Perhaps because of this slight, Schmidt decided to keep our secret channel open despite the international uproar over Afghanistan. But its days were numbered. Brezhnev was nearing the end of his life. Andropov and Konstantin Chernenko, who succeeded him one after the other, were too old and ill to rule for long. When the energetic Mikhail Gorbachev burst onto the world stage, he did everything out in the open. And in Helmut Kohl, the new Chancellor in Bonn, he found an equally dynamic partner ready to take Soviet-German relations onto an altogether higher plane.

The Unwilling Traveller

The exciting new era of glasnost and perestroika still lay ahead, however. In the mid-1970s, East-West relations remained quite tense. Particularly irritating for the Soviet Union was Western criticism of the way we repressed our dissidents. But the persecution of one Russian writer so concerned Willy Brandt that he was willing to risk his friendship with Brezhnev over it. Luckily, through the secret channel, we found a solution to one of the most delicate questions of the day: what to do with the turbulent chronicler of the gulags, Alexander Solzhenitsyn?

The cellist Mstislav Rostropovich had come out to the West with his wife, the opera singer Galina Vishnevskaya, after he had had a row over repertoire with the interfering Soviet Minister of Culture, Yekaterina Furtseva. Ruth Brandt befriended the exiled musicians, who told her how badly the Soviet authorities were treating their friend Solzhenitsyn.

A campaign had started in the Soviet press against the writer, who for a while took refuge at Rostropovich's *dacha*, or cottage, in the countryside outside Moscow. 'Outraged workers' were writing in to official newspapers, demanding that the Kremlin take action against Solzhenitsyn, the 'impudent enemy of the people'. Of course, no real workers had done any such thing. The letters had been fabricated by propagandists working for Mikhail Suslov, the Soviet Communist Party's dreary chief ideologue. But Solzhenitsyn was in danger, and not only of arrest. There was a risk he could be physically attacked by some hysterical person who read and believed the propaganda.

At the urging of his wife, Willy Brandt wrote a memo which I carried to Brezhnev. 'If anything happens to Solzhenitsyn,' the Chancellor warned, 'our relationship with you will be different.'

Brezhnev, who was the party General Secretary, summoned the Politburo to decide what should be done with the writer, who was causing the Kremlin so much embarrassment. The Soviet President, Nikolai

Podgorny, and the Prime Minister, Alexei Kosygin, generally regarded in the West as a kindly figure, were all for sending Solzhenitsyn back to labour camp, preferably beyond the Arctic Circle. 'I don't see what the problem is,' said Podgorny. 'Pinochet of Chile manages to deal with these matters without any discussion.'

Andropov was appalled. His Politburo colleagues were casting him in the role of Beria, the secret policeman who carried out monstrous cruelties on Stalin's behalf. If he refused to do the job, he would be sacked. On the other hand, if he arrested Solzhenitsyn, his image abroad would be blackened forever, which would be a disaster for him, because Andropov nurtured hopes of one day coming to power in the Soviet Union and reforming his backward country.

The next time Valery and I met Bahr in West Berlin, the German side again pressed the matter of Solzhenitsyn. 'Well,' I said to Bahr, 'what do you suggest then?' 'Brandt thinks you should let him out. He's got royalties from his books in a Swiss bank account. He can come and live in Germany.' I grasped at this idea like a drowning man reaching for a rope. Andropov was equally relieved when I reported to him and he sent the following memo to Brezhnev:

'Brandt has said that Solzhenitsyn is welcome to live and work in the FRG. Today, 7 February 1974, Comrade Kevorkov will meet Bahr and discuss with him all the details of Solzhenitsyn's transfer from the USSR to the FRG. If Brandt does not get cold feet at the last minute, then we can reckon on the deal being done by 10 February at the latest.'

Andropov told me to stay in Berlin and await instructions. During this time, I stayed not at the Hotel Am Zoo in the West but in a KGB villa at Karlshorst on the other side of the Wall. I waited and waited. I waited until 13 February and then, when I still had not heard anything, tried to ring Andropov at the Lubyanka. He was in a meeting. The KGB telephonist would not put me through. I began to pack my case for a trip back to Moscow. And then the phone rang:

'The object has flown to Frankfurt,' said a voice. 'Who?' I asked. 'You know.'

Panic stations. The KGB had put Solzhenitsyn on a plane without telling the Germans the number of the flight, the estimated time of arrival, anything. I leapt into a car and sped through the checkpoint into West Berlin to find Bahr. His secretary, Frau Kirsch, said he was in the Bundestag in Bonn. I got through to him on the phone. 'He's flying,' I said. 'Who?' 'You know.' 'Are you mad?' yelled Bahr. 'In Germany you don't do things that way.' 'When you are dealing with the Russians,' I replied, 'you have to be ready for anything.'

Bahr whispered the news into Brandt's ear as he was addressing the

Bundestag. The Chancellor was an important man who did not need to concern himself with details. Cheerfully he announced Solzhenitsyn's imminent arrival to the deputies, who rose to their feet and applauded thunderously. It was up to Bahr and me to sort out the niceties.

Solzhenitsyn would need a visa to enter West Germany. Bahr dealt with that. Meanwhile, I looked through the Aeroflot timetables and found the time of the next flight into Frankfurt-am-Main. We had an hour and a half to prepare a welcome, although that was not too difficult. The boys in dark glasses from the West German secret service would be on the tarmac to receive the writer from our boys in the same dark glasses. Then they would put him in a limousine and whisk him away through the crowds of curious onlookers to begin his new life in Germany.

And that is what happened, the only deviation from the plan being that Solzhenitsyn stayed neither in Germany nor Switzerland but chose, after he was joined by his wife and family, to move on to Vermont in the US, where he lived like a recluse until he was able to return to Russia in 1994.

But that is not quite the end of the story. Some time after Solzhenitsyn came to the West, I found out from a KGB colleague in Moscow the reason why so much confusion had surrounded his flight to Frankfurt. For one thing, according to my colleague, whom I can identify only as K, the Politburo had gone on arguing for some time as to whether the writer should be allowed out. Then, after they had taken their decision, the dissident, who objected to being stripped of his Soviet citizenship and was unhappy about leaving his homeland, had caused further delays by his characteristically uncooperative behaviour.

K was given the task of accompanying Solzhenitsyn on his journey. 'Our officers went to his flat to pick him up,' he said, 'and he made a scandal. He took out his old prison clothes – his padded jacket and his heavy boots – and cried out that the KGB was arresting him, although he knew perfectly well what was really happening.'

The writer was taken temporarily to Lefortovo prison so that the prosecutor could read out to him the decree depriving him of his citizenship because of his 'anti-Soviet activities'. The prosecutor noticed he was badly dressed and rang Andropov to say he could not possibly be let out of the country looking such a frightful mess. The KGB boss ordered action to improve Solzhenitsyn's appearance. Armed with the writer's vital statistics, which were written down in the prison records, operatives went to a special wardrobe which the KGB kept in order to fit out its spies with appropriate fashions for the countries to which they were being posted. Here they chose for Solzhenitsyn a pair of grey flannel trousers, an overcoat in brown herringbone tweed and a fur hat, size 57, to fit his enormous head.

The problem was how to make the writer put the clothes on. The KGB could not use force and risk having Solzhenitsyn arrive in the West covered in bruises. So, letting him think he was staying in Lefortovo and would be getting a prison uniform, officers ordered him to undress in his cell, which the dissident did, being used to the discipline of jail. They then left him naked until he was so cold that he was glad to wear the new clothes.

He looked very smart. 'Right,' they said, 'now take them off for the night. You will wear them for your trip tomorrow.' Solzhenitsyn refused. They were too exhausted to argue with him any more and let him sleep in the outfit. Next morning, it was all crumpled. Solzhenitsyn added to the tramp-look by dribbling porridge down his tie at breakfast. Now he was satisfied with the image with which he would greet the West.

But K's headaches were only just beginning as he met Solzhenitsyn at the airport. He had a difficult journey ahead with an unwilling exile, who was doubly reluctant to travel because he also happened to be terrified of flying. 'I've never been on a plane before. I'm very frightened,' said the writer. 'I'm afraid you have no choice,' said K. Solzhenitsyn was put at the front of the first-class section, which was curtained off. The other passengers on the plane had no idea they were sharing the trip with such a distinguished and troublesome personality.

Throughout the flight Solzhenitsyn, a devout Orthodox Christian, crossed himself repeatedly. He also accepted tranquillisers from a doctor in the KGB team. The writer still did not know his exact destination. 'Where are you taking me?' he asked. 'Abroad,' said K. 'Where?' 'You'll soon find out.'

The nightmare scenario for K was that, when the plane landed, Solzhenitsyn might refuse to disembark and, when forced out, run back up the steps again in front of the world's cameras. K had given his word to Andropov that under no circumstances would he bring the writer back to the Soviet Union. But when the plane dropped down through the clouds and Solzhenitsyn saw the sign 'Frankfurt-am-Main' glinting in the sun, he cried: 'Ah, Germany.' Evidently he was pleased.

There was one final hiccup. The plane taxied to a halt but there were no steps ready on the tarmac because German airport workers were on strike. 'What are we going to do?' demanded K. 'I could lower the emergency slides,' suggested the pilot helpfully. 'Definitely not,' said K, imagining what a field day the press photographers would have if Solzhenitsyn came shooting down one of those. Then, from the open door of the plane, K spotted someone on the ground he knew from the Soviet consulate and called to him to sort out the problem. A little gift of DM100 to an airport worker did the trick and the steps were wheeled up to the plane.

'Your suffering is over,' K told Solzhenitsyn. 'You are free to go.' 'But I haven't got any money for my bus fares,' said the writer. At this K remembered that Andropov had approved an allowance of DM1,000 to help the dissident cope with his initial expenses in the West. The KGB leader was an enlightened man, who had studied the works of Solzhenitsyn, forbidden to ordinary Russian readers, and he had said to K: 'See him off properly. Don't give him any cause to complain.'

But K, a loyal Soviet citizen, begrudged giving so much state money to the irksome dissident and, after extracting a promise that he would pay it back, handed over only half the sum. Do not think for a minute that he put the other DM500 into his own pocket. Oh, no. K was an honest man. He took it back to Moscow and returned it to the fund that would further the work of the Committee for State Security.

The Undisclosed Life of a Secret Policeman

Andropov's treatment of Solzhenitsyn reveals a lot about the KGB chairman's character. He was not a brute like his predecessor Beria but a sensitive man, acting within the limitations of his time – the 'era of stagnation' as the Brezhnev years are now called – and serving the interests of Soviet state security as he understood them. He also had a vision of how life in the Soviet Union could be different in the future.

He was a deeply private man. Although he lived in the same building as both Brezhnev and I – 26, Kutuzovsky Prospekt – I never visited him at home or met his modest wife, who was always kept in the shadows. But I did get to know him very well in our working relationship. The bespectacled Andropov was an intellectual, an ascetic, a man who hated corruption. But despite his dryness, he did not lack human kindness.

I remember once his car ran over a dog in our yard at Kutuzovsky Prospekt. Andropov found out that it had belonged to a little girl and some time later he took her a puppy to replace it. I cannot imagine other Soviet leaders, who used to zoom about in their curtained limousines in special fast lanes, acting with such decency and care for others.

Once Andropov fell in love – and I ended up with the job of extracting him from a potentially compromising situation. Already in his fifties, he had met a slim, beautiful twenty-two-year-old, just out of Moscow University, whom I will call 'N'. I saw them together at a small party at the House of Officers and it was obvious Andropov was infatuated with her, although I am not sure she returned his passion.

N's father was a Communist Party bigwig, so she had nothing to fear from a little romance with the head of the KGB. But probably he should have been more alert to the danger of scandal, for N was flighty and, despite her youth, had already gone through several husbands. Her latest spouse was an actor who had settled abroad. He wanted her to join him, but N was having difficulty obtaining an exit visa.

I was relaxing at the House of Journalists one evening when Andropov's assistant came in and said the boss wanted to see me urgently. I jumped into a car and sped to the Lubyanka, where I found Andropov at his desk, his head in his hands. 'N has rung me. She is having problems leaving the country. I owe her nothing,' he said, denying he had had sex with her. I'm not sure whether she was blackmailing him exactly or whether he just felt that, for a man in his position, he had allowed the affair to get out of hand. But he asked me to meet her and deal with the situation.

I met N on a park bench near the fountain at Pushkin Square. She was in a nervous state. 'Can you live in this country?' she asked me and, before I had time to reply, continued, 'I can't stand it any more.' At that moment, a toddler playing in a sand pit flung sand at her. 'You see?' she said, 'even the children hate me.' Then she delved into her black handbag and pulled out a sheaf of poems. 'Andropov wrote them to me,' she said. I looked at the handwriting. It was indeed his.

> Do not be sad, N, do not be sad,
> Forget everything and forgive them all.

It emerged he had written the lines at a party. Neither he nor N liked alcohol and so, while the other guests had been drinking, they had withdrawn to another room to talk quietly. N had bemoaned her complicated and unhappy love life and Andropov had written the poems to comfort her. 'He told me: "Read them when you are feeling miserable. Perhaps they will help you,"' she said. 'Please tell him they did help me for a while but now they have lost their force. Give them back to him. Tell him I make no demands. I am sorry I troubled him with my phone call.'

I returned to the Lubyanka, where Andropov was waiting despite the late hour. 'I have seen her,' I said. 'She needs help.' 'I won't do anything for her,' he replied. 'I thought you liked her.' 'How do you know I liked her?' I handed him the poems in an envelope. Embarrassed, he tore them up. 'That's a pity,' I said, 'they were good poems. You will not write such lines again.' He thought for a moment, then gathered up the pieces of paper and put them away in a drawer.

'Thank you, I am indebted to you,' he said. 'Not to me, to her.' 'I was afraid she would publish the poems abroad,' he explained, relaxing at last. And then, after all, he made arrangements for N to receive an exit visa.

This petty affair remained secret and did no harm to Andropov's career, which was fortunate because the KGB chairman was a major figure and had an important historic role to play as the grandfather of perestroika.

I believe his conviction that socialism should have a human face, as the Czechs advocated during the Prague Spring of 1968, went back further – to 1956 when, as the Soviet ambassador in Budapest, he witnessed the Hungarian uprising. Andropov and his wife were traumatised by that bloody event. They put quilts up against their windows to block out the screams of Communists being strung up on lampposts by the rebels. Soviet troops crushed the rebellion, of course. But afterwards, Andropov began considering ways of reforming the Communist system.

As KGB chairman, he tried to make changes which would give Soviet citizens more personal freedom within a socialist structure. I remember once asking him why we could not let our people travel. 'Imagine the millions who would build up at the border,' he said. 'There would be chaos.' 'No, there wouldn't,' I said. 'The Western countries would start tightening their immigration controls. We could then say that it was not us refusing to let our people out but the West not allowing them in.' He liked the idea. 'I'll put it to the Politburo,' he said. Of course his conservative colleagues rejected it.

Gradually Andropov began to realise that reform would only be possible when Brezhnev died and if he had the luck to succeed him. He was terrified that his KGB background might be held against him and prevent him from rising to the top job in the Kremlin. When George Bush, a former director of the CIA, became Vice-President of the United States in 1980, he took heart. Bush had set a precedent for a secret policeman to go into mainstream politics.

Andropov did indeed take over from Brezhnev on his death in 1982. But by this time he was himself a sick man, suffering from the kidney problem which would kill him in 1984, and he was unable to achieve much except attempting to tighten Soviet labour discipline. However, for some time he had had his eye on a younger man who, he believed, would be able to carry through his reforms to make the Soviet Union not only more efficient but also free.

Andropov had been going for rest cures to the KGB sanatorium at Kislovodsk in the Stavropol region of southern Russia. After one of his trips down there, I was moaning to him: 'Look at the Germans, they lost the war, but they have recovered thanks to a pleiad of talented leaders – Adenauer, Brandt. Why can't we find leaders of such calibre?'

'Yes, it has been a problem for us,' he agreed. 'But now at last I think I have found someone.' Andropov meant of course the local Communist Party boss who had paid courtesy calls to him during his visits to the Stavropol region, the man who was to become known to the world as the father of glasnost and perestroika, Mikhail Gorbachev.

One Germany

When Andropov rose to become Soviet leader, he advised me to leave the KGB with him. 'There will be nothing left for you there,' he said. He knew that, as always happens when new bosses arrive on the scene, Viktor Chebrikov, his replacement in the top job at the Lubyanka, would bring in his own people to work with him. And so I chose to go into journalism, with which I had always been associated. I became the deputy director of the official Soviet news agency, Tass.

I was still working at Tass headquarters on Moscow's Tverskoi Boulevard nine years later when the hardline attempt to overthrow Gorbachev took place in August 1991. For a while, because of my secret service background, I was suspected of being linked to the coup plotters, who included the KGB head of the day, Vladimir Kryuchkov. But after I managed to convince my colleagues of my innocence, I was posted, as had been planned some months earlier, as a Tass correspondent to Bonn. This was not a demotion, but a pleasant job for me before I retired.

At last I was living in Germany and free to get to know not only Berlin but the whole of this beautiful country. I can recommend tourists to make the journey – by winding mountain road and glass-smooth autobahn – all the way from Bavaria up to Bonn. If you manage to escape alive from the Bavarian health farms – there is one called Dr Schrott's where the overweight are fed on beetroot and swaddled in blankets to sweat off their excess kilos – great pleasure is to be had at a hotel in Spaier near Ludwigshafen where the swimming pool is filled with salty, body-supporting water from the Dead Sea. I suspect some of our New Russians have already found this oasis run by the tanned and hospitable Rolf Ramsteiner.

My favourite hostelry in Germany is the Maternus Club in Bonn, whose landlady, Frau Ria Ailtsen, started out by providing good, homely German cooking to the politicians who descended on the small town capital after the war. It was a recipe for success, which she has not changed to this day.

You will find all the important and influential people in Germany dining here on the roasts and puddings. Look, there's Count Otto

Lamsdorff in the corner. And that chap in the yellow pullover is Hans-Dietrich Genscher, the former West German Foreign Minister. He could tell you a secret or too about the reunification of Germany. But then, so could I.

It was always plain that Germany would, some day, become one country again. I understood that with particular clarity once when Egon Bahr showed me an East German newspaper which was crowing about the fact that the plan for boot manufacture had been fulfilled. 'How dare they?' fumed Bahr. 'West Germany gave them those boots and now they are claiming the credit.' 'Why do you go on supporting them then?' I asked naively. 'Ah,' said Bahr, 'but we are all Germans.'

In the depths of the Cold War, the question of German reunification was discussed in private in the Soviet Union. Once I said to our Foreign Minister, Andrei Gromyko: 'You know, Brandt thinks the status of West Berlin is unnatural.' 'What would be the price for resolving the issue?' he asked. 'Oh, I don't know, if West Germany was to pull out of Nato ...' 'Are they ready for that?' 'No, I don't think so, I'm just thinking aloud.' 'Well, and we can't hurt the GDR,' said Gromyko. 'But reunification will happen sooner or later,' I said. 'Let it be later then,' he said.

I reported on the conversation to Bahr, who was relieved. 'To be honest,' he said, 'we are not ready ourselves yet either.' But we both knew the day would come.

The process started in 1989, when East Germans began fleeing to the West through Hungary, where the Iron Curtain was more porous. Soon emboldened East Germans were tearing the Berlin Wall down with their own hands. Erich Honecker was hoping Gorbachev would order Soviet troops to intervene as they did when East Germans tried to rebel in 1953. But Gorbachev left his ally to sink or swim – sink, as it turned out. When Helmut Kohl saw this, he realised the time was right to raise the question of German reunification.

Complicated talks then began among the World War Two allies. President François Mitterrand of France was categorically against allowing the Germans to come together again and Britain's Iron Lady, Margaret Thatcher, was not keen either. But the Americans knew they would lose their main political partner in Europe if they disappointed Kohl and so they advocated giving him what he wanted. After the US took this line, everyone else fell in behind Washington.

Now Gorbachev had a problem. A matter as weighty as the reunification of Germany should really have been put to the Supreme Soviet, the parliament which was already semi-democratic and included independent MPs along with the Communist place-men. But the Kremlin leader knew if he started a public discussion, he would open a can of worms and nothing would be decided. So there was a 'plot'.

Kohl came out to Moscow with a draft plan for German reunification. At the Soviet Foreign Ministry mansion on Alexei Tolstoy Street, he showed it to Eduard Shevardnadze, Gorbachev's Foreign Minister and partner in perestroika. Together they agreed a mutually acceptable final text. Deliberately, Shevardnadze kept Valentin Falin, the head of the Communist Party Central Committee's international department, in the dark because this veteran Soviet specialist on Germany would almost certainly have raised objections to the deal cut with Kohl. Then the Chancellor travelled down to the Stavropol region for a signing ceremony with Gorbachev in the intimate atmosphere of his riverside country home.

Kohl returned triumphantly to Germany. The bill he had agreed to pay in order to become Chancellor of a united people was DM7 billion for the rehousing of Soviet troops who would be withdrawn from Germany over a four-year period. Germans told me privately that Kohl had been prepared to pay ten times that amount. For the reunification of his country was all-important to him. By achieving it, he knew he would go down in history as the second Bismarck.

Kohl served the interests of his country impeccably. The same cannot be said for Gorbachev. The Kremlin leader had his own eye on history. He wanted to be remembered not like Gromyko, who was Mr Nyet, but as the Russian who could say 'Da'. He also wanted an international agreement to bear the name of his home region. The Artskhis Act (after the little river there) would have a fine ring to it, like the Helsinki Final Act. At the same time, quite simply, he feathered his nest.

I am not saying that Kohl bribed him. It would have been too crude for the Chancellor to turn up at the reunification talks with a bag of money. But, by nod and wink, he gave Gorbachev to understand that he would be a hero in Germany and doors would always be open to him there. So it has turned out. Whenever Gorbachev speaks to German industrialists, he takes a hefty fee. He has also supplemented his Soviet pension by appearing in German advertisements.

In my opinion, what Gorbachev should have done, if he had been thinking as much about the strategic interests of his country as about his own financial position and place in history, was to insist on a quid pro quo for German reunification: a commitment from Nato that it would not expand eastward to take in former members of the Warsaw Pact. The Supreme Soviet would probably have set such a condition if the matter had been discussed beyond the narrow circle which gathered at Gorbachev's house. And I believe the West would have accepted it then. But it is too late now.

Germany was reunited in 1990. Shortly afterwards, the Soviet army began dismantling its bases in what had been the GDR. President Boris Yeltsin extracted a further half-billion Deutschmarks from Kohl for additional withdrawal expenses and the last Russian troops were out by 1994.

I personally witnessed some of the corruption which surrounded the pull-out. I saw members of the Russian 'mafia' coming in their black Mercedes cars to Potsdam, headquarters of the Soviet Western Group of Forces under Commander Matvei Burlakov. This was the scam: senior army officers used Russian middlemen to spend cash received from Germany on supplies, for example bedding, for the troops. The middlemen, who had served previously in the Soviet army in Germany and knew where to obtain local bargains, bought cheaply and sold at inflated official prices to the forces. The corrupt officers and the middlemen then shared the profit.

A young Moscow reporter called Dmitry Kholodov lost his life in a bomb explosion for daring to write about this corruption. He claimed that the former Russian Defence Minister, Pavel Grachev, personally received a Mercedes Benz out of the proceeds of the dirty dealing. That was not the worst of it. When the Germans came to count the weapons that were leaving, they noticed that large numbers of shells were missing. It is generally assumed they were sold through the back door to the Serbs for use in the war in Yugoslavia.

The criminals, who sold everything from bed sheets to weapons, form a part of the community of New Russians in Germany, particularly Berlin. You see them flaunting their ill-gotten wealth and some of them give serious trouble to the German police. They have seen to it that, for the German people, reunification has not been a wholly sweet experience.

Mr Kurt

Back in the days when I was still working in KGB counter-intelligence, an American mole was discovered in the Soviet Foreign Ministry. A Russian traitor called Ogorodnik, he was photographing the reports of our ambassadors around the world and leaving the microfilm for his CIA controllers in a dead letter box on the bank of the Moscow River. When the KGB went to arrest him, he was surprisingly meek, offering immediately to write a confession. But the pen he sucked thoughtfully as he started the first sentence had a poisoned tip and he evaded us by dying in hospital two hours later.

Andropov at this time was keen to romanticise the KGB in the way the British made heroes of their secret agents in books and films such as the stories about James Bond and George Smiley. He ordered me to collaborate with the writer Julian Semyonov on a thriller based on the true story of Ogorodnik. The result was the novel *Tass is Authorised to Announce* ... which firmly established Semyonov's reputation as the John le Carré of the Soviet union. It also cemented our friendship.

Semyonov used to travel regularly to Berlin on private business and I often met him there. Once we were dining on oysters and Chablis in the Restaurant Kempinski on the Kurfurstendamm when an elderly German, very elegantly dressed in a grey suit, blue shirt and maroon bow tie, came up to our table and said: 'Excuse me, but I couldn't help wondering whether you are the writer Julian Semyonov?' It turned out the old man was a fan of *Seventeen Moments in Spring*, another of my friend's books, which had been made into a film and shown regularly on East German television.

We got into conversation. With unusual frankness in front of complete strangers, the old man revealed that, during the war, he had served in the Abwehr, Hitler's military intelligence service, and inevitably had come into close contact with the Gestapo. The reason he so enjoyed *Seventeen Moments in Spring* was that it was about a Soviet spy who penetrated the Gestapo. He invited us to his home for coffee, saying he had many old photographs which he thought would interest Semyonov.

The next day, the writer and I went to visit him at his flat overlooking Potsdammer Platz. Although it was very clean, like all German homes, something in the atmosphere told us our host was a bachelor. Evidently, the old woman who served us coffee was not his wife but his housekeeper.

He kept his promise and showed us numerous albums of wartime photographs and documents, all the time holding our attention with a fascinating running commentary. 'Every one of your stories would make a chapter for a book,' said Semyonov.

When he had satisfied our curiosity, the old man had a question of his own. 'The Gestapo was a closed elite. Even most Germans did not know what went on inside that organisation,' he said. 'But in *Seventeen Moments in Spring*, you portrayed the SS officers as if you had known them. Apart from a few minor details, of course. For example, they would not have drunk water from carafes like you had in the film, they always used soda siphons. But that is hair-splitting. Tell me, Mr Semyonov, how did you manage to depict the Gestapo so accurately?'

'You see,' answered the writer after a moment's thought, 'I know people. I know if they are amused, they laugh. If they are in pain, they cry. I know they are the same everywhere, whatever uniform they wear.

So I work from that. All my characters, good and bad, are doing no more than expressing their human nature.'

After this discussion, we got onto first-name terms. We called our host Kurt and he called us Julian and Slava. He asked us to come again and from then on we visited him whenever we were in Berlin.

Kurt opened up more and more and told us all about himself. During the war, he had served the Abwehr in the Balkans. He was not a major war criminal, but I think he had blood on his hands and the lives of both Yugoslavs and Bulgarians on his conscience. Afterwards, during the de-Nazification of Germany, he was given permission by the Americans to open a law practice.

When the Berlin Wall went up, his wife took fright and fled to relatives in Latin America. But he preferred to stay on in the city of his birth. He had grown up in a house on the Potsdammer Platz, once one of the most beautiful squares in Europe. And so he chose his new flat with one thing in mind, to have a view of the square, although after the war it was a pitiful urban wasteland. 'I decided to stay here until I saw Potsdammer Platz restored,' he said.

We saw Kurt regularly in the stable days of the Cold War, but lost touch after the Berlin Wall came down and dramatic events swept Russia, eventually bringing Boris Yeltsin to power. At this time, Julian Semyonov also died. It was 1992 before I returned to Berlin.

'I thought I would never see you two again,' said Kurt, overjoyed, when I phoned to arrange a meeting. But when he saw me on the doorstep alone, he immediately understood what had happened. 'I did not want to outlive Julian,' he said. We stood quietly at the window, looking down onto Potsdammer Platz, where concrete skyscrapers were going up; America being brought to Berlin, a depressing sight.

About two weeks after this, I received a phone call from the housekeeper. 'Mr Slava?' she said. 'I have to tell you that Mr Kurt died this morning. He left an envelope for you. I will be in all day so you can collect it at your convenience.'

I went straight over to Potsdammer Platz. The flat looked the same as usual except that the housekeeper had put Kurt's photographs everywhere, their frames tied with black ribbons. She handed me the envelope. I drove out of the city and waited until I was in the woods before I opened it.

Dear Slava,
    My loyal housekeeper will give you this letter when I am no more. I thank Fate that she gave me my friendship with Julian and you. It helped me to find peace with my conscience, which had not always been easy

before. I finally understood what I had long suspected – that my generation in Germany and yours in Russia walked an incredibly difficult path. Such a fate could not but deform us. But, as Julian so rightly said, we nevertheless remained people. I thank him for those words. It is a pity that our two countries took so long to find reconciliation. Most of all in my life, I loved Germany and her people. But the great human invention, money, has turned into a virus which is infecting people's brains. Life has become an ordeal. I leave this world without the slightest regret but with hope for its healing. May you live as long as you have the strength for life. Mine has ended. I remain eternally yours – Kurt. P.S. I am leaving you my watch. It is not valuable but tells the time accurately. Put a flower on Julian's grave for me.

The friendship with Kurt also meant a great deal to me. It was not that it helped to ease my KGB agent's conscience, exactly, for unlike him I had never killed anybody. But that was not to my credit. I was just lucky to have had a different fate, that of carrying out a positive mission despite the fact that I worked for an evil organisation. Who can say how I would have behaved if I had been in Kurt's shoes during the war?

Fascism is dead in Germany now. But it could raise its ugly head in Russia in the future. After the collapse of Communism, which gave at least some certainty and social security, many of my fellow countrymen feel humiliated and resentful and long for a strong hand to bring order, just as the Germans did in the 1920s. When it comes to Fascism, no nation can ever afford to be complacent and self-righteous.

TOKYO

Name	Koshkin, Nikolai Petrovich
Born	6 August 1925
Education	Higher
Special Subject	Law
Languages	English, Japanese
Military Rank	Colonel
Worked in	Thailand, Singapore, Japan
Marital Status	Married
Sports	Speed walking
Hobbies	Chess
Favourite Tipple	Vodka
Brand of Cigarettes	LM

A Closed Book

What did I know of Japan when, after I graduated in law, the KGB invited me to learn Japanese with a view to working in Tokyo? Only clichés: Japan, the land of the rising sun; Japan, the home of samurai, kamikaze and geishas; imperialistic, militaristic Japan, where the poor workers could but dream of the good life we enjoyed in the Soviet Union.

Such ignorance may seem laughable today, but in 1951 I was hardly to blame for my benightedness. The Soviet people lived behind an iron curtain which was impervious to information. Japan, itself a closed society until the nineteenth century, was a particular mystery to us. The Second World War had ended a mere six years earlier and all one could read about Japan in Soviet newspapers was hostile propaganda.

I was thrilled and honoured to have been chosen to serve my Motherland abroad, but also acutely conscious that I would need to do a lot of homework before I could say I knew something of Japan, let alone call myself an expert. As soon as I got the news that I was to work for the KGB, I went straight to the Lenin Library in the centre of Moscow to see what books they had on the country to which I was now inexorably linked by fate.

Stalin was still alive at this time; censorship was strict and history was rewritten to conform to Communist doctrine. And yet the Soviet dictatorship never quite wiped out memory in the way George Orwell described. Rather, it stuffed things away at the back of cupboards. The Lenin Library had all sorts of books predating the Bolshevik Revolution, including a fine collection on Japan, which you could ask to be brought out to the reading room. It just failed to advertise this fact and so ordinary citizens never read the books for the simple reason they did not know they were there.

As soon as I began reading, I became fascinated by Japan. Where else in the world can you find a country whose ruling dynasty can trace its line all the way back to the time before Christ? Moreover a monarchy which, right into this century, continued to be regarded officially as divine?

And where else can you find a country which, as late as the middle of last century, was still virtually unknown to foreigners? The rulers of Japan had closed the doors to the outside world so tightly that only the occasional trader or missionary was able to penetrate that secret realm. Not until the 1850s did the American Perry and then our own Russian Admiral Putyatin begin to open up Japan, concluding trade agreements and establishing the first diplomatic relations.

In the Lenin Library, I steeped myself in Japanese history. I read about the feudal warlords who effectively ruled the country from Edo, as Tokyo used to be called, while the emperor lived in a gilded cage in the old capital of Kyoto. I read about the Mongol invaders who, according to legend, were swept from Japan's shore by a kamikaze or 'holy typhoon' in the thirteenth century. This, then, explained the name of those crazy pilots whom I had seen in war films saluting their commanders before they climbed into planes with only enough fuel for a one-way journey.

My knowledge of Japan was becoming a little less pitiful, but I still had to learn the language. That I began to do in KGB school, which I attended for one year after I left the Moscow Institute of Law. The years I had spent learning English in law school were of no use when it came to Japanese, which is a very difficult language. Nor was I excused from the trainee secret agent's other academic and physical disciplines while I sweated over my Japanese and I found I had to do a lot of studying in my spare time.

You could always identify the 'Japanese' at KGB school because they were the ones who sat in the dormitories copying out their hieroglyphs over and over again while the 'English', 'French' and 'Germans', who dealt with nothing more complicated than letters of the alphabet, went off to have a drink and relax. The one compensation for all the difficulties of reading and writing Japanese was that, for me as a Russian speaker at least, the pronunciation was relatively easy. The few Japanese who speak Russian do so almost without an accent except that they cannot pronounce the letter l. When I first met a Russian-speaking Japanese, it took me a while to work out which city he was referring to when he spoke of Reningrad.

The 'Europeans', who laughed at us 'Japanese', left KGB school speaking their languages fluently, but we could not hope to achieve more than an elementary level in one year. 'You will have to keep on working at it for years to come,' said my tutor. 'But when you do finally master it, you will have a high price in the KGB, for English-speakers are ten-a-penny while Japanese specialists are rare.'

After my training, I went to work on the desk in the Asia section at KGB headquarters. Senior officers who came and went on short trips to Japan described the country and brought back literature which helped me with the language. At that time, Moscow had still not restored diplomatic relations with Tokyo after the war – indeed to this day Russia and Japan have not concluded a formal peace treaty because of a continuing dispute over the Kurile Islands – and so there were no permanent Soviet representatives in the Japanese capital. My colleagues travelled under the cover of a state commission which visited Tokyo from time to time to sort out bilateral problems left over after the Second World War.

The Soviet Union was allowed to open an embassy in Tokyo again in 1956. I became optimistic that soon I might go and live in Japan and put into practice all my knowledge of the language and Japanese customs which I had worked so hard to acquire. But my heart sank when my boss called me into his office and said: 'Comrade Koshkin, how is your English? I hope you have not forgotten it after all your Japanese studies?'

'A bit rusty, sir,' I replied.

'Well get yourself on an evening course and have it back up to scratch within six months.'

The problem was that Japan was only allowing in a limited number of Soviet diplomats and there was no place for me at the new embassy. I was being sent to Thailand instead. The KGB was like that. It tried to take into account the qualifications and desires of its agents, but in the end it posted them like parcels to the places where they were needed.

I was disappointed. Japan, which had been a closed book to me, was just beginning to reveal a few of its fascinating secrets and now I must lay it aside and start to learn about another country. I knew that in

Bangkok, I would have no opportunity to practise my Japanese. There were a few Japanese people there, but I could not risk talking to them, as a Japanese-speaking Russian in Thailand would look very suspicious indeed.

For four years, my Japanese went on to the back burner, but I did not give up hope that one day I might put it to use. Finally my patience was rewarded. In 1962, after I returned to Moscow from Bangkok, my boss called me into his office again.

'Comrade Koshkin, how is your Japanese?' 'A bit rusty, sir,' I said. 'Well, I am sure you will pick it up again on the job.' And that was that. I went to spy in Tokyo, passing myself off as a member of the Soviet Trade Mission.

The Glass Wall

My first impression of Tokyo was of orderly crowds. At Haneda International Airport, people moved calmly from queue to queue without pushing and shoving like Russians at airports and railway stations. On week days, the Japanese flowed down the streets, dressed in Western-style clothes and always with immaculately polished shoes, to the ministries and banks and companies where they worked. At weekends many of them, especially among the older generation, changed into the kimonos in which they felt more comfortable. Whatever their dress, they remained unfailingly decorous, restrained and polite.

Although the Japanese had not seen the wheel before 1868, when an American called Gobley introduced the rickshaw, their roads by the early 1960s were busy with Toyotas, Nissans and Hondas, all contributing to the legendary smog of those days before the catalytic converter. Yet the same order prevailed on the highways as on the pavements.

I was particularly struck by a system they had to protect children crossing the street. At regular intervals by the roadside there were metal buckets containing yellow flags. The child would take a flag, hold it up to stop the traffic and deposit it in another bucket when he reached the other side. Flags were never stolen, for it never entered the heads of the community-conscious Japanese to appropriate or damage common property.

Because space was at a premium, the Japanese built multistorey blocks among the spaghetti of the highways. To tell you the truth, after Bangkok, which in the early 1960s was still not a very developed city, I felt overwhelmed in the neon and concrete jungle of Tokyo. How would I ever find my way among the tightly packed buildings? Would I lose myself among the crowds whose politeness was like a glass wall, keeping me forever at a distance?

I was fortunate, however, to have kind colleagues who took me in hand. In a country like Japan where you are obviously an alien, it is far more difficult to be a foreign businessman, correspondent or secret agent than in a country sharing something of your own culture. In such circumstances the outsiders flock together and form a particularly warm expatriate community where mutual help is the rule. My best friend was Boris, who worked with me at the Soviet Trade Mission.

Officially the mission, with its staff of about fifty export-import managers, advertising executives and engineers, oversaw state-to-state trade between Japan and the Soviet Union. Mostly we sold Russian raw materials in exchange for Japanese consumer goods. Those staff who dealt with lucrative Soviet exports such as oil were 'clean' trade representatives because they had to be experts in their field. Responsible trade work was not given to those who were really busy on behalf of the KGB.

Of the secret agents, the engineers with their technical education engaged in industrial espionage, which took on a particular significance in high-tech Japan, while graduates in the humanities, like Boris and I, courted businessmen. In Japan business and politics overlap, for rich entrepreneurs often buy 'pocket people' among the civil servants and influence politics to a far greater extent than in other countries. As a general rule, those who give or take bribes are also not averse to being recruited.

It would be a while, however, before I could court a Japanese businessman in his own language. When I first arrived in Tokyo, I trembled at the thought of having the simplest conversation in Japanese. 'Come on, you have to start somewhere,' said Boris and suggested I go with him to an exhibition of radio equipment being held by a leading Japanese firm.

I prepared with the utmost care for the outing. I sprayed myself liberally with deodorant, then put on a new silver-grey suit brightened by a multicoloured silk tie. An effective contrast, I thought. The door bell rang. It was Boris.

'That won't do,' he said as soon as he saw me. 'Haven't you got a more sober tie?' I changed it for a navy one hanging in the back of my wardrobe. 'Better,' he said. 'You have a chance to meet interesting Japanese businessmen at this exhibition but you don't want to scare them off with your tie. The Japanese abhor vulgar ties.'

This was news to me, although, thanks to my study of local customs, I did know that you had to take care with your footwear in Japan. Scuffed leather and broken-down heels give offence, to say nothing of smelly socks in a country where the people always remove their shoes before they go indoors.

My new black shoes passed muster with Boris. 'I trust you don't have any holes in your socks,' he added.

'You'll be telling me next I have to bow and say "San" [Mr] when I greet a new acquaintance,' I grumbled.

'Better to be told the obvious a hundred times than to make a mistake once,' said my friend.

We went to the exhibition by taxi. Boris was careful not to commit the error I had made a few days earlier of tipping the driver. The Japanese don't accept tips and my driver had run after me to give me the change from a note I had thrust into his hand. It may sound petty, but during an operation such a *faux pas* can give you away.

At the exhibition, Japanese businessmen were bowing to each other in the traditional manner. Some bowed low and held the position for several seconds. Others merely inclined their heads. The deeper the bow, the lower the person's status in the pecking order. I did not need Boris to tell me that.

A more modern but no less important part of the Japanese greeting ritual is the exchange of business cards. Boris had already advised me to keep cards in the jackets of all my suits, for a Japanese will be upset if he hands out his own card without receiving yours in exchange. Scraps of paper hastily torn from notebooks or numbers written in biro on the backs of hands will not do.

Fortunately I had several of my newly printed cards on me, for soon Boris was introducing me to a businessman, the first real Japanese to whom I had ever spoken. It was hard going. I could not understand half of what he said and had to keep asking him to repeat himself. I think he had equal difficulty understanding me as I searched my memory, found a word and glued it clumsily onto the preceding phrase. Our conversation was of the most general nature as my vocabulary did not extend beyond subjects such as family and hobbies.

Glancing at his business card, I noticed that he had graduated in economics from Harvard University. We could almost certainly have slipped into English, which would have been easier for both of us. But it was a matter of honour for me to carry the conversation in Japanese through to the bitter end.

'I'm sorry, I don't speak Japanese very well yet,' I said.

'On the contrary, your Japanese is very good and practice will make perfect. It is I who should apologise to you.'

'Why?'

'Because I do not speak a word of Russian.'

And with that we bowed politely to each other and went our separate ways.

Initiation Rituals

Boris continued to act as a guide to me and my wife Lina. He took us to Gindza, Tokyo's vibrant central district, where we were deeply impressed not so much by the cornucopia in the department stores as by the smiling, bowing service. Back in Moscow in those days, plastic bags were traded on the black market and no poor Russian would believe there was a place where your purchase would be wrapped and you would be thanked for your custom.

'Boris also took us to the Tokyo television tower, a copy of the Eiffel Tower in Paris, only higher, and to Ueno Park, a must, especially when the cherry blossom flowers in April. But I could not rely on Boris for ever. It was time for me to take my own first independent steps in the Japanese capital.

I started out on foot among the chaotic clusters of buildings, where it was almost impossible to keep track of the streets or work out the numbers of the houses. Tokyo twice missed its chance to impose a little logic on the urban jumble which had grown up over the centuries. Much of the city was destroyed in an earthquake in 1923 and again there was widespread damage from the Americans bombing in 1945. But the Japanese just went on building higgledy-piggledy, adding high-rise blocks and motorway flyovers at an increasingly furious pace as the clock ticked away to 1964, the year of the Tokyo Olympic Games.

I floundered at first, but gradually learnt to find my way, as the Japanese themselves do, by following the tram lines and bus routes. Restaurants would provide cards with diagrams of how to reach them and the Japanese, when inviting guests to their homes, would give lengthy explanations and maps instead of their addresses, which had little meaning except for the post.

I was nervous about getting into a car in Japan, where they drive on the left, but I had to conquer that fear. I bought a map and tentatively began exploring various districts: Sindzyuku, Kandu, Asakusa, Ikebukuro. The ubiquitous police booths along the roads, which existed to maintain public order in Japan long before the advent of the motor car, were a bane for secret agents, as at any moment the police could summon the counter-intelligence service if they thought a driver was behaving suspiciously.

Counter-intelligence tails were easy to spot in the Tokyo traffic jams and you could, by changing lanes a few times, throw them off without difficulty. But this was not advisable. By escaping, you showed your opponent that you were up to no good and maddened him, so that he called in reinforcements to find you. It was better to pretend you were on some innocent expedition, such as a visit to the shops, so that he got bored and stopped following you of his own accord. You could catch up with the agent you were going to meet later on, when the coast was clear.

When I first came to Tokyo, however, I had problems with the counter-intelligence service. In any country, the professionals who perform the other, preventive side of espionage work – and whom I always respected as much as my own side – pay special attention to new arrivals until they have got the measure of them. It is a game. The 'cops' maximise their surveillance while the 'robbers' lie low, giving the impression they are not worth watching.

During this initial period, you must be especially careful what you say over the telephone, as counter-intelligence will almost certainly be listening in on a systematic basis. However, do not make the mistake of never using your home telephone, or the opposition will just conclude you are going out to phone boxes and start following you in the street. Also in the first weeks, you must spend more than the usual amount of time driving around on empty errands and be prepared to postpone important meetings until the opposition begins to lose interest in you.

For some reason, my induction in Tokyo lasted longer than usual. Realising that I was being followed, I abandoned one rendezvous with an agent, thinking it did not matter as we had other contingency plans. But the tailing continued, so that I missed other back-up meetings we had arranged in case of failure the first time. I began to worry that I would run out of chances to meet the agent and lose him altogether. Restoring contact with a lost agent is no easy matter as, for obvious reasons, you cannot just pick up the phone and explain why you have let him down.

Luckily I did in the end manage to meet him, but it was a stressful period for me, as I was naturally trying to create a good impression with my new bosses. I was grateful to my wife Lina, who helped me through this trying time.

The ideal KGB wife, she always created an atmosphere at home where I could relax from the pressures of work. The Lubyanka instructed wives before they went abroad that they should not bombard their husbands with questions if they came home late or seemed preoccupied. But not all wives were as wise as my Lina.

I am not saying she was an obedient, Japanese-style wife. I would not have wanted such a passive partner. I always valued her criticism, the more so because she unfailingly picked the right moment to make it.

Only once did I have to give her a reprimand. We had been out together to a park. I met an agent on a bench under the trees while she took our two sons out of earshot to play with a ball on the grass. She took some photographs of the lads and when they were developed in a shop, I was clearly visible in the background together with the agent.

'Don't let that happen again,' I said to her. 'We all make mistakes when we are starting but they must not be repeated.' That was my little lecture to Lina as we began our tour of duty in Japan. She accepted it without making a scene. We were a team, learning together to do a peculiar job in an unfamiliar place.

The Unethical Editor

During my first month in Tokyo, I visited a tea house to enjoy the elaborate tea ceremony. I also tried seaweed and raw fish in the little sushi bars which are to Japan what cafés are to Europe. But most memorable of all was my first set-piece business dinner in a Japanese restaurant, complete with sake or rice wine and geisha girls, professional hostesses who must not under any circumstances be confused with prostitutes.

The occasion was my introduction to 'Tsunami', the editor-in-chief of a leading Japanese newspaper. He disapproved of America's considerable influence over his country after the war and favoured closer ties with the Soviet Union. For the last three years my colleague Igor had dealt with him, not only receiving valuable political information which the editor gathered from a wide range of highly placed sources, but also using him to plant pro-Soviet articles in the press. Now Igor was leaving and I was taking over as Tsunami's handler. I was quite nervous, although I had prepared for the meeting as thoroughly as I could by reading the editor's file.

It was about seven o'clock in the evening when, after driving around for half an hour to make sure we were not being followed, then parking the car outside a supermarket and walking for a further ten minutes, Igor and I arrived at the restaurant in a quiet back street of central Tokyo. We were greeted at the door by a smiling waitress in a kimono, who invited us to take off our shoes, gave us comfortable flip-flops and led us into the hall.

There in a high-backed chair sat a fat little Japanese man of about sixty, dressed in a dark grey suit and smoking a cigarette. Seeing us, Tsunami rose and bowed. Igor introduced me and we exchanged our visiting cards. Then we went upstairs to the dining room, where Tsunami and Igor sat down on the lacquered floor with their legs straight out in front of them under a table no more than two feet high. It seemed I was going to have to do the same.

It really is incredibly uncomfortable to sit bolt upright in this way. The Japanese do it from childhood and so develop strong muscles in their backs. But Europeans soon find themselves wanting to lie back on the floor or support themselves with their hands. In recent years, the number of foreigners visiting Japan has increased enormously and many restaurants now offer tourists low tables with a hole underneath so they can sit on the floor and drop their legs down. The effect is the same as if they were sitting up to a high table on a stool.

But there was no such relief for me back in the mid-1960s. I had just settled myself at the table with Tsunami and Igor when a waitress came up and offered to move us to a small side room where we could sit in privacy. The whole undignified process of getting down on the floor and slotting my legs under the table began again.

The waitress brought a porcelain jug of sake, which we sipped rather than knocking it back as the Russians drink their vodka, then Tsunami and Igor began ordering the food. Steaming bowls of rice and soup were brought out, followed by black lacquered plates of tempura (fish), sushi (raw fish), sliced beef, beetroot, onion, radish, asparagus and bamboo.

Although he knew perfectly well which sauces went with which dishes, Igor kept asking the waitress for advice, as it is part of the ritual in a Japanese restaurant for the diner to seek 'consultations'. I concentrated on not disgracing myself with my chopsticks. And then Tsunami snapped his fingers, the waitress disappeared and we were left alone to discuss our business.

I did not raise the issue at our first meeting, where we just got acquainted, but I knew my long-term task with Tsunami would be to persuade him to reveal his sources. Perhaps it was because of his Japanese reserve or his journalist's ethics, but Tsunami would not say where he got his excellent political intelligence. Although he had worked with him for three years, Igor had never managed to extract this from him. But the KGB needed to know.

A newspaper subscriber is usually satisfied to learn something from 'official sources' because he is reading for his general information and entertainment and quickly passes on to other matters. However intelligence services, informing governments which in turn make policy, must be absolutely sure of the reliability of their data. This is why they need to know its provenance.

There was another reason why the KGB wanted to know to whom Tsunami talked. It was the duty of a paid agent, as our editor was, not only to supply information himself but also to point out to our staff people he knew who might be vulnerable and therefore open to recruitment. For the KGB was constantly trying to extend its network of informers.

'Tell me who drinks, tell me who gambles,' I pleaded with Tsunami when I met him subsequently in other restaurants and sushi bars. He was reluctant at first, but finally he told me about a civil servant in a ministry who needed money urgently because he was deeply in debt.

I had to make sure from Tsunami that this was common knowledge in the ministry and he was not the only person who knew of the man's difficulties, otherwise it would be clear that the tip-off had come from the editor. And of course I did not approach the civil servant myself, leaving that task to a colleague so that there would be no visible link between Tsunami, me and the new informer.

But thanks to the editor who betrayed his journalistic ethics, another poor devil was hooked to work for the KGB.

Vengeance of a Peace-Loving Man

I could not take too much credit for my success with Tsunami because I had only developed him after inheriting him from my predecessor. I had yet to recruit an agent of my own, a difficult task considering that my Japanese was still not fluent.

In Bangkok, the KGB had been more interested in resident Americans and other foreigners than in the Thais themselves, as Thailand was not a particularly important country. That was why I had been able to get away with speaking English there. However the Japanese, our Cold War enemies to the east, were worth targeting in their own right, as their country was becoming a major economic power, one of the leading industrialised nations of the world.

The experience of my colleague Sergei showed that valuable new Japanese agents did not usually just drop into your hands. He attended a political seminar where he saw a Japanese who was obviously very important because the waitresses kept refreshing his glass and bringing him snacks from the buffet. He courted this man for three months, taking him out to sushi bars all over town and politely taking an interest in his family and hobbies, in a vain attempt to get the 'VIP' to say where he worked. He must be a top civil servant at the very least, my colleague reckoned.

While Sergei varied the venue for their meetings, the Japanese always returned his hospitality in the same sushi bar. Perhaps it was conveniently close to his ministry, my friend reasoned. But in the end he found out that his 'prospective agent' was just the manager of that sushi bar. Now it was clear why he had been treated with such respect at the seminar – because he had been overseeing the running of the buffet. My colleague had wasted his time on an apolitical nobody who had been flattered to receive the attentions of a foreign diplomat.

I had more luck, however, in a bar in Gindza where, right out of the blue one evening, I met a Japanese who was to become an asset to the KGB.

Tired after a long tramp through the city, I was quietly drinking a beer and not paying much attention to the man sitting on the next bar stool, reading from a manila file. It was a windy autumn evening. Suddenly a strong gust blew the door open and scattered my neighbour's papers all over the floor. I helped him to pick them up, noticing that they referred to a forthcoming flower show.

'Thank you very much,' he said to me in English.

'Not at all,' I replied in Japanese, which surprised him.

'Are you from Europe or America?'

'From Europe and Asia. I'm from the Soviet Union.'

That surprised him even more. At this point, I expected he would make his excuses and leave the bar, but instead he handed me his visiting card. Hideyo Arita was his name.

We began to chat. I was happy to practise my Japanese while he evidently found it interesting to speak to a real, live Russian. He told me he had a thirteen-year-old son and we laughed about the coincidence of us both having been born in August 1925. When we parted, he gave me his home telephone number, saying it would be better if I did not try to phone him at work. I rang him a week later and invited him to a restaurant. He accepted and we began meeting regularly.

As I gained his trust, I learnt a lot more about him. I found out that he was fanatical about ikebana, the Japanese art of flower arranging. I discovered that he was bringing up his son alone as his wife had died. And he told me where he worked – in a very interesting Japanese government body which dealt with issues of foreign policy. Furthermore, I gathered from a little incident in one of the bars we visited that he strongly disliked Americans. Some soldiers from the US military base at Okinawa were being rowdy and tossing litter onto the floor.

'They have no shame,' he said with a forthrightness uncharacteristic of the Japanese. 'They behave as if they own the place. I hate them.'

I began to see that I might be able to recruit Arita-San. But how? I did not want to be too direct and frighten him away.

At our next meeting, I started to speak in general terms about the way the US was trying to draw other countries into its orbit. Needing no encouragement, my friend launched into a harsh and specific criticism of American policy towards Japan, quoting from a confidential document he had been reading at work.

'I don't suppose I could see that, could I?' I asked with bated breath.

He thought for a moment, then said: 'OK. I will bring it to our next meeting.'

My boss, the *rezident*, was concerned about my initiative. 'It is one thing to get information by word of mouth, quite another to start receiving secret documents,' he said. 'What if your friend gets cold feet and makes a confession to the counter-intelligence service?'

But for some reason I was confident he would not do that and, sure enough, at our next meeting he turned up with the document. For a Japanese to take such a step, I knew, he must have a very serious motive. The KGB would have to reward him with something more substantial than the small presents I had given him up to now as a token of our friendship. Embarrassing though it was for both of us, I offered him money. He hesitated for a while but eventually accepted it.

After that, on a regular basis, he brought me valuable information on US–Japanese relations in exchange for which the KGB gave him cash payments. Several times I also asked him for analytical material on Japanese policy towards South-East Asia and Europe but, although he promised to see what he could find, he never came up with anything. Apparently, he was only prepared to give away secrets whose revelation he thought would damage the interests of the United States. Two years later, it became clear why.

He had just brought another packet of documents and I had slipped him his wages in a small brown envelope.

'No,' he said. 'I won't take money from you any more. While my son was alive, I needed it for his medical treatment. But he died last week. Now I will work for you for nothing. This is as important to me as it is to you.'

I was shocked. He spoke of the death of his son with the same calmness he might have used to refer to the breakage of his favourite porcelain teapot. Such self-possession is typical of the Japanese, who believe they should keep their feelings to themselves and not burden others with their emotions. I persuaded Arita-San to tell me his story.

He said he had known his future wife from childhood and they had grown up together near Nagasaki. In 1942 his father, who worked as a postman, had been transferred to Tokyo and thus he and his parents escaped the atomic bombing of Hiroshima and Nagasaki by the Americans in 1945. But his fiancée, who stayed behind, suffered radiation sickness which led to her death after they married. Genetic defects were passed on to their son, who had fought a long battle with leukemia before he died in hospital.

Arita-San never spoke of his family again after that, but he continued to pass secrets to the KGB, which was his way of taking revenge on the Americans. With me, however, he was always mild and I came to regard him not just as an informer but as a true friend. He gave me what all the books in the Lenin Library never could, an understanding of the Japanese as a hardworking people who thrived and lived in harmony with nature in a land to which nature had not, in fact, been bountiful.

Before I left Japan at the end of my first tour of duty there, I went with Arita-San to a rock garden where the Japanese found beauty in nothing more than the congruous arrangement of stones. It was a place of deep peace. I felt that my friend was as sorry as I was to part. As a farewell gift, he gave me a little Buddha carved out of ivory. It still stands on my mantelpiece in Moscow.

A Traitor in Our Midst

I said goodbye to Japan in 1966, thinking I had seen that enigmatic country for the last time. But a decade later, I returned to serve there again. The Japanese have a New Year tradition which speaks volumes about their work ethic. On the first day of the feast, they go to temples and visit their friends. On the second, they start some new venture. For example, schoolchildren take their first lesson in calligraphy. On the second day of the Japanese New Year in 1976 I started my new job, working under diplomatic cover as the assistant to the KGB *rezident* in Tokyo.

The interim years I had spent in South-East Asia. I rose to be the KGB *rezident* in Singapore, so you might think my appointment as deputy *rezident* in Tokyo was a bit of a come-down. But Japan was a much more important country and so my new position represented a promotion.

You may be wondering how I could now pass myself off as a diplomat, having posed as a trade representative on my first posting to Tokyo. Would the Japanese counter-intelligence service not see something odd in my change of occupation? The answer is that had I been working in an English-speaking country, the KGB would never have risked giving me a different cover, as it would indeed have looked strange. But the Japanese knew that foreigners who spoke their language were few and far between and therefore thought it natural that a foreign state expected its small pool of specialists to be versatile.

I found Tokyo had developed considerably in my absence. By the mid-

1970s, it was really booming. Although Japan is in a region of high seismic activity, many more skyscrapers had been erected, for the Japanese had nowhere to go but up. Their cars were slicker than ever and taxis had pay-TV for their passengers.

The people themselves were taller as a result of better diet. The United Nations said in a report that the Japanese had the highest life expectancy in the world. They had become more relaxed in their behaviour. Young Japanese kissed openly on the streets like Westerners, read comics and went to discos.

And yet the Japanese remained the Japanese.

I was sorry to learn that I would not be dealing with Tsunami and Arita-San any more. The editor was now an old man and, after the death of his wife, had gone to live with his daughter on the island of Hokkaido. Grief had taken its toll on the health of my friend the foreign policy expert and he had died of a heart attack.

However, I had other agents – an economic journalist who was forever in need of money to feed his large family; a civil servant who believed the Soviet Union should hand the Kurile Islands back to Japan but who nevertheless preferred the politics of Moscow to those of Washington. And of course, having risen to the rank of KGB colonel, I spent a lot of time managing the junior officers, giving them the benefit of my experience.

We were a close-knit team and so it came as a terrible shock to discover we had a traitor in our midst. In October 1979 Stanislav Levchenko, who had worked under cover as a correspondent for the Soviet news magazine *New Times*, defected to the Americans. He had gone missing after attending a diplomatic reception. At first the *rezident*, who was based at the embassy but also controlled our non-diplomatic agents, thought nothing of it as it was normal for a KGB officer to go off as part of his job. But then it was announced that Levchenko was in the United States. Evidently the Americans had taken him out through the base at Okinawa.

The rest of my time in Tokyo was spent trying to limit the damage caused by his defection, the first such blow to the KGB since Oleg Lyalin went over to the British eight years earlier. Levchenko had only worked with a few of our informers and was not familiar with the entire network. And yet the textbooks say that in a situation like this, you have to assume the worst – that the traitor knows everything and will tell all to the enemy.

We warned our agents to lie low. We told them to keep their mouths shut if the counter-intelligence service summoned them. We watched to see which one of them were called in for questioning by the Japanese. Some we had to write off, as they had come to the attention of the opposition. Others, who were not sent for, we might be able to reactivate in the future but only after the passage of several years. In the meanwhile, we had to recruit new agents.

Unlike Iran, which has executed 'spies' on hearsay, Japan is a civilised country which will only convict a person of espionage if there is proof. To go to jail for spying in Japan, you have to be caught red-handed with secret documents. Nobody went to prison as a result of Levchenko's treachery. The information he gave to the Americans was probably of no great significance. And yet his betrayal left us feeling hurt and bewildered.

Frankly I did not know what to make of it. But my colleague Arkady, who knew Levchenko as well as I did, had a theory about his motives. Levchenko had joined the KGB relatively late, when he was over thirty. He had studied Japanese at Moscow University's Institute of Oriental Languages. He was really keen on Japanese. After he graduated, he failed to find a job where he could use his skills in any of the prestigious organisations, such as the Foreign Ministry or the newspapers. He had to be satisfied with the position of translator at the Committee of Solidarity with Asian Countries, which gave him access to Japanese visiting Moscow but little hope of ever travelling to Japan himself.

He approached the KGB himself for a job. He came to us for the wrong reasons. He was not interested in being a secret agent, for whom intelligence work comes first and the place and language in which it is performed is almost an irrelevance. He was specifically interested in Japan.

Levchenko was an excellent journalist. He wrote stylishly and pro-lifically for *New Times*. His analyses of Japanese affairs were trenchant. But it cut no ice with the KGB that he was giving satisfaction to the general Soviet reader. Rightly or wrongly, Moscow Centre tended to assume that the more an agent under journalistic cover wrote, the less attention he was paying to his real job. Perhaps it was unfair, but Lev-chenko began to get a reputation as a mediocre agent. He knew this. He feared he would be recalled to Moscow and never be allowed out again.

That was why, in Arkady's opinion, he offered his services to the Americans, who took him on as a consultant on Japanese affairs. He left his poor family behind in the Soviet Union when he went to the West. The Americans crowed about a victory for freedom. But as far as we were concerned, Levchenko had betrayed his own people. And a traitor is a traitor, in any society.

Shortly after completing this memoir, Nikolai Koshkin
died in June 1997.

NEW YORK

Name	Brykin, Oleg Dmitryevich
Born	12 September 1931
Education	Higher
Special Subject	Journalism
Languages	English
Military Rank	Lieutenant-Colonel
Worked in	USA, Indonesia
Marital Status	Married
Sports	Boxing
Hobbies	Collecting beer mugs
Favourite Tipple	Gin and tonic
Brand of Cigarettes	Don't smoke

To my granddaughter K.

Spying Without Insurance

Fear was my constant companion when I served the KGB in the United States of America. I learnt to live with it; it became a dull ache rather than a sharp pain. But the feeling never left me: stress, stress, stress.

I worked under cover as a translator at the United Nations in New York. I carried a Soviet diplomatic passport but the Americans did not recognise it. Only top officials at the United Nations were entitled to diplomatic status as far as they were concerned. This meant I had no diplomatic immunity. My KGB colleagues at the consulate and at the embassy in Washington risked nothing more than an embarrassing scandal and expulsion if they were caught spying. But if I was ever careless enough to give the FBI proof of my espionage activities against the US, it would mean jail for me, or even possibly the electric chair.

I do not know why the KGB chose me for this particularly vulnerable position. 'Ours was not to reason why ...' Perhaps they thought I had strong nerves and a cool head. It was true I had an ability to make split-second decisions. Boxing had given me that. It was an excellent discipline for developing concentration and I had been at the top of the sport. In 1953, I won the amateur boxing championship in Leningrad. But I had no special training to enable me to survive on the KGB's front line.

I came from a poor family. My father Dmitry was a KGB counter-intelligence officer in the Moldavian capital of Kishinyov. When I reached my nineteenth birthday, he lent me a pair of his trousers (for I had no smart trousers of my own) and took me to see his boss, who recruited me. I went to the KGB's Institute of Foreign Languages in Leningrad for a basic education plus intensive coaching in English and then on to the spy school at Balashikha outside Moscow, where all our agents who were being posted abroad received a standard training.

True, I was fortunate to have been involved in a US–Soviet student exchange and spent the 1958–9 academic year improving my English at Harvard University. If I had an edge over other KGB officers, it was that I already had a feel for American life. This, of course, would help me in my dangerous double role. But I had no extraordinary equipment or techniques to protect me.

My job in New York carried no additional prestige for being so perilous and it was certainly not well paid. Usually salaries are built up with bonuses of various kinds, but the KGB found reasons to deduct money from my basic translator's wage of $600 per month. Because I had a low status on our diplomatic scale – I was identified as a third secretary in the worthless passport – they knocked $100 off my salary. And then because I was unmarried at the time, they subtracted another 20 per cent. I was left with $400 a month to live on, and had to pay my own rent.

In short, I was not treated as one of the elite because I was risking my neck for the Motherland. I was rank and file, the equivalent of cannon fodder on one of the main battlefields of the Cold War.

I started work at UN headquarters in 1960. I was extremely impressed by the multistorey glass and concrete skyscraper on the bank of the East River in central Manhattan. The whirring lifts and swish offices belonged to a new age. There was nothing like that in Moscow then, although Stalin's neo-Gothic piles were awe-inspiring in their own way.

The UN was a city within a city. There was no need to go out, for there were restaurants and bars, sports clubs and shops. I made friends and contacts by playing table tennis in the evenings and working as a barman at parties, where the duty-free alcohol flowed in rivers.

I took advantage of the archives and libraries where, although information was yet to be available on computers, there was a cornucopia of reading matter for someone who had come from a closed society like mine. We translators also had fun with the pneumatic internal post system, sending all sorts of documents down the tube to each other, from the Secretary-General's speeches to adverts for patent cures for baldness.

I worked in a team of about twenty translators in the Russian section. Some of them were from the Soviet Union, probably working for the KGB like me, although I never knew for sure because the Lubyanka kept its agents in the dark about the activities of their fellows. Other translators were Russian émigrés and there was a definite tension between the two camps.

I was not good enough to be a simultaneous translator. These were real professionals who could keep up with the cut and thrust of the debates when the UN became like the Tower of Babel. Instead, plodding along at more or less my own pace, I did written translations from English into my mother tongue, the easiest form of translating. Even that was difficult, for my vocabulary was quite limited at first. I could cope with texts on political subjects, but struggled when I had to deal with legal or financial language.

The anti-Soviet émigrés, some of whom were in senior positions after many years in the job, gave me a hard time about this. 'I realise this is not your main work but do try to maintain at least a minimum standard,' said one of the editors contemptuously when I produced a particularly clumsy translation. The émigrés suspected who I really was. But they could speculate as much as they liked. They could not prove anything.

As long as I was inside the United Nations, I was safe. I did a straight translator's job and never risked my cover by introducing disinformation into a text or trying to dig out secrets or recruit personnel. The KGB got nothing out of me here except in the sense that my very presence at the parliament of the world made me a well-informed person, better able than the average Soviet citizen to make political assessments.

From the simultaneous translators' booth, I witnessed two especially dramatic incidents. The first was in 1960 when Nikita Khrushchev earnt world notoriety by banging his shoe on his desk during a session of the General Assembly. Harold Macmillan, the British Prime Minister, was hogging the floor and Khrushchev was trying to get a turn to speak. He banged his shoe in imitation of a chairman banging a gavel. When with withering sarcasm Macmillan said, 'Mr President, perhaps we could have a translation, I could not quite follow,' I found my sympathies were with Khrushchev, who may have been vulgar but at least was not supercilious.

In my own small way, I was involved in the organisation of Khrushchev's visit to New York that year. I was ordered to assist a diplomat from our embassy in Washington in buying three stretch limousines to transport our leader and his entourage. Because we needed them urgently, we had to pay six times the price to a shark in a suit to have them delivered in time for the docking of Khrushchev's transatlantic liner. As far as I know, when the visit ended, the limousines were shipped back to Moscow for the use of Communist Party bigwigs.

Together with Fidel Castro, Khrushchev made a foray into the slums of Harlem, where the two Communist leaders gave speeches expressing solidarity with the long-suffering black population. The US authorities were very irritated, although there was nothing they could do about it.

There was also a funny incident when Khrushchev visited the Empire State Building. Entering an elevator to ride up to the 'roof of the world', our dear leader was immediately surrounded by American security agents and our own boys missed the lift. They dashed for the back stairs and ran up eighty-six flights, only to find as they reached the top panting like dogs, Khrushchev's lift descending once more. Then they had to turn round and run all the way down again.

I stood by the lifts on the ground floor, laughing like a drain. 'What's the joke?' demanded one of our senior diplomats and I pretended I had been amused by the sight of a black man, incongruously dressed in a cowboy hat. Despite the lip service they paid to equality, our bosses were as racist as the Americans and the diplomat believed me and smirked in what he thought was collusion.

The other historic moment I witnessed from the translators' booth was the grilling of Valentin Zorin, the head of our delegation, at the time of the Cuban Missile Crisis in 1962. 'Had Soviet rockets been deployed in Cuba, yes or no?' he was asked by U Thant, the Burmese Secretary-General who succeeded Dag Hammarskjoeld of Sweden who was killed in a plane crash. Zorin tried to dodge this direct question. 'I am not in a US court to be so interrogated,' he said.

But photographs of the missiles taken by a U2 spy plane were produced and Zorin was shown up for all the world to see. I felt very ashamed, not so much because he had lied but because he had failed to handle the situation more elegantly. He was, after all, one of our most senior diplomats Evidently, the Kremlin had not instructed him and he was left looking like a fool, not knowing what to say.

The Cuban Missile Crisis was a very tense time when, for a while, the world seemed to be on the brink of a new war. I lived in Manhattan then and, of an evening, I used to watch the traffic streaming backwards and forwards on the highway outside my window. Usually there were yellow headlights coming in one direction and red tail lights going the other way. But during the crisis there was just an unbroken line of red tail lights from cars, packed with terrified American families fleeing from New York City to the Bear Mountains.

All the TV channels – there were a mere seven in those pre-cable days –

whipped up an anti-Soviet hysteria not seen since the days of Senator Joseph McCarthy's witch hunts against suspected Communists in the 1950s. I remember an image of the Caribbean Sea and a voice saying ominously: 'Soon Russian ships will come over the horizon and war will start.'

Personally, I did not think it would come to that. Confident that a solution would be found, I tried to reassure neighbours in my apartment block, Jewish émigrés from Russia who normally refused to speak Russian with me but suddenly found their tongues and came asking me: 'Oleg, Oleg, will everything be all right?' 'Yes,' I said, 'go home, relax.'

But it was a nerve-racking time, especially for a Soviet spy who knew he could not claim diplomatic immunity if the FBI, jumpier than ever, suddenly decided to tap him on the shoulder.

Streetwise

What was I really doing in the Big Apple? I found out myself what my secret tasks were to be when, shortly after arriving in New York, I reported to the KGB *rezident* who was based at the consulate and received a package of instructions from Moscow Centre. While still at the Lubyanka, I had worked out with my bosses a rough programme of work. So I was shocked on opening the envelope to see they had loaded me down with all sorts of other jobs we had not discussed. But, as the popular Russian comedian Arkady Raikin used to say: 'When you start college, forget all you learnt in school, when you start work, forget all you learnt in college.'

Part of my work was political. I had to talk to people, analyse the press and file reports on American government affairs. In performing this task, I was doing little more than a journalist does in a free society. But remember, in the Soviet Union at that time the newspapers contained mostly propaganda. Only the elite had access to real information. I was a reporter for that elite.

My other work, however, was of a kind no bona fide journalist would ever touch. I was spying on military installations, from rocket bases to chemical and biological warfare laboratories. Often this meant quite simply locating and identifying them. We did not have satellite technology in those days, so I had to go physically to look at them, from the outside of course, and put them on our maps.

Obviously, to carry out such work in a country where the automobile was king, I needed a car. The KGB begrudged me the money for this so the first thing I did after finding a cheap hotel which would be my initial home in New York was to buy a second-hand car out of my own savings. I was lucky. A white Ford was advertised on the notice board at the United Nations for only $100. No need, I thought, for me to brave the sharks otherwise known as car dealers. The Ford turned out to be a wretched banger which I came to call 'the creature'. The heater worked the wrong way round, blowing out freezing air in winter and nearly boiling me to death in summer. But it went and I was absurdly happy.

No sooner had I got it than I lost it. I parked it in Manhattan on a busy Saturday afternoon and was horrified to find it had disappeared when I returned to the spot. What was this? A dirty trick by the FBI? Coming from Moscow where the light traffic consisted of lorries and state limousines with only the occasional private car, I was not used to parking regulations. My 'old lady' had been towed away and the fine to get her back was $40, nearly half what I had paid for her in the first place. It was a hard but useful lesson.

After this, I began to study the city with care. It was one thing to know it in theory – we spent many hours poring over maps of foreign cities at KGB school – another to drive in it. The FBI was likely to be on my tail a good deal of the time, not because they suspected me in particular, just because they kept an eye on all Soviet people in the same way the KGB watched every foreigner in Moscow. To be able to dodge them on the occasions when I was carrying 'hot' material, I would have to know New York like the driver of a yellow cab. Better, in fact, for the taxi drivers were often recent immigrants prone to losing their way.

In one sense, New York is an easy city for a driver, laid out as it is in parallel lines and squares. The dead straight avenues have names while the streets that cross them are numbered – Lexington Avenue, 42nd Street and so on. It all seemed very logical to me compared with the tangle of little lanes inside the concentric rings of Moscow. But the novelty and nightmare for the 1960s Soviet driver was the concept of one-way streets. This, coupled with the problem of parking, made driving in New York anything but a picnic.

My salvation, however, came in the form of the road signs. In Russia, it often seems to drivers that these are made deliberately obscure or non-existent so that the highwaymen who pass for traffic police have unlimited opportunities to trap and extract fines from the unwary. But in America they could not be clearer. The white bar on a red background which means 'no entry' was accompanied in New York by a sign saying 'no entry'. I would have had to have been a cretin to misunderstand that.

I learnt quickly, which was fortunate because soon I was involved in car chases like those in the movies. Once I was travelling with a packet of top secret documents in my car when I spotted two FBI vehicles making no effort to be discreet right behind me. What was I to do? If they stopped me and found the compromising material, I could find myself following in the footsteps of the great Soviet spy Rudolf Abel, who was sentenced to twenty-five years in an American jail. (He was later swapped for Gary Powers, the pilot of the U2 spy plane downed over the Soviet Union in 1960.)

My mind raced. I could not eat the package because it was too bulky. If I tossed it from the window, the FBI men would be sure to see it through their binoculars, retrieve it and find out what secrets the KGB had stolen. Instead, I drove round and round the city and its outskirts like a plane circling an airport when it is waiting for permission to land. As long as I did not commit a traffic violation or give the FBI any other reason to stop me, the game could go on. I drove 400 km in the city that day, filling up with petrol three times, until finally I managed to get clear of my pursuers for long enough to dart into the United Nations compound, where I was safe.

The FBI agents must have been grinding their teeth with frustration. My suspicious behaviour must have alerted them that I was up to something. But they had not been able to pin anything on me. That was all I cared about.

In the Lions' Den

I hung on in my precarious position in New York for three years. During that time, I recruited my share of traitors ready to betray their country, usually for financial incentives. The KGB may have been mean with its own staff, but it spared no expense on foreign moles as long as they provided top-quality classified information. That is still the case today, so if you would care to work for the Foreign Intelligence Service, as the overseas branch of the old KGB is called in post-Communist Russia, I could do a deal with you.

Back in the days when I was preparing for my assignment to New York and wondering whom I might recruit, I had formed the idea that black people, still oppressed by a system which came close to apartheid, were 'progressive', in other words pro-Communist. I think my stereotype was created by the singer Paul Robeson, a friend of the Soviet Union and the only black man most Russians had ever seen. But in New York I discovered that, on the contrary, blacks tended to be regular churchgoers and great believers in free enterprise. I never managed to recruit a single one of them.

Neither did I have any success with the Russian émigrés, who in the early 1960s had yet to form their famous community at Brighton Beach and were scattered all around New York City. You might have thought the fact that I spoke their language and could play on their nostalgia for home would have given me some leverage with them. But they were almost invariably fiercely anti-Soviet; indeed quite a few of them hated Communism to such an extent that they cooperated with the CIA and FBI.

Ironically I had most success with the 'WASPs', the white Anglo-Saxon Protestants who formed the American establishment and should have been, one would have thought, the most patriotic. But there were those who had reason to feel resentment against the United States and were not averse to being disloyal if the price was right. For example, I befriended a clerk at a naval base on the west coast who regularly leaked secrets to me for cash. I did not spell out to him that I was from the KGB, although he must have understood what he was doing. Not all spy scandals were reported in the press and so I cannot be completely sure but, as far as I know, he was never caught and he probably died peacefully of old age.

Unfortunately I am not at liberty to reveal any more about his case and must likewise censor myself in telling you about my other operations. Even if I wanted to be more open, there are some secrets I cannot tell you, for the simple reason that I do not know them myself.

'The less you know, the safer you are', was a favourite KGB maxim. The bosses kept the rank and file agents in ignorance of what their colleagues were doing. We would perform parts of operations, but never see the whole picture. We were like horses, blinkered so that we could only see the particular track down which we were running. The thinking behind this was that if we cracked under pressure, we would only be able to give away a limited number of secrets and the KGB's losses would be minimised. Actually, I suspect our bosses were similarly blinkered themselves. Probably the only people who saw the entire show were the spectators at FBI headquarters at Dulles.

In my blinkers, then, I might for example deliver a package without knowing its contents, or choose a knot in a tree trunk for another agent to use later as a dead letter box, or myself take a route which had been selected for me in advance by a colleague but about which I was only told on a need-to-know basis at the last minute.

The system may have protected us, but there was endless scope for confusion. Once I was sent off like a messenger boy to meet an agent called 'Roger' at a pre-selected place which I would never have been so stupid as to choose myself – the lions' cage at the Bronx Zoo. Anyone who has ever been to the Bronx Zoo knows that the animals are not kept behind bars but allowed to roam freely in an extensive wildlife park. Even though I had a good description of Roger – blond hair, fringed suede jacket – it could take me hours to find him in the mock savannah. 'No buts,' said the resident. 'I want the job done. It's your problem how you do it.'

I entered the park and wandered around in the sunshine among the skateboarding teenagers and families feeding the squirrels with packets of nuts sold at the gate specially for the purpose. It was an idyllic scene, but I was not there to look at the pretty squirrels. What on earth was I going to do? Suddenly I noticed bicycles for hire and my spirits rose. I rented one and rode through the park among the elephants and rhinos, which ranged as freely as American citizens in their great free country. At last I found an agitated-looking Roger. 'Do not feed the lions,' I said, quoting the password. 'They may bite,' he replied and handed me a package. I took it back to the resident who, had I returned empty-handed, would certainly have bitten my head off.

On another occasion I was ordered to make contact with an American traitor called 'Larin' who was flying in from West Berlin with some juicy secrets. The KGB in Germany had chosen the place for the rendezvous but whoever had done it obviously did not know New York because he had picked the corner of Madison Avenue and 35th Street at rush-hour. He must have just stuck a pin in a map to come up with that ridiculous venue. I, of course, knew that where Madison Avenue crosses 35th Street there are four corners and that in the early evening there would be thousands of New Yorkers there rushing to catch the subway home after work. Spotting Larin would be like finding a needle in a haystack.

I went to the crossroads twice before I was due to meet the agent and scrutinised the whole area. I worked out that he was most likely to stand by one of the two exits from the subway and of those, one looked more convenient than the other for waiting. I decided to put my money on this exit. I knew Larin had instructions not to hang around for more than five minutes. By a miracle, I picked him out of the crowd in that short time and signalled to him to follow me, for there were too many police patrolling in the area for comfort. When we reached a more secluded spot, he handed over his package. How fortunate that I found him because his envelope contained coordinates for some forty military installations across the United States, some of which it would fall to me to check out on my peregrinations beyond New York.

On the road

As a translator at the United Nations, I was entitled to travel freely around America, but I tried not to let the FBI know when I was going away so that I could work incognito in other cities. A trick I often used was to turn up at the last minute at airports and buy one of the standby domestic tickets which were sold at the steps of the plane to latecomers. In this way, I did not need to go through check-in, where I might come under surveillance.

I successfully played this game on one occasion when I had to do a job in Boston. On arrival I hired a car, showing my UN card and driver's licence which bore my name and address but gave no indication of my citizenship. I spoke English with a slight accent but that hardly mattered as every second American had an accent. Then I booked myself into a small hotel using the name Hamilton which, judging from the telephone directory, was as common as Smith and Jones in that city. It was a comfortable little establishment with a television in the room, a swimming pool downstairs and, most exotically for a visitor from the Soviet Union, a vibrating bed.

As a horse in blinkers, my task in Boston was simple enough. All I had to do was select two or three places where microfilm could be safely hidden, pick a quick route from the railway station to the dead letter boxes and choose another couple of venues where agents could conveniently meet, all for colleagues who would come here in the future on missions about which I would know nothing. Then I was free for the rest of the weekend. It was really rather pleasant.

I used to love going to restaurants. In New York, I revelled in the variety of ethnic food and fulfilled my own personal plan of trying every national cuisine by visiting over eighty restaurants in my time there. But Italian and Chinese were my favourites. In Boston, I chose a small Chinese restaurant, ordered a selection of fish dishes and relaxed in the cosy ambience.

As I slurped the crab and sweetcorn soup and chased the sweet and sour prawns with my chopsticks, I allowed my memories to come flooding back. For it was here, as an exchange student at Harvard University, that I had my first taste of America.

Back in 1958 I had been a pioneer, joining the first ever group of Soviet youths to study in the United States. There were seventeen of us in all, including the young Oleg Kalugin, who was to go on to have a major career in the KGB and then blow the whistle on the organisation when free speech came to Russia, and the young Alexander Yakovlev, who advised Mikhail Gorbachev during the heady days of glasnost and perestroika. I studied English Language and Literature, squeezing as much benefit as I could from the American educational system but not, at that point, doing any active work for the KGB. I was a sleeper, waiting for my time to come.

But while I slept, what a magnificent time I had. The authorities watched me – there was an American student who lived in the room opposite mine and always kept his door open so he could observe my comings and goings and report on me to the FBI – but it did not worry me because I knew I was doing nothing wrong. It was hardly my fault that once, when I was lying on the beach with two local girls, a helicopter landed nearby and the naval pilots who jumped out invited us all to go for lunch on board the aircraft carrier *Enterprise*, not realising that I was a Russian!

At Harvard I went to all the parties, where the guests drank beer straight from the cans, and made many friends. There was a girl called Linda with whom I danced rock 'n' roll and even won an inter-university jive competition. There was a boy called Jack from a wealthy WASP family, who invited me home for Thanksgiving. I remember being disappointed by how thinly his mother sliced the turkey. 'So rich and so mean,' I thought at the time, although I realised later that counting every cent was the secret of accumulating wealth. We Russians who scorned the economising mentality and put everything we had on the table with no thought for tomorrow would always be the poor ones.

And there was a Korean boy called Kim, also from a very rich family. His multi-millionaire father rented five rooms for him at Harvard. He had four fridges, all filled with food and bottles of bourbon. For his birthday, he received a light plane and landing rights at Boston airport which cost more than the plane itself. But he was a great guy, not stingy in the least.

How I longed to see them all again, even Jack and his cheese-paring mother. How I wished I could just walk on the campus once more. But I did not dare risk it. I did not want to be recognised at the university while I was on a job for the KGB. I paid the bill at the restaurant and then went back to the hotel to pack my bags for the return journey to New York. Along with fear, loneliness was another of my frequent companions.

Do not think I am complaining, however. Being in the US was a great adventure, a privilege I am conscious the majority of my fellow Soviet citizens never enjoyed. And I travelled all over that vast, fascinating country.

On another occasion, I went to Chicago, the city where everything is billed as 'the biggest in America'. My job this time was to reactivate an agent who had lapsed. For a change I decided to take the train. I could not afford to use the buffet car so I took a large bag of sandwiches and a bottle of whisky and settled down to enjoy the twenty-hour journey from New York.

Early in the morning I was overcome by an instinctive sense of danger. I could not understand what it meant at first, but I felt it in my gut like a hunted animal. Suddenly I realised what the problem was. Of the eight trains which plied between New York and Chicago, seven took a direct route but one made a brief detour into Canadian territory. I had made the mistake of boarding that train.

My UN documents entitled me to go anywhere in the US, but not into Canada. I was not among the lucky Americans and Canadians, for whom there was effectively no border control, but a Soviet citizen. If the Canadian frontier guards, who were even as I contemplated my situation coming down the corridor towards my compartment, caught me, there would be trouble. Of course, I would not be arrested as a spy because there was no proof of that. But a scandal would be bad enough, because in my position it was very important that I did not draw undue attention to myself.

My brain worked overtime. Suddenly I had a bright idea. I put my ticket in my hat band, took a long swig from the whisky bottle and dribbled the rest of the alcohol over the seats so that the compartment, where fortunately I was alone, stank like a distillery. Then I stretched out on the floor with the hat pulled down over my face, pretending to be dead drunk.

An American ticket inspector and a Canadian border guard came into the compartment together. 'Well, he's displaying his ticket. I guess we should leave him to sleep it off,' I heard the inspector say and they both left, laughing.

When I arrived in Chicago the old agent, whom I had not been able to risk telephoning in advance, was away from home and I had to make a second trip to the city. The next time I went with a colleague, planning to check out a couple of the military installations on Larin's list as well as to see the agent. We hired a car, but we must have slipped up somewhere because the FBI were soon on our tails. We had to abandon the operation and pretend we were tourists, come to admire the beauties of Lake Michigan. This was par for the course. So often our important work for Soviet state security descended into something more resembling a farce.

From a personal point of view, the most satisfying trip I made was to New Orleans. This expenses-paid outing was a real gift from the KGB. All I had to do was read an agent's signal, which could not have been easier. A signal was something simple like a chalk mark on a wall or a stone left in a certain position, although it could carry enormous significance, for example alerting us to the fact that some important new military secrets were available. I read the signal and then I was free for three whole days in the jazz capital of the world.

Whereas Harlem was threatening, more dilapidated than any other place I have seen in peacetime, and was virtually a no-go area for whites, New Orleans was more mellow, although even here there were parts where it was inadvisable for a white man to venture as I quickly discovered when I got bodily thrown out of a bar popular with local blacks. But if you stuck to the centre, thoroughfares like Bourbon Street in the heart of the French quarter, you were safe enough. And it was pure heaven to walk in the balmy evenings with the sound of jazz coming from every doorway.

I tried a Cajun restaurant and took a ride on a paddle steamer down the Mississippi River with the spirits of Tom Sawyer and Huckleberry Finn. But the highlight was the jazz. Words cannot adequately convey how exciting this was for me.

You see, back in the Soviet Union jazz was illegal. The authorities said it was a corrupting influence and the domestic branch of the KGB used to persecute enthusiasts. Despite my loyalty to the Lubyanka, I was a huge fan of Benny Goodman and Louis Armstrong and Ella Fitzgerald. But it was nearly impossible to get their records. Instead, like other devotees, I was reduced to listening to homemade copies scratched on used film taken from hospital X-ray departments and passed from hand to hand on an underground network. We called it 'jazz on bones' because very often you could literally see a spinal cord or a femur on the makeshift record.

Now at last was a chance to hear the liquid sound of a live saxophone instead of the rattle of old bones.

Little Cinderellas from the Bolshoi

I relocated my home in New York from the hotel to a one-room apartment in Queens, the rent on which ate up a third of my meagre salary. But it was clean and I had a second-hand television, at least until it went on the blink and I was laughed out of the repair shop by a rude assistant who said he had never seen anything so antediluvian.

I did not have much of a private life because I always had to think of friends as possible recruits for the KGB. Once at a UN party I met an American woman who shared some of my interests, like sport and jazz. We got on well and I went back to her flat for the night. I think she was quite keen on me and I liked her in a way. I suppose it was a budding romance. But I felt it my duty to report the affair to the *rezident*. 'Go on seeing her, you can kiss her, but don't let it go any further,' he said. How could I tell him that it had already gone a good deal further?

I continued to meet the girl, whose name was Mary-Ellen. After a while, she told me her contract at the UN was coming to an end and she was being transferred to the State Department in Washington. I informed the *rezident*, who ordered me to hand her over to another agent for handling. So cynical was the KGB in matters of human relations. But I had to obey. I pretended I did not want to see her any more, which offended her greatly, and I left my colleague to take over the courtship.

He had no success with her, however, which was hardly surprising because she had liked me. So the *rezident* ordered me to go to Washington to look her up again. The boss thought we had no feelings and he could just switch us off and on like machines. I made a half-hearted effort, hanging around in cafés near the State Department in the hope of catching her at lunch, but I failed to find her. Later we heard that she had been posted to a Scandinavian country. KGB agents there approached her, introducing themselves as my friends and passing on regards from me. But by this time she had got our number. 'All Russians are spies, even Brykin,' she said. 'Tell your masters to call off the dogs.'

I may have proved a bitter disappointment to Mary-Ellen but at least I was able to make some Russian girls very happy during my stay in New York. The Bolshoi Ballet came out on a tour and after they had performed *Swan Lake* and *Cinderella*, the dancers had some free time to see the sights of the Big Apple. They could have gone to any number of theatres or museums but what they really wanted to do was to shop until they dropped.

Unfortunately they had limited funds. The American impresarios at the Hurok agency and the management of the Bolshoi Theatre had exploited them, paying them only $350 each for a whole months gruelling work. But the *rezident* evinced a little generosity for once and gave me some extra money to show the girls a good time. Within reason, naturally.

The ballerinas could not have been in better hands. From experience, I knew where all the cheap shops were. My rule of thumb was: the more cluttered the window, the cheaper the shop. Stores displaying just a single black dress draped elegantly against a stark background were to be avoided at all costs. The poor should look out for heaps of junk and garish advertising stickers.

Purely for academic interest, we did go into Alexander's department store and flick through the rails of expensive jackets and trays of silk scarves. To the girls and me, the shop might as well have been a museum for we could only look, not dream of buying anything. We also went into Tiffany's where the jeweller, who had seen and loved the ballet, thrilled the girls by giving them little gold chains which they could not possibly have afforded themselves.

But we were really making for a shop called Yasha's, run by a Jewish émigré from Odessa. The girls wanted fake fur coats, which were all the rage in Moscow in the early sixties. You might have thought that buying fur coats in New York to take back to Moscow was like carrying coals to Newcastle. But it was very difficult to buy coats, or indeed any other consumer goods, in the Soviet Union in those days. Russians had some money in their pockets then unlike now when, as a result of President Boris Yeltsin's market reforms, people are struggling to make ends meet. But there were few available goods on which to spend cash, Soviet industry being geared to arms production rather than satisfying consumer demand, and people had to wait years for the privilege of being allowed to purchase a car, say, or even a coat.

Yasha had the answer. There were mounds of fake fur coats in his shop and the girls soon snapped them up. Silently I prayed that the coats would not turn out to be sub-standard, like a load we bought in another discount store called Grisha's for the dancers of the Beriozka folk troupe. When a representative of the consulate went back to the shop to complain, he saw a sign hanging on the door: 'Gone bankrupt.' A few months later, a 'new' store opened down the road with a different name but exactly the same personnel and goods.

Anyway, for a while at least, the ballerinas were blissfully happy and I was content too. These charming dancers had brightened the life of a solitary spy.

Split Personality

I prepared a welcome of a very different kind when a famous Russian artist who had defected to the West came to perform on Broadway. I found out from my friend Joe, an impoverished young man who earned his bread as a 'pearl diver' washing up in a restaurant but who lived for his evenings at the theatre, that the artist was in town. 'I've got two tickets,' he said excitedly, 'up in the gods but never mind. What a golden opportunity. You must come with me, Oleg.'

Personally I was more interested in the cinema than the theatre but I wanted to see this particular artist, whom I would rather not identify. 'I'll get good seats for us,' I said, 'up at the front.'

We went to the show and the artist – I cannot even say if he was an actor or a singer for fear you will recognise him – performed beautifully. Joe sat spellbound, tears rolling silently down his cheeks. But I was hatching a plot to do something very unpleasant to this entertainer, not assassinate him of course but create some disturbance which would throw him off balance and make him nervous for the rest of his performances in New York. For as far as I was concerned, he was no genius but a lousy traitor to his country.

I sat there fuming. What right did he have to come and bask in the applause here when his proper place was in front of a Soviet court? The Motherland had invested in his education and this was the gratitude he showed.

Eventually I hit on what seemed to me at the time a bright idea. The artist would be appearing a few evenings later at a reception laid on for him in a fancy Manhattan restaurant. I would gatecrash the event, leaving Joe out of it of course, and throw a stun-grenade at him while he was dining. That would spoil his visit to New York!

I went as far as to buy myself a false beard and dark glasses to disguise myself when I went into the restaurant to reconnoitre. I sat in a corner drinking whisky and worked out that the best time for the attack would be around midnight when the waiters turned out the main lights and lit candles to create a more intimate atmosphere for the floor show. I already knew where I would get the grenade. There was a gun shop in New Jersey where such a weapon could be bought over the counter.

I assumed my bosses at the KGB would be pleased with this plan, as they were always telling us that defectors were the lowest form of life. But to my surprise, when I put it to the *rezident* he was not enthusiastic and the answer from Moscow Centre was categorical: 'Stop this idiocy at once.' Now, of course, I see myself that it was lunacy.

At the time, I felt real burning hatred towards that artist. I was still a fervent Communist and it had been drummed into us during the Second World War to despise traitors. I myself had come close to starving to death as a teenager in Central Asia, to which my family was evacuated. A doctor had said there was no chance for me. But my father saved my life by coming back from the front with some glucose.

After the war, I followed in his footsteps, joining the KGB, without really asking any questions. I was immature and ignorant and desperate for a job. To begin with I was a loyal and unthinking Communist. But gradually a struggle developed inside me.

Various things made me begin to doubt that our Soviet system was perfect. The first was seeing the files of people who had been executed under Stalin when I worked for the KGB in the city of Gorky in the mid-1950s. This was the period when Khrushchev was beginning to speak of the atrocities of his predecessor. The files were all suspiciously thin. 'Such and such an officer found guilty of spying, sentence death; another officer convicted of treason, sentence death.' There were too many people and too little evidence of their guilt for it to make any sense.

Going abroad, of course, was the biggest shock to my certainty. When I saw how people lived in the West, I immediately understood the double standards of my own country. I also hated the arms race and could not see why, if Communism was so great, it had to be imposed by force.

But it took a while for these doubts to become fully conscious. When I was planning to throw the grenade at the artist like some crazed anarchist, I was still a Jekyll and Hyde figure, a hardline Communist with a human being inside, fighting to get out.

Now I am a pensioner, living with my life Lyudmila in a one-room flat in the Moscow suburb of Chertanovo. The high-rise blocks were built as part of an American–Soviet joint venture which predated perestroika, but the fountains and shops and sports complexes we were promised never materialised as the money was siphoned off for other projects such as a luxury hotel for top Communists. My monthly income today is less than the salary I received in New York in the early 1960s. Prices, however, have risen astronomically. It is not easy to be poor in Boris Yeltsin's Russia.

But I am not one of those pensioners who feels nostalgia for Communism. I would not want to restore that hypocritical system, even if it were possible to go backwards, which it is not. The path of reform is difficult but we have no alternative.

My posting to New York came to an end in 1963. After that I went to Indonesia as a diplomat – immune at last! And in 1980 I supervised the 2,500 translators who worked at the Moscow Olympic Games, boycotted by the US over the Soviet invasion of Afghanistan. I was sad to leave the Big Apple, where I spent some of the best days of my youth. But I was also mightily relieved. Considering how risky my job had been, I had done well to survive.

MEXICO CITY

White Power

Knowledge is power. The Indians who lived in Mexico before the Spanish conquest understood that, respecting their medicine men and magicians even more than their warriors. In Soviet society, those who ruled thanks to their access to information were the leaders at the top of the Communist Party pyramid. My job as the 'Tass correspondent' in Mexico City was to supply them with the facts that kept them in a position to command.

Journalism and intelligence-gathering are really very close. The only differences are the arenas in which reporters and secret agents work and the audiences they serve. Journalists work in the open for a wide readership. Spies want classified as well as publicly available information for a more exclusive circle.

The KGB was always in the market for secrets but in pre-glasnost days, much of the information which Tass, the official Soviet news agency, sent to the Communist hierarchy differed little from what Western people could read in the free press. The fact that it was unavailable to the mass of Soviet citizens gave our leaders their grip on power. The Tass which came ticking over the wires to newspaper offices, television and radio stations and other ordinary subscribers was not the Tass received by Leonid Brezhnev, the Politburo and the Central Committee of the Communist Party. For this elite, there existed a special Tass service known as 'white Tass', 'white' because of the quality of the paper on which it was written. Tass also sent despatches with specialised information for the military.

In Mexico City, I would write four or five short news stories a day which were transmitted over the open teletype machine for all, including my minders at the Mexican Interior Ministry, to see. But once a month, through the diplomatic bag, I would send a package with longer and more detailed typewritten reports for the masters of the Kremlin. For example, when presidential elections were held in 1976, I wrote a page or two for general readers, informing them that Mexicans were going to the polls to choose from among a number of candidates and giving them a brief account of the issues. But by 'white Tass', I sent sixteen pages of news and analysis, with biographies of all the candidates and a prediction of who was likely to win. My political judgement turned out to be spot on. This was the election in which Lopez Portillo replaced Luis Echeverria as President.

The stories on the open Tass wire were not only short but slanted, giving a view that was ideologically acceptable. 'White Tass' told the truth, even if it was unpalatable, for our rulers needed to know the real state of affairs in the world in order to prolong their time in power. For instance, plain Tass would paint a rosy picture of Soviet–Mexican friendship, becoming ever closer and warmer. But 'white Tass' would speak honestly of the tensions in bilateral relations.

Our leaders' attempt to monopolise knowledge was doomed, of course. It worked up to a point, for a while, but in the Brezhnev years, when Russians began to lose the fear instilled in them by Stalin, cracks appeared in the monolithic system. Soviet citizens tuned in to the BBC and Radio Liberty and heard the news that the Kremlin tried to keep to itself. Glasnost could no longer be resisted.

Knowledge is power, as the old Mexican Indians knew. But twentieth-century communications technology compels a wider sharing of these benefits. The Soviet empire foundered on its own lies, leaving only monuments to intrigue archeologists.

Undesirable Connections

How did humble Pavel Yefremov come to the attention of the KGB, for whom I was really working under the cover of Tass? Although I did not know it at the time, I was spotted in Havana where I went in 1964 to learn Spanish and agitate among Cuban students on behalf of the Komsomol, or Soviet Communist youth organisation. I was a committed Communist in those days, when Communism had not yet become a dirty word. I still am at heart, although I see now the ideals do not work in practice.

After graduating in law from Leningrad State University, where I had been secretary of the Komsomol branch, I set sail on a cruise ship with young Communists from various Warsaw Pact countries. We passed safely through the Bermuda Triangle on our way to Cuba, where we were to work as volunteer political missionaries among our Caribbean brethren.

I am an amiable soul, ready to befriend all kinds of people. In Cuba, I knew Raul Castro, the brother of Fidel, and Che Guevara. I also had two friends of whom the stuffy Soviet embassy did not at all approve – Princess Sonia Ukhtomskaya, a white Russian émigré who had ended up in pre-Castro Cuba after passing through China, Japan, the Philippines and New York in her flight from the Bolsheviks, and her companion, the opera singer Mariana de Gonich. Both were elderly when I met them. The princess, who had known Rasputin, must have been in her eighties while the diva, who had sung with the legendary Russian bass Fyodor Chaliapin, was not much younger.

Having spent their lives fleeing from Communism, you could say they were unlucky to settle in Cuba where, after a three-year guerrilla war, the playboy President Fulgencio Batista was overthrown by Fidel Castro's 26 July Movement in January 1959. But the Russian aristocrats, who had shown their patriotism by raising money for the Soviet Army during the Second World War, found a *modus vivendi* with Castro and lived comfortably in Havana. They mixed with senior Cuban officials and knew everyone in the diplomatic corps. Indeed, in 1967, their extensive connections were to prove of great use to the Soviet authorities. The Six-Day War between the Arabs and the Israelis had just taken place. Although the Soviet Union broke off diplomatic relations with Israel as a result of it, Castro was not satisfied and accused Moscow of having encouraged the Arabs to fight and of then abandoning them. Relations between the Soviet Union and its Cuban ally became very frosty; indeed we were not talking to each other at all on an official level. At this point my friendship with the aristocrats, who were the leaders of a 200-strong

Russian émigré community, became the only channel of information about what was going on in Cuba. A month before it occurred, the princess tipped me off to an impending split in the Cuban Communist Party. I mentioned it in passing to the consul at the Soviet embassy, who suddenly took a favourable new attitude to my 'undesirable contacts'. Thus Moscow was forewarned that comrades who remained loyal to the Soviet Union despite the row over the Middle East were to be expelled from the Cuban party.

The embassy continued to rely on the white Russians until normal relations with Cuban officials were restored in 1968, when the Soviet Union invaded Czechoslovakia. Fidel Castro was an even more orthodox Communist than Leonid Brezhnev. When tanks were rolling to 'save socialism' he was happy again and Cuban–Soviet relations were back on track.

All this came flooding back to me when the telephone rang at Komsomol headquarters in Moscow, where I went to work after my four-year stay in Cuba, and the former Soviet consul in Havana came on the line saying: 'Aren't you tired of doing kids' work? We think it's time for Pasha Yefremov to come and work for the "office".' I realised the 'consul' was from the KGB and he was inviting me to join Soviet foreign intelligence.

Frankly, I was not very keen at first. I enjoyed motivating young people, 'kids' work' as he put it. On my return from Cuba, I had been involved in organising a Communist song festival in the Black Sea resort of Sochi. It was fun, and rewarding too. The Komsomol had just arranged for me to get a Moscow *propiska* or residence permit and my own flat in the capital, the fulfilment of a dream for a provincial boy like me. But the 'consul' did not give up easily. Working for the 'office', I would be of greater use to my Motherland, he said. That convinced me. I began to hope for the honour of serving in the secret war, although I was not sure the KGB itself would want me when it found out the truth about my background.

I was born in 1939 in the southern Russian port of Novorossisk. In 1942, the Germans bombed the city prior to entering it. My mother, Anna Kolyada, saved me by covering me with her own body. I was pulled from the rubble with nothing worse than an injured arm but she was killed. My father, Alexander Yefremov, remarried a woman called Vera Kolomytseva and we went to live in the northern Caucasus.

For reasons only someone who grew up in the Soviet wonderland would immediately grasp, my parents changed my birth certificate to make it appear that I came into the world in Beslan in the region of North Ossetia. I still live with this forged document to this day.

My father, who was a military intelligence officer, drummed it into me from school age that I must stick to this version of my origin at all costs. He feared that, like millions of other Soviet citizens who happened to fall under Nazi occupation, I would suffer discrimination in college and job applications in the future. I might only have been two years old when I survived the bombing of Novorossisk but the fact that I had been in a German-held zone made me forever 'unreliable' in the eyes of the authorities. By lying, I got into Leningrad University and the Komsomol.

However, I felt that if I were to serve in the foreign intelligence service, I should do so with a clean conscience. I told the truth on my KGB application form and waited for an answer without much optimism. I was amazed when the KGB accepted me for what I was, although now I know that the bosses of the foreign intelligence service were not as bone-headed as other Soviet bureaucrats and were capable of flexibility and imaginative decisions. The weakness in my arm that was the consequence of my injury in Novorossisk was not held against me either by the KGB's medical commission. I went to study for a year at the Krasnoznamyonny Institute, which was later renamed the Andropov Academy and which still trains officers for the post-Communist Russian foreign intelligence service. Then I joined Tass and went out to Mexico City in 1972.

In at the Deep End

Rebuilt in modern times, Mexico City stands surrounded not merely by mountains but by the live volcanoes Popokatepetl and Istaksiuatl. The metropolis of 15 million people is saved from disaster by the fact that it is cushioned by an underground lake, although in 1986 it suffered the world's worst earthquake this century.

As I and my wife Nellie and son Sasha came in to land at Benito Juares Airport, however, we saw nothing of the volcanoes and, in the car afterwards, little of the palm and acacia-lined boulevards either, for Mexico City was, as is often the case, covered in thick smog which cut visibility down to only a few yards.

We moved into a flat with an office attached in a green suburb called Condesa. On my salary of $500 per month, we lived in luxury compared with ordinary citizens back in the USSR. I had a car, a yellow Ford Maverick, which was a sporty two-door vehicle a bit like a Mustang. Later I sold it for a coffee-coloured Dodge Dart imported from Detroit.

It was not far from home to the Soviet embassy where my boss, the KGB *rezident*, was based. The embassy, a mansion with fountains in the garden, had a fascinating history. Mexico was the first country in the

Western hemisphere with which the young Soviet Union established diplomatic relations after the Bolshevik Revolution. From 1926 to 1927, our ambassador was Alexandra Kolontai, the daughter of the Tsarist-era governor of St Petersburg, a famous beauty, an ardent supporter of Lenin and the first woman ambassador in the world.

Other colourful characters were associated with the embassy. During the Second World War, ambassador Konstantin Umansky, later to die tragically in an air crash, channelled the funds raised by Princess Sonia on Cuba to Red Army troops resisting the Nazi invasion of the Soviet Union. And in the early 1960s, a famous villain turned up at the embassy. Lee Harvey Oswald, an American student who had married a woman from Belorussia, came and asked if there was anything he could do to express his love for the Soviet Union. He was shown the door, which was fortunate in retrospect, as he went on to assassinate US President John F. Kennedy, a crime with which the KGB would not have wanted to be linked.

But all this was before my time.

I was the only correspondent working for Tass in Mexico City, although two people replaced me when I left in 1978. In other bureaux round the world, Tass employed several staffers, both 'clean' journalists and undercover KGB agents. The journalists, who were all Communists of course even if they were not spying, wrote the news stories for both plain and 'white' Tass while the KGB officers did a mixture of journalism and the usual intelligence work of meeting agents and emptying dead letter boxes. Being alone, I had to run round doing everything. 'The Tass man is like a wolf, his legs feed him,' Leonid Zamyatin, the director of the news agency, told me before I set out on my posting.

I came to Mexico at an unfortunate time. The country could not help but be influenced by its giant neighbour, the United States, and its policy was sometimes anti-Soviet. On the eve of my arrival, five Russian diplomats had been expelled from Mexico including – and this was a below-the-belt blow from the Mexicans – the senior diplomat who was deputising for our ambassador in his temporary absence. Ambassadors are usually immune in tit-for-tat expulsion scandals.

Even without this complication, I would normally have eased myself gradually into intelligence work, doing more straight journalism at first in order to convince the Mexican Interior Ministry, which controlled correspondents by requiring them to renew their visas at six-month intervals, that I was a bona fide reporter. In view of the tense atmosphere, however, I had instructions from my KGB boss in Moscow, a grey-haired man nicknamed the Silver Prince, to refrain from spying for a full six months until my first visa was renewed and it was clear the Mexicans had accepted me.

'That's the theory,' said Yuri, my *rezident*, who was grey-haired too, prematurely so at the age of thirty. 'But the Silver Prince also wants us to make contact with agent Tomahawk and you should be the one to do the job because you're going to be handling him in future. So you're in at the deep end.' Yuri was a nice guy for a boss. I still go to the *banya*, or Russian steam bath, with him in Moscow now.

And so, against all the rules, I went straight to meet an underground contact within hours of stepping off the plane. Yuri helped me. Since I did not know the city at all, he took me in his car to the meeting with Tomahawk, an exile from a Fascist dictatorship elsewhere in Latin America who cooperated with the KGB not for money but from ideological conviction. 'You'll recognise him,' said Yuri, 'because he'll be standing outside the restaurant with a newspaper under his arm. Now get out of the car and walk the rest of the way. You can come back to the embassy afterwards on your own by metro.'

The meeting went off without a hitch. I got acquainted with Tomahawk, who served us as an 'agent of influence', and passed on to him some pro-Soviet texts which we wanted him to plant in the Mexican press. But the trip back to the embassy turned into a nightmare.

I was in the metro car, riding to Takubaya, the nearest station to the embassy, when the lights went out. A voice came over the loudspeaker telling all the passengers to vacate the train and start walking up the track. I don't know what caused the scare but it was an unpleasant experience. Finally we emerged at Balderos station where crowds of people began competing for taxis. But I could not have taken a cab even if I could have flagged one down, for I did not know the city and the only instruction I could have given to the driver would have been, 'Take me to the Soviet embassy', which would have immediately given me away. Neither could I buy a map as it was past midnight and the street kiosks were all closed.

I racked my brains. I vaguely remembered the layout of the Mexico City metro system. If I was not mistaken, Balderos was on a straight line to Takubaya, the terminus, so if I kept walking I should eventually come to the suburb of Condes and the embassy. I walked half the night and, as far as I know, nobody from the Mexican Federal Department of Security followed me. Eventually I reached base, where the *rezident* had already started to wonder why his new member of staff had gone awol.

'All's well that ends well,' he said when I came in at last. 'Yes,' I agreed, 'but perhaps I had better follow Moscow's instructions now and lie low for a bit.' 'That's the theory,' said Yuri, 'but we've got more work for you.' And so I began my job as a secret agent in Mexico City without the six months I was supposed to have to settle in and lull the Mexicans into complacency. Nevertheless, the Interior Ministry renewed my visa that time and another eleven more over the following five and a half years. They seemed to like me, or perhaps it was the vodka and caviar I used to give them that they liked.

Committed Communists

'You kept your secret all these years. I don't see why you had to reveal yourself at all,' said my wife Nellie when I contributed to this book of memoirs. I did it because I wanted the world to know that some decent people worked for the KGB.

In Mexico, I was not operating against my host country but against the interests of our Cold War enemy, the United States. Gathering political information not only about Mexico but also about other Central American countries such as Nicaragua, which was boiling with revolution at that time, I was helped by many Mexicans and other Latin Americans who regarded the Soviet Union as a friend. All in all, I had over ten paid agents and scores of more casual contacts, a wide network.

Like Tomahawk, many belonged to the older generation who had been young before Hitler was defeated and Stalin's atrocities were exposed, when all the brightest and best-hearted people in the world considered themselves Communists. It was inspiring for me to work with such people. Our Communist struggle, which by the 1970s had become a fight against US imperialism, gave our lives meaning.

Mexico was very generous to political exiles. In Mexico City, I knew Bussi de Allende, the widow of President Salvador Allende, who was overthrown when General Augusto Pinochet seized power in Chile in 1973. She was not a KGB agent, of course, but other exiles from Latin America were, including 'Comandor', a charming, intellectual man on whom the KGB had to press money for his services as a Soviet lobbyist because really he did it for love.

On one occasion, I had to travel to Cuernowaca, or the City of Eternal Spring, in Morelos State to give Comandor his wages and some texts on 'trade unionists who had sold out to American capitalism', which we wanted him to publish before a regional trade union conference which was about to be held. He was well placed to do this because, since coming to Mexico, the former politician had found work in journalism.

Vasily, a new KGB agent who had just arrived at the embassy, acted as my chauffeur on the one-and-a-half hour drive south from Mexico City on a mountain road with hairpin bends and viewing places which were perfect not only for enjoying the scenery but also for checking to make sure Mexican security were not on our tail. We passed the waterfalls near Cuernowaca, where local divers copy their heroes from Acapulco and plunge from the rocks, the only difference being that at Acapulco the daredevils dive into the Pacific Ocean, while here they leap into a stream only a few feet wide. As we came into Cuernowaca, students were holding up the traffic, begging for money to feed a group of American hippies who had come to camp near the city.

Vasily and I checked into the Hotel Popugayo (Parrot) on the main Mexico City–Acapulco highway. My meeting with Comandor was set for the next evening in a nearby restaurant called the Don Quixote, chosen because it was conveniently close to where the elderly agent lived, so he would not have far to walk to the rendezvous. We killed time by drinking beer in open-air cafés in Cuernowaca's picturesque old town.

When the time came for me to meet Comandor, Vasily dropped me off near the restaurant and went to wait for me a few streets away. My Spanish was so good that I was taken for a 'gringo', not a Russian, but Vasily's accent was heavier. 'If someone asks you for a light and then gets chatting with you, tell them your friend has gone off to meet a woman,' I said.

With only minutes left before the rendezvous, I approached the Don Quixote when, to my horror, I saw that the restaurant was surrounded by police and crowds of onlookers. My first thought was that Comandor had been arrested and that I should make a run for it, but then it occurred to me that the police would not have done that; rather they would have waited for me to turn up too, to catch us both *in flagrante*. I decided to hang about, although it was risky. If I was stopped, how would I explain that I was carrying $3,000 dollars in cash, an allowance from the KGB which Comandor would have to make last for several months? I would say it was my own journalist's wages. I would have been glad to earn such a salary!

Eventually I spotted Comandor making his way to the restaurant. 'Follow me,' I hissed at him through the side of my mouth. He did so, walking several paces behind. When I was sure nobody was following us, I passed him the texts and money right there on the street. 'I'm sorry but we'll have to skip dinner tonight,' I said as we parted.

Afterwards, when the crowds thinned, I realised the police had been attending a traffic accident. The Mexico City–Acapulco bus had crashed into a lorry outside the Don Quixote. My precautions had been unnecessary but in intelligence work it is always better to be safe than sorry.

On other occasions, I came to Cuernowaca to visit the artist David

Alfaro Siqueros, who was not a KGB agent but simply a friend whom I loved and deeply respected. He had a house called Tres Picos or the Three Peaks in Mexico City, but his summer house and studio were in the City of Eternal Spring and it was here, working up a ladder at an enormous easel, that he painted his political panoramas. He belonged to the muralist school of painters and was most famous for a series of frescos called *The March of Humanity in Latin America* on a gigantic mushroom-shaped structure called the Poliforum in Mexico City. It was his ambition to paint a fresco in Moscow but sadly he died of cancer before he could fulfil his dream. Nevertheless, every self-respecting Russian art lover has heard of Siqueros.

Not only was he an artist but also a committed revolutionary who in his youth had travelled to the Soviet Union to attend meetings of the Comintern, or Communist International movement, and met Lenin in person. In 1939, on orders from the Mexican Communist Party Central Committee – but really on orders from Stalin – Siqueros attacked Leon Trotsky, firing a machine-gun at him in his flat. Trotsky saved himself by diving under his bed, only to die in a better-known incident a year later when a Spaniard called Mercader killed him with a blow from an ice pick.

For his bungled attempt to assassinate Trotsky, Siqueros was jailed. The Chilean poet Pablo Neruda, who in the 1940s worked as his country's consul in Mexico, used to meet Siqueros, who was allowed out of prison for an occasional drink in a bar. Once over the tequila, Neruda persuaded Siqueros not to return to jail and quickly issued him with a visa so that he could escape to Chile. He lived in Santiago for several years before returning to his native Mexico.

All that was ancient history when I used to visit Siqueros and his wife Anjelica, although we sometimes remembered Chile in our conversations, bemoaning the situation in the country since General Pinochet had taken over.

Once at his studio, Siqueros introduced me to Monsignor Mendes Arseo, known as the 'Red Bishop of Cuernowaca' because he preached liberation theology, and he became a friend of mine as well. The walls of his cathedral of San Francisco, one of the oldest Catholic churches in Mexico, dating back to the time of the Spanish conquest, were constantly spray-painted with abusive graffiti by Mexican Fascists, who would have liked to prove he was a KGB agent, although I better than anyone knew that was not true.

The bishop, whose thick-set frame and shaven head belied his gentle nature, was a man of few words when he was not in the pulpit, but I gathered that graffiti was the least of his problems and he also suffered

Leonid Kolosov: before and after
recruitment by the KGB.

Kolosov's car after an accident intended to kill Khrushchev's son-in-law.

Lev Bausin pondering the mystery of Egypt.

The late Nikolai Koshkin in Tokyo standing between two geisha girls.

Left Oleg Brykin as a young man. He had overcome a poor childhood and was set to become a boxing champion when the KGB spotted him in the 1950s. *Below* In retirement.

Brykin targeting young American blacks, whom the KGB had mistakenly believed might be pro-Soviet.

Pavel Yefremov in Mexico.

Above Nikolai Urtmintsev, the KGB's man in Latin America.

Left Oleg Brykin drinking away his tropical ennui in Jakarta.

Leonid Kolosov in Paris by the freshly dug grave of the émigré bard, Alexander Galich. Kolosov was on a mission to bring him back to Russia but arrived too late, just days after his mysterious death by electric shock.

death threats and physical attacks from the far-right. Nothing deterred him, however, and he continued to tell his congregation every Sunday that had Christ been alive today, he would have been a Marxist insisting on social justice in the world.

Picnic at the Pyramids

Just as Vasily acted as my driver and back-up man when I travelled to Cuernowaca to meet Comandor, so I was also required from time to time to assist my KGB colleagues in their operations. Once the *rezident* ordered me and Vladimir, a junior diplomat at the embassy, to gather our families together for a weekend picnic that would provide cover for a delicate operation which another operative named Gennady had to carry out in the Teotehuacan National Park.

Gennady, who unlike me had diplomatic immunity, had the highly responsible job of dealing with the KGB's illegal agents in Mexico. They would rarely meet face to face, for that was too risky, but communicated via dead letter boxes. My colleague had to go the national park to dig up a canister buried at the foot of a pine tree. I did not even ask what was in the canister, for we KGB agents knew we had to mind our own business. Together with Vladimir, my task was simply to create a diversion so that Gennady could retrieve his consignment.

Our wives and children were thrilled at the prospect of a picnic. We set out in a convoy of three cars, heading northeast from Mexico City on a road lined with maize plantations. We had not gone far when we came to a peasant market with knitwear and pottery which our wives just had to inspect. But we did not complain as the stopover also gave us a good opportunity to check we were not being followed.

We resumed our journey. The landscape became more barren. Corn gave way to different kinds of cactuses. Mexican Indians make controlled use of hallucinogenic drugs derived from cactuses for spiritual development. I did not give this much thought when I lived in Mexico – the only drug users I saw then were pathetic teenage junkies smoking marijuana in Mexico City – but I have since become interested in the subject as, in my retirement, I have discovered Carlos Castenada, the US anthropologist who wrote about the Yaqui Indian guru, Don Juan. I believe that I myself have extra-sensory perception and in Moscow now I sometimes heal the sick with the energy that radiates from my hands. But I digress . . .

We were on the road to Teotehuacan National Park to empty a dead letter box. The park lies along the San Juan River, not far from the ruined Pyramids of the Sun and Moon, evidence of the advanced civilisation of the Toltec Indians who lived in Mexico centuries before the Aztecs. The Mexican pyramids are not as large as those in Egypt, but possibly of even greater significance as they were not used to bury the dead but as temples, observatories and centres for the administration of Toltec society. We duly paid our respects at this important cultural site.

Then we found the place where we were to have our picnic. In a pretty meadow, Vladimir set up an easel and began giving an excellent impression of an amateur landscape painter. Our wives spread a table cloth on the grass and busied themselves with the food while the kids played tag. Gennady and I set off in the direction of a clump of pines, consulting a little hand-drawn map like treasure hunters in a children's adventure story. We pitched a tent where X marked the spot, at the foot of one particularly noble pine. I was to act as the look-out while Gennady did the digging inside the tent.

He took out his spade and immediately came up against a problem. The tent which we had bought in a sports shop turned out to have a tough canvas bottom to keep out moisture from the ground, so before he could start digging Gennady had to cut this away. Then he began excavating for the canister. 'It's OK,' I said, 'there's nobody about.'

Gennady dug and dug and failed to find the canister. We moved the tent a few feet and he started to burrow again. Eventually his spade hit metal. Heavy rain had washed the earth down from the foot of the tree and the canister had been carried away from point X. We were lucky there had only been a small slippage, otherwise we might have had to dig up the entire field.

'I'm coming out with the canister now,' said Gennady. 'Is the coast still clear?' 'No, stop,' I cried, for I had suddenly become aware of a man in shorts sitting in the lotus position on a cliff on the other side of the river, which gave him an eagle's eye view of the whole field. 'Oh, ****,' said Gennady.

The yogi was probably just some hippy on holiday, but we had to be cautious in case he was from Mexican counter-intelligence. We stayed in the tent for about half an hour until the observer stood up and left. He was indeed just an innocent tourist. We sighed with relief, then quickly got the incriminating canister into the boot of Gennady's car and joined the picnic to make everything look natural.

What would we have done if the busy-body had approached us and wanted to know what we were up to? Personally, I would have invited him to share a sandwich and a glass of wine with us, disarming him with our hospitality. Serendipity: that's the secret of espionage.

Briefing for Brezhnev

The telephone rang. It was my pal Ruslan from *Izvestia*. 'Sergo Mikoyan's coming out with a delegation from the Peace Committee,' he said gloomily. Who was Sergo Mikoyan? Nobody special, just the editor of a Soviet journal called *Latin America*. But his father was the great Anastas Mikoyan, a minister under Stalin who ended his political career by briefly playing the role of Soviet President when Leonid Brezhnev became General Secretary of the Communist Party. I would have to roll out the red carpet for this son of a 'bump', as we call bigwigs in Russian slang.

Although it interfered with my own work, I entertained Sergo royally. I took him to several of the best restaurants and introduced him to various Mexican public figures. I even managed, after considerable string-pulling, to arrange for him to interview the then President of Mexico, Luis Echeverria.

I was going to have to attend the interview as Sergo's translator, a nightmare job because the poor chap had a stammer, so I reckoned I might as well squeeze maximum benefit from the occasion for the KGB too. As things turned out, I was to get not only a revealing political interview but also a lesson in the rivalry of the different branches of power in the Soviet system.

Feeling rather pleased with myself for securing the interview, I went to consult my boss, the *rezident*. Yuri had left Mexico City and the new *rezident* was not so well disposed towards me. Because I did not have much time, I called on him in the evening at his home, which was a bit risky for me because his house was probably under surveillance and also, quite simply, not the done thing. He opened the door in his dressing gown and slippers.

'I've got an interview with President Echeverria,' I said brightly.

'Congratulations,' he replied gruffly, 'but what use is that to the KGB? The President is hardly going to reveal any secrets. It will just be polite chit-chat.'

I was a bit offended by that. 'Allow me then,' I said stiffly, 'to make use of the opportunity for Tass.'

'No objections,' said the *rezident* and closed the door.

The rejection by my KGB boss and main master was something of a blow. You see, a lowly functionary like I did not have the right to interview the head of a foreign state without agreeing in advance the questions to be asked with someone more senior in the Soviet hierarchy. There was no time for me to get through to Moscow to consult the editors at Tass, to whom I reported after the KGB and who also had the authority to sanction my proposed questions.

But then Nellie cheered me up by saying that Nikolai Konstantinovich, the Soviet ambassador, had just rung and wanted to see me first thing the next morning. When we met, he was only too happy to give his seal of approval to the questions I planned to ask President Echeverria.

'Just be sure to come and brief me afterwards,' he said at the end of our chat.

With the ambassador's blessing, I went with Sergo to interview the President, who lived in a mansion called Los Pinos set in Chapultepec Park. Families were picnicking on the lawns around the National History Museum housed in Chapultepec Castle, where the Mexican army made a stand against the Americans in the US–Mexican war of 1846–8. The President's residence was more homely, with surprisingly little security. We were shown into an oval room painted pale lilac.

I did not get much out of the interview at first. Sergo received formal answers to his rather obscure questions on Latin American affairs, which he had presented in advance in writing, then President Echeverria gave him some art books and a set of records to help him learn Spanish. It was not too difficult for me to translate, as the President did more of the talking than the stammering Sergo. Echeverria made a good impression on me. I had thought he was very pro-American but in the course of the conversation I realised he was a wise man who walked a difficult political path and defended Mexico's interests as best he could.

When Sergo had finished, I asked if I could put three questions for Tass. My questions were simple and designed to extract spontaneous answers on global rather than purely Latin American matters. President Echeverria had just returned from a visit to the Soviet Union. First I asked him what impression he had of our leaders and second how he saw Mexican–Soviet relations developing. Third I asked him for his views on a summit which was about to be held in Washington between President Richard Nixon and Leonid Brezhnev.

After the interview, Sergo and I paid a courtesy call on Nikolai Konstantinovich, the ambassador.

'What answers did you get to your questions?' he asked me.

'You know I ought really to report to Tass first,' I said. Since the KGB had shown no interest in the meeting the President, my next duty was to inform the news agency which provided my cover and only then could I assist the ambassador, who represented the Soviet foreign service.

'I understand,' said Nikolai Konstantinovich. 'Let's agree that you will file your story and then you will let me have a copy.'

This I duly did. Then Sergo and I went off for the weekend to Cuernowaca, where I introduced him to my friend, the artist David Siqueros. We got back very late on the Sunday night and I was still in bed at nine o'clock on Monday morning when the telephone rang.

'Who the hell do you think you're working for?' said an angry voice. It was the KGB *rezident*, who wanted to see me in his office immediately. When I arrived, he demanded to know why had I reported on the results of my meeting with President Echeverria to the Foreign Ministry and not the KGB.

'I didn't,' I said. 'I wrote a story for Tass. And anyway, I thought you weren't interested in the interview.'

'Pack your cases. You're leaving,' said the *rezident*.

You can imagine my feelings as I went home to tell Nellie we were being sent back to Moscow in disgrace.

Two hours later, the *rezident* rang back. I could stay after all, he said, but without much grace. He had discovered I was telling the truth and that the report of President Echeverria's interview which went out on the Foreign Ministry's lines of communication was merely a rewrite of my article for Tass, quoting the news agency throughout.

The KGB *rezident* was later to kick himself for his own bad judgement, however, because the report, which could have come from the KGB and gained him credit, was appreciated by none other than Leonid Brezhnev himself. This was in 1973, when the Kremlin leader was in Washington, preparing for his talks with Nixon who, only a year earlier, had broken the Cold War ice by being the first US President to visit the Soviet Union. Brezhnev was encouraged to hear that a country like Mexico which, because of its proximity to the US was obliged to support the Western super power, nevertheless felt some sympathy for the Soviet Union as well and wanted to see international detente. The outcome of his second meeting with Nixon was that Brezhnev declared the Cold War over, perhaps in part because of the intelligence he received from me in Mexico City.

I should have glowed with pride, but instead I felt sad as the realisation sank in that different Soviet organisations, which were supposed to cooperate for a common cause, were often at each other's throats. The KGB mistrusted the government ministries; the ministries hated the KGB, which was seen as a power unto itself.

I did not allow myself to become cynical, however. A foreign intelligence officer is no good when he becomes hard-bitten and pessimistic.

I continued to serve in Mexico City until 1978, when I returned to Moscow to help control the Latin American region from KGB headquarters. I was offered other foreign postings but Nellie and I did not want to put our son into a boarding school.

My work in Moscow was interesting. I was involved in thinking up disinformation, for example the suggestion that the AIDS virus had been created in an American military laboratory. Once I had a dream that I was in Guatemala, a country I never visited in my waking life, handing out bread to the poor. A peasant said: 'What should we do?' and I replied: 'Continue the struggle.' The next day, inspired by this, I wrote an article about Guatemala. A few hours later my boss came in and said: 'We need something urgently about Guatemala to get into the American press before a Congress debate.' The subconscious always plays an important role in creative work, which I consider the intelligence officer's job to be.

I would probably be working for the KGB today had the *putsch* against Mikhail Gorbachev, led by hardliners including the KGB chairman, not failed in August 1991. After the coup the powerful KGB, which had combined internal policing with foreign intelligence, was split into two organisations. Many staff were pensioned off, including myself in 1992. Now I supplement my pension by working as a legal consultant to the Russian Supreme Court while my spare time is devoted to literature. Recently the Macedonian ambassador to Russia asked me to translate his country's classic poems into Spanish. Macedonian is close to Russian and I was glad of an opportunity to immerse myself once more in the Spanish language which, over the years in Spanish-speaking Mexico, I had come to love as much as my mother tongue.

LONDON

Name	Lyubimov, Mikhail Petrovich
Born	27 May 1934
Education	Higher, Masters degree in history
Special Subject	International relations
Languages	English, Swedish
Military Rank	Colonel
Worked in	Britain, Denmark
Marital Status	Married
Sports	Swimming, volleyball
Hobbies	Walking
Favourite Tipple	Glenlivet
Brand of Cigarettes	Don't smoke

Mr Weller's knowledge of London was extensive and peculiar.
Pickwick Papers, Charles Dickens

The Spy's Return

The road from Heathrow is drab and dull and hardly excites the heart to a faster beat. My friend Chris is chatting with the taxi driver, a burly Scot who politely stops for an old lady hobbling over a zebra crossing. He faithfully obeys all the rules of the road. This is not Moscow, where drivers zoom through red lights, so far has our Russian democracy progressed.

'Do you realise who you have in the back of the cab?' Chris asks jokingly. 'A former KGB colonel, a dangerous spy who got thrown out of Britain. Do you know what he got up to, this chap who looks like a kind old uncle? He recruited our Tories right and left.'

The driver catches my phizog in his mirror and exclaims, 'Good on yer! You did right! That's the way to treat 'em! Those damned Tories have brought the country to its knees!'

People from the impoverished north, where Scotland lurks among its castles and whisky fumes, have little love for the Conservatives or prosperous London, which amiably regards the Scots as layabouts. Hearing the driver's outburst, I feel satisfied. So it was not in vain, then, that I devoted my ardent revolutionary soul to trying to subvert the Establishment in the Britain of Harold Macmillan.

Now I am back visiting London for the first time since the Foreign Office declared me persona non grata in 1965. Chris has invited me to stay with him and see how England has changed in the thirty years I have been away.

Greetings, inscrutable Albion! I remember racing my car down Pall Mall before dawn, hurrying to my first meeting with my newborn son, Sasha. My wife Katya gave birth in a maternity hospital in Mile End because we had more faith in the Communist obstetricians of the East End than in the hospitals of the bourgeoisie.

How divinely we lived in a cellar in Earls Terrace with a view out over the rubbish bins of the Soviet diplomatic community. As a junior diplomat, my pay was low and we had to share a rented flat with another family. Who could have guessed then that Sasha would become one of the television stars of the perestroika era and a TV mogul? Good Lord, how long ago it all was!

Greetings to Marks and Spencer, not charging the earth like pompous Harrods but a cheap, democratic shop. Some people still think that, together with the philosopher Spencer, it was Karl Marx himself who founded the store. Sometimes, when I used to visit M & S, I was taken for an assistant by the shoppers, who asked me where they could find the vegetable graters or the jackets. My face must have borne the stamp of obliging service, for I grew up under the dictatorship of Stalin.

Greetings to the Ritz Hotel, cumbersome jewel of Piccadilly – 'Goodbye Piccadilly, goodbye Leicester Square, it's a long way to Tipperary but my heart is there' – and to the deer grazing in Richmond Park. It is an eternal mystery to we Russians, but we cannot fathom how come, despite all the crowds that trample and lie on it, the grass of England always springs up freshly while at home, where it is strictly forbidden to walk on the grass, it is crushed and muddy.

Greetings, too, to the Georgian cottages of Chelsea with their window boxes and leather Chippendale divans, under which I was always wanting to take a peek and see if there was a corpse, as in an Agatha Christie novel.

London impresses me with its gravity and variety; London is wise; London always comes with a subtext.

When I spied there in the 1960s, I wore out my shoe leather tramping over the city. The eighteenth-century Russian aristocrat and writer Nikolai Karamzin might have been able to afford to ride everywhere in a cab, but we poorly paid Soviet intelligence agents had to walk down winding streets, checking and rechecking that we were not being followed. With an open *A–Z* in my hands, I would hurry to meet my agent, sweating and getting lost, fearing that I might be late to the rendezvous and miss 'our man'.

Everywhere I went I saw Englishmen; indeed there were times when I became distressed at the huge numbers of Englishmen I had still not managed to recruit. Arrogant Tories, privy to top secrets on which the fate of superpowers hung (everything was super in those days), moved in packs down Oxford Street or walked their shampooed dogs, the very sight of which offended those like me, who were struggling for human happiness. Or with their briar pipes, they smoked themselves silly in cinemas. Fortunately it is forbidden now but in those days the screen used to disappear in the smoke, especially during the last sitting, after which the retired colonels from the colonies would leap from their seats and bellow 'God Save the Queen'.

Tories were everywhere and among them waved the tail of my lucky goldfish.

Shameful Passion

With England I fell strangely in love; the more I admired her, the more nervous I felt, literally as if I was doing something shameful, and I admired her more and more. I loved the regatta at Henley and Cheney Walk, where Dante Gabriel Rossetti had his house and my favourite poet, Algernon Charles Swinburne, also lived. The English were far from being stiff types out of Thackeray – although there were a few dreadful snobs – but were for the most part open and friendly.

My forbidden passion for Albion threw me into a fever and the whole flirtation began to smell almost of treachery. I tried to relieve my feelings by writing bitter verses, satirising the dabauchery of Soho, the boring clerks with their bowler hats and inevitable umbrellas and the excessively polite and hypocritical English ladies.

Had not the British preserved their monarchy in order to distract the masses from the path of socialism? I argued with myself. And was this not also the real reason behind their cult of tradition? Westminster Abbey and the little toy palace guard and even the restaurant of the Ritz Hotel that, as we all knew, was open to rich and poor alike? Ha, ha!

I was infuriated by the nannies pushing prams and leading beribboned little girls by the hand in Hyde Park. These well-fed children irritated me (I thought of the starving in Africa) and as for the nannies, I wanted to tell them they had no reason to look so proud. They were just servants of the idle rich, who had no time for their own children, let alone the problems of the working class, but only cared if the Veuve Clicot was properly chilled. I was proud that such a disgrace was impossible in my country, where we had kindergartens, equality and brotherhood.

My Albion! The cab takes me down Memory Lane and I hear the paper boys shouting in their rough Cockney: ' 'Ank you, sir.' I remember Stratford-upon-Avon and the statue of Hamlet (to spy or not to spy became my dilemma). I also remember being interested in the Serpentine Lake in Hyde Park because Shelley's wife drowned there. ('Whose wife?' asked an embassy colleague. 'You don't mean that bow-legged fellow at the reception the other night who wolfed a whole bowl of caviar all to himself?')

Early in the mornings, I used to jog in my shorts in Hyde Park – I was a fitness fanatic. There, too, I pushed the pram with my son and saw him take his first shaky steps on the grass, looking with wonder all around him.

I revisit the Etoile restaurant in Soho. I was eating snails there with an American professor of history – he saw me casting covetous looks at the silk handkerchief blossoming in his breast pocket and gave it to me with a generous flourish – when a man rushed into the dining room and shouted: 'Kennedy has been assassinated.' The rest was a piece of silent theatre.

On another occasion, I was dining at Chez Isaacs with Dick Crossman, a Labour Shadow Minister, when the waiter came up and brought us a note: 'Your table is bugged.' My unflappable companion read it, raised his eyebrows and passed it to me. I shook with a vague premonition of disaster. Although we had not been doing anything criminal, we quickly finished our meal and went out on to the street. There someone slapped me on the back and laughed. It was only that joker, my old friend the cinema director Jack Levine, playing a prank. But I for one had gone pale.

Spying as a profession widens one's understanding of human nature, but it coarsens one and turns one into a cynic. Could any decent person peep through keyholes and gather, crumb by crumb, information that his neighbour would prefer to keep to himself? The worst aspect of the job is that you come to see man, created by God and with all his human joys and sorrows, as nothing more than an object for recruitment, to be sniffed and licked, ensnared, seduced and finally hooked.

And yet they are always with me, my agents actual and potential, devoted and unfaithful. Hand in hand, they pass in a procession, laughing, crying, greeting me or threatening me with their fists. I float above, a curious spectator of my own life. Long ago I knew how the whole show would end and yet I went on playing and replaying all the moves of the game.

Here comes the flexible diplomat, who promised gold but gave only dross. And the experienced wolf who taught me more about life than all the universities (it was he, I think, who gathered the evidence that led to my expulsion). I see him thumbing his nose at me and calling: 'Hey, old man, I fooled you good and proper!'

Here is the thin lady who could not make up her mind: should she give me the secret documents or live poor but happy? She was afraid to meet me but later opened up in the embrace of a Western correspondent who, unbeknown to her, also worked for the KGB. Now she gives me an ironical smile. 'How are you, conqueror? How did you manage to set me up with that rogue? You know, if you had only had more patience, I would have given you those damned documents in the end.'

If only you knew, dear lady, if only you knew. If only we could read the book of fate in advance. Oh Lord, how long ago it all was, thirty years have passed!

And now I am in London once more, a pensioner and writer. To get here I had to go through the horrifying procedure of applying for a British visa.

Interview with an Indifferent Bobby

At the British consulate in Moscow, I meekly filled out a form that reminded me of the huge sheet I had to complete years ago when I joined the KGB. Also, since the British had once caught me engaging in activities incompatible with my diplomatic status, I had to fill out another small form for ex-criminals. The form-filling was preceded by the romance of standing in a long queue of the kind we used to have outside shops but now only outside Western embassies.

There is no guarantee you will reach the head of the queue the same day unless you spend the night there. You can warm yourself around one of the little campfires or wear a Siberian fur coat. Or, like me, you can pay $80 to an old granny to keep your place in the queue until the consulate opens. Thus these delightful Russian pensioners make money and ease their suffering.

After I had handed in my application forms, I had to go to the consulate again on another day (more queuing) to have an interview. I was in a cold sweat lest they arrested me, stuffed me in a box and took me to England to be interrogated by Scotland Yard.

A very nice man, who reminded me of a London bobby, conducted the interview. Ready for a thorough interrogation (I am, after all, a famous spy), I launched into a long monologue about my triumphs for the KGB, but the 'bobby' smiled politely and said: 'Just answer my questions, sir.' With delight, I recognised the uncompromising style of the Home Office!

I answered several questions, mostly about my host Chris, but not a single one about my past illegal activities. Then the 'bobby' smiled and announced that the decision about granting me a visa would be taken in London. Well of course London, I had not expected anything else. And yet I was a little hurt that the 'bobby' had taken so little interest in my work for the KGB and not even listened to my nervous babble. I suppose so many former Russian spies are flying to London these days that the British have become blasé.

It took a month for the visa to come through, then I was able to fly to London. We Russians are provident. In his memoirs, Churchill wrote that when, during the War, he ordered a search of the hotel room where the visiting Soviet Foreign Minister, Vyacheslav Molotov, was staying (naturally for the safety of the minister, why else?), to their surprise the British found a Krakow sausage, a loaf of black bread and a pistol. Basically I have the same luggage, except instead of the pistol I am carrying a bottle of vodka. The Cold War is over and I am eager to embrace England.

At Heathrow, I fell into the hands of a very strict immigration official, who gave me a thorough interrogation for a full fifteen minutes. Only now do I realise why he latched onto me. Stupidly I said I had once worked for the KGB and that woke him out of his routine. He questioned me with great curiosity, I think from a purely personal interest. At last my vanity was satisfied. The indifference of the British authorities had been starting to upset me.

And now I am living like a poor relation in the mansion of my old friend and fellow writer, Chris, right in the middle of Hampstead, that district adored by the intelligentsia. Here is the house of Keats, who died of a surfeit of epigrams, while on the Heath there still lives the famous writer and ex-spy, John le Carré. Everywhere there are memorial plaques to the famous. Picturesque Kenwood is nearby. But most of all, it is just good to walk on the Heath.

We have breakfast in the kitchen. Chris brings out several plastic containers. With amazement, I discover that they contain all kinds of cereals about which we knew nothing in the sixties, with raisins and nuts and the devil knows that.

Karamzin cautioned: '... we also dined like Englishmen, that is we ate nothing but beef and cheese. The English do not like salads. This diet thickens their blood; it makes them phlegmatic, melancholy, intolerable to themselves and quite often suicidal. To the physical causes of their spleen one may also add others: the endless mists from the sea and the interminable smoke from their coal fires.'

Slowly we savour our coffee, real mokka and not instant coffee – that is for plebs. By the way, coffee drinking is not a bad way to make contacts, especially at large functions and buffets where you can stroll about the hall, cup in hand. The method is very simple: as you come up to your target, you have to spill some coffee on the floor and give a little cry. The object naturally tenses slightly and this gives you the perfect excuse to apologise for your clumsiness, introduce yourself and get talking. If you are nervous, you may spill the coffee over someone else's suit or dress (or worse still over your own) but do not despair. In this situation, it is even more natural to get acquainted as the victim thanks you effusively for sprinkling salt on the stain or rubbing him down with vodka.

Chris offers me a cigar and we sit puffing importantly like two Winston Churchills. As Kipling wrote: 'A woman is only a woman but a good cigar is a smoke.' Cigars are also useful tools for a spy. They are good for assassinations: you can stuff explosives in them or darts with poison which instantly enters the blood stream and causes a heart attack. (I am joking naturally. In the course of my career, I never killed even a fly.)

After breakfast, I put on my English mackintosh that reaches almost to my heels. I had to buy it in Moscow as people do not wear such raincoats in London any more but go around in anoraks. Chris switches on the burglar alarm and we are ready to go out.

I wonder whether MI5 is keeping tabs on me. Surely they have not written off the legendary Lyubimov. After all, I could still do it.

Of Brussels Sprouts and Left-Hand Driving

We get into Chris's grey Jaguar, the favourite model of James Bond. Just to be on the safe side, I check the car thoroughly, even bending down to look underneath – the special services love to put explosives into the exhaust pipe – especially good for this is a condom stuffed with a mixture of chlorate and sugar.

We drive around and eventually stop not far from Portobello Market, beloved of the Russian community because here you can buy everything from flea powder to aeroplanes. Oh, Portobello! Every Saturday I used to put my wife and son in the car and rush to this cornucopia. I would buy armfuls of Granny Smiths ('an apple a day keeps the doctor away'),

Brussels sprouts and broccoli and dump them in the boot while surreptitiously taking out the folding pushchair.

When I was sure I had given a good impression of family shopping to whomever might be watching me, I began my spying operation. I would send my wife and son off to walk through pretty Holland Park back to our humble abode on Earls Terrace while I sat at the wheel and quietly drove into a side street (from tension, my nose would run). Like a cat with its tail in the air, I glided up and down the streets and back streets, then transferred to public transport, putting on an arrogant English expression to mix with the natives on bus and Underground.

It was nerve-racking but great fun to fool others (if I wasn't fooled myself).

However I must admit that at the start of my spying career I could not get used to driving on the left side of the road and often, during my manoeuvres, forgot that I was not in Russia and once even drove against the stream of cars. The police chastised me in a very English way. Once at night a bobby stopped me: 'Excuse me, sir, perhaps it would be a good idea if you put on your lights.' I thought I was talking to Sir Walter Scott.

Remembering all this, I lightheartedly potter about colourful Portobello when suddenly I hear a heart-rending song. 'You ruined me with your black eyes . . .' A young man in the uniform of a Soviet army colonel is pouring out his soul. He plays a guitar, his cap lies on the pavement and passers-by toss coins to him.

My whole soul is turned inside out: My God, have we come to this?

Back in my day, the lad would have been taken by the seat of his pants, despatched back to Moscow and sent to labour camp for insulting the glorious and invincible Soviet Army. And now . . .

Before, we had law and order. One of our agents, a Chinese local governor, said something he shouldn't have said about Stalin and was taken straight away to dine at the Soviet embassy. Only they did not give him pilau rice but a bullet in the back of the neck while a lorry ran its engine in the yard to drown out the sound of the shot. For convenience, he was buried in the cellar of the embassy.

In those days, you only had to sneeze and you were buried on the spot. And this scoundrel is singing . . .

We continue on to the Russian embassy in Kensington Palace Gardens, where I spent some of the happiest days of my life.

In the 1960s, we were packed into the building like sardines in a tin. I did not even know many of my fellow diplomats and I could only pity British counter-intelligence having to keep tabs on such a tireless crowd.

In 1971 the British lost their patience and expelled more than 100 diplomats – if they had not been so decisive, we would probably have gone on to build a huge complex like the Lubyanka and create something like the Ministry of Love. Probably we would have bored a tunnel into neighbouring Kensington Palace and seduced all the royal ladies-in-waiting.

How to Court a Lady in Hyde Park

I stride out across Hyde Park, which did not slip the attention of Karamzin. In his day, the park was regarded as suburban.

The writer admired the young English ladies on horseback, accompanied by their riding masters, and when they galloped under the shade of some ancient oaks he tried to speak to one of them in French. The English girl looked him up and down, said 'Oui' twice and twice said, 'Non', and that was it. If Karamzin had been acquainted with the basics of espionage, he would have known that introducing oneself in such a way is not the done thing, it is tantamount to talking to a stranger on the bus or Underground. Furthermore, there is nothing more pointless than speaking to the English in foreign languages, for they only recognise English and compliment foreigners who know a smattering of their tongue: 'How wonderfully you speak English.'

Karamzin behaved like a bad spy whose station chief dresses him down every day for having insufficient contacts.

I myself suffered many knocks and setbacks. On several occasions I tried to get to know someone in Hyde Park and once chatted with a girl who was on the staff at Conservative Party headquarters. On discovering that I was Russian, the poor lass nearly fainted on the age-old lawns, so afraid of us were the English in those days. (Now Russian spies have been replaced by the Russian Mafia.)

Then I got wise and introduced myself to strangers as a visiting Swede. Thus once, during my morning run in Hyde Park, I overtook an old chap (then only rare idiots went in for jogging), got talking to him and introduced myself as a Swedish journalist. Imagine my embarrassment when the sportsman answered me in perfect Swedish. Naturally I quickly recovered myself, saying that in actual fact I was only half-Swedish, but the very grass of Hyde Park blushed to hear such an apology.

Before I know it, I have reached Knightsbridge. Of their own accord, my legs carry me to the most fashionable shop in the world, Harrods.

For the work of a secret agent, shops are no less important than buses and the Underground. The enormous Harrods building has dozens of entrances and exits; huge crowds are always milling there and, if you spot someone on your tail, then it is the easiest thing in the world to melt into the throng. What could be more natural than the role of avid shopper, whose eyes nearly pop out at the overwhelming selection of goods?

Run like a lost dog from floor to floor, change from lift to lift, turn back down an emergency exit. Try a jacket on in a fitting room, then dash up a flight of stairs ... Almost certainly, in a few minutes, you will see behind you the mugs of British counter-intelligence, flushed and panting.

But I would advise those of you who like to do a little shoplifting to think twice – because of the Irish terrorist threat, Harrods has as many security guards as there are currants in a bun.

I remember that in the 1960s the assistants in big department stores never left you alone (and back in the USSR we told stories about the wonderful service in England). Now it is all horrible, self-service. The main thing about this system is not to lose courage.

Under the penetrating gaze of the assistant, I choose a pair of flannel trousers (another of my anglophile attachments; my last pair I kept for thirty years). Then I go into a fitting room, try the trousers on, find to my surprise that I have put on weight and go out for another pair. You are only allowed to try on three pairs at any one time but it is not easy as the sizes in England are different from those in Europe. It's hot in the cubicle; every time I emerge for new trousers I have to get dressed again; the whole process drives me crazy and I want to go out in my underpants.

At last, clutching the trousers to my heart (the harder the purchase, the more valuable it becomes), I return through Knightsbridge to Buckingham Palace, where once I drank tea at one of the Queen's garden parties. At the gate, as usual, there is a huge crowd for the changing of the guard and a band is playing.

In England the monarchy has long since ceased to be regarded as holy and anybody can trample on it just as he pleases. Take for example those terrible scandals about Princess Diana and Fergie, the Duchess of York. I cannot understand why the public is so obsessed with the private lives of the royals, as if we ourselves were not falling in love or divorcing every day.

At one time the keeper of the Queen's pictures was our agent Anthony Blunt, one of the secret Communists of the 1930s. However, by the time he went to the palace, he had already broken relations with Moscow and in any case the royal family was of no particular interest to Soviet intelligence: the KGB was a serious organisation concerned with politics, not gossip. And we knew perfectly well that the Queen reigns but does not govern.

Catching My Firebird at Downing Street

I come into Downing Street, home of the Foreign Office, the holy of holies of the British Establishment. The clerks from that institution feared Russians like fire, seeing in every one of us a spy (how right they were!). But the KGB *rezident* thumped his fist on the table and demanded that we hook and recruit these minions. From time to time, in a gloomy mood, I would hang around outside the ministry, on the off-chance that my firebird would suddenly fly out.

Once I followed a fat man in a pinstripe suit from the Foreign Office into a pub and observed him biting on a sandwich as if he had not eaten for days. From naivety but more from despair, I tried to get into conversation with him. But the fat man only mumbled something, sending crumbs and saliva flying, not wanting to break off from his meal. Why were they so hungry at the FO?

Now here I am at Westminster Abbey: many spies are buried here, including Major John André, who was hanged by the Americans during the War of Independence.

Not only spies but also the victims of espionage lie here, for example the Lake poets Coleridge and Wordsworth, who fell under the surveillance of government agents. Coleridge probably deserved such attention. Had he not distributed pamphlets calling for the overthrow of the system and given wicked speeches at local meetings? Had he not made sketches of the landscape?

Whatever happened to Coleridge and Wordsworth, D. H. Lawrence, author of *Lady Chatterley's Lover*, and his German wife Frieda, suffered worse harassment during the First World War, when they lived in Cornwall down by the sea.

Lawrence was suspect not only because of his German wife but because he wore a beard and wrote, which was odd behaviour as far as the average man was concerned. Once, when the Lawrences were returning home, they were searched, although their rucksack contained not a camera but vegetables and a packet of salt. All the local people spied on the couple: Frieda could not hang out the washing, take out the rubbish or light the fire lest these acts were taken as signals to German aviation. It was believed that the writer and his wife took food and fuel to German submarines coming in to the old smugglers' coves.

On another occasion, when Lawrence was sitting on the cliffs, Frieda came striding out, exalting in the sea air and sun, the white scarf at her neck blowing in the wind. Reduced to a state of nerves, Lawrence cried out in despair: 'Stop, stop, you fool! They'll get it into their heads that you are giving a signal to the enemy.'

In the end, spy mania forced them to leave Cornwall.

And here is the tomb of Kipling, bard of spies, an anathema in the Soviet Union because he defended imperialism. This is his 'Spies March':

> There are no leaders to lead us to honour, and yet
> without leaders we sally,
> Each man reporting for duty alone, out of sight
> Out of reach, of his fellow!

The English always respected the profession of espionage (it is said that even Shakespeare did it) and the statesmen lying here could not have imagined life without it: Disraeli, Pitt, Palmerston and Gladstone.

But I have not honoured every spy. My favourite still remains, although he does not lie in this Pantheon but rests in the cemetery of Bunhill Fields.

We professionals love cemeteries. There you can not only rest from life's hurly-burly and escape from the boss's displeasure over your failed recruitments but you can do real work. How convenient to sit grieving by a stranger's tomb while you await the arrival of your agent. Your hand trembles as you put it down the back of the tombstone to retrieve the contents of a dead letter box. What if a skull nips your fingers? Or a rattling skeleton jumps out from behind a tree and cries: 'I am your old boss, General Ivanov!'

Bunhill Fields is the last resting place of the famous spy Daniel Defoe. He is remembered now for *Robinson Crusoe* but his career began rather differently. Arrested for writing a scurrilous Whig pamphlet, he only got out of jail after he agreed to run a network of spies for the Tory minister, Robert Hardy. Near the grave of Defoe lies another victim of espionage, William Blake. Government agents threatened him with arrest if he did not stop making maps for the enemy (that was what they called the landscapes of this wonderful artist and poet).

But why am I talking about the past? Did I not myself work with Englishmen who chose to serve the KGB?

General John

'Michael, have I ever told you about the time when I was fighting the Germans in the Ardennes? We were starving, we did not even have any corned beef. And then the cook invited me into the mess. "What is this wonderful meat?" I asked him. "Cat, sir'," he said, "I boiled it myself."'

In his cups (whisky was his poison), 'General John' always liked to tell this story.

One of my best agents, the 'General' was an anti-Fascist and Communist idealist. The show trials and purges in Moscow in the 1930s gave him pause for thought about Stalin, but then the war started and again he put his faith in the Great Leader. After the war, he broke relations with us because of the occupation of Eastern Europe but returned to help Soviet intelligence after Stalin's death in 1953, saying that it was no fault of the sacred red flag that dirty hands had besmirched it.

The 'General', who hated the intellectuals of Oxford and Cambridge and especially the British press, adored the proletariat. 'Nothing is too good for a fellow worker,' he used to say. He put his whole heart into his work for the KGB. He never missed a rendezvous and, although he knew me well, always insisted on using the password (what if MI5 had sent my double to the meeting?). He had contempt for money and only accepted cash to cover his expenses, not to enrich himself. His unconditional belief in Communism even frightened me a little, for I was starting to be weakened by easy English living.

'Don't judge by the shops, Michael,' he would say. 'Look how the working class lives. You can't imagine how terrible it is to live in Britain.'

When I tactfully replied that the Soviet Union had its share of problems, he said: 'Of course you have problems, but they are temporary. Look how far you have come in a short time. Churchill himself wrote that Russia has progressed from the plough to the space rocket in the blink of an eye. But England is sleeping. While the whole world marches towards socialism, she is dreaming about her past. It is suffocating here. What hope is there of revolution when every morning at eight the milk is delivered to the door?'

I suggested that if he found England oppressive he might travel to Europe, but his dream was to see the Soviet Union. This was difficult to arrange because British counter-intelligence kept lists of those who went to Moscow and we did not want to lose such a valuable agent. But some years later, when I was already back in Moscow myself, he did manage to come for a visit.

Bad hotel service, broken lifts and dripping taps were enough to make the playwright John Osborne lose his faith in socialism when he visited the USSR. The KGB knew that such small details could be decisive and so laid on VIP treatment for 'General John'. He was driven around in a black ZIL, shown the clinics for the elite, taken to the Bolshoi Theatre and, for good measure, fêted in the hospitable southern republic of Georgia. I remember his beaming face in the company of the Georgian KGB chief and myself after a couple of bottles of wine. We gazed at the mountains and sang the 'Internationale', holding hands, tears in our eyes.

Could he not see that he had been given a pair of rose-tinted spectacles?

Perhaps he was the sort of man who only saw what he wanted to see.

Not long ago a colleague returned from London and I asked after 'General John'. 'He's fine,' he said, 'still full of life and delighted about the success of Russian democracy. He is sure that the free market will improve living standards and bring about the final victory of his socialist ideals. He thinks England is sleepy but in Russia it is never boring. Oh yes, and he told me some story about the war as well ...' 'About how he ate boiled cat?' 'Yes, that was it, boiled cat.'

These memories bring on a wave of Communist nostalgia and I rush to Highgate to pay my respects at the grave of Karl Marx. He is still a money-spinner with 75,000 visitors paying to see him each year. A herd of Chinese in padded jackets files past, evidently a Communist Party delegation. Two Trotskyists in tweed jackets and red scarves linger at the grave.

Around the huge bearded head, next to which you feel as small as an ant, are the graves of lesser Communists, mostly revolutionary leaders from former British colonies. I stand by the tomb of one such leader. Years ago in the Soviet Communist Party Central Committee hotel in Moscow I gave him advice on how to organise a conspiratorial network in his homeland and helped him to get money from us.

From Highgate I go to the West End. On Jermyn Street I drop into Trickers, the most famous shoe shop in England. Here the boots of Admiral Nelson are on display and there is a thick, leather-bound album with the outlines of the feet of great Englishmen. I find the soles of Guy Burgess, who was a spendthrift, dandy and snob, but that did not lessen the significance of his services to Soviet intelligence.

Next door is Berry and Rudds, the best wine shop in London, which sells both cheap and vintage wines. The prices are lower than in Russia and so is the water content in the bottles.

In Piccadilly I marvel at the imposing Ritz Hotel, which evokes a complex mixture of memories. Here I used to meet an English lord, who was the embodiment of snobbery. He would order his food with painful slowness, endlessly consulting with the waiter, then when he was not satisfied, call the chef and discuss *ad nauseam* the ingredients of the salads and garnishes.

After the food had been ordered came the most excruciating moment, the choice of the wine. He would make the waiter open at least ten bottles and after each sip pull a face, complaining that instead of a Mâcon 1948 he had been given a Mâcon 1958, until finally he summoned the manager and made a scene. (Though a lord, he usually drank moderately. Only once, when he was on a visit to Moscow, four of us had to carry him out of a restaurant because he was as drunk as a lord.)

This time I am lunching at the Ritz with a journalist who is rather nervous about the fact that I used to work for the KGB. I try to put him at his ease by telling him an old Soviet joke: a Frenchman, an Englishman and a Russian are discussing the respective merits of their women. 'When my Mary sits on her horse, her legs reach the ground,' says the Englishman. 'But that is not because the horse is small, rather because our English girls have the longest legs in the world.' 'Ha,' says the Frenchman, 'that's nothing. When I dance with my Nicole, my elbows touch. But that is not because I have long arms, rather because our French girls have the slimmest waists in the world.' 'Well,' says the Russian, 'when I go to work I slap my Masha on the backside and when I come home her bum is still wobbling. But that is not because Russian girls have the fattest backsides in the world. It is because we have the shortest working day.'

He guffaws with laughter and relaxes his guard. Telling jokes is an old spy's trick.

But during the Cold War, how MI5 used to spoil my appetite with their surveillance! They would follow me into the restaurant and sit down at the next table, ears wagging. Where are you now, my dear minders, who were always on my tail, especially when I travelled outside London? Do you remember how once I got lost and could not find the way to my hotel and in the end just gave up and asked you for directions? You went ahead, guiding me to my destination, then stopped and even drank a beer with me while I promised not to run off to any secret meetings. I kept my word, for we spies were gentlemen. Where are you now? Retired like me? If only we could get together for a few drinks and remember the old days. You would tell me about my stupidities and failures and I would have a thing or two to say to you.

From the Ritz, I go back to my home from home in Hampstead. I need Chris to help me choose some trousers (the ones I bought with so much suffering in Harrods turned out to be too short when I tried them on again at home).

How to Buy Glad Rags

Next morning, we set out on this great mission.

Chris swears that Hampstead has the best pubs and the best shops – and that altogether it is the most beautiful spot on earth.

At first we pop into a French café ('Are you French or just pretending?' he flirts with the waitress), then saunter into an outfitters run by an Indian. After a good lunch with excellent wine, choosing clothes is a doddle: not only do I find the right trousers but fall in love with a tweed jacket to go with them.

The only problem, which I could never solve without Chris, is that the trousers need taking up a little. The shopkeeper measures me. I pay for the jacket but decide to leave it at the shop and pick it up together with the trousers the following day.

'Come tomorrow at four,' says the Indian, bowing politely. 'Would you mind leaving a deposit?'

'How much?' I ask.

'A hundred and fifty pounds.'

'What?' interrupts Chris, 'but that's the price of the jacket and trousers and we're leaving the jacket with you. What kind of arrangement is that?'

'It's the system here,' says the Indian.

'What do you mean "here"?'

'In this shop,' says the assistant.

'Then I will never come back to your shop again,' snorts Chris.

'Thank you, sir,' smiles the Indian.

We try another shop where the owner, who looks like an aristocrat, offers me aubergine-coloured trousers. Aubergine, indeed!

So, since trousers are more important to me than pride and principles, there is nothing left for it but to go back to the Indian the next day.

'Take the trousers if you must but refuse the jacket or the bastard will take you for a mug,' says Chris. 'And be a man. Insist on trying them on. You can't trust his type.'

My time in Hampstead is coming to an end. Soon, at the invitation of a newspaper, I move from Chris's (he has gone to visit relatives in Bristol) and settle in at a hotel that suits me perfectly, the Royal Horse Guards. It has many advantages: proximity to the Ministry of Defence and all of Whitehall. I could spy on them again. But Scotland Yard is also nearby; there is no avoiding that. The hotel is popular with retired English colonels but have I not, if only indirectly, been part of their world?

In the romantic atmosphere of the Royal Horse Guards, I feel like a character out of Thackeray or Fielding, an old squire or an old colonial in a cork helmet. They even address me here as colonel: 'Excuse me, colonel, but would you prefer toast or porridge?' I love it and would awfully like to have a batman in livery.

Suddenly I am overcome with an inferiority complex: looking as I do, do I blend into the atmosphere of this old-fashioned hotel? Am I too scruffy? Or, on the contrary, do I look too formal? Blending with the environment, melting into the crowd, those are the laws of spying. Wear a pinstripe suit in a working-class pub and you are a dead man.

After a few seconds of panic, I calm down. At last I have bought my flannel trousers (oh, idiotic joy!), I have got my tweed jacket and my classic shoes from Church's. They all go tastefully together and I fit in. In ecstasy, I merge with the royal horse guards.

I put on my new outfit, fan out a silk handkerchief in my breast pocket and confidently go down to lunch.

There I hear muttering in Russian. I am so amazed, I do not even understand what is being talked about. The muttering continues. I turn my head and see a dark-haired woman in an elegant black dress. She is in her prime. Her face is a little capricious and therefore beautiful. She is holding a child by the hand like a typical Russian mother. (They endlessly muffle, fuss over, restrict and overfeed their children and then wonder why their offspring suffer from disturbances of the metabolism and can never shake off the flu.)

The Russians are here, even in the heart of the Establishment. Now all we need is for the guitar-playing colonel from Portobello to turn up!

What a paradox: when we had our great empire, you could always tell visiting Russians by the way they clung together, terrified to lose sight of their KGB group leader, and by the way they looked enviously in shop windows and counted their pathetic hard currency. But now that the Soviet Union has collapsed, they come to London in herds and behave as if they owned the place.

I meet more Russians on Charing Cross Road. I overhear their conversation, peppered with swear words. I am intrigued. What do the New Russians talk about after all? I am afraid they will recognise me, for there is also something indefinably Russian about my appearance, but nevertheless I tag along behind them, listening in.

'At first sight, everything looks great,' a long-legged woman in jeans is telling a couple who have obviously just arrived in London. 'But in actual fact ... for example, I pay outrageous prices for their television. But it is complete shit compared with ours. Soon I am going to put up a satellite dish.'

This patriotic bluster touches me.

Do Not Tread on an Englishman's Tail

I walk down the Strand, past the BBC and the statue of Dr Samuel Johnson, heading for the City and the Tower – a marvellous itinerary.

Immediately I run into three more Russians. I can tell them from their slouching gait (hands in pockets) and from the indifference, even contempt, with which they look in the shop windows along the way. These are very rich people, the kings of business.

They wear top-class suits from Bond Street, where it is regarded as vulgar to hang price tags on the goods, perfect shoes, Italian silk ties and one even has the archetypal English umbrella with bamboo handle.

But you can't fool an old KGB pensioner!

Under that brilliant disguise I can see a Communist Party functionary, a former director of a state factory, and his accountant who, in his old age, unexpectedly came into a fortune. And who is the third young man with tattoos on his arm and an aggressively confident walk? An ex-labour camp inmate, obviously.

They regard the English as poor idiots, unable to make money and trembling before the law. They have become as rich as Croesus in a matter of months or days and simply cannot imagine that wealth might be built up over centuries by honest means. They love money but do not know how to spend it. They are already bored by the fact that you can buy a beautiful woman and the most expensive luxuries, champagne from the cellar of some duke, the duke himself and his castle. They laugh at the hardworking English.

With some help from Kim Philby, I once wrote a dissertation for the KGB entitled *The Traits of the English National Character and its Use in Operational Work*. So I think I know a thing or two. And my advice to these New Russian thugs is this: do not push the Englishman too far. He looks tolerant, loves cricket and fair play. He hides his feelings, minds his own business and compromises when he can. Tread on his toe and he will apologise to you. But tread no further. The English lion roars when you tread on his tail.

From the Tower, I take a boat back up the river to Westminster. There I see a Russian submarine, a former Soviet I-475 from the Baltic Fleet, taking on tourists for £8 a visit. And now I am the one who feels an insult to his national pride. After all, like the British, we did once have a mighty empire and a great navy. My God, what happened to them?

Why Not Get Drunk in a Pub?

Our empires have collapsed, so why not get drunk in a pub, my friend? Because in England people do not often get blind drunk in the way we do in Russia. It is difficult to get drunk when there exists such a unique phenomenon as the pub, where you can play darts and billiards, have not too bad a meal and even drink a coffee. And a better place for spying you will not find. You can hide away in a corner and quickly agree everything with your agent or, if necessary, go out with him to the toilets to pass him a note with instructions and a purse full of Mongolian tugriks.

I am in Baker Street at the Sherlock Holmes pub where, for the entertainment of the drinking tourists, there is a cabinet with waxworks of
Holmes and Doctor Watson. After a couple of glasses, you can imagine
you are Sherlock Holmes; if you drink a bit more you can turn into the
doctor.

When I first came to London, I found it painfully difficult to adapt from
vodka to whisky, especially as the scotch sold at a discount in our
embassy shop was Canada Club, a disgusting swill like American
bourbon.

Real Scottish whisky is an acquired taste, like the music of Richard
Strauss. However, once you have got into it and stuck with it for several
years, a whole new world opens up. How pleasant it is to sit with a friend
and drink Scottish whisky. You start with simple Johnny Walker and
Grant, then graduate to twelve-year-old Ballantines and more Johnny
Walker, only with the black label. You swim in Chivas Regal, the drink
of prime ministers and KGB *rezidents*, and in Glenfiddich and Glenfiddich ... and finish with a glass of vodka.

In the Sherlock Holmes, I order a double Teacher's because it's cheaper.
I remember another evening in the autumn of 1964 in another London
pub whose name I cannot for the life of me remember. So I will call it
the 'Lyubimov and Boot'.

It all began with a modest tea party in the house of William Penn on
Balcombe Street, where the Quakers ran a programme of lectures (I think
Professor Max Beloff was speaking). We were mixing and I was moving
among the guests with a cup of tea in my hand when I bumped into my
old friend Mr X, a modest and rather absent-minded person who reminded
me of a librarian.

Mr X was a head of department at the Foreign Office and was linked
with GCHQ at Cheltenham – a tasty morsel for Soviet intelligence. He
was a respectable family man and my wife Katya and I often ran into him
taking his children for walks in Hyde Park. Neither the KGB *rezident*
nor I had the slightest doubt that Mr X was linked to MI5, if not an
actual staff member of the counter-intelligence organisation, although
he happily met me, even invited me to his home and gave me a book by
the impenetrable philosopher Whitehead. I put it on my shelves to
impress guests.

At one point the KGB, which had suffered setbacks with the Profumo
scandal and the arrests of George Blake and Gordon Lonsdale, had the
idea that I should build up our network again by trying to recruit Mr X.
Moscow's foolish plan was that I should take him away for a weekend to
a luxury hotel in Hastings and drug him with a cocktail of psychotropic
drugs and vodka. What then? Moscow presumed he would divulge secrets

and I would record them. But I had visions of the hotel staff looking suspiciously at two men in one hotel room and found a good pretext to turn down the whole mad adventure.

And so, after the reception in Balcombe Street, Mr X and I went on to a comfortable pub, ordered whisky and started chatting. We had already dipped into that paradise and drunk two whiskies when my companion excused himself, got up and, as he delicately put it, went to wash his hands, a natural enough thing to do.

I was in a good mood, thinking of my family who had just returned from Moscow, and smoking a cigarillo (Castro and Che Guevara had long ago convinced me that a love of cigars need not mean a surrender to the bourgeoisie). The barman smiled and the pub filled up with drinkers.

'Your career is over, sir.' All of a sudden I heard these words and felt rather than saw that two gentlemen had sat down beside me. But no, they were not gentlemen. 'You have no alternative, sir. You have been caught. We know about your secret contacts. We have photographs. You have no alternative but to ...'

I could not take in what they were saying, I was so shocked. We had been taught that British agents were aristocratic and intellectual like the former spies Somerset Maugham and Graham Greene and here instead were two ugly plebs like caricatures out of Gogol. One was unshaven and could have passed for the sort of tramp who stands on an orange box at Speaker's Corner. The other, who had unhealthily red cheeks, slumped like a sack and smelt of fried potatoes. I was unable to take note of any more details, as this was clearly not a moment for making literary sketches.

They were trying to recruit me! When I understood this, I did not bellow the 'Internationale' or deliver a withering Ciceronian rebuke, but simply acted according to instructions and shouted (well, whimpered actually): 'It's a provocation!' Then I pushed the table aside and dashed for the exit.

In shock I ran to the car. Nobody followed me and no bomb went off when I started the ignition. I flew to report to the *resident* hurt that I had been treated not like an ace secret agent but like a petty thief.

In those glorious times, the Soviet Union had not lost its teeth and, although there was no doubt I had broken the law, the KGB decided not to give in to those Englishmen (or else they would become completely impudent). Soon our ambassador was off to see the new Labour Foreign Minister, Patrick Gordon Walker, with a memorandum about the 'barbarous provocation against an innocent Soviet diplomat'.

'One moment, sir,' the minister interrupted him and took out of a file his own memorandum, which stated that your hero had clearly been involved in activities incompatible with his diplomatic status and must leave Albion. The tactful British did not set a date and promised not to make the scandal public. In Moscow this was seen as weakness and the KGB decided not to give an inch but to keep me on for another six months!

I wound up my work and enjoyed a period of leisure, walking in Pimlico and Chelsea and visiting galleries – an observer might have thought that the KGB had sent me to London to study pictures.

But after a few weeks, at a reception at the Soviet embassy, the head of the Russian section of the Foreign Office, a man called Smith, came up to Ambassador Soldatov and delicately enquired ... could he be mistaken or was that young man over there, the one gorging himself on sturgeon, the same fellow who ... about whom the memorandum ... and had he not left Britain yet?

We took the hint, the penny dropped, and we lifted anchor with hardly time to pack our suitcases, taking a ferry across the Channel. Thus 1965 witnessed two important events: Winston Churchill died and Captain Lyubimov became persona non grata.

England died for me then, but she did not die in me. On the contrary, she became brighter and more attractive. In my memories she emerged in more detail and colour. I loved her more and more and love her still as a symbol of my youth, of my beautiful illusions and serious insights. It seems to me now indecent that I engaged in spying in such a wonderful country, my Albion, who is always with me.

I order another whisky, Glenfiddich this time, and consider how I have changed over the years.

Of course, I used to be more afraid when I was younger, and of many things. Fearing temptation by passionate English girls, I was especially nervous in hotels and always locked the door but still worried that they would fly in through the window and jump into my bed. I was also wary of men who came across as anti-Soviet. With them I immediately engaged in ideological arguments so that nobody would doubt my loyalty. I refused all presents and, of course, all dubious offers.

In every Englishman I saw an agent. But I was also afraid of my own people in case they informed on me, for someone had told tales to Moscow when I bought a spotted Formica coffee table at about the same time as Khrushchev made his famous speech condemning abstract art. Now I fear neither my own side nor yours, but some people are afraid of me. Russians living in England avoid meeting me lest the British mark them down as my agents, even though my past is common knowledge and it is obvious I am retired.

Are MI5 really not following me at all? It's even a bit hurtful. (Now I am on the Chivas Regal, it's softer.) No, they must be keeping an eye on me; it's just that I don't see them, I am out of condition.

Suddenly I take it into my head to try and find the pub where I was set up thirty years ago. I lurch out of the Sherlock and get swept away in a crowd of young people with painted faces. 'Chelsea,' they yell. One cheekily splashes red paint on my nose and they laugh. What are young people coming to these days?

'Taxi!' I stamp my feet in annoyance.

The taxi drives off and it seems we quickly find the pub I am looking for. But I cannot get out; the door handle is so cunningly hidden away that I cannot find it. And where the devil am I?

In a completely different area outside a completely different pub; it just looks from the outside like the Lyubimov and Boot but is in actual fact the Rat and Parrot.

There is nothing left for it but to take another taxi and go to Leicester Square. All the way, I hum to myself a favourite tune from the time when I was young in London: 'Que sera, sera, whatever will be, will be...'

A Visit from 'Them'

Much later I return to the Royal Horse Guards and collapse, exhausted, into bed. Almost immediately, the telephone rings: 'You are back, colonel? Can we come up to you now?'

My heart stops: who is it? Who are 'we'? And why do they want to come up? There must be some mistake. But no, they said colonel. So what is this all about?

I leap up and pace the room like Napoleon before Waterloo. I rack my brains. Good Lord, why did I not think of it before? Of course, it is British counter-intelligence! They have been following me all along. They pretended they were not there; they bided their time, and now they are going to spring their trap.

And I, fool that I am, completely relaxed and allowed myself to drop my guard! Now, keep a cool head. It is obvious they are coming to try and recruit you, don't panic and stop running round the room like a goat!

What compromising material could they have on me?

I search my memory for all the sins I have committed in recent years. There are so many of them that I do not know where to start. But they were all committed in Russia; in England I have behaved impeccably. I have not strayed from the laws of morality. I did not bring hash or weapons into the country; I did not get up to any machinations in London; I did not dig out any secrets. I did not even – strange as it may seem – share my bed with anybody.

Pull yourself together, old man, face the enemy with dignity as becomes a Communist (I forget that I am an ex-Communist)!

If they attempt to tie my hands, I will swing out through the window on the chandelier. If they behave like gentlemen, I too will be polite and try, like a cunning fox, to discover what dirt they have got on me.

> If you can meet with triumph and disaster
> And treat those two imposters just the same...

That's from 'If' by Kipling, the favourite poem of many Russians, not only the English.

I quickly smarten myself up, splash eau de cologne on my face (it's BOSS, a present from my wife; I think about her at critical moments), carefully comb my thin hair and put a white handkerchief in my breast pocket. In my tweed jacket with a hint of red, the tie with cherries on (it provokes envy in my friends, hatred in my enemies) and the grey flannel trousers, under which my shoes, also cherry, peep out, I look like a hero, ready to rebuff the provocateurs.

Courage old man, you only die once!

There is a knock on the door. I put on a determined expression. Once again I check in the mirror (I notice the sclerotic redness of my cheek) and stomp out into the hall. A black porter is standing at the door, holding a silver tray with a note on it. He bows and quickly retreats. I am so nervous, I do not have time to rejoice that he did not punch me for not giving him a tip.

It's a message to say that from tomorrow the newspaper will stop paying for my stay at the hotel. The Royal Horse Guards is beyond the means of a retired KGB colonel. Now there is nothing left for me but to get undressed again, sadly admire the cherries on the tie, look at the evening newspaper and go to sleep. It will be a pity to leave this hotel, to go from being a colonial colonel to a poor but genteel lodger. But in Russian, we say 'Better to be poor than ill.'

In the morning I shave and chuck into my suitcase all the little hotel soaps, shampoos, gels, balsams, lotions and plastic bath caps. Typical Soviet sponger? Yes. And so what? As if the English never do it!

My last breakfast in the fashionable hotel is like the last breakfast of my life and I am a suffering king, being humiliated by the mob and sent off into exile. But why so bitter, colonel? Grieving over lost porridge and marmalade?

Did not my teacher Karamzin, although an aristocrat, share a room in a pub with some upstart in black silk breeches who was always strumming on the guitar and playing cards? All in all, Karamzin was unlucky in London. He was always being touched for money by scoundrels and was almost cleaned out by beggars in Richmond Park. His hairdresser cut his cheek with a blunt razor, rubbed his head not in hair oil but lard and, adding insult to injury, powdered him with cooking flour. And in answer to the poor chap's protests in many languages, the hairdresser invariably replied: 'I do not understand.'

The thought that someone else was in a worse situation always cheers one and I go out to look for accommodation. In the Earls Court area, I go from cheap hotel to boarding house. They are like hostels. The facilities are shared, but cheap, only £20–30 per night. There are some for £10 but I fear to meet the guitarist in silk breeches.

I stand in the hall of one, waiting for help from the receptionist, but she is tied up. She is speaking on the telephone in fluent, filthy Russian. She does not even look at me! Very like at home.

While I wait, I learn all the details of her complicated relations with a certain Charles. The bastard does not want to marry her although he is loaded with money. The main thing is she must avoid getting AIDS from him (and here we get a cascade of details about her contraceptive methods). After this I feel awkward about addressing her in Russian and, stammering in an Oxford accent, enquire as to whether she has a vacancy.

Not very politely, the lady answers in the negative.

Another half-hour of lonely wandering.

But at the next boarding house, which is called The Nest, I am in luck: a plain little room, a narrow iron bed and hand basin. There is even a window by which I can sit and sigh.

Poverty is No Vice

I soon settle in at The Nest, such is the adaptable Russian nature. I have a knife, fork and, most importantly, a bottle opener with me, also an electric water heater. After all, this is not my first foreign assignment.

It is getting dark, time for me to think of food; the local shops should have all I need. As I leave the boarding house, the concierge looks at me indifferently. Evidently I do not resemble a killer or robber, but just an old pensioner on holiday. How cleverly I have put on a new disguise.

In the corner shop I buy two tins of sardines (one for morning), several triangles of processed cheese, two apples and (so has not to hang myself in the room with my own belt) two bottles of inexpensive wine. With a grey shopping bag in my hand, I feel even poorer, even uglier (it seems I am giving off the smell of old age) and ill with every imaginable ailment.

Back at The Nest, I break my nail pulling the bottle opener out of the penknife. But after the first gulp of wine, the dreary room takes on a rosier hue. Sweet memories float into my mind: how I strutted down Piccadilly; how I bought a checked scarf in Carnaby Street; how I ate roast pheasant in quail sauce at the Café Royal.

On a copy of *Pravda* (in which my slippers were wrapped) I lay out the viands I have just bought. They look delicious, especially if I keeping taking a swig of the wine from my shaving glass. The processed cheese reminds me of the Fatherland, of the travels of my youth. With perfect timing, the telephone rings and an insinuating woman's voice asks after the state of my libido. I am tender and gentle, ready for a relaxing conversation, but the voice is practical and not inclined to chat for long and the telephone mercilessly clocks up the pounds.

Remembering my old self, I imagine what horror such a telephone call would have aroused in me in the past. 'Stop this provocation,' I would have shouted into the receiver and put my ear to the door, trying to hear the rustle of the provocateurs ready to burst into my room with clicking cameras. From honesty, I would probably have reported to my boss and he would have asked: 'And why do you think they chose to call you? Nobody ever rings me in English hotels.'

My God, I have already polished off the second bottle of wine. I need a breath of air. I might buy some yoghurt. I'll decide on the way; after all, you only live once, don't you?

I go out into the night. Sunk in my thoughts, I walk down a poorly lit street. Suddenly a drunk springs out of the shadows and starts to mimic me like a monkey. He makes me out to be a supercilious snob, walking with my belly stuck out, face like an upturned potty.

'He's going to hit me,' I think with resignation, 'a perfectly worthy end to the evening.'

What a pity I have forgotten all the sambo techniques that I learnt at KGB school. I could, without any effort, have given him a kick in his tender parts. But the fellow laughs and offers me his hand. I quickly shake it. Then, like a frightened giraffe, I dive into the nearest shop. Instead of yoghurt, I buy another bottle of wine (oh, the power of the unconscious mind!)

Love in the Hotel

My Nest has turned into a noisy palace: footsteps sound on the marble staircase, the crystal chandeliers blind me, in the assembly hall there is a mountainous banquet, the ladies wear crinolines; the gentlemen are in tails.

'Take that old goat for instance ...' says a lady in fluent Russian. I freeze. She is talking about me. I become aware that the hotel is full of Russians, many of them drunk, especially the men. A passage from T.S. Eliot comes to mind.

> Grishkin is nice: her Russian eye
> Is underlined for emphasis;
> Uncorseted, her friendly bust
> Gives promise of pneumatic bliss ...

I adopt a stony English face (that of an old colonial walking through the desert with his suit buttoned to the neck) and calmly go up to my room.

Down in the hall the merriment continues. They are singing a Siberian drinking song about a wanderer, who curses his fate but plods on with his sack on his back. Is not that the Russian fate?

Maybe I should go out and have fun with them? No. They are sure to come up and invite me, they will not leave me out.

I lay on the bed in my rust-coloured cords with a bottle of wine beside me.

'Oh cursed Fate of the Wanderer ...'

I doze off and dream about a cat. She scratches at my door, then taps more insistently with her claws, painted in red nail varnish.

I open the door. 'Excuse me, sir,' says a woman in barely comprehensible English, 'but could you see your way to lending me until tomorrow ... until later today ... until this evening ... £50?'

Disappointed, I pretend not to understand.

'Just look at him, Masha,' says a male voice in Russian behind her, 'he's got "mean bastard" written all over him. A typical English arsehole.'

'I'm sorry, miss,' I say in my Oxford accent (I'm afraid I'm going to break down and cry), 'but unfortunately I only have a credit card ...'

'There's a cash dispenser down on the street,' she interrupts. 'It's not very far and it's only three o'clock ...'

'Bugger him,' says her husband and adds a few other strong expressions.

I get undressed and finish the wine.

'Oh cursed Fate of the Wanderer ...'

And suddenly (but why suddenly?) I am overwhelmed with sentimental emotions. I want to go out, embrace them, confess my love for Russia and all my fellow countrymen, sing the national anthem and drink!

I cannot sleep; London has disappeared; I have returned to Russia, where everything is at the crossroads, and I do not want to sleep at all.

When it grows light, I dress and go out onto the street.

Preoccupied passers-by are already rushing to work; newspaper sellers are shouting and cars are honking. In the Underground, I see only sullen morning faces. We rock along, thinking our own thoughts.

At Green Park I emerge to waking Piccadilly. She is snuffling and stretching, lighting up her windows. Has she slept at all? Or does she just pretend to sleep while really she changes her clothes and puts on fresh make-up?

'Que sera sera,' sings a voice inside me, 'whatever will be will be.'

And yet it is a pity. A shame that there are no longer great empires and holy ideals, though chimerical, and I am no longer that soldier, always at the ready.

I walk past the Ritz and the Royal Academy of Arts, past playful Eros on the square. Nearby, on Shaftesbury Avenue, the old Trocadero Hotel used to stand. They pulled it down to build a shopping centre.

Everything dies sooner or later, other buildings appear and other people and other states, but the world remains the same, enormous, beautiful and cruel, and always mysterious like the stars above.

A cold wind blows. At Leicester Square, I see the ghost of a thin youth in a pinstripe suit, ridiculously proud of his spy's mission.

It is a pity.

'Que sera sera ...' A little orchestra is playing in my head.

For an instant, it seems that London once more belongs to me.

Translation by Helen Womack

COPENHAGEN

Name Lyubimov, Mikhail Petrovich	
Born 27 May 1934	
Education Higher, Masters degree in history	
Special Subject International relations	
Languages English, Swedish	
Military Rank Colonel	
Worked in Britain, Denmark	
Marital Status Married	
Sports Swimming, volleyball	
Hobbies Walking	
Favourite Tipple Glenlivet	
Brand of Cigarettes Don't smoke	

Boss At Last

The cipher clerk knocked on the door, timidly, as if he were entering a tiger's cage, tiptoed across the carpet and put a telegram on my desk. In the top right-hand corner was a 'top secret' stamp, underneath a VIP's signature. The telegram instructed me to go urgently to the town of Helsingborg and remove a container from a dead letter box down on the shore. Silently, the cipher clerk withdrew.

Oh, how satisfying to be the KGB *rezident* at last. Only my wife Tamara failed to appreciate my importance, calling me pet names and making me do the hoovering. She might forget that I was the station chief, not some small fry, but in the office I was a god.

A black Mercedes brought me to the embassy each morning, where a trembling doorman pressed the button to open the automatic gates. In the vestibule I shook hands with the lower orders like a member of the Politburo surrounded by infatuated collective farmers during a visit to the Exhibition of Economic Achievements. Then up the polished wood staircase I climbed, taking global decisions as I went – one member of staff needed time off work to have his teeth fixed, another wanted to know when the furniture store should deliver my leather suite. And finally I reached my office, hung with portraits of Lenin and Kim Philby. In the corner was a safe. On the desk, a diary, a beaker of sharpened pencils, a magnifying class, not for catching the murderer in the style of Sherlock Holmes but for studying microfilm in the manner of the KGB.

I put the telegram on one side and started to read a letter from Philby, once the star of MI6, now the pride of our intelligence service. I had made friends with him back in Moscow, when I was heading the British section at KGB headquarters. After I was made *rezident* in Copenhagen in 1976, I continued to correspond with him because I knew he felt isolated in his exile, although he was happy with his Russian wife Rufa. Sometimes I would use the diplomatic bag to send him whisky and Oxford marmalade, essentials unavailable in the socialist Utopia. Most recently I had sent him an album of erotic graphics by the nineteenth-century British artist Thomas Rowlandson. The book was outrageous by prudish Soviet standards and I was eager to hear his reaction.

'The Rowlandson I have not yet seen,' Philby wrote. 'Our friend Viktor, with a discretion wholly appropriate to our profession, delivered it in a sealed brown envelope, explaining to me its contents. Unfortunately, my mother-in-law is around, helping us to settle in after a holiday in the Crimea, and I don't know how she would respond to erotica. Rufa, of course, is less old fashioned, so at the first opportunity we shall take a surreptitious peek. You can be sure of one thing – I won't burn it or return it to you. On the contrary, I will cherish it as my very own; or, if the worst comes to the worst and inflation erodes the value of my pension, I shall sell it to one of those shady black-marketeers who lurk in the corners of our Central Post Office at a very high price.

'I have been disgracefully long in thanking you for the new stream of wonders that we have received in instalments since the New Year began. The replacement jeans were perfect, the glasses also. Not to mention the Haig, Harper and Co., the Maxwell House, the soy sauce, mustards and other goodies. You have at last solved the problem which has baffled the arithmeticians over the past year or two. All Rufa needs now is to lose another of the few kilos which she put on during trips to Bulgaria and Hungary and the jeans will be perfect. You say you want me to keep the earlier ones for your secretary. OK – provided you produce her so that I can persuade myself that they really do fit her. No doubt I shall fumble a bit, but then I fumble most jobs.'

I would have to reply to Kim and find something else to entertain him, for I knew how hard it was for him, living in a golden cage.

But now, how was I going to carry out this secret operation in Helsingborg? Moscow Centre would, naturally, have taken into account the fact that although Helsingborg was only about twenty kilometres from Copenhagen, it was on the other side of the Oeresund Sound on the territory of an entirely different country – Sweden. A difficult assignment but then, what were we senior officers for? I would have to think about it, starting with an examination of the ferry timetables.

Meanwhile, there was plenty of other work to keep a *rezident* busy.

I began my day exchanging great ideas with my deputies. I had three of them, fewer than the Soviet Prime Minister it is true, but still I felt I was somebody. Then I had a short meeting with my other operatives before going into the ambassador's room to analyse the morning papers. There everyone knew his place and nobody had the nerve to sit in the *rezident*'s leather chair.

The bona fide diplomats, who made up roughly one third of the forty or so embassy staff, the others coming from the GRU or military intelligence and the KGB, regarded me with deference if not fear, convinced I was not only managing the course of Danish affairs but listening to all their domestic conversations. Really, the myth of all-knowing intelligence had been brilliantly thought up and it never occurred to anybody that more often than not, the *rezident* was not heading for some rendezvous with an agent but rushing with his wife to a suburban market where the tomatoes were cheaper. As Brezhnev said: 'The economy should be economical.'

Discussion of the press lasted about an hour, then I went back to my fortress to confirm logistics with the operatives. The set-up was the same as under Stalin – without a summons, underlings did not cross the threshold. For serious brain work was going on in here. What the devil was I going to do about Helsingborg?

Time enough to deal with that later. Today I had a lunch at the Gyldne Fortuna on Gammel Strand with a member of the Folketing. Portentous conversation would be helped along with Remy Martin, followed by a thoughtful walk back to the embassy, stopping off at the bookshops along the way, and then again the ascent of the polished wood staircase. In the afternoon I would devote my experienced pen to paper work.

The Mermaid's Tail

Nobody liked staying on at the embassy after six. Most of the diplomats went to our club where there were Russian-language film shows, singsongs and, most important, duty-free booze. A few went fishing or took their families for walks along the shore to breathe the ozone. That night

I went home and remembered my impressions when I first came to Denmark in 1965, *en route* to Moscow after I had been expelled from my beloved Britain.

Proudly I stepped from the Soviet liner which brought me to Langelinie and unfolded my map like Doctor Livingstone or Captain Cook. Andersen's famous Little Mermaid was right there on the shore and of course she was charming. But could you really compare her with Admiral Nelson in Trafalgar Square?

I surveyed Amalienborg, the Danish royal palace, with its guards like toy soldiers, thinking all the time about Buckingham Palace as if I had drunk tea with the Queen there every afternoon. I walked round the National Kunst Museum, sighing constantly for the Tate and the National Gallery. I slipped into Nyhavn but it was a poor den of vice compared with Soho. The Danes had an opera house, I noticed. Hardly Covent Garden. Stroeget, with its little boutiques, was pretty enough. But where were Harrods and Selfridges?

On Raadhuspladsen, I looked at the map again and realised I had already seen almost all the centre of Copenhagen had to offer. The miniature city was touching but the entire excursion had taken little longer than I would have needed to walk round Hyde Park. All that remained was to take a boat trip along the canals. I did that too. It was romantic but short.

In time, however, my Anglophile snobbery melted into an admiration for the Danish capital. I came to appreciate Stroeget with its colourful buskers and wonderful shops, Illum and Du Nord, no worse than my favourite English stores as it turned out. Nearby was the university, the Nikolaj Kirke and Gammel Strand, where fish traders in great white aprons used to sell fresh cod and mackerel. In particular, I loved a first-class fish shop by the memorial to the founder of the city, Bishop Absalon. It brought to mind a line from the Russian poet Anna Akhmatova: 'Sharp tang of the sea in a plate of oysters on ice.'

It was pleasant just to stroll down Stroeget, turning into side lanes to look in the little book shops on Pilestraede and fortifying oneself with Danish sausage and Tuborg along the way. In 1967, when Denmark was the only country in Europe with pornography on open display, I reeled from shop windows with pictures of bearded satyrs frolicking with real goats as well as engaging in the more routine ravishing of virgins, who apparently enjoyed every minute of it. It was a bit difficult to pass these images with my son Sasha, then six years old, and maintain the fiction that babies were found under gooseberry bushes. However, after a while, the Danes lost interest in pornography and the sex trade dwindled to a few specialist shops.

Copenhagen did not knock me off my feet like London but gradually stole my heart. Denmark, I discovered, had a world-class ballet, better than in London, and Danish cuisine with its forty ways of preparing herring was not so insipid after all and the Danish Queen was a nice woman, who even rode her bicycle into town. Once I nearly trod on her toe when she was shopping with the general public in Du Nord.

The country might lack great art galleries but it boasted some impressive sculptures by Bertel Thorvaldsen in the museum bearing his name. The Ny Carlsberg Glyptotek exhibited not tins of beer but works by Gauguin, Monet and Van Gogh and you could see some decent Renaissance stuff in the National Kunst Museum.

Copenhagen without its surroundings is, of course, like a kebab without the meat. I loved the dunes down at Gilleleje and Tisvildeleje and lakes Furoe and Farum. There were castles here and splendid restaurants, perfect for softening up potential recruits. Koege, Helsingoer, Hilleroed, Humlebaek. Most of all I loved the sea, which was sometimes green and sometimes iron grey, sometimes angry, sometimes just a little dishevelled, but always the Baltic.

At evening, the sea was especially beautiful and I wanted to drop everything and just live in a little house by the shore; forget about Moscow Centre and spying, about agents and cipher clerks; drink milk for breakfast and eat croissants spread with jam; fall in love and write great novels like Lev Tolstoy cosseted by hi wife Sofia Andreyevna; well, try my hand at a little poetry perhaps.

I was in love, you see. It happens to even the best of spies.

The Gentleman Traitor

But back to the matter in hand, I had to think about Helsingborg. I had never been there before, which for a secret agent was a big disadvantage. Finding a dead letter box in an unfamiliar place by following someone else's instructions was always difficult. Perhaps Oleg Gordievsky could advise me?

Of course in 1977, I never suspected that my deputy on the political side had already been working for MI6 for three years. I first met him in Copenhagen in 1967 when he was just starting his career, working with our network of illegal agents. Now he had risen in the service and gathered political intelligence.

He had recently recruited an African diplomat – poor fellow, immediately after his contact with Gordievsky he was probably arrested and carted off home to be strung up by the genitals – but unfortunately my deputy never brought in any serious catches, only left-leaning figures who more or less shared the Soviet world view. In retrospect, I understand why.

At the time, I was impressed by Gordievsky's learning. A graduate of my Alma Mater IMO, the Institute of International Relations, he was very knowledgeable about history and religion, the latter a forbidden narcotic for the mass of Soviet people. His love of Bach and Haydn inspired respect, especially when set against the Soviet colony's general mania for shopping. It was natural that I should consult him when I had to make tricky decisions.

However, I also valued the less erudite members of my staff. While it never entered my head to question the loyalty of any of my agents, it just seemed their more practical brand of cunning made them better than the intellectuals at recruiting. They did not need to quote Kirkegaard to worm their way into the simple souls of Americans, whom we regarded as our 'main adversary' and hunted on every continent.

Every secret agent has his style. Personally, I thought of myself as a spider, patiently waiting for flies to catch in my web. Sometimes, after watching Western films about the KGB, I imagined I was an evil, hairy spider, chomping on my prey.

With PET or Danish counter-intelligence though, I became a gentle joker. Chatting on the telephone, I would give my fantasy free rein, imagining the girl in earphones (it was all for her) running the tape back and typing out my nonsense. There were limits to this entertainment, however. For at the other end, they knew that I knew that they knew my little game and one fine day they could lose their tempers and boot me out, as the British had in 1964.

Life in the KGB station in Copenhagen was no less fantastic than a fairytale by Hans Christian Andersen. As *rezident*, I dealt with all manner of incidents. It might be a Soviet student who had hanged himself in his dormitory or an 'Englishman' coming to the embassy offering secrets. In the latter case, I was fairly sure it was a set-up but, just to be on the safe side, I put one of my agents on the job. When he went out to meet the 'Englishman', who stood with a thick file under his arm, he was immediately surrounded by PET agents as well. The 'Englishman' ran after him, trying to thrust the compromising documents into his hands.

On another occasion, two intelligence operatives, nationals of a Nato country, came to the embassy, seeking asylum in the Soviet Union in exchange for classified information about the Western alliance. Feverish activity in the KGB residence ensued: coded telegrams to Andropov in person; preparation of the Lyubimov lapel to receive a medal. The would-be traitors were put on a Soviet cargo ship, taken off by helicopter in the middle of the Baltic and rushed via Leningrad to Moscow, where Andropov was said to be sleepless with excitement. But when they were interviewed, our heroes showed decided symptoms of mental imbalance and there was nothing left for the KGB but to send them through East Berlin back into the fairytale land of Andersen.

At this time, Moscow Centre was constantly upbraiding us for failing to recruit a sufficient number of Americans. Part of our problem, as Moscow thought, was that Gordievsky spoke German as well as Danish but no English (I can imagine how MI6 laughed about that!). Even routine contacts with our US opposite numbers were difficult, as they rarely ventured through the graveyard which separated our embassies (was this symbolic?) to attend our receptions or invited us to theirs. However, occasionally we were lucky and the damned Yankees would be tempted over for a film show. Twice we managed to organise liquid lunches for CIA staff on board a Soviet ship docked in Copenhagen harbour, although our guests were nauseatingly abstemious and the Bacchanalia fell flat.

Healthy volley ball might be a better bet, we thought, and tried that too. The Americans came, played, drank a little light beer, thanked us politely and declined our invitations to meet later in town. We also had a football match to which the US embassy sent its strapping young marines. We, on the other hand, had to field older diplomats, trained at lunching for the most part like your faithful servant. I puffed and panted up and down the pitch until, by a miracle, I scored our only goal. KGB honour obliges me to admit that my subordinate had kicked the ball so that it just bounced off my foot into the goal. The crowd went wild. Three minutes later, I staggered off, bathed in sweat.

Apart from well-fed Americans who with a few exceptions refused our bait, we did have, mercifully, the rest of the diplomatic community in which to fish. A couple of quite good specimens from non-Nato states landed in our net. But Moscow Centre was never satisfied. 'Don't get distracted, Comrades, when the main adversary is always under your nose.' Don't get distracted...

Now, how was I going to get the times of the ferries to Sweden? An ordinary mortal could just ring the Danish side of the service at Helsingoer, as the locals called Hamlet's Elsinore, and find out when the next boat was crossing to Helsingborg. But for me that would be tantamount to committing suicide as, I knew perfectly well, all the embassy phones were bugged.

The next morning I went straight from home to Lyngby, where I duped anyone who might be following me by disappearing into a department store, then continued through Holte with its low hills to the woods of Hareskov. Health-conscious foreigners were afraid to pick the mushrooms here and thank goodness for that, for we Russians used to come every weekend and gather so many whites and chanterelles that we were even able to send samples, pickled in jars, back to our relatives in Moscow.

There was a time when I used to come to Hareskov for a more furtive purpose. The Central Committee of the Soviet Communist Party allocated funds to foreign comrades including our Danish breathren and it fell to the KGB to pass on the money. I still get goose pimples when I think how I used to hang about on the edge of the forest, waiting for the Danish General Secretary's car to pass slowly by, its accident warning lights flashing, so that I could lob a briefcase of cash into the open boot. It was really incredibly risky. If a police patrol had come along, how on earth would I explain what I, a Soviet diplomat, was doing in the woods in the middle of the night?

Later I just invited the General Secretary to come and pick up his money at the embassy. It was much simpler. He signed a receipt, we drank a bottle of vodka to the solidarity of the proletariat and he tottered back to his party headquarters, which was only just down the road. After the failure of the hardline coup in August 1991, Central Committee statistics came out in Moscow, showing that in the decade from 1981, the Danish Communists received Kr20 million or about $3 million. Not a princely sum when you consider that Moscow regarded the Danes as the leading Communists in Scandinavia.

On my latest visit to Hareskov, however, I confined myself to wandering about in the woods to confirm I was 'clean' of any PET tail before I made a break for the coast. There I discovered that the ferries to Sweden went every hour. Returning to the embassy, I passed the meadows at Taarbek to which all the Soviet children, including my son Sasha, were bussed out in summer by the teachers from our special Russian school.

I had hardly got my feet back under my desk when, almost as tentatively as the cipher clerk, Gordievsky knocked on my door, bringing in a sheaf of telegrams. His delicacy used to endear him to me, for he was not, after all, the embassy sweeper but my number two and could have walked in more boldly to see his boss. Later, I realised he had masked his perfidy with consummate acting skills. He never poked his nose into matters that did not concern him, on the contrary he maintained a respectful distance from his chief. Yet he always told me what he was doing, even down to informing me of his plans to play badminton after work. Probably this was when he met his controllers from MI6.

It was years before I found out the truth about Gordievsky. I was retired when he came to my home in Moscow in the summer of 1985, just before he made his escape to the West. He was in a terrible state. Normally a teetotaller, he had obviously been drinking heavily. Shaking, he told me the KGB had found works of Solzhenitsyn in his home. He worried me so much that I wrapped my own copies of Solzhenitsyn in plastic and buried them in my garden.

But unbeknown to me, Gordievsky was really panicking lest the KGB, which already suspected him, arrested him before he managed to get away to the West. On the telephone, which he knew was bugged, he made an appointment to meet me in the town of Zvenigorod outside Moscow. But he never showed up. Instead he crossed the Soviet border, hidden inside a British embassy removal van. In retrospect I realise he used me to distract the KGB but I do not hold it against him. In his position, I would have done the same thing.

It was hard to explain to the KGB that I was innocent, however. They dragged me to Lefortovo prison and interrogated me. Evidently they suspected that I had been working for the British since the early 1960s. I sweated for quite a long time before they released me for lack of evidence.

All that was still in the future. The telegrams which Gordievsky brought me that day in Copenhagen were gratifying. Moscow Centre might complain about our poor catch of Americans but when it came to Danish internal politics, we did not disappoint. What did Moscow really need to know about Denmark anyway? Norway, outside my patch, was important because it guarded Nato's northern flank. But dinky little Denmark? We in the embassy might follow every nuance of policy under the Social Democratic Prime Minister, Anker Joergensen, and inflate the country's importance because it was our patch. I doubt, however, that Comrade Brezhnev even knew where Denmark was. Somewhere near Kenya, perhaps? As a matter of fact, many Russians confuse Denmark with Holland to this day because in English the inhabitants of the Netherlands are called the Dutch and that begins with a d too, doesn't it?

Ferry to Helsingborg

Now, what about that operation in Helsingborg? I decided not to delay any longer. There were no particular complications, as far as I could see. The border between Denmark and Sweden was more or less open and nobody checked peaceful foot passengers going on and getting off the boat. Of course it was another matter if you took your car, especially if it had diplomatic number plates.

Two years later, I was to go to Stockholm on business, with a visa naturally. Then when I drove off the ferry, I was immediately joined by a tail from the Swedish counter-intelligence service SAEPO. Along the way, I wanted to see Göteborg and the little house of my favourite childhood writer Selma Lagerloef and Millesgaarden, the sculpture park near Stockholm. But I did not know the roads and, as I got myself more and more lost, my pursuers must have concluded that I had come to Sweden to meet an important agent or put a bomb under the Riksdag. When I came down to my car after spending a restful night in a hotel on the shores of Lake Vaettern, I found that all four of my tyres had been punctured. It was a familiar trick. The KGB used to do the same thing to irritating foreigners in Moscow.

As a foot passenger on the ferry, I would have no such problems. But what if Sod's Law applied and I was, nevertheless, asked for my documents? It would do no good to play the fool and pretend I was unaware I needed a passport because I would just not be allowed on the ferry. Period. And what if they demanded to see my passport in Helsingborg? Then it would become clear that I was a Soviet diplomat in violation of the rules. Why had I come to Sweden? To look at the landscape?

No, I would need some kind of cover story. And then I remembered that in the Russian school there was a conscientious teacher of about fifty, a morally upstanding member of the Communist Party. She had dyed blonde hair and an indeterminate figure, feared the KGB like fire (and rightly so!) and led an impeccable private life. Not once had we caught her receiving the attentions of men, not even the randy Soviet sailors who used to come into port.

Maria Ippolitovna – let's call her that – sometimes requested my help with school matters, for I was a member of the embassy's powerful Communist Party cell. Why should I not invite her for a short trip to Helsingborg? I could pack her off to the cinema or somewhere while I conducted my business. If anything happened, what would look more natural than a diplomat being coy about the fact that he was showing the sea to a woman who was not his wife? The sex-obsessed Swedes would never suspect me of anything so cerebral as spying.

You may not believe me but, in all honesty, I can tell you that I had not the slightest romantic interest in Maria Ippolitovna. For one thing, she was much older than I was. For another, I was desperately in love with another woman who was not my wife, although she was to become so later.

In the lunch break, I asked the duty clerk to ring the school and invite the teacher to the embassy. He did not say who wanted her – conspiracy, conspiracy – but brought her straight to my office. She was visibly nervous. What had she done to find herself on the carpet before the KGB *rezident*? We had our share of scandals at the embassy – either a junior diplomat had a drink too many and wrapped his car around a lamppost or the wife of an attaché was caught trying to smuggle jewels out of

Russia to sell in Denmark. Maria Ippolitovna probably thought I was going to accuse her of heresy in her classes.

'I have a little business in Sweden,' I said, grinning like the Cheshire Cat. 'Would you care to come with me? It will only take a few hours.' At this her face lit up and she asked: 'To what do I owe this honour?'

'I'm thinking of getting the Party committee to organise an excursion for the kids but first I must look at Helsingborg myself. Since you are one of our most active staff, I naturally thought . . . I'll see you tomorrow at two, then. Outside Klampenborg metro station.'

The flabbergasted teacher left and I began working out the details of the operation. I would go home for lunch as usual. It was unlikely counter-intelligence would follow me as they knew the bosses liked to command and not expose themselves to undue risk in the town. But to be on the safe side, I would transfer to the car of one of our experienced chauffeurs, who would drive me round until we were sure there was no tail. Then we would pick Maria Ippolitovna up at the metro station, make one more check, head for Hamlet's castle and . . . to sea.

The night before the operation I slept peacefully. I had refrained from drinking my usual Glenlivet, after which I felt as carefree as Robert Burns bounding through the heather, because I knew the value of a clear head at times like this. The next morning, like clockwork, I was at the embassy at quarter to nine. I lunched at home on half a pheasant, which I had shot recently on a hunting trip with one of my Danish friends. Then loudly and at length, so the girl in earphones would be sure to hear, I discussed with my wife an outing to the cinema.

Two o'clock. Klampenborg. Divine deer park. It is hard to think of a more romantic place in Copenhagen. I used to come here in secret to meet Tatyana, my third and evidently my last wife, when I was still tied to my second spouse. Like a magician, I would produce from my attaché case . . . a folding tent! My beloved, also following the rules of conspiracy, would arrive by bicycle and fall straight into my embrace. In the shade of the tent, we would drink Chablis. 'Life is meaningless, meaningless, meaningless without you,' I wrote then in a poem dedicated to her. She still sometimes quotes the line at me.

Maria Ippolitovna was on time at the metro station. She was dressed in her Sunday best, as if we were going to a banquet at a yacht club or for tea at the Queen's summer residence at Fredensborg, another jewel in the environs of Copenhagen. This worried me slightly, as did the smirk on the face of the chauffeur, who behaved somewhat unnaturally, as if he were privy to the *rezident*'s Big Romantic Secret.

To confuse the opposition – if indeed they were paying us any atten-tion – we looked in at the Louisiana art gallery and open air sculpture exhibition, where figures by Henry Moore evoked creatures that had crawled out of the Stone Age. Sculpture really does benefit by being displayed in nature. For all their great galleries, neither London nor Paris has anything to compare with Louisiana in its seaside setting. The walk in the park inspired my companion rather differently and she began to flash me flirtatious smiles.

We reached the ferry without incident, bought two return tickets and went up on deck. 'Oh, how green the sea is,' trilled Maria Ippolitovna, suddenly grabbing me by the elbow. Involuntarily, I recoiled but quickly recovered my manners. 'Excuse me,' I said, 'but I have to collect my thoughts.' Although, at that moment I had not a thought in my head. Like most of humanity, I was lucky if God granted me a thought once a month (or a year).

She removed herself to a tactful distance and I sat with a notebook on my lap, staring out to sea. I must have looked like Napoleon on the eve of the Battle of Austerlitz. Actually, I was going into battle in a way. Everything looked easy enough but I could not take it for granted that the operation would go smoothly. How many of my colleagues had been caught red-handed near dead letter boxes with the damning material? The men in mackintoshes would arrive and the press photographers and then you were on your way to Moscow, persona non grata. That is, if you were lucky enough to have diplomatic immunity.

At this point Maria Ippolitovna interrupted me again with her fussing. The devil take it. Why had I brought her along? On the other hand, perhaps I had been right. Operational requirements came first and we Communists and KGB agents knew we should always sacrifice our individual interests to the common cause.

The ferry docked. The cars began streaming off. On duty was a single Swedish border guard who looked bored until his eyes suddenly fell with interest on us. I tensed, took Maria Ippolitovna by the arm and held her close. She responded joyfully and for a second I felt her extraordinarily hot thigh against me. I was concentrating so hard on making our exit appear natural that I did not, perhaps, draw the full conclusions from this. The border guard turned his attention elsewhere and we disembarked.

Helsingborg in high summer was like an Italian resort with white yachts bobbing on the sparkling harbour. Maria Ippolitovna looked up at the azure sky and herself lit up the grey cliffs with her radiant smile. Jumping about like a girl, she took my hand and exclaimed: 'How beautiful, how beautiful!'

'I've got to go and see the Mayor on embassy business,' I said. 'Why don't you wander off and take a look at the town? See if there are any interesting museums for the children. We'll have a bite to eat later.' She beamed by way of reply but looked no more attractive for it.

Down the Rabbit Hole

After leaving her outside a shop, I set off in search of the dead letter box which, according to the map from Moscow Centre, was a shallow pit under an oak tree about fifty yards from the sea. To begin with I carefully studied the general area. It was 4.15, holiday-makers were strolling along the shore and fishermen were sitting all along the bank, just like in Copenhagen. I was slightly disturbed at the sight of a young couple kissing about twenty yards from the dead letter box. For it was a classic trick of counter-intelligence agents to relax the inexperienced spy by playing the part of lovers.

I pretended I was enjoying the sea air, then walked up the path past the dead letter box, all the time watching the couple out of the corner of my eye. When it became clear they were completely absorbed in each other, I sighed with relief but something else worried me. My plan told me to look for one hole in the ground but here were several. And was that an oak or an ash? Obviously some KGB trainee, still wet behind the ears, had written these instructions.

While the couple went further with their love-making – evidently it was the Swedish weakness to do everything in public – I doubled back to the dead letter box. The container I had to pick up would be a large pebble with a hole into which microfilm had been stuffed. I would pretend to tie my shoelaces while I poked around for it, then drop it into a plastic bag which I had brought with me specially for the purpose. What if the lovers were after all from SAEPO? What if they signalled to colleagues hiding in the bushes? Where was the guarantee ...? There was never a 100 per cent guarantee. Just get on with the job, Lyubimov.

I put my hand into the hole and felt about but found no stone. Idiots! Could they not have placed the pebble nearer the surface? I plunged my arm in again, down to the elbow this time, and suddenly: Oh horror! I felt something warm, like a human body. I drew my hand back as if from scalding water.

What was it? The corpse of a murder victim that had not had time to cool? Except that the pit was too small for a full-length body. On the other hand, if the corpse had been ... My mouth was as dry as the Sahara, my pulse was racing.

Then suddenly something brown shot out of the hole, an ugly little dwarf with long ears. A fat rabbit ran past me into the bushes. I shook for five minutes before I tried the pit again as well as all the neighbouring holes. But I never did find the pebble. Later it turned out that the officer at Moscow Centre who had written the instructions had confused Helsingborg in Sweden with the Prince of Denmark's home port of Helsingoer. What a farce!

I found Maria Ippolitovna again with no trouble, however. She had bought herself a Flora Danica brooch in the shape of a sprig of heather. 'Is something the matter?' she asked as we boarded the return ferry. 'No, everything's fine,' I said, going up on deck.

Kronborg, 'Hamlet's castle', loomed on the horizon. I loved that place. It did not matter that the real seat of the doubting Danish prince had stood, according to the Icelandic legend on which Shakespeare based his play, on the neighbouring peninsula of Jutland. For we happily believe in other myths, do we not? Sometimes British actors came here to give outdoor performances of *Hamlet*. I attended one on a summer's evening when the skies opened. The audience were thoughtfully provided with plastic raincoats but the actors had to continue, their make-up streaming down their faces.

Thinking of Hamlet, I completely forgot that I should be attentive as we got off the boat in case Danish border control unexpectedly woke up. With great distaste, I again took Maria Ippolitovna by the arm – oh, that hot thigh – and we set foot once more on Danish soil. 'I'm ravenous,' she then announced, inspired by our reunion.

I had no appetite whatsoever but the *rezident*'s promise is law. I took her to the restaurant Ophelia in the Hotel Hamlet and ordered beef tartar for myself and lobster for her. I counted on drinking most of the accompanying Chablis myself but Maria Ippolitovna turned out to be a worthy companion and I had to ask the waiter to bring a second bottle.

However, this appeared to be her first encounter with lobster. She had no idea how to use the special forks but tore it with her hands and crammed it into her mouth. How I hated her! 'Oh, what a lovely time I'm having with you,' she enthused. 'I never dreamt you would take me out. Maybe we should order another bottle of wine?' 'No, it's time for us to leave.'

Outside, she grabbed my arm again. 'You know, I've been wanting to tell you for ages but I couldn't .. I love you.' And then she actually took my hand and kissed it. The shock was worse than when I touched the rabbit in the hole. My reaction was instant and I pushed her away. In acute mutual embarrassment, we walked down the street, straight past a porn shop with a cartoon of Sigmund Freud with naked women on the brain and, next to it, a gigantic plastic phallus with a bra strapped to the balls. Maria Ippolitovna could take no more. She burst into tears. Was it the Chablis?

The embassy car was waiting for us at the corner. We drove back to town in silence. All the way, the chauffeur kept eyeing us in his mirror and smirking to himself.

What a relief to get home after this fiasco. When I went into the kitchen, I found my teenage son Sasha sitting there, strumming his guitar and singing the words to a little ditty I had written for him. We called it the Danish national anthem and it cheered me up to hear it:

> Two tourists strolled through Copenhagen,
> The shops were filled with cheese and bacon,
> Danish ham and Danish fat,
> 'Look at that, will you look at that!'
> But the peasants live on bread and lard
> While the cream is exported abroad,
> For the pigs rule here, they are the lords,
> And the proles eat scraps so they can gorge.

I joined in with the refrain: 'Andersen, Andersen, all in the land of Andersen.'

So long ago now since I was in the land of Andersen, so much water has passed under the bridge since then. How fortunate it is that we do not know our fates. I did not know then that I would divorce and remarry for the third time, be fired by the KGB as a consequence, start to write and struggle for recognition in literature.

I did not know that many of my friends would die and some, like Gordievsky, prove to be adversaries. Or that perestroika was coming, with all its upheaval. Or that the Soviet Union itself, for which I had worked all my life, would collapse and disappear from the map of the world.

Denmark I remember fondly as a gentle country, where the people appreciate nature and good food and measure their happiness not by the number of private cars per capita on the roads or the level of their incomes but by something they call 'quality of life', a concept which could include something as simple and beautiful as the tapping of a lilac branch against a cottage window.

It is made for pleasure, this magical land of Andersen, and not for the grubby business of espionage. Although in espionage there is a subtle enjoyment.

As for that cursed rabbit, that fat jumping ball of brown fluff, I sometimes see him in my dreams, waving his long ears at me. I look at him and recognise myself, which only serves to sadden me ...

Translation by Helen Womack

WASHINGTON

Name Yakushkina, Irina Alexeyevna	
Born 12 August 1925	
Education Higher	
Special Subject Linguistics	
Languages English, French	
Military Rank None	
Worked in USA, Britain, Australia	
Marital Status Widowed	
Sports Swimming, gymnastics	
Hobbies Sewing	
Favourite Tipple Don't drink	
Brand of Cigarettes Salem Lights	

The *Rezident*'s Wife Goes Shopping

Washington is a steamy city. When snow falls here, it is an event. Cars stuck in snow drifts top the television news and the newspapers report on the tiny band of heroes who made it into work. Life grinds to a halt.

On just such a winter's day my husband, who was the KGB *rezident* or station chief, telephoned me with the 'good news' that I could have an embassy car for the afternoon to 'go and do my shopping'. Public transport is minimal in the US capital and usually my excursions were limited to what I could do on foot. My favourite shopping malls – Tyson's Corner and White Flint – were out in the suburbs, twenty to thirty minutes' drive from the city centre.

The chauffeur came to pick me up in an Oldsmobile. Cars were moving with difficulty on the snowy streets. Some had spun round to block the traffic, others were having to be dug out of deep drifts at the kerb. Our progress was slow and that made us nervous.

We crawled through town and I popped into a couple of stores, then we headed out to Rock Creek, the woodland park that cuts like a wedge into the north of the city. At weekends in summer, Washingtonians come here for picnics, although it is not advisable to stroll in the park alone.

Suddenly we stopped. What happened next was like a scene from a silent movie. Without saying a word, my driver got out of the Oldsmobile and opened the capacious boot. A man rolled out and, without the slightest embarrassment, came round to sit in the front passenger seat. I looked out of the window, pretending to be studying the winter scenery. We drove in complete silence to the nearest bus stop, where we dropped our passenger. He had nearly frozen to death in the boot but evidently had had no choice but to travel like luggage.

This was the only time I became involved in my husband's work. Having been married to a Soviet intelligence officer for many years, I knew better than to ask him questions about his operations. I accepted that there was a part of his life which had to be secret and waited for him to tell me what he thought it was appropriate for me to know.

I guessed the mysterious man in the car boot was an American citizen who had just turned up and knocked on the door of the Soviet embassy, offering his services. Americans sometimes did this, although such a direct approach was risky because the FBI watched the embassy and kept a card index with photographs of everybody who called. After the passage of years, if the FBI suspected someone of treason, they could look back through the cards and see if he had ever visited.

This man must have interested the KGB enough for them to smuggle him out of the embassy. How they managed to get him unseen into the car boot I do not know as the embassy, an old mansion on 16th Street, had no underground garage. I only know that the operation turned out to have been for nothing. In the end, the KGB concluded that the man was not trustworthy.

It could have been otherwise, however. Then for ten or fifteen years the recruit would have spent his time photographing documents, communicating via dead letter boxes and flying to quiet European countries to receive instructions and money from his KGB controllers. Until the dreaded day when, thanks to someone else's alertness or treachery, he was found out. Or his own wife gave him away to the FBI.

Such was the downfall of John Walker, a naval officer who for eighteen years provided the KGB with classified information about the movements of the American fleet and the codes it used. His wife had to denounce him to the FBI twice. The first time they did not believe her. They thought she was just settling a marital score.

Parallel Careers

My late husband, Dmitry Ivanovich Yakushkin, was appointed to the post of *rezident* in Washington by Yuri Andropov himself. The KGB Chairman offered him the job just after Leonid Brezhnev and Gerald Ford had discussed arms control at their summit in Vladivostok in November 1974. The leaders of the superpowers were due to meet again on American soil the following summer.

This was the era of bell-bottomed trousers and Afro hairstyles. The United States and the Soviet Union were friendlier than they had been at any point since their wartime alliance. American senators and Soviet dignitaries flew backwards and forwards on exchange visits. In space, Soyuz prepared to dock with Apollo. Among the stars on earth, Elizabeth Taylor appeared in a jointly produced film called *Blue Bird*. Russians drank Pepsi Cola in exchange for which they gave the Americans Stolichnaya vodka. The world was bi-polar and seemed stable.

Yet the new relationship remained uneasy. Each side interpreted the fashionable word 'détente' in its own way. For our part, we wanted to be closer but objected to the way America interfered in our affairs by accusing us of human rights abuses. Another factor was that President Ford was preparing for his re-election bid (unsuccessfully as it turned out, for he was defeated by Jimmy Carter in 1976) and he knew that his policy of befriending Moscow did not make him universally popular. The US Congress was divided into 'hawks' and 'doves' when it came to relations with the Soviet Union; indeed there was even a restaurant near Capitol Hill called 'Hawks and Doves'. If, as it appeared, the short pause in the Cold War was coming to an end, then more than ever Soviet intelligence would have to busy itself in the American capital.

My husband was briefed about his new job when Andropov summoned him to his bedside in the Kremlin hospital. The KGB Chairman, later to become Soviet leader, had already begun to suffer from the kidney ailment which was to kill him in 1984. Perhaps for Andropov the meeting in the hospital was a routine affair but it made a deep impression on my husband. He was being asked to leave the Britain and Scandinavia department, where he had been trying to restore some order following the defection of Oleg Lyalin to Britain in 1971, and move quickly to take up the top KGB post in the country most important to Moscow Centre. He was filled with a sense of the responsibility of his mission, which I of course shared.

Andropov did not speak to me, indeed nobody from the KGB invited the new *rezident*'s wife for a chat. I know that prior to foreign postings some wives were called in and given little lectures on how they should behave abroad but I never experienced this, perhaps because I had had a higher education and a career of my own. After the war during which, as a teenager, I helped to build the anti-tank defences around Moscow, I attended the prestigious Maurice Thorez State Institute of Languages, graduating in English and French in 1949. I went to work as the personal interpreter to the Minister of Agriculture, an interesting job which took me on trips with trade delegations all round the Soviet Union and even to Britain and Australia.

Never a member of the Communist Party, I had no desire to work for the KGB myself, even if such a job had been offered. I trusted my husband's judgement, however, when he told me he had accepted an invitation to join the KGB. We were already married at this stage and working together at the Ministry of Agriculture.

Dmitry's first foreign posting was to New York, where he worked from 1963 to 1969 as the director of conference services at the United Nations. I followed him and looked after our son, Dmitry junior, but I did not give up my own career. To test myself, I decided to sit the fiendishly difficult 'Proficiency Test' for translators who aspire to work at the UN. Candidates normally study for two years but with my degree it was enough for me to join the last course. I was interested in the teaching methods.

The day of the exam came. We gathered nervously in a cavernous hall. I remember one of the tricky items we had to translate was an announcement of a UN outing, which had to be tactfully worded so as not to offend spouses who were not invited to participate. It was usual for candidates to take the exam three or four times before they passed. But I was pleased to pass first time with high marks, after which I worked as a translator in my own country's UN mission.

In Washington, I was also to keep up my profession. As well as helping out part-time at the embassy, I translated literature for Soviet publishing houses. My husband and I both loved books and we would go to sales held periodically by the State Department to dispose of the unwanted volumes owned by American diplomats who were always on the move. While Dmitry rooted around searching for rare editions of Tolstoy and the war memoirs which he collected, I would be on the lookout for American and British literature worth translating for Soviet readers. Irving Shaw, Susan Hill and Norman Lewis were among the authors I rendered into Russian.

Now in my seventies, I still work as a translator from my home which, coincidentally, overlooks the American embassy in Moscow. Like all men, my husband was not really keen on having a working wife. But I have always believed that a woman should work.

On Edge in a Des Res

My husband and I flew out to Washington in 1975. If you are planning to visit the US capital, prepare yourself to land in the middle of fields at Dulles Airport, built by the Finnish architect Eero Saarinen and resembling an ultra-modern farm more than an airport. Later I found out that FBI agents always waited at Dulles to see who came in on the Aeroflot flight from Moscow and to wave goodbye to departing Soviet personnel. Who knew, perhaps one of them might take it into his head to defect at the last minute?

Just before we came in to land, I remember seeing the numerous swimming pools in the Washington suburbs, which served as a socio-economic introduction to life in the US. I know some Soviet women who lost their minds at the first sight of a supermarket, but I had been to the West and indeed to America before and so reacted calmly to the contrast with Soviet reality. I thought of Anastas Mikoyan, the Soviet Deputy Prime Minister who, after he had attended the funeral of John F. Kennedy in 1963, was taken to see a branch of Safeway in the Washington suburb of Rockville. 'It will be like this in the Soviet Union,' he said and after a pause added: 'Some day.'

Although I was not reeling from culture shock, I did have to adapt to a new place. The humid climate was the first thing that struck me the very moment I emerged through the automatic glass doors of the airport. I breathed in the clammy air and it was as if I were unable to breathe out again.

A noiseless limousine took us from the airport along the Beltway to the suburb of Chevy Chase in Maryland. I could smell freshly mown lawns and see bicycles dropped casually in the drives of white clapboard houses. But there was not a soul in sight.

We came to a block of luxury flats on Willard Avenue. Automatic doors lifted and our car plunged into an underground garage. An elevator with mirrors and piped music but no button for the unlucky thirteenth storey took us to our floor. The flat was stuffy until I opened a few windows. I switched on the television. The broadly smiling newscaster reported on a local murder and the prospects for the Red Sox impending match. Then the weather forecast: thunder.

I was pleased to learn that our new home was in a building called Irene, which is the English form of my name Irina. The complex, complete with a swimming pool and tennis court on the roof, was a state within a state. Video cameras and doormen guarded the property of the rich Americans who lived there.

Rules were rules inside Irene. Flats were not rented to people with dogs, cats or children (our son was a student by this time and only visited us occasionally). The residents were obliged to cover at least three quarters of their flats with carpets so as not to disturb the neighbours with the noise of their footsteps. All misdeeds were recorded in a book which was kept by the concierge along with spare sets of keys. Once an entry was made in the name of Yakushkin. The neighbours complained because I had fed the birds from my balcony and they had left marks on the windows of the floor below.

This strict regime did not, however, prevent FBI agents from entering our home when we were out. These gumshoes made no attempt to be imaginative, leaving cigarette butts in ashtrays or moving objects around to let us know they had paid a call. Once I came in to find cigar smoke still hanging in the air after what was obviously a recent visit. I called the concierge, who was at a loss for words. But after that complaint, the FBI at least had the decency not to smoke cigars in our flat any more.

Washingtonians seemed to fall into two categories. The doormen and the mechanics and the hairdressers and the shop assistants were ordinary citizens who reacted with remarkable calm and lack of hostility to the knowledge that we worked at the Soviet embassy. Even when anti-Soviet hysteria was at its height and vodka was publicly poured down drains and Aeroflot planes were banned from landing, I never felt hatred from these people. But the other category conducted a war of nerves against my husband which also affected me as his wife. These were professionals and it was no coincidence when our carpet was stained or our car boot was broken into even though the vehicle was kept in a locked garage.

Once in our mail box we found some letters addressed to Richard Helms, the former director of the CIA, from which we deduced that he had lived in the flat before us. This could hardly be coincidental. Of the hundreds of apartments in Irene, ours must have been made available for rent to the Soviet embassy because it was already riddled with bugging devices. Helms, CIA director under Richard Nixon and then the US ambassador to Iran, had somehow been involved in the Watergate scandal and it was probably this that put him under the surveillance of his own secret service.

The Big Apple and the Small Town Capital

'Washington,' wrote the French writer Georges Simenon, 'is a great capital and at the same time a small provincial town where everybody knows each other. Actually it's not even a town, it's a royal court.'

Certainly for me there was a strong contrast between Washington, the seat of government where everybody was either engaged in politics or interpreting and commenting upon politics, and cosmopolitan New York where we had lived before.

I had experienced some tense moments in New York. For example, when President Kennedy was shot and people began mumbling on the buses that perhaps the Russians were behind the assassination, I judged it was safer for my son and me to be at home than out on the streets shopping for Lego. But in the Big Apple, I usually felt free.

My life in Washington was more restricted. Partly it had to do with the fact that if you did not have a car, it was as if you were a second-class citizen. So much could be achieved on foot in New York, which was a European city in that sense, but Washington was true to the American tradition in which the car was king. The bus and metro services were limited. You rarely saw pedestrians, except the crowds of white-shirted government personnel in the centre during working hours.

Quite apart from the distances involved, walking was not always a pleasure because crime was a worrying factor. With perhaps admirable honesty compared to the Russian habit of building 'Potemkin villages', the Americans allowed the impoverished black ghetto to extend almost to the door of the White House. Washington had one of the highest crime rates in the country. The man in charge of the domestic running of the Soviet embassy was shot dead only two blocks from the embassy during a raid on a shop by a robber who apparently thought he was reaching for a gun to defend himself when he was only putting his hand inside his jacket for his wallet.

All Washingtonians lived with the fact that their city was not pedestrian-friendly. As Soviet diplomats, we suffered added restrictions.

Working at the UN in New York, my husband had been considered an 'international civil servant' and so we were not subject to the requirement to inform the State Department two days in advance whenever we planned a trip twenty-five miles or more beyond the city limit. In Washington the rule was strictly applied and the Soviet embassy dacha at Pioneer Point on the Chesapeake Bay was the only place we could visit without having to ask for permission. (The CIA headquarters at Langley, Virginia, was actually within the twenty-five-mile zone but my husband and his colleagues censored themselves and never went there anyway.)

Travelling to the dacha in a car with diplomatic number plates which immediately gave us away, we had to stick to the straight road however enticing the side lanes looked. We could not even turn off to the nearby town of Annapolis because of the naval academy there. It was frustrating, but on the other hand we enjoyed diplomatic immunity, which we had not had in New York a decade earlier.

Then I really did worry about my husband. If he rang up and said he was leaving work and I should get the dinner ready, it meant the opposite, that he was going out on some operation of unknown duration. In Washington, he was the one who sat at base and worried about his operatives in the field.

He held the rank of counsellor, the number three position in the embassy. The FBI knew perfectly well who he really was but this was by no means apparent to the many guests who used to come to our parties. Gradually we built up a circle of Washington friends. One of my regular companions for shopping trips and other outings was Inna, the wife of the Czechoslovak ambassador. We also had contact with a few friends from our New York days. One was an Australian woman called M, who came to look us up in Washington. In the 1960s she had had a prestigious job at the UN but now she was down on her luck. She told us she was working as a cleaner to rich people in South Carolina and was grateful when they left uneaten food for her in the fridge.

We were pleased to see her again after so many years, but unfortunately there was no coincidence in our reunion. Over dinner in an expensive restaurant on Connecticut Avenue she made a proposal on behalf of the FBI that my husband and I should defect to the United States. Our driver said that while we were eating, the restaurant was surrounded by FBI cars waiting to whisk us away if we agreed. Dmitry, of course, declined the offer. Then we took M back to her hotel where we said polite goodbyes, knowing we would never see each other again. Personally I felt sorry for our old friend, who had yielded to FBI pressure because she desperately needed a green card.

Exploring Washington

If at first I hankered after New York with all its vibrancy, I came to appreciate the peace of Washington. Eventually I concluded it was fun to visit New York but better to live in the capital, where people used to feed wild racoons on their back lawns. From Chevy Chase, we drove into work not past motorway junctions and industrial estates but gardens and the colonial-style houses of the upper middle class.

KGB staff and diplomats were packed together in the old embassy at number 1125 16th Street, a building which was often shown in glossy magazines accompanied by the caption: 'Nest of Spies'. The four-storey mansion bristled with communications antennae.

It is widely known that the FBI used to pore over the rubbish in our dustbins in case it contained secrets. But naturally the Americans also used sophisticated equipment. It is said they bombarded the embassy with electromagnetic impulses from a nearby roof in order to overhear conversations and, from the tapping of typewriter keys, decipher documents as they were being written. My husband protected himself from eavesdropping by working in a room within a room surrounded by an electromagnetic field, which could hardly have been good for his health.

I took an interest in the history of the mansion, a listed building which boasted one of the first electric lifts in the city. The house was built in 1911 for Pullman, the Chicago railway magnate. The architect was Nathan White, who also designed the Oval Office in the White House. In 1913 the Tsarist Russian government bought the mansion, but after the Bolshevik Revolution and the ensuing rupture of diplomatic relations it stood empty until 1933, when ties with the US were restored. Then began the era of Stalin's ambassador Alexander Troyanovsky, who may have been a Communist but who knew how to throw parties in the grand old Russian style.

The embassy was only three blocks away from the White House, which I visited at the first opportunity. I explored Washington with my husband when he was free, with Inna sometimes, but most often on my own. That was how I saw the White House. The building was started in 1792 but America's first President, George Washington, never lived there and its first master was John Adams, the second US President. In 1952, in the depths of the Cold War, an atomic bomb shelter was added to the American leader's official residence.

My personal impression was that it was beautiful but smaller than I had expected and I was disappointed that the Oval Office was out of bounds to tourists. I did not see the mistress of the house, Betty Ford, then or on any other occasion.

I derived more pleasure from visits I was able to make in the car with Dmitry to the Virginia plantation houses of George Washington and Thomas Jefferson, the author of the Declaration of Independence. Despite pronouncing that all people are created equal, Jefferson was a man of his time and kept slaves on his estate of Monticello, as did Washington at Mount Vernon. For fans of Scarlett O'Hara, both museums are well worth a visit.

Jefferson's house on the hill gave me particular satisfaction because of its restrained good taste. He designed it himself after returning from France, where he studied the style of Paladio. He came home with eighty trunks filled not with souvenirs but with books for the library and seeds for the garden. He installed lifts so the slaves could send food up from the kitchens and hid the staircases from view behind cupboards. The result was a house which is both beautiful and functional.

Jefferson, who was inspired by Paris, made his mark on Washington too. In accordance with his wishes, Congress passed a law banning buildings higher than the dome of the Capitol and so Washington is atypical of American cities in having no skyscrapers. Only the obelisk memorial to George Washington breaks the rule. Around Jefferson's own memorial on the bank of Tidal Basin, 3,000 cherry trees grow, attracting thousands of tourists when they blossom in April. They were a gift from the Japanese government to the wife of President William Taft.

I went to see the graves of John and Robert Kennedy in Arlington Cemetery, America's pantheon, but was perhaps most impressed by the memorial to the American Marines. Based on Joe Rosenthal's Pulitzer Prize-winning photograph of soldiers raising the American flag on Iwo-Jima in 1945, it is dramatic and not, like most memorials, deader than the dead themselves.

In a straight line from Arlington, rising on a hill over the city, stands the Capitol, seat of Congress and the political symbol of Washington and America as a whole.

My own interest in Congress was in its wonderful library, which was originally built for the exclusive use of lawmakers. But after Jefferson bequeathed his personal collection, the library opened to the public and grew into one of the best stocked in the world. There is a rich Russian section, including volumes which belonged to the last Tsar, Nicholas II.

I found Russian treasures at Hillwood, the home of the late Marjorie Post who, while her husband served as US ambassador to the Soviet Union in the 1930s, went round second-hand shops in Moscow buying up art confiscated from Russian aristocrats during the Bolshevik Revolution. Also in the National Gallery there are some fine paintings which the American millionaire Andrew Mellon took from the Hermitage Museum in Leningrad for his own private collection.

I was standing in the National Gallery one day, looking at a picture by an Italian master of a beautiful woman being observed from behind a curtain by a lascivious Moor. It hung not on a wall but on a stand in the middle of the hall. Suddenly an FBI agent poked his head round the screen to look at me in just the same way as the Moor. Unlike my husband and his colleagues, I never tried to seduce anybody on behalf of the KGB but the FBI occasionally followed me just in case.

In general I would say that Washington in those days was not particularly well endowed with culture. It was as if the Muses had passed this political city by. Until the beginning of the 1970s, there was not even a large stage to accommodate touring opera and ballet companies. However the cultural scene became livelier after the John Kennedy Arts Centre opened in 1971. This was one venue at least where I did not feel overdressed in evening wear. There was also the little Ford Theatre where Abraham Lincoln was shot. It was restored and used to stage plays.

Our nightlife further improved when we discovered Georgetown, a former river port on the Potomac which had been gentrified by intellectuals and politicians and which provided the nearest thing in Washington to a bohemian lifestyle. We went to the cinema here and to French and Italian restaurants.

One of them was the scene of a strange incident in Cold War history. In 1985, the KGB agent Vitaly Yurchenko disappeared while on assignment in Rome, only to pop up later in the US. It seemed he had defected. But one evening when he was eating with American agents in the Au Pied du Cochon, he excused himself to go to the toilet, slipped through the back door of the restaurant and ran all the way to the Soviet embassy.

The Western press suggested he had been put under pressure to return by the KGB. He said he had been kidnapped in Rome by the CIA. In short, it was an odd story, one which to this day had not been fully explained.

A Break in Las Vegas

My husband's delicate position as KGB *rezident* prevented him from travelling to represent the Soviet Union in different American cities, something the bona fide diplomats were always doing. He felt that if he went away, the law by which the sandwich always falls buttered side down would operate and some emergency would happen in his absence. However on one occasion the ambassador, Anatoly Dobrynin, did ask him to go and represent Moscow at a US–Soviet boxing match in Las Vegas. It was a rare chance for us to have a weekend outside Washington. Actually it was more than that; it was the trip of a lifetime.

Rich Russian tourists may flock to Las Vegas now but then the gambling mecca was strictly closed to most Soviet visitors because the top-secret nuclear test site was not far away in the Nevada desert. Only for our boxers did the US sometimes made an exception.

Dmitry applied to the State Department for permission to travel as a sporting representative and received it. Because he was not planning to do any of his usual business, he did not inform Moscow Centre that he was making the trip. At KGB headquarters they only found out that he was in Las Vegas when they switched on their televisions in Moscow and saw his face among the other spectators with ringside seats. He received a pointed telegram about that afterwards.

The match, which I attended too, was just like the fight in *Rocky IV* except that the American was black and in reality the Soviet champion beat him by six points to four.

Afterwards, Dmitry and I were able to enjoy a short holiday. I was amazed by Las Vegas from the moment we landed at the airport. Hundreds of thousands of gamblers fly in for the weekend and many, unable to restrain themselves, fall immediately on the one-armed bandits in the arrivals hall as on a fountain in the desert. Surrounded by a real desert and planted with palm trees, Las Vegas is surprisingly beautiful for all its vulgarity. For many people, it is an oasis where they can forget work and family problems, lose all sense of time and give themselves up to the passion of gambling.

We stayed in the Hotel Sahara, which had a gigantic flashing and jingling casino in the basement. Youths under twenty-one are not allowed to play but there is no age ceiling and elderly people in wheelchairs are left for hours in front of the one-armed bandits while their relatives go off to play blackjack and roulette.

Dmitry and I had a flutter and lost a small amount, which was probably to be expected in view of the saying that those who are lucky in cards are unlucky in love. The majority of people lose, of course, otherwise the casinos would go out of business. The manager of the Sahara told us about a Japanese visitor who lost so much that he could not pay the bill for his room or his air far home. The hotel paid for him and regarded it as money well spent because he was addicted to gambling and would be a regular guest in future.

Like vampires returning to their coffins, the gamblers leave the casinos and rush home to bed when the sun rises. There is not much to do in Las Vegas during the day unless you want a quickie wedding or divorce, which Dmitry and I did not. We went shopping, had a look in the famous Caesar's Palace and found a surprising number of churches, presumably to console those who had nothing left but to turn to the Lord.

American puritans and Soviet Communist propagandists alike would fulminate against Las Vegas but personally I found it fascinating. I did not make moral judgements, but was just curious to see another side of life.

Honourable Return Without a Backward Glance

The era of political correctness in America was a little before our time, but my husband and I nevertheless witnessed various sexual scandals when we lived in Washington. One of the most amusing was the case of Congressman Wayne Hayes who, like many US politicians, employed his secretary for her looks rather than her skills. Eventually it emerged that his personal assistant, a curvaceous blonde called Elizabeth Ray, was such a bimbo that she could not even type. After she and her boss were exposed, she went and posed for *Playboy* while little lapel badges became popular in Washington with the catchphrase of the year: 'I can't type.'

Just as American politicians sacrificed privacy to enjoy power, so Soviet personnel had to accept that if they worked in the US, their private lives went under the microscope. The only difference was that in our case it was usually the FBI rather than the press that did the prying. They knew about all our love affairs and financial problems, everything that made us susceptible to recruitment. One KGB officer could not stand this pressure and had to be sent home after he had a nervous breakdown.

Another sad case involved the assistant to our naval attaché, who, like many staff from the Soviet embassy, used to patronise a Russian émigré bookshop called Kamkin's. At first he was just interested in the kind of books which were difficult to obtain back in the USSR, then he became interested in the salesgirl, an attractive young woman of Russian extraction whom everybody called 'Fresca'. Matters developed predictably from then on. The Americans showed the young man photographs which corresponded with his feelings, but not with his position at the embassy. He was sent home to a distant garrison, while for Soviet diplomats the bookshop became a 'zone of heightened danger'.

Although my husband had made clear to our Australian friend M that he was loyal to the Soviet Union, the FBI did not give up hope of seducing him too. One lunchtime we went shopping together in Safeway in Georgetown. Whilst I was looking for cornflakes, an FBI man went up to Dmitry, who at that precise moment was choosing a cabbage. I only saw the agent's back. Dmitry told me afterwards what he said.

In his book *Inside the CIA*, the American author Ronald Kessler suggested that the FBI offered my husband $20 million to defect. In fact the agent offered Dmitry nothing more than a chance to meet his bosses. My husband replied that he was quite happy to have such a meeting provided it took place inside the Soviet embassy. After that he heard nothing more from the FBI.

My husband was an erudite, decent, generous but above all patriotic man who would never have dreamt of betraying his country. In a backhanded way, the Americans expressed respect for him when our time in Washington came to an end. At least that is one interpretation that can be put on an article which appeared in the *Washington Post* by none other than Bob Woodward, one of the two ace reporters who broke the story of the Watergate scandal. The other possibility is that the FBI,

which must have been the source of Woodward's report about my husband's departure, wanted to embarrass him in front of his KGB bosses
by saying too many flattering things about him.

'One of the best known of Washington's important persons is expected
to leave this month after a six-year assignment here,' Woodward wrote.
'Few Americans have heard his name. He works exclusively behind the
scenes and there is probably no-one in the US whose secrets are more
coveted by the US government. He is Dmitry Ivanovich Yakushkin,
according to the diplomatic register one of ten counsellors at the Soviet
embassy. Mr Yakushkin is a moderate of refined temperament. He is said
to have voiced concerns about human rights issues and the need for arms
control. With a degree in economic science, he is said to keep up with
literature and other cultural developments.'

As far as I know, Woodward never actually met my husband, although
he came to the embassy, evidently looking for him and for me too one
day when we were both out. I returned to find a signed copy of his book
All The President's Men on my desk, which perhaps he wanted me to
translate for Soviet readers. Unfortunately, I was not able to do so as the
publishers in Moscow were not interested at that time.

Dmitry and I left Washington in 1982 before the Cold War was quite
over. There is a famous Soviet spy film called *The Dead Season* which
ends with an exchange of Russian and American spies on the Glienecke
Bridge in Berlin. The two agents are ideological enemies yet at the same
time colleagues who feel no hatred on a personal level. They link their
fortunate return home with the fact that they have honestly carried out
their missions. Perhaps that is how we felt when we returned to Moscow.

After he retired, Dmitry was not inclined to reminisce about his career.
Serious people in the intelligence profession tend, as a rule, to say little.
Their silence breeds legends. The reality was usually simpler. Traitors
were governed by motives as banal as they were base and successes were
often the result of pure luck.

On our very last day in Washington, only hours before the flight, I took
it into my head to go to my favourite hairdresser in the Statler-Hilton
Hotel. The hairdresser greeted me with a question which seemed to have
a strange subtext: 'You just want a hair cut?' 'Yes,' I said. A TV crew was
hanging about by the entrance to the salon. Whilst I was having my hair
washed, it dawned on me that they were waiting for me to come out and
make a last-minute request for political asylum. The Americans could
not believe that I might, without any ulterior motive, just want to have
my hair done before my flight. They never gave up.

DELHI

Name Timofeyev, Vasily Ivanovich

Born 10 June 1945

Education Higher, Masters degree in history

Special Subject History

Languages English

Military Rank Colonel

Worked in Thailand, India

Marital Status Married

Sports Football

Hobbies Photography

Favourite Tipple Beer

Brand of Cigarettes Java

Among Friends

Indira Gandhi and Leonid Brezhnev had a famous political friendship as strong as the regard which, years later, Mikhail Gorbachev and Margaret Thatcher were to show for each other. I saw Brezhnev and the Indian Prime Minister together once, long before I was posted to Delhi on a permanent basis. The year was 1973 and I was a junior KGB agent on a short assignment which coincided with the Kremlin leader's official visit to India.

Brezhnev was not then the senile wreck who made Russians feel ashamed of their leader but a sprightly and charming politician. In the picturesque setting of Delhi's Red Fort, he was giving a speech about an oil refinery which was to be built with assistance from the Soviet Union at Mathura just outside the capital. Peasants had been bussed in from the provinces to swell the crowd and give him a good welcome.

Brezhnev spoke at length about international cooperation and the solidarity of the Soviet and Indian peoples. His speech was translated into Hindi. The crowd stood silently. They did not understand a word he was saying. It was not because the translation was bad but because they were uneducated people and could not grasp his jargon. The lack of response became embarrassing.

And then Mrs Gandhi, beautifully dressed in a silk sari, stepped in and began speaking to the peasants like a primary school teacher explaining simple things to young children. Her words were to the effect that this was nice Mr Brezhnev all the way from Russia. He was going to build them a factory to give them jobs. They would work and earn money and be able to feed their children. The factory would make petrol to make the buses go.

At this, the crowd burst into ecstatic applause. They really were very poor people, desperately in need of employment opportunities. The oil refinery was to provide jobs for thousands of labourers, who still worked on building sites without any machinery. They carried baskets of sand and piles of bricks on their heads, balancing with the skill of yogis as they climbed the scaffolding.

I remembered Brezhnev and Mrs Gandhi when I returned to India at the end of the 1980s to work under journalistic cover for Soviet foreign intelligence. They were both dead by then, Brezhnev having succumbed to old age, Mrs Gandhi having fallen victim to Sikh assassins, but the special relationship between India and the Soviet Union continued and was to determine the way in which I operated.

In Thailand, where the United States had had strong influence and even military bases, my job had been to dig out secrets, which amounted to hostile behaviour towards the host country, although personally I loved and respected the Thais. In India, which was a friend of the Soviet Union, the KGB did not want me to spy but to exert influence in political circles so that, as far as possible, decisions taken in Delhi suited the interests of Moscow.

India was not a formal ally of the Soviet Union like East European members of the Warsaw Pact, but in some ways it was perhaps closer to us, for the friendship was voluntary or at least based on the principle that my enemy's friend is my enemy. After India was partitioned to end Muslim–Hindu bloodshed, the young Islamic state of Pakistan looked to the United States for help. And so predominantly Hindu India cooled towards America and befriended the other super power. In 1971, India and the Soviet Union went so far as to sign a mutual defence agreement in which it was stated that an attack on one could, in certain circumstances, be interpreted as an attack on both. Friendships do not get much closer than that.

Moscow did not want to undermine this trust; friends do not have secrets from each other and yet ... the Soviet Union felt its partner needed a little guidance. My task was to find Indians who would act as lobbyists for socialism at home and lean on the government to support Soviet positions in world bodies such as the United Nations and the Non-Aligned Movement. There were few thrills and spills in this work and I admit honestly that I was no James Bond. But there was satisfaction to be had when my 'agents of influence', as the KGB called them, helped events to go Moscow's way.

For example, I had a paid lobbyist who was a Member of Parliament for the Congress Party. He was not committing any crime by advocating Soviet policies. Nevertheless, I tried not to be seen meeting him in public, as an agent of influence is not much use if everybody knows he is Moscow's man.

On one occasion I read in the papers that the Americans were preparing to conduct naval manoeuvres off the Indian coast. Following instructions from Moscow Centre, I persuaded the MP to raise an objection to this in parliament. He recruited other influential politicians, who whipped up such a fuss that the US exercises were cancelled. I cannot be sure this was as a direct result of the KGB's hidden interference in India's affairs. Perhaps Delhi would have stopped the manoeuvres anyway. But I had a warm feeling about the fact that the Americans had been frustrated.

The tasks which were given to our agents of influence were always decided by Moscow. Seeing the day-to-day situation on the ground, I was in a position to make recommendations to headquarters, but I did not have the global overview they enjoyed and was therefore only ever a middle-man passing on instructions. Just suppose I started some propaganda campaign against American policy at precisely the same moment that elsewhere in the world delicate Soviet–US negotiations were going on. You can see why KGB staff at my level were not allowed to take any initiatives.

In the Soviet Union before glasnost, information was power and only those at the very top were fully in the picture. It was the Central Committee of the Communist Party itself which decided which questions should be raised in the Indian Parliament. Our senior comrades, only one rung down in the hierarchy from the Politburo, used the KGB to try to orchestrate debate in the biggest democracy in the world. This was the special treatment Moscow reserved for its partners. This was how the KGB operated when it was among friends.

At Home with the Indians

The mark of the Mogul emperors can still be seen in the Red Fort, the Jama Masjit mosque and the other sixteenth- and seventeenth-century monuments but Delhi was largely rebuilt after King George V announced in 1911 that the capital of British India was to move from Calcutta. I lived just inside the Outer Ring Road of New Delhi in a comfortable residential district called Vasant Vikhar. I rented my house, complete with servants, from the 'Milk King' of India.

In Russian, we use the word *krysha*, or roof, figuratively to mean a spy's cover. Gurbash Singh never knew that he was giving a roof in the literal sense to an agent of the KGB. Believing I was just a Soviet journalist, he was very friendly to me. I did not abuse his friendship by trying to recruit him, but enjoyed his hospitality. Often he would invite me to his lavish parties.

He is dead now, but in his day my landlord was a prominent personality. He made his money in the early 1970s when, during a conflict with Pakistan, the Indian Army went into what is now Bangladesh. Like their British imperial masters before them, Indian Army officers are creatures of habit and lovers of comfort. They were extremely put out that in war-torn Bangladesh there was no milk for their tea, so upset in fact, that the government had to take urgent measures to prevent a mutiny. Tankers of milk were sent up to Dhaka, but it went sour on the long journey. Enter Gurbash Singh with an original solution.

He knew the secret, also known to Russian peasants centuries ago, that if you drop a frog into milk, it will keep it fresh. He took a huge overdraft from the bank and contracted to supply the entire Indian Army in Bangladesh with fresh milk. Of course, he did not advertise the fact that frogs were swimming in his tankers or there might indeed have been a revolt. The officers only knew that there was fresh milk for their tea. After making his fortune in this way, Gurbash Singh invested in real estate. I think he owned half of Vasant Vikhar and rented out his property to many other foreigners as well as me.

I did not mix with them, however, in the same way as I had courted diplomats, visiting businessmen and, above all, foreign journalists in Thailand. Delhi has a Foreign Correspondents' Association like Bangkok. Sometimes I saw the BBC's legendary correspondent, Mark Tully, there. But I did not need my 'colleagues' from the press quite as much as I had done in my previous posting.

Thailand, you see, was a dictatorship. Just as journalists in the pre-perestroika Soviet Union used to share what they knew with each other because the authorities released so little information, so reporters in

Bangkok hunted in a pack and pooled their knowledge. It was necessary to talk to other journalists to find out something as simple as when a foreign minister would be arriving on an official visit.

But in democratic India, which had gained something from being under British rule, everything was published freely. This made the correspondents more competitive and inclined to work on their own. I met them rarely because they were often away on long trips around the vast and varied country which, like Mother Russia, defies reason and cannot be understood in one lifetime. But I managed without them because all I had to do was open my morning paper to find the information which would be the starting point for my peculiar work.

I would say that roughly thirty per cent of what I did was for the editors at the news organisation which provided my cover while seventy per cent was in the service of the KGB. My journalism, then, was just the tip of the iceberg.

In Thailand, I had devoted a lot of time to pursuing Americans and other foreigners, but that was not a big part of the job in Delhi. US citizens in the Indian capital were almost all diplomats, who rarely left their embassy compound with its swimming pool and other fine facilities and, when they did, knew better than to do more than drink a polite reception cocktail with anyone representing the Soviet Union.

The British were no longer a significant presence in Delhi either. After granting the Indians their independence, they left them to make their own way and the only Englishmen I came across were isolated business people who had stayed on, like a man with a little jeweller's shop which my wife Svetlana used to like to visit.

Almost all my work was with the locals and I usually met them in their own homes, something which would have been unthinkable in Thailand where the counter-intelligence service listened in to conversations. In Asia, to avoid the walls with ears, I took my sources out to restaurants or chatted them up in bars, of which there was a wide choice. Some streets in Bangkok were lined with bars and restaurants from end to end.

It was not so in Delhi. The Hindus are not supposed to drink alcohol and therefore bars are few and far between. Cheap and cheerful Indian restaurants may be popular in London and other Western cities, but in India itself they are mostly so filthy that it is not advisable for Europeans to eat there.

Of course, Delhi does have some excellent high-class restaurants, often in hotels. But the home-loving Indians don't go into hotels much and it looks odd to see a European dining with a local in such a context. From my point of view, the good restaurants in Delhi were purely for family pleasure. Svetlana and I loved tandoori chicken and other Indian dishes and often had a night out in our favourite Moti Makhal. If we fancied a change, we would go to the 'Chinese' restaurants, where the chefs and waiters were in actual fact Tibetan exiles.

My agents of influence, whom I inherited from my KGB predecessors except for one man whom I recruited myself, preferred the privacy of their own homes, where they offered me tea and Indian sweets. We did not need to fear that our conversations were being overheard for Indian counter-intelligence was too poor to use expensive eavesdropping equipment unless it had reason to believe a person was spying, which a Soviet 'friend' of India would not do. The *choukidar*, or gate man, might inform the police that Mr Timofeyev had visited his master, but he would not know the substance of our discussion. However most Indians, when they moved to Delhi from the provinces, brought their own *choukidars* with them and could be sure of their loyalty.

The Indians as a whole are a helpful and friendly people, very hospitable to foreigners, with whom they like to mix as they think this confers prestige on them. Once I was invited to the wedding of a young woman whose father, an army officer, I had only met twice. Of course I did not miss the chance to go and see the colourful ceremony in which the impression was given that the couple were seeing each for the first time although in fact they had courted in a modern way, arranged marriages being largely a thing of the past.

But the genial Indians have one defect – they do not keep their promises. Unlike the Thais, who wriggle out of making a commitment but generally keep it if it is once made, the Indians will cheerfully promise the earth and then not deliver. In particular, they like to drop names and hold out the possibility of introductions to famous people. I do not think I ever met an Indian who did not claim to be related to the Gandhis. In this, the Indians are like the Arabs and Afghans and unlike the Chinese and peoples of South-East Asia. Evidently it is a tribal trait. 'Everyone in my tribe is linked to me even if there are millions in the clan.'

You can imagine how frustrating it was for me. But a KGB agent must be flexible. Instead of getting enraged, I learnt to work with this particular national characteristic. I knew that the Indians, good-hearted despite their boasting, would always do what was within the range of their capabilities. The skill was in assessing what they could actually accomplish and in giving them realistic tasks. A backbench MP could not be expected to recruit the Prime Minister, but there was no reason why he should not raise some awkward questions in parliament.

The Soviet Lobby

Those who lobby in the interests of foreign powers are to be found in many assemblies around the world. For example, the Israeli lobby has a loud voice in the US Congress. This is accepted as normal because the pressure group is registered and above board. The Soviet lobby in India, however, did not declare itself.

The KGB used MPs from the Congress Party to promote policies deemed desirable by Moscow. After Rajiv Gandhi was assassinated, like his mother before him, the opposition came to power in India but the KGB continued to work through the Congress Party, reckoning that the Nehru–Gandhi dynasty had the best long-term political prospects in the country.

Before my time, the KGB had had a very senior agent of influence, a minister in one of Indira Gandhi's cabinets to whom Moscow gave the codename 'Dik'. Originally from Bombay, he had spent time in jail during the struggle for independence. He was one Indian who could say truthfully that he knew Pandit Nehru.

He did not betray his country by giving away state secrets, but he influenced government decisions. For example he might argue that India, which tried to avoid becoming dependent on any one country by buying arms from Britain, France and even the US as well as the Soviet Union, should favour Moscow for a certain contract. The KGB rewarded him not only with money but by paying for his wife to travel to the Soviet Union for eye treatment.

When I arrived in Delhi, Dik was living in Agra as he had lost his seat in parliament. But then the papers reported that he was thinking of making a comeback at the next election. Naturally, the KGB was keen for him to return.

My family and I got a wonderful expenses-paid trip to see the Taj Mahal by moonlight so that, under the cover of tourism, I could visit Dik and find out his intentions. He was indeed considering putting forward his candidacy and I encouraged him heartily in this. The KGB could not afford to finance his election campaign, but he found a rich business sponsor instead. He succeeded in getting back into parliament, where he continued to lobby for Moscow, although by this time he was quite old and never reached ministerial heights again.

Another of our top agents of influence was a Congress MP named 'Shiva', who had also been on the KGB's books for years when I began handling him. He was paid a regular salary for bringing up in parliament issues of interest to Moscow, for example the question of US meddling in the Punjab, and for organising seminars, often on anti-American and anti-Chinese themes.

His positions were well known. When he stood up in parliament, fellow MPs may well have groaned and said: 'There goes that Soviet apologist again.' But as long as I was never caught actually handing over money to him, it could not be proved that a hidden hand controlled him or that he represented anybody but his poor constituents.

To some extent, I was also motivated by considerations of Shiva's welfare in being discreet about our relationship. He was not risking his freedom but he was putting his reputation on the line by cooperating with the KGB. If ever an anti-Soviet regime came to power in India, he could be persecuted in the future. Therefore I used to pretend that we met to discuss the innocent subject of Indian–Soviet cultural ties.

Our talks took place at Shiva's home in central New Delhi in one of the villas which were originally occupied by British colonial administrators. After independence, they were taken over by the Indian political elite, who all lived together conveniently close to parliament, the presidential palace and the various government ministries. I would drive down to town from my garden suburb of Vasant Vikhar in my silver Hyundai, taking a back route via Lodi Road to avoid the counter-intelligence service which kept its gaze concentrated on the country's political hub. But once when I was going to give Shiva his latest task from Moscow, I ran into unexpected trouble on the road.

Delhi was witnessing the worst unrest since Hindus attacked Sikhs in the wake of Indira Gandhi's killing by her Sikh bodyguards in 1984. This time the students were revolting because the government had introduced positive discrimination to ensure that a certain percentage of public-sector jobs went to 'untouchables' and not only to candidates from the higher castes. This may sound progressive, but the students objected that the talentless would get ahead of the well qualified purely to satisfy notions of political correctness.

Hooligans under the influence of hard liquor had joined the students with a genuine grievance in the riots, which had been going on for several days. Barricades had been thrown up all over the city, manned by students who wrapped themselves in blankets and sat round camp fires to keep out the relative cold of an Indian January. Passions were inflamed by the suicide of one student, who poured petrol over himself and set himself ablaze. Dozens of people were injured when the police opened fire on some students who tried to storm the presidential palace. Our ambassador ordered members of the Soviet colony to cut their trips to town down to a minimum as one diplomat had had his windscreen smashed by rampaging students wielding baseball bats. But the work of the KGB had to go on.

I faced the first group of student pickets almost as soon as I drove out of Vasant Vikhar on my way to call on Shiva. Their rucksacks were piled up on the grass verge, from which I gathered they were school kids who thought it fun to join in the protest of their elders. They linked arms and blocked the road, but dispersed when I gave a long blast on my horn and made clear I was not intending to drop my speed. Clods of earth and small stones rained down on my Hyundai as I drove through. That was only the start of it.

On the ring road I saw a bus with smashed windows full to overflowing with students, some of whom sat on the roof waving banners. The bus was escorted by police motorbike riders who carried bamboo canes for crowd control. Just before the exit I needed to take me into the city centre, a huge traffic jam had built up. I got out of my car and walked a few yards up the road to see what was causing the hold-up. Students were lying in the road, ignoring the shouts of a single policeman who did not dare to use his cane until reinforcements arrived.

Soon a dark blue bus drew up and dozens of policemen came to the aid of their colleague. A pitched battle ensued, the students flailing bicycle chains, the police whacking with their canes. The forces of law and order got the upper hand and the road was cleared for me to continue my journey.

Near Lodi Road, however, I encountered youths older and tougher than the school kids who had given up at the sound of my horn. Seeing they were armed with bricks, I decided I had better retreat. One brick bounced off my bonnet although fortunately it did not hit my windscreen.

Circling to find a different approach to Lodi Road, I saw another traffic jam and concluded there were more pickets ahead. My first thought was that I should abandon the car and walk the remaining mile to Shiva's house. That was until I saw the wrecked and burnt-out vehicles of other drivers who had had the same idea.

And then I spotted a garage offering to respray cars. The mechanics were sitting around looking bored as the student unrest had deprived them of work. They were delighted when I asked if they could touch up the scratch the brick had left on my bonnet and I was pleased too, for in the two hours it would take them to do the job, I would be able to conduct my business with Shiva, confident that my car was in the safest possible parking place.

'I did not expect you today,' said Shiva when I finally arrived at his house. He led me into his living room where sweets and fruits were laid out on the table. 'The caste system is the great ill of India,' he mused. It was not as rigid as it had once been, he said, but it survived because professions were associated with castes and for generation after generation the same castes performed the same jobs.

And then we turned to our own business. Shiva was due to fly to Washington as a member of an Indian parliamentary delegation. Moscow Centre wanted him to have a quiet word in the ears of a few American Congressmen. 'You must tell them your brother works in Indian intelligence,' I said, 'and through him you have found out that Delhi is worried Pakistan is using US military aid to develop nuclear weapons. Get them frothing at the mouth about that.'

This was the technique of the KGB, to spread rumour and disinformation, to mix lies with a certain amount of truth, to get other people fighting our battles for us, until in the end nobody could distinguish between truth and falsehood or say who had started the whole hullabaloo.

Lost in the Labyrinth

You may have come to the conclusion that the KGB cynically used people, but it was not entirely so. Just as the devil looks after his own, so the Soviet intelligence service took care of those who served it with loyalty.

One of my agents in Delhi was a journalist called 'Sabur'. He had been useful to Moscow for over a decade, not only because he supplied us with information on Indian politics but also because he slipped into the pages of his newspaper stories which the KGB wanted to see in print. He had a large family and was grateful for the extra income that he could earn from us.

Sabur was one agent whom I did not visit at home. Unlike the politicians who had fine residences in New Delhi, he lived much more modestly in the warren of streets in the old town where, if a white man walked, he would stick out like a sore thumb. It is often said that India has one foot in the twentieth century and the other in the sixteenth. The old town has more than historic architecture. It has historic open sewers and historic smells. However, when Sabur suffered a personal tragedy, I found myself abandoning my Hyundai, through the windows of which I usually saw Indian reality at a bit of distance, and making an unexpected walking tour of the old town.

In Delhi's chaotic traffic, where lorries mingle with sacred cows, Sabur had been knocked off his motor scooter by a car whose driver just left him lying on the dusty road. It had all happened in a split second and he had been too badly hurt to notice what the driver looked like or to memorise his registration number. His own newspaper reported the accident, mentioning that he had suffered complicated leg injuries and would need an expensive operation if he were to walk again.

Moscow Centre did not hesitate when the KGB *rezident* in Delhi suggested Sabur should be helped and immediately approved the payment of a lump sum for his treatment. The only question was how were we going to deliver the money. Visiting him at home, where he was lying bedridden, seemed to be the only option, but it was important that his family did not start asking awkward questions about where so much cash had come from.

I had the idea that Sabur could say the driver of the car had regretted his callousness and, having read the newspaper article, sought the reporter out to pay him compensation. That would sound plausible. Indians often do make amends to each other without using insurance companies; indeed swindlers sometimes deliberately put their legs under car wheels in order to extort money. Perhaps one of our Indian agents could play the part of the contrite driver and take the cash to Sabur? But no, that would not do. It would mean revealing to the agent the role the reporter had played for the KGB and there was a risk the jour-nalist, who had contacts everywhere, would recognise the visitor, for the majority of our agents were active on the political scene. In intelli-gence work, it is most undesirable to let different agents meet each other.

That left me. I would have to go into the old town and see Sabur in person. He could tell his wife that I was an English businessman whose chauffeur had been responsible for injuring him. The Englishman had not been in the car at the time of the accident but when he had seen the damage to the vehicle, he had demanded an explanation from the driver and then fired him.He had read about Sabur in the newspaper and got his home address from the hospital which had treated him. I rang the reporter and warned him to expect a visit from an 'Englishman'. 'OK,' said Sabur. 'I get the message.'

Sabur lived on one of the little lanes running off Chandi Chouk, or Moonlight Street, in the very heart of the old town. There is a famous bazaar here where beggars and shoe-shine boys mix with the motley crowd buying everything from spices to cloth, from cheap jewellery to radios. It all looked simple enough on the street plan. I parked my car at a safe distance on Asaf-Ali Road, took a taxi to the Red Fort and then set out confidently on foot. Immediately I got lost in the labyrinth, where the streets were all unmarked and twisted and turned in complete defiance of the map.

I was going to have to ask somebody for directions, which was not ideal when I was trying to keep my mission secret. Apart from that, I knew the Indians did not like to admit ignorance, especially to a foreigner, and I was likely to be sent off on the wrong route by a smiling person who would have done me a much bigger favour if he had just said: 'I'm sorry, I don't know. Why don't you ask someone else?'

I stood mesmerised by the passing crowd. Eventually I picked out a middle-aged man with a file under his arm who looked like a clerk going home after work. Thinking he would probably be reliable, I approached him when he stopped to drink a glass of sugar cane juice at a little stall. The clerk thought for a moment, then told me to take the next lane to the left, look out for a workshop with 'lots of metal pipes' and turn right. There I would find the house I needed.

The workshop with the metal pipes was easy enough to find. I heard the clashing sounds coming from within before I saw it. But in the street to the right, which was so narrow that residents could stand in their upper windows and shake hands with their neighbours on the opposite side, I could not for the life of me find number 6A.

I sought help again, this time from a Sikh who was sitting in the metal workshop reading a greasy newspaper. The street I needed, he said, was on the other side of the old town. I had gone wrong because its name sounded like that of the one just round the corner. Seeing the helpless expression on my face, he decided not to confuse me with any further directions but offered to take me to my destination on the back of his motor scooter.

Clasping the case containing Sabur's money, I hung on for dear life as the scooter swerved round corners and wove in and out among the crowds. It was hot and noisy. The air stank of spicy food, dung and exhaust fumes. We came out onto a small square. The Sikh began consulting in Punjabi with one of his fellows, a leather trader. We turned to go back the way we had come. I began to worry that perhaps my guide was not as expert as I had first thought. But finally he did deliver me to Sabur's door.

The family was expecting the 'English' guest. One of Sabur's sons, a thin lad of about sixteen, led me upstairs to see his father. The reporter cried with gratitude when I gave him the money and pressed me to stay, but I had to be getting back. It was dark when I emerged on to the street, but I anticipated no difficulties in finding the square again. If I could just reach Chandi Chouk, I could take a taxi from there.

In minutes, though, I was lost again. The streets all looked identical. From the back of the scooter, I had kept my eyes open for possible points of reference, but now I could not see anything that might help me to get my bearings. Two youths loomed out of the darkness. How would I like, for only two hundred rupees, to enjoy myself with a young girl? When I refused their offer, they deliberately misdirected me and I ended up further away than ever from anything that was familiar, hopelessly lost in a maze of back alleys and dead ends.

I began to feel anxious. I knew the *rezident* would be worrying about me by now, for I had left hours ago carrying a large sum of money. In India and other Third World countries, a person can easily be killed by bandits and disappear without trace. My worst fantasy was that the KGB would think I had defected and take reprisals against my family back in the Soviet Union. These black thoughts were all going through my head when suddenly, as in a fairy tale, I came out through a snicket onto a wide road with traffic. I flagged down a cab and was astonished to find that we were soon passing the Kashmir Gate, yards from my parked car, which only moments before had seemed to be on another planet.

The *rezident* gave me a reprimand when I reported back, but made allowances for the fact that I had only been in Delhi for three months and, in any case, even more experienced KGB staff rarely ventured into the labyrinth of the old town.

Curse on the House of Gandhi

I was not in Delhi when the murder of Indira Gandhi by the Sikhs she had entrusted to protect her shocked the world in October 1984. But I was there when her son Rajiv, who succeeded her, was blown up by a female kamikaze bomber who presented him with an explosive flower garland when he attended an election rally near Madras in 1991.

I was shocked. I had known Rajiv slightly, having met him and his Italian-born wife Sonja at official receptions. A Russian colleague woke me up to tell me the tragic news. I quickly dashed off a dispatch to my editors, then thought more carefully about what I would write in my report to the KGB. For the secret service always received far more detailed and revealing coverage than general readers back in the USSR.

I needed to speak urgently to Ram, a relatively new source whom I had cultivated myself. Hindus are not supposed to drink but Ram, a Congress Party worker, historian and freelance writer, was partial to whisky. He considered himself my friend and did not accept cash payments but I gave him gifts in exchange for his useful insights into Indian society. Best of all he liked whisky from the Soviet embassy duty-free shop.

The Indian press seemed inclined to believe that Rajiv's assassin, a Tamil woman, had acted to revenge her ethnic sisters who had been raped by Indian soldiers sent as 'peacekeepers' to the island of Sri Lanka when fighting broke out between the Sinhalese majority and the separatist Tamil Tigers. But Ram, who had been a close friend of Rajiv, suggested another version of events. According to him, the same people who had killed Indira Gandhi had pursued her son. The Sikhs, who wanted their own independent state of Khalistan, had sentenced the whole Gandhi family to death to punish Indira for having sent troops into their sacred Golden Temple at Amritsar. The Sikhs had simply used the Tamil woman to cover their tracks.

Interesting though all this speculation was – eventually a group of Tamils were executed for plotting the murder – the KGB did not really care who had killed Rajiv Gandhi. The deed was done. Others might be concerned with history, but the Soviet intelligence service looked to the future. My job was to analyse how Indian politics were likely to develop. In this too, Ram helped me by giving me the benefit of his knowledge and experience.

In my report to Moscow Centre, I argued that little would change in India as a result of Rajiv's death. Leaders might come and go but India endured. It was like an elephant, making its plodding way regardless of the tumult around it, to a destination only it understood. In that, India is very like Mother Russia which, we Russians say, is too mysterious to be grasped by the mind.

The KGB expected more than waffle and mystification from me, however, and so I also predicted that, after a transition period in which the opposition would rule, the world would see the return of the Gandhis. Indians respected the line of Nehru like royalty. To the poor and unedu-cated, they were almost divine. Whenever a Gandhi stood for election again, Indians would vote for him or her.

Rajiv, who had been a pilot, had never wanted to go into politics. It was only because his playboy brother Sanjay, the chosen successor, had been killed in a plane crash that he had reluctantly accepted the mantle of power when his mother Indira was assassinated. After Rajiv's death, Sonja was left. She was much loved by the Indians, having adopted their ways including their Hindu religion. But she concluded then that she could not take power in India. It was not because she was a woman. Indira had shown that a woman could manage this vast country as well as any man and, together with Golda Meir of Israel, had given hope to women would-be politicians around the world. Rather it was because, despite her efforts to integrate, Sonja remained a foreigner and felt she had no right to lead India.

But Rajiv and Sonja had children, I reminded the KGB in my analysis. They might well come to power in the future and the world could see the resurrection of the House of Gandhi.

The Mysterious Sikh

In view of what Ram had said about the Sikh vendetta against the Gandhis, I decided to pay more attention to the Sikh separatist movement, which had radical activists in Assam, Kashmir and Punjab. The common people in India believed that the US government was financing terrorism in those states and, although it had no proof this was true, the KGB was quite happy to let Indians go on thinking that. But it was my job, if at all possible, to provide Moscow Centre with facts.

It was certainly highly likely that the Sikh diaspora in the West was sending money for the struggle for an independent Khalistan. The turbaned Sikhs, followers of the sixteenth-century guru Nanak who outraged the multi-theistic Hindus by proclaiming there is only one God, are the equivalent of the Jews in Indian society. With their flair for engineering and mechanics, they often own small businesses and you rarely see a poor Sikh. In postwar Britain, Sikh immigrants began by driving the buses, but quickly rose to become some of the richest members of the Asian community.

Among the Sikhs, the KGB did not have a single agent. For some reason, they avoided contact with representatives of the Soviet Union. And then one day a Sikh began appearing regularly in the restaurant of the Delhi Press Club. He would come in at about nine o'clock in the evening, order a beer – Sikhs do drink although they are not allowed to smoke – and sit quietly in a corner until closing time. Nevertheless, with his bright red turban, he really stood out, for you do not often come across Sikhs in the profession of journalism. I was keen to get into conversation with him, but there were always other people around him.

One evening I was dining alone in the club when the Sikh came in. It was busy in the restaurant and the only free seat was at my table. He asked politely if he could join me. We started chatting. Soon we were exchanging cards. His name was Dilip Singh. He was about thirty, with regular features and burning eyes. He spoke excellent English, although he said he had never been outside India. He was living in the Vikram, a three-star hotel, and using a hire car, luxuries that not every foreign correspondent could afford. It was all rather suspicious. I said I would like to discuss the subject of Sikh separatism with him and he readily agreed to meet me a few days later in the cafeteria of the Ober Hotel.

During our next conversation, he made no attempt to hide the fact that he ardently supported the idea of an independent Khalistan.

'Winning political independence is not so hard,' I said. 'The difficult thing is to achieve economic independence.'

'Easy,' he replied. 'As soon as we have our own state, we will declare war on the Soviet Union, rapidly lose and become one of the richest countries in the world. Just look at the experience of Japan and Germany.'

'Joke,' he added, seeing the puzzled expression on my face. 'That's what the pessimists say. But I believe Khalistan can thrive. The Punjab is the bread basket of India. We can export not only grain but leather products and textiles. Foreign investment will flood in. Our currency will become convertible. It is India which is stifling our potential. Many of our people cannot make ends meet. There is high unemployment, especially among the young. I myself was unemployed.'

'You seem to have a good job now,' I said. But he did not want to go into that.

At a nearby table, I noticed three young Indians drinking orange juice through straws. When we got up to leave, they also paid their bill and came out after us. Singh got into his car and drove off, followed by the *troika* in a black Ambassador saloon. When I had come to the café, I had checked nobody was trailing me, even though Indian counter-intelligence rarely bothered with me anyway, and on the way back I was 'clean' too. If there was a tail, it was Singh who had brought it with him.

My boss, the *rezident*, decided to check. He launched an operation involving several KGB drivers, who watched Singh closely as he moved about town. It rapidly became clear that he was being followed the whole time by Indian counter-intelligence, which meant there was no point in me seeing him any more. The *rezident* cabled Moscow Centre, seeking permission for me to end the relationship with Singh, but it ceased of its own accord when the mysterious Sikh disappeared. He stopped coming to the Press Club and his room at the Vikram was occupied by someone else.

At about the same time, we received a tip-off from one of our highly placed Indian agents that the government had asked an American diplomat to leave Delhi. Except when alleged Pakistani spies were caught, India tried to avoid expulsion scandals, preferring to request in a quiet way the withdrawal of those who abused their diplomatic status.

We guessed that the American might have been using the Sikh as his agent, although we had no proof. Neither could we prove that the departure of the American was linked to the disappearance of the Sikh. There was never any announcement that Dilip Singh had been arrested. Perhaps he just went home to his family in the Punjab. But the coincidence was intriguing and we naturally reported it to Moscow Centre. If we could not give the bosses facts, we could at least give them food for thought about possible US involvement in the armed struggle for a free Khalistan.

All Tied Up In Knots For The KGB

We secret agents had to be ready to try anything if we saw a chance of making a catch for the KGB. I even practised yoga in the hope of recruiting Vincent Melville, a devotee to this ancient Indian art of posturing and meditation. He was the exception that proved the rule, the only American I went after when most of my attention, as I have already said, was focused on the Indians.

He lived in my suburb of Vasant Vikhar and for a long time we only knew each other by sight. Often of a morning I would see him jogging under the trees or just standing on the grass, breathing deeply. Once when I was passing Jawaharlal Nehru University in my Hyundai, I noticed him waiting on the side of the road, apparently trying to flag down a taxi. I offered him a lift and it was then that he introduced himself. He said he was teaching international jurisprudence at the university. After that, I began inviting him to my home.

The KGB thought it worth studying all Americans who came within its sights, however unlikely they were to be of use. The mere fact that they were holders of the dark blue passport and smiled like toothpaste adverts was enough for Moscow Centre. They must be probed, just on the off-chance they could prove helpful or, on the contrary, dangerous. I wanted to find out if Vincent Melville were malleable. Another possibility was that he was really working for the CIA.

My usual recipe for loosening a person's tongue did not work with Vincent. He refused my offer of a drink, saying he was teetotal.

'Have you never drunk?' I asked.

'Oh, if only,' he replied. 'I used to drink like a fish and smoke marijuana. That was when I was in college back in the States. I probably would not have finished my course and I might not even be alive today if I had not met my guru, Prapata Mekhtu. He got me into yoga and that saved me.'

'And that's how you came to India?' I asked.

'Yeah, I decided I had to see the homeland of yoga. I've been here six years, working on my postures in every spare moment when I'm not teaching law. Are you interested in yoga?'

'Yes, I've always found it fascinating,' I lied.

'Then why don't you come with me to an international yoga seminar that's held every year in Rishikesh? It's a beautiful place, at the foot of the Himalayas.'

Actually I knew very little about yoga, which was not one of the subjects taught in KGB school. Football had been my chosen form of physical education. I had always thought yogis were charlatans who fooled the public by appearing to eat fire, walk on broken glass and lie on beds of nails.

There was one famous con-man when I was in Delhi called Lakshman Rao. His face appeared in all the papers and he promised the public that as soon as he had finished perfecting himself, he would walk on water. Commercial sponsors built a special swimming pool for him in Bombay. They reckoned the place where Lakshman Rao had repeated Christ's miracle would attract tourists and pilgrims and bring in a good income for years.

The yogi trained and trained at the pool and then the day arrived when he was ready to perform his feat. Tickets sold like hot cakes, although they cost from 100 to 500 rupees at a time when the average salary was 270 rupees a month and 30 rupees were worth one US dollar. The yogi demanded that he should be paid in advance.

Frankly I was surprised that he appeared before the public at all as I had assumed he would just run away with the money. But he came to the pool, stood on the edge, called for silence, made a big show of his deep breathing, stuck his foot out and . . . fell with a great splash into the water.

He got out, towelled himself down, went to the microphone and apologised, saying that two days earlier, during a rehearsal, he had fallen and lost his inner balance, which meant he could not hold the necessary amount of air inside himself to walk on the water. But he would do it soon. The tickets would still be valid if the audience cared to come back in two months' time.

And then he dropped out of sight. Notices appeared in the newspapers saying he had been diagnosed as suffering from cancer. He lay low for several months until he popped up again, this time standing as a candidate for parliament.

'That has nothing to do with real yoga,' said Vincent. 'Come with me to Rishikesh and you will see.' I agreed. I was always glad of a chance to travel outside Delhi, for the capital is hardly representative of the country as a whole. Once I had been to Jaipur, the city of rose-pink buildings, just because the *rezident*, for some reason unknown to me, wanted a letter posted there. Now here was a chance to see Rishikesh in the state of Uttar Pradesh.

We travelled for five hours in a battered bus full of hippies. The town was truly beautiful, standing on the Ganges not far from where the sacred river rises.

People had come from all over the world to attend the seminar. Many of them greeted Vincent, who was obviously a well-known figure. We sat listening to a long philosophical speech from guru Aiengar and then broke up into small groups. I was sent off to join the beginners' class and lost sight of my friend.

Wearing a long grey cotton shirt and baggy trousers, which I still have –
they make good pyjamas – I twisted myself into knots. I stood on one leg
with my hands clasped behind my back. I sat in the Lotus position, well
half-Lotus to be precise, and did the Cowface, Cobra and Modified Fish
postures. And I breathed.

'Well, what do you think?' said Vincent when we met during a break.
'Yoga's very good for your health, but it demands an enormous input.
You must do it for at least four hours a day, preferably five or six.'

I realised I was wasting my energy with Vincent. He was a yoga fanatic
and nothing more. He simply did not have the time to work for the KGB
or the CIA. Neither did I find any other potential recruits among the
visitors to Rishikesh. I returned empty-handed to Delhi.

After the seminar, I did not continue with my posturing. Intelligence
work is very stressful and perhaps yoga would have been good for my
body, mind and spirit. But I was too busy. When I needed to unwind after
work, it was easier just to reach for the whisky, then walk over to the
fridge for the ice. It was a professional weakness. I think most of my
colleagues were like that.

RIO DE JANEIRO

Name Urtmintsev, Nikolai Nikolayevich

Born 16 January 1932

Education Higher

Special Subject Journalism

Languages Spanish, Portuguese

Military Rank Colonel

Worked in Colombia, Panama, Brazil

Marital Status Married

Sports Swimming

Hobbies Woodwork

Favourite Tipple Cuba Libre

Brand of Cigarettes Marlboro

Name Leonov, Nikolai Sergeyevich

Born 22 August 1928

Education Higher, PhD in history

Special Subject History, international relations

Languages English, Spanish

Military Rank Lieutenant-General

Worked in All countries in the Americas except Canada and Paraguay

Marital Status Married

Sports Swimming, skiing, shooting, chess

Hobbies Growing flowers

Favourite Tipple Daikiri

Brand of Cigarettes Montecristo

When Nikolai Urtmintsev was based in Latin America, Nikolai Leonov used to come out on working visits from Moscow Centre, where he held a senior position. Urtmintsev is the narrator in this joint account of an operation they carried out together in the dream setting of Rio de Janeiro.

Our Man in Rio

One hot June day I was lying by a stream in the grounds of a sanatorium outside Moscow. My reverie was interrupted by a woman's voice: 'Excuse me, but where did you get that tan?' 'In Rio de Janeiro,' I replied languidly. 'I asked you a serious question and you ...' The pretty young woman flounced off, offended. If I had told her I had been in Ethiopia or some other Third World country friendly with the Soviet Union, she might have believed me, but Brazil was just too fantastic.

I had spoken the truth, however. After serving the KGB in Colombia and Panama in the 1970s, I went to work in Rio de Janeiro in 1982. Every day it was my good fortune to see the famous Sugar Loaf Mountain and sunbathe on Copacabana Beach. Why did I need a holiday in a Soviet sanatorium, you might well ask. Because field work, even in the most glorious setting, was stressful and sometimes it was good to go home.

My leave passed quickly. After relaxing among the pine trees and seeing friends and relatives, I paid a duty call to the bosses at Moscow Centre. 'When you get back to Rio, we want you to make all the necessary arrangements for a meeting between someone from the Centre and a valuable agent who will be flying in from the United States,' they said. 'We can't risk a rendezvous with this agent in North America. But in Rio, who will notice us among the crowds of tourists?' I promised to give the matter my full attention and to come up with a logistical plan for the meeting.

The next day I flew back to Brazil on a flight which went via New York. Even when he is in transit, a good intelligence officer never sleeps. Like a whale filtering plankton, he studies and sorts out the people around him to see if anybody might be of use. On the eighteen-hour transatlantic crossing, I had plenty of time to take in my neighbours.

My attention was drawn to a man in his thirties, deep in the passages of the *International Herald Tribune*. 'Aha,' I thought, 'this comrade knows English and takes an interest in politics. He might be my man.' I deliberately dropped my cigarette lighter under his seat, excused myself, burrowed for it and got into conversation with him. He was a diplomat from a European country, going out for the first time to his embassy in Brasilia. 'If I can be of any assistance ...' said I, the experienced Latin

America hand. (As things turned out, I did not help him myself but passed him on to KGB colleagues at our embassy in the Brazilian capital.)

'Ladies and gentlemen, please fasten your seat belts,' said the pilot of the Boeing. We were coming in over Guanabara Bay. On New Year's Day 1502, when Portuguese explorers first saw the bay, they took it to be the mouth of a wide river and called it Rio de Janeiro or January River. With the building of Brasilia this century and the growth of Sao Paulo as an economic centre, the old Portuguese capital has lost some of its significance but to Brazilians Rio, the 'Cidade Maravilhosa' (miraculous city), remains the heart of the country.

The Soviet Union had a consulate and trade mission in Rio as well as a bureau of Tass, where I worked under cover as a correspondent. 'Reuters is reporting a teachers' strike. Why have you not filed?' demanded a telex from the editors in Moscow shortly after I returned from holiday. Because, gentlemen, I was out meeting an agent on behalf of the KGB. But I could not say that. Only the senior management at Tass knew of my double workload, while the editors on the desk expected me to perform as well as my bona fide journalistic colleagues.

I quickly dashed off a report to 'match' Reuters, then headed for a meeting of all the KGB staff based in Rio. We had plenty to discuss – the latest orders from Moscow Centre, who was going to meet which agent, where we were going to set our dead letter boxes. In addition, one colleague had got a new car and I still had not had a chance to test drive it.

From bitter experience, I had learnt the importance of being familiar with all the cars in the KGB pool. The *rezident*, or station chief, had once asked me to help him bring a VIP from Moscow Centre safely to a villa, where he was to meet a local agent. The idea was that the *rezident* would ferry the visitor in his Mercedes to the entrance of a department store. The guest would get out and walk through the shop to the back exit where I would be waiting to pick him up and take him on to the villa. In this way, if Brazilian counter-intelligence agents were tailing us, we would throw them off. But the plan went disastrously wrong.

My Dodge Dart, in which I was cruising about town prior to the operation, broke down. I ran to the store just in time to catch the Mercedes drawing up at the front. The *rezident* gave me a murderous look. I quickly explained the situation. 'In that case,' he said, 'you had better take the Mercedes, check you're not being followed and go straight to the villa.' I did not like to mention that I had never driven a Mercedes before and was not even sure if it had four gears or five.

I was tense at first but soon began to feel confident at the wheel of the boss's limousine. It flew like a bird along the coast road. Darkness fell.

Seeing no headlights in my mirror, I concluded we were alone.

We neared our destination. I turned up a lane, at the top of which stood the villa. Putting the handbrake on, I got out to ring the bell. The gate opened for me to drive into the courtyard but, back behind the wheel, I could not find the lever to release the handbrake. I got out a second time. Standing with my feet on the ground and the rest of my body leaning into the car, I fumbled around for the lever. I pressed some button. Suddenly the Mercedes started rolling backwards down the hill. The open door threatened to knock me off my feet as I tried to scramble back inside the moving car. I managed to bring the situation under control only when the limousine, with the VIP sitting in the back seat, was inches from a deep ditch.

I did not want to repeat that hair-raising experience, particularly when the new bigwig from Moscow Centre came out to meet the prized agent from the United States.

I prepared carefully for the coming rendezvous, choosing a suitable venue for it, considering the best routes to and from the meeting place and so on. But I heard nothing more from the bosses in Moscow. The rainy Brazilian winter, during which I had taken my summer holiday in the northern hemisphere, turned to high summer and still Moscow Centre was silent. I assumed they had called off the operation and concentrated on other work. I had plenty of Brazilian agents of my own to keep up with. The KGB was most interested in what the US was up to in a region which Washington considered its own backyard; it was also curious about Brazil itself.

And then one day in February, just when I had forgotten about the business that had been discussed when I was on home leave, I received an urgent coded telegram informing me that the representative from Moscow Centre was arriving the next day. Tomorrow! Why could they never give me a bit more notice? I would have to rearrange all my plans in order to meet the visitor at the airport.

The good news was that my guest, Nikolai Sergeyevich Leonov, although a KGB general, was an active agent and not some armchair commander who never got up from behind his desk. More than that, I had known him for years and worked with him several times before, although this was his first trip to Rio de Janeiro. He was coming out posing as a journalist on a feature-writing trip. That was a good cover, at least from my point of view. It would look natural that I, as a resident correspondent, should shepherd my colleague around, indeed spend days on end with him hanging out in the bars and on the beaches of Rio.

The Boss Flies In

The next morning I drove to Aeroporto de Galeao, where NS was due to arrive at 9.30. With time to kill, I went up to the viewing gallery and café on the third floor. 'Coffee, please,' I said to the waiter.

After the coffee I had a cold beer as, despite the early hour, it was already extremely hot. I fell into my spy's habit of observing the crowd. Young man with a bouquet, meeting a girlfriend probably. Brood of children pestering their mother: 'When is Dad arriving?' No prize for guessing who they were, then. Man in a suit and tie. He had to be meeting his boss, for only a subordinate would wear a tie in such heat.

A voice over the tannoy announced that NS's flight had landed. I went down to the arrivals hall where, a short time later, I could see him through a glass screen although he did not spot me in the crowd. He had passed successfully through passport control and was waiting to collect his luggage. In view of his rank, we could have had the Soviet consul meet him at the steps of the aircraft, but that would have drawn undue attention, so he was having to look after himself like an ordinary mortal. The consul was on hand, however, in case a problem developed.

Soon the general emerged into the hall. Not a muscle in his face twitched, although I knew what he must have been feeling. The fact that he had not been stopped at passport control meant that the Brazilians suspected nothing – and this despite the fact that their counter-intelligence service cooperated with the all-knowing CIA. We embraced and made for the exit while I gave a little wave to the consul to indicate: 'Everything's all right. Thanks for your help, mate. You're free.'

'Welcome to Rio,' I said when we were settled in the car. 'How was your flight?'

'Fine.'

'What's new in Moscow?'

'I'll tell you later.'

'Any letters for me?'

'Yes. One from your daughter, a couple of others.'

'How do you want to go the hotel? The straight way or the exotic way?'

'Show me the exotica.'

Other Soviet colleagues had been disappointed on seeing Rio for the first time. Their disenchantment was due to the fact that they had been taken by the most direct route from the airport, in an industrial zone north of the city, to the southern suburb of Leblon, where our trade mission and consulate as well as the Tass office were situated. The 'exotic way' lies through the city centre, down Atlantic Avenue and along the five kilometres of Copacabana Beach.

We set off on the Rio–Sao Paulo motorway, which was choked as usual with traffic. Our eyes began watering from the smog. My guest looked glumly out of the window at the factory chimneys and *favelas*, or slums. 'It gets most beautiful further on,' I assured him.

We drove up onto a flyover from which we could see containers and cranes in the docks at Niteroi. Suddenly the picture was transformed. The whole of Guanabara Bay opened out before us. We were on the fifteen-kilometre bridge linking Niteroi to Rio proper. If the bay was wide enough to accommodate all the fleets of the world, then the bridge was high enough to allow the tallest ships to pass under it. It was a stunning sight, which made me think that San Francisco could keep its Golden Gate Bridge.

From the bridge we could see the sixteenth-century Catedral da Candelaria at the start of Vargas Avenue which crosses Rio Branco, the modern banking district of the city. Rio's poshest restaurant, the Albamar, is here but if you want my opinion, the food is overrated.

Eventually the bridge brought us down to a coast road running alongside a series of small bays. Yachts bobbed on the water and ahead we could see Sugar Loaf Mountain. To the right a hill came into view, topped by the white Igreja da Gloria church. At night it is lit up and appears to be floating above the city.

We drove on. Flamengo and Botafogo districts were behind us now. The car dipped into a tunnel and emerged again, no longer on the shore of Guanabara Bay but by the edge of the Atlantic Ocean. Copacabana Beach was to our left.

The seafront is lined with boutiques and bars, casinos and discos. The crowds come and go in the flimsiest swimwear. Further down, past the Arpoador Fort where Brazilian independence was declared in 1822, the sands become the Ipanema Beach, not as famous as Copacabana but just as good for catching the powerful rays of the Brazilian sun.

When the beach ran out, we were close to our destination. We crossed a bridge under which the waters of Lake Rodrigo de Freitas flow into the sea and entered Leblon district in the shadow of Mount Dois Irmaos.

'It's amazing,' said NS as we walked into the Hotel Leblon, 'but wherever we were on the road, I never lost sight of Christ.' He meant the famous statue of Christ on Mount Corcovado, which is to Rio what the Eiffel Tower is to Paris or the Statue of Liberty to New York.

'That's right,' I said. 'It's impossible to lose yourself in Rio. Just look up at Christ and from the direction his hand is pointing, you can orient yourself wherever you are in the city.' Then I left my guest to freshen himself up.

While NS was in the hotel, my wife Lyudmila and I debated where we should take him for a late lunch. Avoid Chinese restaurants outside Asia and Mexican cuisine in Europe, that's the advice of an old spy. We decided he could not come to Rio without trying a *churrascaria*, or traditional Brazilian meat restaurant, but which one? Eventually we settled on the Restaurante Porcao (wild boar), which has achieved great popularity among tourists without losing the loyal custom of the locals.

Altogether the churrascaria serves twenty-four different cuts of meat from beef and lamb to pork and chicken. For the set price, you can eat as much as you like. I always had second and third helpings of cupim, the hump of the cow which, in Brazil, is a humped animal like a camel. I am told the secret of its tenderness is that it is baked in banana leaves but, although I have tried to do this myself at home, I have never produced anything as tasty as in the restaurant.

'How much has this set us back?' NS asked at the end of the meal.

'Ten dollars each for the meat. Drinks extra.'

'Incredibly cheap,' was his verdict.

After the meal NS had a few hours to rest in the hotel. In the evening, we were due to meet at the KGB *rezident*'s to discuss preparations for the visit of the important agent from the United States. Meanwhile I went into the trade mission. As I parked my car, I looked up at the windows of the hotel, where the general was doubtless asleep. I envied him. I could have done with a post-prandial nap myself. But today was the day the post arrived in the diplomatic bag and I had to check if there were any orders from Moscow Centre. In fact it contained only routine messages. However there was a thick envelope addressed to NS. Instructions for our operation, no doubt. But the rules of conspiracy as well as elementary good manners forbade me from opening it. In intelligence work, everything is done on a need to know basis. The rest of the afternoon I spent talking to more junior KGB colleagues who wanted to report their successes and failures to me.

In the evening NS came and opened the thick envelope. I was right. It contained a list of questions to discuss with the agent from America.

'The Centre is happy with the logistical arrangements you have made. Furthermore, it has been decided that in future you should handle the agent. On this occasion, I will introduce you,' said the general, who had met the mole on different continents several times before.

'As if I did not have enough work already ...' I thought.

'Here is a photograph of the agent,' NS continued. 'In case of danger, destroy it immediately.' He passed me a small envelope.

'But Nikolai Sergeyevich,' I exclaimed, 'it's a woman!' And what a woman, I said to myself as I looked at the picture of the dark-haired beauty. 'Perhaps I should take flowers to the meeting?'

'If you think that will help to make things look natural.'

The general put several questions about the planned route to the rendezvous while I continued to study the photo. Having performed my military service in the Soviet navy, I knew what the sailors say: 'A woman on board means disaster.'

'Tomorrow,' said NS, interrupting my brooding, 'we will have a look at the place you have chosen from which to observe our agent and check she is not being followed. A tail is unlikely because nobody in the US suspects her and the Brazilians are hardly going to be interested in an American tourist. But we must be sure.'

The briefing was over. We parted until the following morning.

Beach Bums

The next day we made our reconnaissance, then back at the hotel I asked NS how he wanted to spend the rest of the time until we were due to go into action. Actually I knew what he would say, for a man who has just come from Moscow to the tropics in February can have only one desire – to lie on the beach and swim in the warm ocean. I suggested we try the sands at Barra da Tijuca rather than following the herd and going to Copacabana.

'No,' he said firmly. 'It must be Copacabana. Nobody in Moscow has heard of Barra da Tijuca, but if I say I have been to Copacabana, my colleagues will be green with envy.'

Having seen the Brazilians walking the streets dressed in nothing more than bikinis and g-strings, NS was soon in his trunks with a towel tossed over his shoulder. It was 30 degrees in the shade and I knew his snow-white skin would be burnt to a crisp in half an hour if he went out like that. He was obviously annoyed, but took my advice and put a light shirt and trousers over his swimming things.

The trip to Copacabana suited me well because I had a small job to do on the way there. I had to check a lamppost on Rua Visconde de Piraja to see if one of our illegal agents had left a signal for me. Strictly speaking, I should not be doing this with an important guest from the Centre in tow as I was putting him at risk. If anything went wrong and we were caught together, I would be hauled over the coals later by the KGB bosses. But it was such a trifling job. 'Go ahead, don't mind me,' said the general.

I bow down to the illegals, the tiny band of heroes who just merge into a society instead of working under cover like me and risk far more than expulsion if they are arrested as spies. For years, they live a lonely underground life without a chance of speaking their native language or meeting anyone from home. Signals are their only way of communicating with the Motherland. A horizontal chalk mark on a wall might mean 'I need money', a vertical line 'I'm in trouble' and a wavy line 'I've made a drop at the dead letter box.' On this occasion, there was no mark at all on the lamppost, which meant my agent was all right and NS and I could go off and enjoy ourselves.

I have seen many beaches in my life, in Peru and Cuba, in Panama and Colombia, but none can compare with those of Rio. Often I have asked myself why this should be. I think it is because the Brazilians have a talent for making a feast out of the simple activities of sunbathing and swimming. Brazilian society is a colourful mixture of the carioca or whites of European descent, native Indians and blacks whose forefathers were brought over from Africa as slaves. Perhaps because slavery was only abolished last century and remains a painful memory, the Brazilians can be very touchy if they perceive a slight to their honour, but otherwise they are warm and outgoing and can always find a reason to have a party.

On the beach, they not only tan themselves and bathe but surf and go delta-planing. The young women show off the latest fashions in swimwear and take it as a compliment if you comment favourably on their bronzed bums. The sun shines on rich and poor alike, the water-skiers and the kids from the *favelas* who carry heavy baskets of drinks for sale. Among the children playing football, there are dozens of new Pelés in the making.

We joined this carnival, picnicking under a parasol and splashing in the waves of the Atlantic. But we stayed within sight of the lifeguards, mindful of the fact that back in 1962, before our embassy moved to Brasilia, the then Soviet ambassador to Brazil, Ilya Chernyshov, drowned after swimming out of his depth from a beach in Rio. A Brazilian guard of honour accompanied his cortège to the airport and he was buried among the famous politicians and great men of Russian letters in Moscow's Novodevichy Cemetery. He knew the pitfalls of diplomacy but under-estimated the ocean, with its powerful breakers and hidden currents.

Nothing spoilt our day on the beach, however. The next two days we were free for sightseeing too, as our agent had not yet arrived from the States.

After Copacabana, NS naturally wanted to have a closer look at the statue of Christ, towering 700 metres above the city. A funicular railway runs up Mount Corcovado, but we preferred to drive up to the car park and walk the rest of the way to the viewing platform. Souvenir sellers hawked crocodile skin handbags and collections of Brazilian butterflies on the path up to the statue.

On the way down again, we quenched our thirsts with a Coke in a café and I gave my boss a pep talk about the dangers of pickpockets in Rio. A Soviet delegation had been robbed on the street by a group of women thieves but the Russian poet, Yevgeny Yevtushenko, had been luckier on a recent visit. Mobbed by admirers at the airport, he had forgotten all his luggage at the taxi rank. Miraculously it was still there when friends went back to look for it. Evidently a trolley-full of bags was more than the pickpockets could handle.

The visit to Christ did not satisfy NS's hunger for heights, so we also made an excursion to the top of the Sugar Loaf Mountain. An eight-year-old cable car creaks from sea level to the summit of Mount Urca, the intermediate stage, then on to the peak of the Pao de Acucar. I am told that in James Bond films, there is always a fight in a cable car resulting in a fatal plunge for the baddy. But NS and I rode up sedately and, if we were working at all, it was only to prepare ourselves mentally for the operation ahead.

I left NS to go by himself to visit the celebrated Estadio do Maracana football stadium, the biggest in the world when it was built in 1950 to host the World Cup Final and still an impressive sight. Football is everything to the Brazilians, more than religion, more than politics. At a low point in the Cold War, it was enough for the Russian goalkeeper Lev Yashin to visit Rio and troubled Soviet-Brazilian relations were back on track. I shudder to think what the Brazilians would say if they knew I had used their sacred football terraces for meetings with my agents because it was so easy to merge with the crowd. They would be less angry if they discovered that I had slept with their wives.

By the way, on the subject of adultery, I have to tell you that the Brazilians are astonishingly liberal. If you have a lover or hire a prostitute, female or male, you can go to one of the many motels in Rio where privacy is guaranteed. You register at the gate, drive into an underground garage, go straight up into your own closed suite complete with bedroom, dining room and plunge pool, entertain yourself, then drive out again and pay at the exit. Nobody sees you, not even the waiters who bring champagne because you order it by telephone and they leave it in the dining room.

I had experience of the Brazilian motels, although I am thankful that the KGB never required me to compromise anybody in bed, for that is dirty work indeed. Of course, I did not take NS to see a motel. We were friends but still he was my boss and such a jaunt would not have been appropriate. Besides, we had a serious job to do.

Sideshow at the Carnival

The annual Rio carnival had just started. The whole city had gone completely mad. From the constant banging of drums and the never-ending processions of samba dancers in kaleidoscopic costumes, my head was spinning. How wise of the bosses at Moscow Centre to arrange for our American agent to turn up in the middle of the carnival, when the last thing the Brazilian authorities would be thinking about was the activity of Soviet spies.

Late in the evening, NS and I planned to take Lyudmila to the 'Sambodromo', the special stadium where the official carnival ceremonies take place. Hopefully by then we would have something to celebrate, for at two o'clock in the afternoon we were due to meet our agent. Her name was Maria. Would she be as beautiful in the flesh as she was in her photo?

All the arrangements for the meeting – the time, the place – had been worked out long before and the participants knew them by heart. If anything went wrong, we would abort the operation and rendezvous at the same location twenty-four hours later.

Three hours before the meeting, NS and I set off on a convoluted journey up the winding mountain roads and back into the labyrinth of the town to check that we were not being followed. All was clear. The clock was ticking towards 14.00. Time to park the car and transfer to a taxi.

A few blocks further on, we paid off the taxi driver and walked the rest of the way through the carnival crowds to the Odeon Cinema. Soon Maria would approach and pretend to study the posters advertising the films. I went across the road to the restaurant where we were going to eat in order to double-check that nobody was sitting there watching us and to choose a quiet table at the back from which we would have a clear view down the dining hall to the entrance. NS waited on the street to meet Maria. He did not need a password because he already knew her well.

I was sipping a Spanish sherry and considering the menu when NS brought Maria in. Although they were in command of themselves, I could tell that they were both nervous, like lovers who had not seen each other for a long time. Within the KGB, Maria was indeed much admired because for many years she had leaked secrets from inside an important US state body which dealt with policy towards the USSR.

NS introduced us. She was a charming woman who could have been any age from thirty-five to fifty. She was dressed with classic good taste in a white blouse and charcoal skirt. The conversation was in Spanish because Maria was a Puerto Rican American.

I do not know much more about her, for example how she was recruited by the KGB in the first place. It was not my business to know the details of my predecessors' work. I can say that she accepted money from us. It is a rare person who refuses money. However I had a strong impression that she was motivated more by political conviction. I did not feel that we were buying her or that she was selling herself. Rather we had a shared belief in the sacred idea of socialism.

We ordered lunch and talked animatedly like close friends. At least that is how our troika would have looked to the customers at the other tables. In fact NS was giving Maria advice and instructions for her next operations.

She listened attentively, then opened her bag and handed him a button covered in rose satin exactly like the ones which fastened her pink cardigan. Seeing the general's eyebrows rise questioningly, she said: 'To be on the safe side this time, I have brought you the material on microfilm. It's inside the button. There are about 1,000 frames.'

'You could have lost the button. Your handbag might have been snatched on the street and you would have lost it,' said NS.

'No, I had the button stitched on my person.' She indicated the place where the V-neck of the cardigan came down to meet over her breasts. 'Just before I came to the restaurant, I changed it for a spare one.'

We finished the last course of lunch and ordered coffee. Maria announced that she was going to the Sambodromo that evening and then flying on to Brasilia to visit a friend at the US embassy, which was the reason she had given her American employers for coming to Brazil. 'What do you advise me to see in Brasilia?' she asked me.

I began to waffle about the interesting modern architecture of Oscar Niemeyer. Maria fixed me with her black eyes, all attention. I remember that look to this day. It penetrated to my very heart and I forgot about spying and the restaurant and the people around us. It seemed that there was no one in the whole world but her and me.

NS brought me down to earth again by calling for the bill. Operational meetings should never last too long, even if everything seems quiet and there is a temptation to go on chatting after the business is completed. We made preliminary arrangements for Maria's next trip to Rio, when I would be the one to meet her. On the street we said a correct goodbye although we would have liked to embrace like comrades. Then Maria got into her hired Volkswagen and merged with the stream of traffic.

Cars honked their horns and revellers leaned out of the window waving flags. Everyone was going to the carnival.

Described by the French writer Pierre Ronde as the 'marriage of Brazil and Africa', the Rio carnival has its roots in the time when the Portuguese colonists allowed their black slaves a few days to vent their frustration through dance and drumming so that they would go back to the plantations ready to work all the harder. In 1990, the city authorities decreed that it was acceptable for revellers to parade naked, provided they painted their bodies in bright colours. During the carnival, husbands are freed from their wives and vice versa. Madness rules.

We were heading for the Sambodromo, built to accommodate the main parades when Vargas Avenue could no longer cope with the crowds of spectators. The show was scheduled to start at ten in the evening and would go on without a break until noon the next day.

With difficulty we found a parking place, quite a long walk from the Sambodromo.

'Senhor, senhor, I will guard your car,' said a little voice. It was a black boy of about twelve.

'OK,' I said. 'Take good care of it.'

'You have to pay in advance.'

'In advance?'

'It's the carnival.'

It was useless to argue with him about this, or indeed about the price which was five times higher than the self-appointed parking attendants usually charged.

We reached the Sambodromo just as the spectacle was starting. The drums deafened me at first, but gradually I got used to the noise. The rhythm permeated my body until I was nearly in a trance.

Ladies in rainbow-coloured wigs and crinolines and gentlemen in glittering top hats and tails opened the parade, after which each group of dancers became more fantastic. The crowd roared its approval and moved in time to the music. Somewhere in this throng was Maria.

Lyudmila, NS and I stayed most of the night but lacked the stamina to keep going until noon. When the sky lightened in the east, we decided it was time to go home. On the street outside, the black kid was still guarding our car.

'All in order, sir,' he said.

'Obrigado amigo, you have done an honest night's work.'

We slept in that morning. The next day NS was due to fly back to Moscow. Already today Maria would be in Brasilia. The very thought of her made my heart flutter. When would I see her again? I was supposed to handle her from now on but who knew what the future would bring? 'Pull yourself together,' I told myself. 'Today you have to take NS to Niteroi, maybe find a nice little restaurant down on Guanabara Bay.'

The satellite town is not particularly pretty, although the palm-fringed shore is beautiful. Here we found a restaurant and ordered lobster and beer. The conversation was dead. We were each thinking at our own thoughts.

Suddenly NS looked at his watch. It was half-past two.

'In an hour, Maria will fly to Brasilia,' he said, as if to himself.

I was thinking the same thing.

'You know,' he went on, 'we really should have seen her off to make sure she was OK.'

I looked at him. Our eyes met. We understood each other without words.

'Let's go. We can still make it.'

We threw our money on the table and rushed for the exit. 'Oh, to see Maria, to see Maria again, if only for a few minutes.' I knew he was thinking the same.

The car flew towards Santos Dumont, the airport for internal flights. Finally we screeched to a halt outside the airport and ran into the departures hall. We could not see Maria. A voice over the tannoy was announcing that the flight to Brasilia was ready for boarding. We went up to the glass screen separating the passengers from those waving them off. And there she was on the other side. Maria. Maria.

Whether because she sensed our presence or because she had been hoping we would come, I do not know, but she turned for an instant, smiled sadly and waved. To both of us? Or to one of us in particular?

'Goodbye Maria,' I whispered as she disappeared down the corridor. It was the last time I saw her. The best-laid plans go astray and, as things turned out, she could not come to Rio again but went to other cities to meet different KGB agents. I have never forgotten her, though, and neither has my boss whom shared experiences made my friend.

JAKARTA

Name Brykin, Oleg Dmitryevich	
Born 12 September 1931	
Education Higher	
Special Subject Journalism	
Languages English	
Military Rank Lieutenant-Colonel	
Worked in USA, Indonesia	
Marital Status Married	
Sports Boxing	
Hobbies Collecting beer mugs	
Favourite Tipple Gin and tonic	
Brand of Cigarettes Don't smoke	

On Safari with Two Suitcases

In tropical Indonesia, I hunted for wild boar, sea turtles, tigers and Americans. The KGB *rezident* asked for a tiger's tail when he gave me leave to pursue my hobby. In working hours, he expected me to deliver Yanks. Only live Americans would do.

Indonesia is a nation of incredible variety. With its 13,677 islands, it is the largest archipelago in the world, wider than the US from coast to coast, wider than the whole of Europe. Yet as far as my narrow brief for the KGB went, this exotic country was just a hunting ground, a place to trap citizens of the United States which, throughout the Cold War, Moscow called the *glavny protivnik*, or main enemy, and confronted in every corner of the world.

'How do you feel about going to Indonesia?' asked my boss at Moscow Centre where I had been stationed on the desk for three years after finishing my previous posting to New York. 'Always at the ready,' I replied like a Young Pioneer, the boy scouts of Communism whose eager motto that was. 'Good, you'll be going to our consulate in Surabaya,

Indonesia's second city,' he said. 'As usual, the task will be to target the *glavny protivnik*. Take the files and read up on the country. You'll be leaving next month.'

Down in the archives at the Lubyanka, I discovered that the file on Surabaya was unusually thin. I soon understood why. The port had been turned into a Russian naval base when the Communist-leaning Indonesian President, Achmad Sukarno, invited Soviet military specialists into his country after independence from the Dutch in 1949. There were no Americans in Surabaya. My KGB predecessor there had had nothing to do but spy on his own people and drink whisky. Perhaps he had kept quiet about this in order to prolong his stay abroad. But I felt I should say something.

'Excuse me, sir, but ...' At first the boss refused to believe me. He thought I was trying to blacken the reputation of the previous agent. But when I showed him the file, he had to agree. 'Well, if there's no *glavny protivnik*, there's no point in sending you there,' he said. 'You'll have to wait until a slot becomes available at the embassy in Jakarta.'

It took a while for a position to open up. Of the fifty or so Soviet diplomats, trade representatives and military advisers in the Indonesian capital, only about one third were working for the KGB and I had to wait my turn. More dreary desk work. But at last, in May 1967, I flew out to Jakarta to take up a post as second secretary at the embassy.

I travelled light. My first marriage was breaking down and my wife did not want to accompany me. This would have been a problem a few years earlier, but the KGB had relaxed its rules about only sending safely married men to face the temptations of life in foreign climes. So I was able to set off on my secret agent's safari carrying nothing more than two suitcases.

Emerging from the Aeroflot plane into the tropical heat at Jakarta airport, I felt as if I had entered a *banya*, or Russian steam bath. Indonesia is a wonderful place to have a holiday but a hothole in which to work. In this sweltering climate, I would have to carry my peculiar Slav version of the white man's burden for four years.

The Europeans lived separately from the Indonesians in luxurious compounds with swimming pools and servants. I had a flat in a two-storey house some distance away from the rest of the Soviet community, which suited me fine. The apartment consisted of a living room and a bedroom with a balcony overlooking highly scented tropical flowerbeds and a grove of banana palms. Later I would help the gardeners who carefully cut down the trees at nine-month intervals and put the bananas into sacks to ripen. New palms soon sprang up in place of the old. The tiny bananas of a variety called 'royal' had a rich aroma and strong flavour.

When I went on leave, I tried to take them back to Russia, but they rotted on the long flight. Call me spoilt, but I have never been able to eat the big Latin American bananas that have become a staple in post-Communist Russia since tasting the delicious little Indonesian royals.

Apart from harvesting bananas, drinking cocktails became a way of life in the tropics. My colleagues threw a party for me when I arrived and from them I learnt that foreigners could easily get round the alcohol restrictions in Muslim Indonesia by ordering crates of duty-free wine and whisky from Australia, the nearest continent. When the sun went down at six o'clock, regardless of the season, it was a relief to drink scotch with ice and coke. To tell you the truth, I sometimes made darkness and the drinking hour fall earlier by drawing the living room curtains.

The tropics induced a languid pace of life. List-making Westerners are frustrated in bureaucratic Russia, where they must be satisfied if they achieve one goal in a day. But in Indonesia, if you ticked off one task in a week, you were doing well. However, the *rezident* did not see it that way. His peptalk was the same for all new arrivals. 'You think time has stopped. A month passes in this heat and humidity, six months, a year. But what have you done today for the KGB? What trophies have you brought your *rezident*?'

It was time for me to start hunting.

A Narrow Escape from Wedlock

I arrived in Jakarta only one year after President Sukarno, a friend of the Soviet Union, was forced to hand over power to General Raden Suharto, an anti-Communist, following a short war in which some 300,000 people were killed. Suharto's 'New Order' government looked to the West and was smashing Indonesia's Communist Party, which had been the biggest in the region after China's. The Americans were in favour now, while the political climate was not very auspicious for Russians. But it was sheer hell for Indonesian Communists, who were being herded into jails and executed.

I assumed some of my KGB colleagues were liaising with the local Communists, who had been forced underground. I was not involved in this work and consequently know nothing about it. The Lubyanka only gave its staff information on a 'need to know' basis. My task, as I have already said, was to try to recruit Americans, who were beginning to swagger in Jakarta now that Indonesian politics had taken a turn that suited Washington.

It was not easy. True, having worked as a translator at the UN in

New York, I spoke good English and knew the ways of the Americans. Presumably that was why I had been chosen for the job. But I could not just walk up to the US embassy, knock on the door and ask if anyone wanted to become a traitor. My first task on arrival in Jakarta was to build up a network of contacts, which I had to do more or less from scratch since my KGB predecessors had not been generous with their address books. I need Indonesians and foreigners who could introduce me to Americans in circumstances which would at first seem innocent.

I socialised tirelessly, accepting invitations to every diplomatic cocktail party going. Soon I latched onto Ron, who was a second secretary at an African embassy which must remain nameless and, like me, a fancy-free bachelor. Ron, who spoke both English and French fluently (so if you are trying to guess whether he came from an English-speaking or Francophone African country, you are wasting your time), was a very merry fellow and a bit of a Don Juan. He used to invite women for drinks in the middle of the afternoon. Air hostesses, touring actresses, Christian missionaries, embassy secretaries and even senior diplomats' wives attended his hen parties. Sometimes we had sex with the girls. Why not? We were both single.

Of course, I tried to make my own private dates with the women, but I did not have much success. One guest from a Western embassy told me straight out: 'We are not allowed to go out alone with Russians. We know you are all spies.' Later Ron himself said to me as we were dining together in a Chinese restaurant: 'Oleg, I know you're a Soviet agent and you need contacts. I'm also an intelligence officer. I'm trying to get information on the attitude of Western countries to my homeland. You're a nice guy, a good drinking companion. So let's keep it friendly. Don't get in my way and frighten off my customers.' I laughed and tried to turn the whole thing into a joke.

Unbeknown to Ron, however, I had managed to date one of the women, a beautiful calm, blue-eyed Dane called Molly. She worked as a secretary at her country's trade mission. She had been to my home but made clear she was not prepared to sleep with me as her regular boyfriend was a marine at the US embassy. That was just fine by me, I said.

The three of us started going out to bars and restaurants together. The marine, a freckled redhead called Bob, was a big, brawny lad with a very small brain located somewhere between his enormous shoulders. For him, a whole bottle of whisky was just an aperitif. Often, at the end of the evening, I would help poor Molly to carry him home. Once, when he was exceedingly drunk, I managed to photograph his identity card. Moscow Centre said they had no information to suggest Bob or Molly were *provocateurs* and gave me the go-ahead to pursue the young Yank.

I did not have high hopes for Bob himself, for he really was incredibly stupid, but I thought he might lead me to more interesting Americans at the embassy, so I continued to entertain him and his girlfriend. One evening I asked him jokingly if he was not afraid to be dining with a Russian, as it was a well-known fact we were all spies. 'Not at all,' he said. 'I am reporting all our meetings to the head of security at my embassy.' That was that, then. Bob must be written off. But it was not quite the end of the story with the lovely Molly, who had come to regard me as a close friend.

Her mother fell ill and so she broke her contract in Indonesia to return urgently to Denmark. Our agents in Copenhagen courted her for a while but Moscow Centre decided I should pay her a visit in person. On my next leave, I flew out to Copenhagen with instructions to make her a direct offer of work as a KGB informer. She was not an American but she was from a Western country which was not to be sniffed at. Popping the question was not easy, as her mother was sitting in the flat the whole time, but when we got a moment to ourselves I said: 'Molly, how would you like the help Soviet intelligence?' Her reply astonished me so much that I nearly dropped my whisky.

'Oh, Oleg,' she said. 'I love you, I love you. I will help the KGB if you will marry me.' She was sincere, I am sure. It was not a joke or a honey trap by the Western intelligence services. My mind raced. What should I do? At last I said I was sorry but I was still married and, as I was not a Muslim, I could not take a second wife.

I was ready to do almost anything to ensnare poor souls into working for the KGB. But not if that meant allowing myself to be recruited as a husband. I had had enough of wedlock.

On and Off the Cocktail Circuit

Back in Jakarta, I was back at square one. I had drawn a blank with Bob and Molly's price had been too high but the *rezident* still wanted results. I returned to the cocktail circuit, chatting, smiling, drinking too much, always hoping to make a catch.

It was hard work, although others might not appreciate it. 'You've got nothing to do,' said the ambassador one day. 'Come and translate *War and Peace* for me.' He was giving a film show for his guests and needed a simultaneous English translation of the epic movie. Evidently I satisfied him, for he had me back in the unventilated projectionist's booth several more times to do the English voice-over for his films. In the end, the only way I could get out of this time-wasting obligation was to invite his wife into the booth, at which he became jealous and stopped asking me.

On another occasion, diplomatic colleagues who thought I had nothing better to do sent me off to buy Wiener Schnitzels for 400 guests invited to a reception the Soviet embassy was holding to celebrate May Day. Indonesian food was highly spiced and the foreigners often preferred European dishes for their parties. The chef at the Hotel Indonesia, a jovial Dutchman called Frans, helped me out with the schnitzels in exchange for which I gave him my recipe for Chicken Kiev. If you go to the Hotel Indonesia, you will find Chicken Kiev à la Oleg on the menu to this day, evidence that we KGB agents were involved in more operations than James Bond ever dreamed of.

I'm sorry, I'm being sarcastic. Do not think I am complaining, however. My life in Jakarta was much easier than it had been in New York, where I lacked diplomatic immunity and risked arrest at any moment. Here I was secure. I was also materially better off for, although my salary was no higher, my spending power was greater in this developing country where foreigners were kings compared with the locals.

After independence from the Dutch, Sukarno had turned Jakarta into a city of grandiose monuments, dominated by Monas Square, one of the biggest piazzas in the world. Khrushchev, who wanted to encourage Indonesia as a counter-balance to China, helped him to modernise, giving him money for a giant stadium. Yet much of the old character and ethnic colour remained in the city, which was home to communities of Chinese and Indians as well as Indonesians.

I loved the bazaars, where the traders and customers argued in a dozen different languages and dialects – Malay, Javanese, Balinese. Braving the maniacal rickshaw drivers, who would lynch any motorist careless enough to knock one of their number off his pedal car, I would drive my Volga saloon to Glodok, the market where you could buy anything from fried frogs' legs and the stinking durian fruit, to pork. Yes, pork. Indonesia was a Muslim country but the Chinese were allowed to sell pork, so pigs were kept in cages at the bottom end of the market.

When I tired of Jakarta, which was not only hot but also dirty and full of biting insects, I went up into the nearby Punchak mountains to find relief in the cooler air. Often I would rest in the luscious botanical gardens at Bagor and watch the myriad brightly coloured butterflies flit over the bamboo. Close by was the presidential palace where, in his day, the 'progressive' Sukarno had kept nearly as many concubines as there were butterflies in the garden.

Occasionally my job brought me benefits for which the word 'perk' is wholly inadequate and which compensated me for all the Wiener Schnitzels and other humiliations life as a servant of the Soviet cause could throw at me. Once, for example, after I had gone with a colleague to meet an Indonesian agent in Surabaya, stopping on the way to visit the ancient Buddhist temple of Borobudur in central Java, I had a few days spare for a holiday on the paradise island of Bali. Pity me. The KGB paid my expenses because I was on an assignment, but what work could I do in paradise?

Such trips were rare, however. Mostly, I spent my time standing with a gin and tonic in one hand, a bowl of peanuts in another, saying, 'So how do you like Indonesia?' and always hoping to hear the reply: 'Just fine, come and meet this fascinating American who has just arrived.'

One representative of the 'main enemy' I met with tedious regularity was Charles, the head of station for the CIA. I knew his role, although he did not advertise the fact, and likewise he knew perfectly well who I was. It was a game. But he broke the rules of play in a very crude way.

'Hi, Russian spy,' he used to say in a loud voice whenever I arrived at a reception and the guests would move away from me, as if I had a problem with my personal hygiene. I have no doubt that, just as we saw the Americans as our principal opponents, so they regarded us as the 'main enemy' too, although I do not know if they actually used that term. But to embarrass me in such a way was not the done thing. I decided I would have to teach Charles a lesson.

I took a piece of card, drew the stars and stripes on it and wrote underneath: 'I am an American spy.' Then I engaged a colleague to assist me. At the next cocktail party, I went up to Charles and clapped him on the shoulder while at the same instant my friend ran up from behind and stuck the placard on his back. Thus adorned, he walked around for half the evening with the guests sniggering behind his back until the host, the Dutch ambassador, whispered something in his ear and he withdrew to attend to his appearance.

That was not all, however. At the end of the party, I persuaded the Indonesian who called out the numbers of the limousines arriving to take the guests away to make a special announcement: 'CD 3864, car for the CIA station chief at the door.'

Probably I should have left it at that. But, although I have become relaxed and sweet-natured in my retirement, I was a pugnacious little guy then and I had one more punishment up my sleeve for Charles.

Near the botanical gardens at Bagor, there was a Chinese restaurant which also used to serve *blinis* or Russian pancakes. I suspect this was a hangover from the days when the Indonesians catered for the hundreds of Russian construction workers and advisers who helped Sukarno. The Americans loved this restaurant as much as we did and, sure enough, I soon ran into Charles dining there. I was having *blinis* with black caviar myself. They were delicious but the plate had not been warmed to keep them hot. I called the waiter over, sent my compliments to the chef, said I wanted to treat my friend at the table in the corner to some of these delicious pancakes, but would he be sure to have the plate piping hot this time?

The *blinis* were delivered on my behalf to Charles. He looked up questioningly, wondering if I was trying to be friendly, and burnt his fingers on the red-hot plate. He had his answer. I left the restaurant, laughing like a drain. As far as I was concerned, my cocktail party adversary and I were now quits.

A Trophy for the *Rezident*

When they were not mixing and fulfilling the requirements of protocol, most of my colleagues at the Soviet embassy passed the time shopping for gold jewellery or snorkelling to build up their coral collections. I was not an acquisitive person – I arrived in Jakarta with two suitcases and left with two when my four years were up – and I preferred to spend my free time getting to known Indonesia. It was not essential for work, which was dominated by the search for potential American recruits, but it seemed to me a shame to live in a country and not make an attempt to learn its language and see its life. I wanted memorable experiences, not souvenirs.

A course of lessons with an Indonesian teacher enabled me to communicate with the locals and soon I had several friends outside the expatriate community. One was a Chinese businessman called Chang, who had made his money from rice, tapioca and tobacco. He took me on an expedition into the jungle near Bandung on the island of Java. I was the only white man, cosseted by about twenty native porters and other servants as in colonial times. Chang was using me as a guinea pig. He believed there was serious tourist potential in jungle adventure holidays. 'If you can stand it, I will start to advertise,' he said. I survived and he went into the business. Many tourists who go into the Javanese jungle today are following a path first beaten by this KGB agent at leisure.

Another friend was a senior Indonesian policeman called Anwar. I had met him in a swimming pool and asked him to find a guard for my house, which he did. He introduced me to his fellow officers, who showed me how the locals lived and several times took me hunting.

The chase for wild boar was conducted in a most unusual manner. We found a river bed, dry as a bone outside the rainy season, and erected reclining chairs along the banks. Local dog handlers, whose beasts were normally kept in cages and starved until their ribs showed through their coats, released their animals to chase the boar down the channel. Without even rising from our chairs, we shot several pigs with rifles. I got the meat, since neither the policemen nor the dog handlers ate pork and only hunted for the sport. After we had killed the boar, we turned our guns up into the palm trees overhead and brought down a shower of dead monkeys to reward the dogs.

It was rather barbaric. Personally, I preferred another outing when the policemen took me looking for turtles' eggs on the shores of the Indian Ocean. We travelled by jeep, which soon turned off the smooth highway into another dry river bed, down which we bumped for what seemed an eternity. But it was worth all the discomfort to see the dreaming ocean in the pink light of sunset.

We did not dare to light a camp fire for fear of frightening off the turtles so we ate a simple picnic in the dusk. Soon the moon came up over the water. And then the turtles began emerging from the waves, gentle giants crawling across the sand to a place where they all laid their eggs together. It was more like a ceremony than a process of nature. The stately turtles paid us spellbound human spectators no attention whatsoever.

Later, when they had withdrawn back to the sea, we did light a fire and fried some of their eggs, which are treasured in Indonesia as an aphrodisiac. I went down to the water's edge, where a few turtles were still splashing in the foam, and two of them let me stand with a leg each on their broad backs and carried me along the shore. The policemen did not approach the ocean, but stayed well up the beach. It is a strange thing, the Indonesians being island people, but many of them are afraid of the sea.

An angry tiger seems to me more terrible but the Indonesians say: 'He who kills the tiger will inherit his spirit and live forever.' On another occasion, the policemen invited me to go with them on a tiger hunt. At first I thought they were joking, but they were deadly serious. They were planning to fly by helicopter to the island of Sumatra, where the king of the jungle still reigned, albeit shakily, for he was becoming an endangered species. 'You're welcome to join us,' they said. 'Make your mind up.'

For a venture at once so dangerous and so useless from a KGB operational point of view, I needed the permission of the *rezident*. 'Yes, you can go,' he said coolly. 'Take care and bring me back a tiger's tail.'

The tiger hunt turned out to be the worst nightmare of my life. The first night we stayed in a guesthouse consisting of a group of wooden huts on the edge of the jungle. We ate a huge meal of shark's fin soup, bat kebabs, fried frog legs and spicy carp pie, washed down with beer which was nearly hot from the can. I tossed and turned on the board that

was my bed, nauseous from the stink of the pillow on which dozens of
people before me must have lain. Half a bottle of Johnny Walker finally
knocked me out and I slept. The next morning I was woken by the
laughter of the servants. It turned out that what I had taken for the pillow
was in fact a bolster that people in the tropics put between their legs to
absorb the sweat when they sleep. This piece of information put me off
my breakfast.

We tramped for five or six hours into the jungle, the servants slashing
at the bamboo. When we arrived at a place deemed to be suitable, they
dug a deep pit and built a stockade beside it. They had been carrying two
lambs, which I assumed would be killed and roasted. But no, they were
tied to stakes down in the pit to lure the tiger with their bleating. We sat
behind the stockade, guns at the ready.

The deal was the policemen would get the meat of the tiger, which
was said to enhance male potency, while I would get the skin, a valuable
prize. We waited, all day. The tiger did not appear. 'How long do we have
to stay?' I asked. 'Three days, a week, as long as it takes.' I was appalled.
We could not move outside the stockade, for fear of disturbing the tiger.
The conditions inside were hellish. The heat was indescribable, clouds
of insects buzzed all round and we had to go to the toilet where we stood.
I kept drinking whisky to blot out the horror but that turned out to be a
mistake. In the end, I started to have hallucinations and had to be air-
lifted out by helicopter.

The policemen stayed on until they finally shot a tiger. It was illegal,
I am sure, but busy as they were pursuing Communists, the authorities
did not have time to care about wildlife protection. The Indonesian
police, like police in most poor countries, were corrupt and could have
got out of trouble with a bribe anyway.

Because I had not stayed the course, my friends were not able to give
me the tiger skin, not even his tail for the *rezident*. As a consolation,
they gave me the skin of a boa constrictor which, with a simper, I
presented to my boss instead.

'Very nice, Comrade Brykin,' he said. 'Now, when are you going to
bring me an American hide?'

To Catch a Yank

I had established, by this time, some productive agents including a
Japanese source who gave the KGB political information on the whole
South-East Asian region. He was based in Jakarta but thought it was safer
to meet me in third countries, so on different occasions I flew to Sydney,

Singapore and Kuala Lumpur to see him. He provided particularly valuable intelligence on the activities of the Americans in the Philippines. You see, you did not necessarily need a Yank to tell you what the 'main enemy' was up to. And yet, the Lubyanka wanted to hear it from the horse's mouth.

Always I was on the lookout for a top-class US traitor. I could never forget my task, even when I went with my Dutch shipping friends to the fantastically diverting Jakarta all-night prostitutes' market or when I visited the volcanic spa at Bandung. After the steam bath, the blind masseur – one of a special caste of Indonesian masseurs who, I was told, were blinded in childhood to intensify their sense of touch – would roll me out like pastry. And all my thoughts would melt away, except that one. What should I do to catch a Yank?

One American came my way without making any effort. I was driving into the embassy when I spotted a hairy young white man standing by the roadside. It was quite a rare sight in Indonesia in the 1960s and I pulled over to see if he was in trouble. He was just a hippy, one of the first of a wave of Western backpackers which was to hit the Far East in later years. But he was a US citizen. 'Take a seat, Mike,' I said, for that was his name.

He had come out to Indonesia on a one-way ticket, hoping to find casual work to finance his further wanderings, but he had not had much luck and, when I picked him up, was without a cent. I took him home, fed him, made a bed up for him in my garage and gave him a little money. It was not a promising investment, I knew, but my mind began working on the question of how Mike or perhaps friends of friends of Mike could somehow, one day be useful to the KGB. That was how I worked, with such will-o'-the-wisps. You can imagine how frustrating it was, how I longed for a concrete result.

I was due to go on leave. I gave Mike a bit more pocket money and told him I would see him when I got back. Imagine my surprise when, on my return, I found an invitation to his wedding in my mailbox. In the month I had been away, he had worked fast, getting himself engaged to a young woman from a very rich Chinese family. He was asking me to be his witness, as I was the only other person he knew in Jakarta.

The wedding reception was lavish. Dressed in cloth of gold, the bride and groom sat on thrones while some 300 guests queued up to give them presents, mainly envelopes containing money. The American ambassador attended as a friend of the bride's family, although much good that did me. I could hardly try to recruit such a public figure. Our Chinese hosts offered us a delicacy – boiled monkey's brain, which we were invited to suck up out of the skull with straws. The ambassador and I

dashed for the bar, neither of us sure whether this was an example of
Chinese hospitality or black humour.

The Chinese family was of course using Mike to facilitate emigration
to the United States. Whether he understood that or not, I do not know,
but he seemed happy enough with his fortune. I wished him well. I had
missed my chance to exploit him, been too slow, allowed the Chinese to
get ahead.

Luck was waiting for me instead in a sleazy downtown bar. What else
was there to do but drink in the middle of the monsoon season? I had
gone out with a colleague from the embassy and it was he who first
spotted the solitary American ordering himself another whisky. But it
was I who spoke English and had all the best chat-up lines. My new
friend turned out to be a US serviceman called Rogers. We got on so well
that he invited me to visit him the next day at his hotel. If hotel was the
word. In a run-down one-storey building, in a filthy room in which the
sluggish overhead fan barely stirred the humid air, he was lying on a
pallet, reading a book. He brightened when he saw me and, over whisky
and a tin of black caviar which I had brought along, told me his sad story.

Rogers was serving in a unit responsible for supplying the US army
but, as his contract with the forces was due to run out, he was trying his
hand at other business. He had bought three cranes cheaply, expecting to
sell them at a good profit to a client in Singapore. But the customer had
gone bankrupt and he had been advised to come to Jakarta instead. Here
nobody wanted the cranes. He was out of money and the US embassy,
which he had approached for the air fare home, had shown him the door.

He was ripe for the taking but how best should I do it? Back at the
embassy, I discussed the problem with the *rezident*, who was excited
about Rogers but concerned lest I scare him off with a hasty move.

At one of our next meetings, the American mentioned in passing that
he had taken part as a mercenary in the overthrow of Sukarno, keeping
a diary about the events of 1965 and 1966 when a Communist coup
failed and subsequent anti-Communist riots gave the pro-US Suharto
the excuse to take power. It was history now and of no great interest to
the KGB but I offered Rogers a few hundred dollars for the diary as a
means of hooking him.

Then he himself began to ask what he might do for us. The Lubyanka
wanted information about the American army. He said he could give it
for $100,000, in advance. Naturally, I refused those impudent terms but
gave him $500 and told him he would get more when I had assessed the
quality of the material he brought. He went away to Singapore and
returned a month later with a file of secret documents which Moscow
Centre valued at $10,000.

I paid him. He was pleased. So was the *rezident*, which made me happy. It seemed that Rogers and the KGB were in business.

Thirty Pieces of Silver

Some months later, in the wee small hours of the tropical morning, I was drifting off to sleep to the monotonous sound of the air conditioning when my guard raised me with a telephone call. I had had a few security problems in the past. Thieves had stolen my talking Bea bird, although they hardly got any secrets for I had only taught him to say 'who's a pretty boy?', and a deserter from the Indonesian army had broken into my flat. What could it be this time?

I went out onto the balcony and saw a car parked below. 'Who's there?' I shouted. In reply, I heard the voice of my agent Rogers, but it did not reassure me. On the contrary, I was overcome with an instinctive feeling of danger. On my way downstairs, I switched on a tape record that I kept hidden in the hall. 'Come in,' I said. Rogers was with a companion, whom he introduced as Günther, a second secretary from the West German embassy.

I poured out the whisky. We talked about this and that. Rogers said he had been in Singapore again. The German didn't say much. The spools of the tape recorder turned silently. I sensed they were going to try to turn me. I was right.

'Oleg,' Rogers began rather sheepishly, 'we have a proposal for you. Here's an air ticket and $30,000 in cash. We'll fly with you to Singapore, from there you will go to the US where you will receive another $30,000 and political asylum.'

Why me? Did the Western intelligence services sense that I was vulnerable? I think not; they were just trying it on. They could not have known of the growing doubts I had about Communism because I kept them strictly to myself. Besides, I might hate the Soviet political system, but I was always a patriot of my Russian homeland. I could not for one moment imagine myself betraying my country.

I reacted immediately and very angrily. The offer of $30,000 made me think of the thirty pieces of silver Judas received for betraying Christ. 'How dare you?' I shouted at Rogers, throwing my whisky in his face. The German ran for the door but Rogers stayed to listen to my tirade of abuse. I was genuinely furious. It was illogical, I know, for Rogers was only trying to do what I had done to him. He was the hunted, turning on the hunter. But I could not see it that way then.

'You lousy scum, I helped you when you were down, found you work, and now you have the nerve to insult me etc etc ...' At which Rogers began to cry and justify himself. He was sorry, he said. He would never have approached me in this way but the CIA had forced him. They had found out about his shady business deals and threatened him with court martial if he did not try to trap me.

'Who sent you, exactly?' I demanded. 'Mr Forsyth,' he said. 'He's waiting at the airport now to see you off to Singapore.' I realised he meant Charles Forsyth, the CIA station chief in Jakarta, my old sparring partner on the cocktail party circuit. At this, I exploded with rage, took Rogers by the scruff of the neck and literally booted him down the stairs.

I lay awake for the rest of the night, wondering if I had handled the situation correctly. One thing I knew for certain: even if I had been offered a million dollars, I would not have gone over to the Americans. I could not have stood life in exile, never able to see my beloved Russia again.

The next morning, I had to make my report to Moscow Centre. It must be carefully worded for my future career depended on how the bosses interpreted the matter. Previously, whenever the CIA or FBI so much as approached a Soviet citizen working abroad, he was immediately called home because Moscow considered that the spotlight had fallen on him. This was a wasteful policy because a replacement had to be prepared, which took time. The Americans were not so cautious. They did not automatically withdraw their personnel from countries just because the KGB had made an advance. Gradually the Lubyanka began to see the sense of the opponent's policy and changed its own to match.

Clearly there had been no disloyalty on my part. The tape, recording my angry scene with Rogers, proved that. But would the bosses conclude that I had been lit up too brightly or was my position in Jakarta still tenable?

I waited nervously for an answer. Finally they decided that I could stay on but I must move from the flat, where I had had considerable independence, to the compound where the rest of the Soviet community lived. This I did and, keeping a low profile, worked out the rest of my tour of duty in Indonesia, which ended in May 1971.

The incident with Rogers did not end my career with the KGB but, back in Moscow, office politics did. After twenty-one years in the service, I chose to retire with honour rather than resist. I got a new job, welcoming foreign delegations on behalf of the State Committee for Science and Technology, which was less exciting but also less stressful than intelligence work.

I have not been abroad again since 1971, but I have no regrets. My career took me over much of America, including Alaska, and half of Asia, not to mention Australia. That is more than most people see in a lifetime.

LISBON

Name Kovalyov, Eduard Vasilyevich	
Born 12 March 1932	
Education Higher	
Special Subject International Relations	
Languages Spanish, Portuguese, English	
Military Rank Colonel	
Worked in Cuba, Portugal	
Marital Status Married	
Sports Basketball, table tennis	
Hobbies Reading	
Favourite Tipple Gin and tonic, Cuba Libre	
Brand of Cigarettes Don't smoke	

The Right Place at the Right Time

Soldiers with red carnations protruding from their rifles greeted me when I arrived in Portugal in 1974. I had flown into a country in the middle of a revolution, a bloodless one which was to change not only Europe's westernmost nation, a backwater which had been under fascist rule since the 1920s, but my own professional life as well.

I heard about the revolution on the radio in Moscow, where I was sitting at the Foreign Ministry, making last-minute preparations to go under diplomatic cover to work for the KGB in Peru. My air ticket was already in my pocket. I was due to fly out to Lima on 10 May to continue a Latin American career which had started when I served in Castro's Cuba in the 1960s. I was interested in Latin America, of course, but secretly disappointed that I was going to miss the events in Portugal. 'Never mind,' I told my wife Valentina, who had rung me at work and excitedly told me to switch on the radio, 'perhaps we will get a chance to go there in five years' time.'

On the eve of the Soviet May Day holiday, I received a telephone call from my KGB boss, General P. I was to come out immediately to Yasenevo, the modern concrete complex on the edge of Moscow which replaced the old Lubyanka as the headquarters of the foreign intelligence service at the start of the 1970s. So urgent was the matter that I was allowed to take an ordinary city taxi to Yasenevo, which KGB staff normally approached in special limousines or by bus and then on foot so that cab drivers did not find out what the new building was. The plaque on the wall identified it as the National Research Centre, but the world was not fooled for long and soon everyone knew it was the new KGB HQ. I felt nervous in the taxi, for I did not know why I was being summoned by General P and imagined the worst, that I had done something wrong and was about to be reprimanded.

'Have you heard about the events in Portugal?' said my boss, coming straight to the point. 'Indeed I have,' I replied, thinking how fortunate it was that Valentina had alerted me to the radio broadcast, enabling me to sound intelligent on the subject of Portuguese politics. Also in my favour was the fact I was the only KGB officer available at that moment who spoke some Portuguese. 'Forget about Peru. Andropov wants you to go to Lisbon,' said General P, referring to the KGB head himself. I was thrilled.

There was a small problem, however. Portugal and the Soviet Union had not enjoyed diplomatic relations since the Bolshevik Revolution and so I could not go to Lisbon under my usual diplomatic cover. However, I had worked as the Soviet press attaché in Havana. 'That's close enough to journalism,' said General Petrov. 'Perhaps we can get you in as a Tass correspondent if Zamyatin will have you.' He meant Leonid Zamyatin, director-general of the official Soviet news agency.

'Mmmm,' said Zamyatin, reclining in a leather armchair in his office on Tverskoi Boulevard. 'I had a chap in Asia with the same surname as yours. I don't know you, of course. But I gather Andropov is keen to post you. All right, you had better go and do your KGB business in Lisbon but don't forget to send Tass a news story from time to time.'

So it was that, thanks to the Portuguese revolutionaries, I not only moved from the Third World to Europe, which was considered a more prestigious sphere of work within the KGB, but also shifted from the diplomatic field into journalism. There is nothing more exciting for a journalist than being in the right place at the right time and in May 1974, Portugal was *the* place to be.

The Lisbon Spring

Unfortunately I was not allowed to take Valentina with me when I set out on what I expected to be a short mission of six months at the most. Instead, I travelled with Vladimir Kuznetsov, who was a bona fide journalist for the government daily *Izvestia*. We flew via Paris as there were no direct flights from Moscow to Lisbon in those days. We would have liked to linger a little in Paris, but Moscow Centre was impatient for us to plunge into the maelstrom of revolution.

When we went to the Portuguese embassy in Paris to apply for visas, we found it had been closed since 25 April, the day the revolution started, and all the diplomats loyal to the old regime had fled. Only an elderly Bulgarian émigré remained to guard the building. 'Lord, I've spent my life running from the Communists and now the Russians have come to Paris,' he cried. We tried to calm him, explaining that all we wanted was to get into Portugal.

At this point, we were joined by Vadim Polyakovsky, a thrusting young journalist from the Soviet magazine *Za Rubezhom* (Abroad). 'I'm going to Lisbon without a visa,' he declared. It was all right for him. He was only a hack who could afford to take risks but I, as a KGB officer, had to be careful to avoid any international scandal and stick to the official channels.

Back in the hotel, I telephoned Raul Rego, who had been the editor of the opposition newspaper *Republica* when the Fascists still ran Portugal. In Lisbon the phone was answered by Vitor Dias, assistant to Señor Rego who had become the new Information Minister. I asked if he could help me and my colleague from *Izvestia* to receive visas. 'Soviet journalists can come to our free country without visas,' said Señor Dias. 'We will meet you at the airport.'

The funny thing was that the eager beaver Polyakovsky, who had gone ahead of us, had his flight diverted to Faro in southern Portugal because of thunder storms over Lisbon, so Kuznetsov and I were the first Soviet reporters to reach the capital in revolution. In fact, I think we were the first Soviet citizens to reach Lisbon since 1917.

The Portuguese welcomed us with open arms. Soldiers were everywhere but their guns were silent, not shooting but sprouting the carnations which were the symbol of the revolution.

Señor Dias installed us in the President Hotel near Marquis de Pombal Square, an establishment which was quite basic despite its three stars. It was not that Kuznetsov and I wanted luxury, but we needed good telecommunication links, so we moved to the five-star Altis Hotel on Rua Castilho, where the operator could get us a line to Moscow via Paris.

I dictated my reports to the copy taker at Tass headquarters. She hated me because I sent reams of stuff. 'I hope your tongue blisters like my fingers,' she said to me after one particularly long session.

My first dispatch for Tass was devoted to the appointment of General Antonio Spinola as head of the Junta for National Salvation or 'Soviet for National Salvation' as I preferred to call it. For in the Soviet Union, 'junta' was a dirty word and Moscow was of course hoping that Portugal would take a leftish path.

My instructions from the KGB, however, were to observe, not interfere. The Soviet Union was taking part in negotiations to enhance security and cooperation in Europe, which in 1975 were to culminate in the signing of the Helsinki Final Act. One of the clauses of the act states that countries should respect each other's territories and refrain from interference in each other's internal affairs. In view of this, Leonid Brezhnev himself was insistent that Portugal should be left to develop in its own way and under no circumstances be pushed towards Communism. He was probably as tempted to meddle as an alcoholic is to have another vodka, but the Kremlin leader who had promoted Communism around the world and, when it looked like slipping in Czechoslovakia in 1968, sent tanks in to preserve the system, really did keep his hands off Portugal.

The country had been a monarchy before 1910, when King Manuel II was deposed in a popular revolution. There followed sixteen years of anarchy, in my opinion like the socially unjust free-for-all in Boris Yeltsin's 'democratic' Russia, until Marshal Antonio Oscar de Fragoso Carmona took over in 1928. Carmona invited Dr Antonio de Oliveira Salazar to become Minister of Finance to sort out the economy, and within a short time, power passed entirely to Salazar, who became a dictator like General Franco in neighbouring Spain. For an astonishing four decades and more, Salazar held Portugal in his grip, breaking up protests and jailing left-wing opponents. Western propagandists portrayed Portugal as a 'sunlit house in a peaceful garden' but the people lived in grinding poverty. The regime kept them docile with a diet of the three fs – football, *fado* (Portuguese folk song) and Fatima (the place where a cult of the Virgin Mary developed after three Catholic children saw a vision of her in 1917). 'All evils on Earth come from Red Russia, do not admit into your homes and hearts the Communist Satan,' the regime claimed that the Mother of God had told the children. But the real F was for Fascism.

Eventually Salazar became old and incapable but he continued to rule through his protégé Marcello Caetano, who was appointed Prime Minister in 1968. Salazar finally died in 1970 at the age of eighty-one, but the revolution did not take place until April 1974, when Caetano was ousted by a group of some 200 army officers from Movimento das Forcas Armadas (MFA). The uprising was triggered by the high death toll in wars to prolong colonial rule in Guinea, Angola and Mozambique. The army officers took Lisbon in twenty-four hours with hardly a shot being fired. Their success was due to the fact that they mobilised the crowds and managed to surround the headquarters of PIDE, the Portuguese equivalent of the GESTAPO, so that the Fascists were unable to resist.

General Spinola was chosen to head the subsequent military junta, in which four out of the six members were left-wingers. Palma Carlos headed a civilian government in which various parties were represented, including the Socialist leader, Mario Soares, who took the country into the EC. Alvaro Cunhal, the Communist leader, was made a deputy premier.

Lisbon had still not lost its euphoric atmosphere when I hit the streets in mid-May. It was very inspiring. Everyone was glowing with enthusiasm and goodwill. Even the prostitutes were giving their services free to soldiers and marines in honour of the revolution. The workers were in a good mood because they had received pay rises from the gold reserves accumulated by Salazar. The most impressive thing was that in the midst of revolution, there was perfect public order.

Many people told me the stories of their lives under Fascism. Dias Lourenco, a metallurgist and leading Communist activist, recounted how he had spent years in jail for his political beliefs. In the new free Portugal, in which the Communist Party was legalised, this decorated hero of the resistance became editor of the newspaper *Avante*. He was to help me a lot in the months to come. In his seventies, he was thirty years my senior and called me *filho*, which means 'son' in Portuguese.

Most touching of all were the stories of the simple people. The porter at the Hotel Altis told me how he had gone all his life in fear of the informers who reported to the dreaded PIDE political police. At last he was free. It was as if a weight had been lifted from him, he said.

All popular revolutions, particularly if they are peaceful, give this initial sense of liberation. I do not know, because I was not there, but I imagine the fall of the Berlin Wall gave a pure thrill to those who witnessed it. To me, the Portuguese revolution seemed like the overthrow of Mussolini or the Cuban revolution in its early, visionary days.

So why do revolutions go sour? The Portuguese revolution was no exception. I stayed on in Lisbon to witness increasing wrangling and intrigues among the generals and an anti-Communist backlash. As an idealist who hated the way Brezhnev distorted Communist principles in the Soviet Union, felt hope when Mikhail Gorbachev first came to power but then was disappointed, I still dream of revolutionary change for the good of ordinary people. But now I think I will probably not experience this Utopia of freedom and equality in my lifetime.

Getting Established

Running around covering the Portuguese revolution for Tass and the KGB, I soon had the evidence of my own sore feet to confirm what the guidebooks say, that Lisbon is built on seven hills. My hotel was near the palm-lined Avenida de Liberdade in the district of town reconstructed by the Marquis de Pombal after the earthquake of 1755. Sometimes I would save my legs by taking the funicular railway or the iron lift built by Eiffel, more famous for its tower in Paris, to the Bairro Alto or upper part of the city. Nevertheless I lost pounds in weight in my first months in the Portuguese capital.

Exploring is all part of a KGB agent's job but I had an added reason to range over the city as, immediately after the revolution, various artists and public figures from the Soviet Union visited to demonstrate their solidarity and I had to show them round. The singer Josef Kobzon and Valentina Tereshkova, the first woman in space, were among my guests. I would take them to the palaces and churches dating from the time of the great sea explorer Vasco da Gama, when Lisbon was the richest city in the world. Or to the hothouses in the Edward VII Gardens, named after the son of Britain's Queen Victoria. For centuries, Britain and Portugal were close because of their common enmity towards Spain and to this day Lisbon evinces a curious mixture of British and Latin culture.

Another of my guests was the famous Soviet poet Konstantin Simonov. I took him to my favourite place, the ruins of St George's Castle, which was the stronghold of King Alfonso Enriquez where he liberated Portugal from the Moors in 1147. The ruins stand on Lisbon's highest hill from where you get a magnificent panoramic view of the city. Simonov was an old war veteran but he still beat me up the steps to the castle. Afterwards we went to enjoy beer and prawns in a downtown bar.

I had been in Portugal several months by this time and was missing my wife Valentina. I asked Simonov to take a present back to Moscow for her, some jewellery which I had bought on Lisbon's famous Rua do Ouro or Street of Gold. Simonov was very kind and not only went straight from Moscow airport to our flat to deliver the package, but also penned a poem to Valentina in the taxi on the way.

I did not have to wait too much longer, however, before Valentina joined me. Because I had proved satisfactory as a 'fireman' attending a hot news event, my bosses decided to extend my posting so I could go on monitoring the progress of Portuguese democracy and I became the resident Tass correspondent in Lisbon. We were both very pleased.

I went to meet Valentina in Paris, which was a double pleasure because I always liked to stop over in the French capital. In preparation for her arrival in Lisbon, I had rented a flat with two bedrooms and a balcony on Campo Pequeno. But the area, though respectably middle class, was noisy and later we moved to a suburban villa with a garden on Avenida dos Descubridores (Avenue of the Explorers).

The house, more luxurious than the *dachas* of some members of the Soviet government, was like an English club. It even had a billiard table in the cellar. Miraculously, it cost no more than the flat because the landlady, a genteel woman whom we called the 'Marquisa', had fled from Angola and needed to make money quickly by letting her property. So Tass did not balk at the rent which they paid on top of my salary of $400 per month.

Soon we got a grey cat called Pequenino ('little one' in Portuguese) or Pika for short and that made us feel at home. I have noticed that many KGB agents are cat lovers. Perhaps it is that the devious feline mentality appeals to us more than the stupid sincerity of dogs. In my case though, I found that stroking a cat helped to relieve the stress of the job.

Both Valentina and I worked as well as lived in the villa. The telex machine was next to our bedroom on the second floor so that I was able to go and read the messages first thing in the morning, still wearing my dressing-gown and slippers. Tass roped Valentina into working as a teletype operator. That was the lot of women married to correspondents from Tass, which did everything on the cheap.

The Portuguese were able to read whatever went out over the telex. 'Perhaps you are working for the KGB?' a revolutionary official called Souza e Castro said to me once. 'Just look at the number of telexes I send out to Tass and you will see that I don't have any time for spying,' I replied.

On the whole, I think I was in the good books of the new authorities, although I did have one little problem with the police. All the Russians who were coming out to establish a Soviet community in Lisbon – Portugal and the Soviet Union restored diplomatic relations in June 1974 and we opened an embassy soon afterwards – had visas and work permits. I only had the simple *entrada* stamp which had been put in my passport when I arrived in the heat of the revolution. I thought nothing of it until one day the police said to me: 'How come you are here without a visa?' Valentina feared they were going to 'take me away in handcuffs' but a call to the Ministry of Information, which was always very helpful to me, sorted the matter out.

The Deputy Information Minister, an aristocrat called Sancheso Osorio, was a particular friend and I was always dropping in to see him and his charming secretary Maribel in the Palacio Foz where they had their offices. Osorio was close to General Spinola himself and through him I got introductions to many leading Portuguese politicians.

Of the politicians in military uniform, I knew General Mario Firmino Miguel, the chief of the army staff, who at one point was tipped to become prime minister but who died in a road accident. At least, I think it was an accident. I also knew General Carlos Fabiao, chief of ground forces and a key player in the revolution who lost out later because he was a shy man unable to keep up with all the political intrigues. Once he invited me to his home where he had a collection of guns including a Kalashnikov AK-1 automatic rifle. 'I took it from a partisan in the war in Guinea,' he said bashfully when he noticed me looking inquisitively at the famous Soviet-made weapon of choice for liberation movements around the world.

My military friends were just the kind of contacts all journalists have and not paid KGB agents, although one whom I had better not identify did break his side's rules by arranging for me to listen in during a session of the junta. He smuggled me into a side wing of the building where the meeting was taking place and I was able to overhear the discussion. Very interesting.

Apart from army sources, I also had a wide range of civilians friends. I am eternally grateful to Ferreira, the owner of the Hotel Altis, for introducing me to people in high society who recommended me for membership of the prestigious Gremio Literario or Literary Union. In the restaurant of this club, I conversed with many useful Portuguese intellectuals including Miguel Urbano Rodriguez, editor of the left-wing *Diario de Lisboa*, and the writer and fashion designer Vera Lagoa. She was a fascinating woman who had been moving steadily to the left by marriage. Her first husband was a Fascist, her second a socialist and her third a Communist. Rumour had it she was really an agent of Britain's MI6.

Like the army officers, these intellectuals were just friends, not my paid agents, but to a spy such open contacts can be as helpful as clandestine informers in throwing light upon the mysteries of a foreign society. Membership of the Gremio Literario opened doors for me in Portugal. When I had my backside firmly in one of the club's deep leather armchairs, I could say that I had established myself in Lisbon.

'Tricky Dickie' in the Azores

You may be beginning to wonder how my work differed from that of a bona fide foreign correspondent. It is true that in the early days of the revolution, the greater part of my output was straight journalism, a pure response to a dramatic event. But I did have another hidden agenda, which was not, as I have already said, to work against Portugal, but rather to foil our 'main adversary' the United States and to spy on Nato, whose Iberian and Atlantic Command (Comiberlant) was situated just outside Lisbon.

The Americans were very worried by the revolution in Portugal, a founder member of Nato which played the strategically important role of guarding the approach to the Atlantic Ocean. So committed to non-interference in Portuguese affairs was the Soviet Union that we refused a request from the peasants for tomato seedlings when drought ruined their crop and the prospects for their vital tomato paste exports. But the same could not be said of Washington, which meddled actively – and came up with the tomato seedlings.

In the wake of the revolution, Lisbon was twice honoured with a visit from Vernon Walters, then the deputy director of the CIA. Ambassador Scott left and was replaced by Frank Carlucci, whom the KGB believed was also the CIA *rezident*. It is not the usual practice for the job of ambassador and intelligence service station chief to be combined but we are pretty sure that Carlucci was the exception to the rule.

We believe that the Americans financed extreme Maoist groups in an attempt to discredit the revolution. Philip Agee, a former CIA operative, admitted in his *Letter to the Portuguese People* published in 1975 that the CIA aimed to create chaos in the country so that 'moderate pro-American politicians' would come to power.

From time to time, I was aware of the Americans – or their lackeys – on my tail. Straight after the revolution Portugal had no counter-intelligence service as such, making Lisbon a paradise for spies. For example the phones were not bugged, although the French probably listened in to international calls routed through Paris. But after lying low for a while, former officers from the PIDE secret police found new American pay-masters. They would follow me when I drove round town in my beige Peugeot-504.

They may have been behind me when I popped in to see Sanches Osorio one day in the summer of 1974 but they did not know the substance of our talks. The kindly Deputy Information Minister told me that the Portuguese side had decided to include me in a group of about twenty-five foreign correspondents being allowed to accompany General Spinola on a trip to the Azores to meet US President Richard Nixon. The security and public relations men from Washington went 'ape shit', as I believe the American expression is, when they saw me, a Soviet correspondent, taking part in the media circus on the Nato base of Lajes. 'Who is that goddamn Russian?' they wanted to know. They had no choice but to accept the Portuguese guest list, however, because I was already there with my notebook at the ready.

I behaved impeccably, deliberately leaving my camera behind so that nobody could accuse me of taking illicit photos. I listened to a briefing by General Spinola, nicknamed by the press 'the man in the monocle'. He was friendly, smiling and handing out autographed copies of his book, although later he was to show the world a very different face. Then I joined the welcoming party at the steps of Nixon's plane. The thing that struck me most when I first saw the American President was the amount of make-up he wore, although nothing could disguise the fact of his age.

The press conference given at the end of the summit was confined to polite generalities which my Tass editors would have scorned, let alone my bosses at the KGB. But I had not been sleeping during my short stay on the rocky Atlantic island. I had not needed a camera, for my brain did just as well, taking in the details of the military base, which was up to date and equipped to take Galaxy heavy transport aircraft. Also I had a mole in the American entourage who leaked me the details of Nixon's conversation with Spinola. The US President said Nato was concerned about possible Soviet influence in Portugal after the revolution and especially worried lest Soviet ships started appearing in Portuguese ports, undermining the Western alliance's Atlantic defences. 'We should all understand,' my source quoted Nixon as saying, 'that change is not always for the best.' Spinola assured Nixon that Portugal would not only continue to support the US but tighten cooperation. After this Nixon promised financial aid for Lisbon.

This was hot stuff, the first really secret material which I had obtained since coming to Portugal. I would need to transmit it to the KGB urgently. But I could not send it immediately when I got back to base as I had no access to a code machine. As we still had no embassy in Lisbon, there was nothing for it but to travel to Madrid.

Together with Miroslav Ikonovich, a genuine journalist from the Polish news agency PAP, I set off by car through the picturesque Algarve to Spain. The astonished Spanish frontier guard, who had never seen a Soviet citizen before, said, 'Have a nice holiday,' as he stamped the tourist visa which the Spanish embassy in Lisbon had issued.

I cannot claim to have been the first Soviet citizen in Franco's Spain. My KGB colleague Leonid Kolosov had already been in Madrid sounding out Spaniards on what was likely to happen when their aging dictator died and laying the groundwork for the establishment of diplomatic relations between Spain and the Soviet Union. But in 1974, this break-through had still not occurred. There was no Soviet embassy in Madrid, just an office of the Soviet Shipping Agency equipped with a code machine. Here I finally relieved myself of my secret report and then relaxed.

After my working holiday, I returned to dramatic events in Lisbon. Evidently as a result of his peptalk with Nixon, Spinola, who had never really been a committed reformer, attempted a right-wing coup on the night of 28 September. Maribel, the secretary at the Information Ministry, rang me and said: 'If I were you, I would not go out on the streets tomorrow.' She feared for my safety in likely clashes between Spinola's anti-Communist Mayoria Silenciosa (Silent Majority) and those who still supported the radical officers of the MFA.

Spinola's plot failed and a few months later he showed his true colours by fleeing to Spain, where Franco gave him political asylum. His chosen Prime Minister, Palma Carlos, was replaced by Vasco Gonsalvez and Costa Gomez became President. Both were leftists. Meanwhile in America that August, President Nixon had been forced to resign in disgrace over the Watergate break-in. Knowing what I did about his talks on the Azores, I had a different reason to think of him as 'Tricky Dickie'. But his attempt to put pressure on the Portuguese backfired and their revolution continued to move in a 'progressive' direction. This state of affairs suited Moscow admirably, although it had done nothing to bring it about.

The Perfect Holiday Destination

At Cabo da Roca, the westernmost point in Europe, the wind blows straight off the Atlantic and the waves crash with the force of a whole ocean behind them. On an outing there one summer's day, I strode over the headland and breathed in the ozone until, when I was sure nobody was watching me, I bent to retrieve a bright red drinks can glinting among the stones on the path. Then I walked to a small wooden hut to claim a tourist certificate declaring that I had been at the edge of the continent beyond which, apart from a few islands, lies only the coast of America.

Somewhere in Europe there is another man with a certificate like mine. He arrived after about half an hour ahead of me and also enjoyed the view before dropping the can containing microfilm. To this day I do not know his identity, just that he was one of the KGB's paid agents bringing secrets for me to pick up and deliver to the Soviet embassy.

Because I was not attempting to undermine the government in Lisbon, I had not recruited a single Portuguese to betray the country. But I dealt with quite a number of Western citizens, working either from ideological conviction or for money for the KGB, who came from elsewhere in Europe to Portugal to meet or communicate with me.

Portugal is the perfect holiday destination. It has sandy beaches and a rich history and, in those days, was still so cheap that unemployed people from Britain could afford to come out and live in the sun on their dole money. Nothing looked more natural than our agents, who might be working in France or West Germany, choosing to come to Portugal for their holidays. An added advantage was that Portuguese counter-intelligence was weak and unlikely to be able to distinguish West European traitors from tourists.

The little lanes, back alleyways and cul-de-sacs of old Lisbon were ideal for communicating via dead letter boxes. I would take a stroll, glance in the window of a boutique and out of the corner of my eye look to see that nobody was behind me, then surreptitiously drop a cigarette packet containing instructions for one of the visitors. Or at the crowded Campo da Santa Clara flea market, where everybody was too busy shopping for bargains to notice me, I would make a chalk mark on a lamppost to let an agent know that our evening rendezvous was on in one of the cheap and cheerful fish restaurants down by the Tejo River.

Unlike Soviet personnel in other Western countries, which repaid Moscow for the travel restrictions it imposed on their citizens in the USSR by not allowing Russians to go more than twenty-five miles outside their capital cities, I was not confined to Lisbon but was able to visit many interesting places such as Sintra, Coimbra and Estoril. Often I would invite the visiting agents to meet me outside the capital, where we were even less likely to be observed.

I met 'Max' in the casino at Estoril, an elegant resort which is the Portuguese answer to Cannes or Nice. He was a journalist from a former imperial power. We conversed in Spanish but he was not a Spaniard. Neither was he British. I will leave you to guess which country he came from. I had never met him before and the KGB *rezident* at the embassy had given me what I considered an inadequate description. 'He'll be wearing a white bow tie. He looks like a journalist. What more can I say?' But once I was in the casino, it did not take me long to spot him sitting among the gamblers at the roulette table. It was not the white tie, of course, for all the men present were wearing them. Neither was it the cigar he was smoking. Rather it was his lively, communicative manner, which I think is essential for the profession of journalism.

'I'm out of luck. How about you?' I asked. 'You can rely on me when the chips are down,' he replied. It was the correct password. We moved off together for a quiet cognac at the bar.

When the barman's back was turned, he slipped me an envelope containing some secrets of a political nature. I left soon afterwards to deliver it to the embassy while he went back to the roulette wheel. I had not paid him, but he had received a handsome amount of 'holiday spending money' from the KGB in the country he came from. I do not know whether gambling was the weakness that enabled the KGB to hook him in the first place. I took the attitude that the less I knew about Max the better and, after our business was done, I never had anything more to do with him.

Roughly every four months – it depended on the situation abroad, of course – my journalistic routine would be broken by such a rendezvous with an agent from outside Portugal. On another occasion, I passed myself off as a pilgrim and went to meet 'Ali', a spy bringing economic secrets from North Africa, in a chapel at Evora near the Spanish border. It was built by the Inquisition out of sinners' bones and the walls are literally constructed out of skeletal remains, which glow eerily in the candlelight.

I had a merrier time in Madeira, where I met yet another of my visiting agents, a man called Hans who worked for Nato somewhere in Western Europe. It was the eve of 8 March, International Women's Day, so nobody in Lisbon raised any eyebrows when I said I was taking my wife away for a special treat. Hans also had no problem convincing his employers that he needed a break from the grey northern weather and where better than Madeira, off the African coast, where it is pleasantly warm all year round?

I decided to get the business out of the way first and went straight to meet Hans. Since we were on an island far from any counter-intelligence services, I did not have to take any special precautions but just picked him up at his hotel. He was standing in the lobby, middle-aged, balding, just as he had been described to me. I took him to a fish restaurant for our sordid hand-over. Then I was free to relax with Valentina who, asking no questions, had entertained herself while I was busy.

We were like children, excited to be on this beautiful island. We went tobogganing, not on snow but in wicker carts which slid down the steep streets. Such was the local transport. We also walked the mountains and sampled the island's famous wine.

For Women's Day, I gave Valentina some orchids. I think for her they made a welcome change from the hothouse-grown red tulips which unimaginative Soviet husbands usually give their wives on the one day of the year when women are special.

All History Now

Envious Russian friends used to say that my time in Portugal must have been like one long holiday and in a way it was. The job of an intelligence officer is demanding, however, and I had mixed feelings of regret and relief when I returned to Moscow in 1978. My parents were happy, as they had only seen me on one home leave in the whole four years I had been in Lisbon.

I had come to Portugal in the midst of a revolution but when I left it was turning into a bourgeois democracy like any other country in Western Europe. Some radical Portuguese officers had favoured the Cuban political model for their country but gradually traditional anti-Communism and Catholicism reasserted itself. In 1975, there were pogroms in which the homes of known Communists were burnt in Braga, the town famous for the Bom Jesus do Monte church which pilgrims approach on their knees until they bleed. Communism never had much chance there.

Also in 1975, Portugal held its first free elections since the 1920s. Mario Soares emerged as the country's most powerful politician. He was a socialist in the safe mould of West Germany's Willy Brandt or François Mitterrand of France and when he became Prime Minister the Americans must have sighed with relief. I spent the remainder of my time in Lisbon following the activities of his new government.

When I returned to Moscow, my old Tass boss, Leonid Zamyatin, who went on to head the international department of the Soviet Communist Party Central Committee, asked Andropov to release me from the KGB so that I could go and work for him as an analyst of southern European affairs. From time to time at conferences I would meet the former Portuguese president, Costa Gomez, and his premier, Vasco Gonzalves, who continued to champion the cause of world peace.

At the Central Committee, I also became a specialist on methods of combating terrorism, which is one of the priorities of the post-Communist Russian secret service. After the collapse of the Soviet Union, I worked for a while as press secretary to the Communist leader, Gennady Zyuganov, in the State Duma. Now at the end of my career, I am a public relations consultant to a Russian commercial organisation.

I went back to Lisbon only once, in 1990, when a television company invited me to take part in a discussion programme to mark the fifteenth anniversary of the end of the Portuguese revolution. I sat in the studio along with various other guests. Participating by satellite from across the Atlantic was Frank Carlucci, the former American ambassador in Lisbon.

'Do you think he was also the CIA *rezident*?' the presenter asked me provocatively. 'Well you know,' I said tactfully, 'it was really not the practice for the ambassador to get involved with intelligence work as well.' I had got Carlucci off the hook, in exchange for which he then moved the conversation on before the presenter had a chance to ask him what he thought Eduard Kovalyov had been up to in Lisbon.

I had left Portugal in 1978 in the belief that nobody had rumbled me. But a few days after I returned to Moscow, a fellow journalist handed me a copy of the French newspaper *Le Figaro*, which carried the following short item: 'On 24 September, Portugal at last said goodbye to Eduard Kovalyov, a lieutenant-colonel in the Soviet intelligence service working in Lisbon under the cover of chief correspondent for Tass. It is interesting to speculate what and how much this "journalist" contributed to the Portuguese democratic revolution.'

How did they know who I was? I can only guess that the French counter-intelligence service, which I had suspected of bugging international calls routed through Paris, listened in to my conversations. They may have shared their knowledge with the Portuguese who, if they knew, perhaps preferred to live with a familiar devil rather than expelling me.

Had I been publicly exposed when I was still working in Portugal, it would of course have been a disaster. But by the time the *Figaro* report came out, the KGB did not really care. It was water under the bridge and 'our man in Lisbon', as my bosses used to call me, had passed into history.

MADRID

Madness, Intuition and the Course of History

When May comes round I pack my bags and jet off to Spain, where I own a time share in a seaside villa near Malaga. It is a luxury a KGB pensioner can afford if, like me, he also has a few royalties from his writing. But I would not be taking Spanish holidays now if my first planned trip to Madrid had gone ahead. Indeed Spain itself would probably not be the flourishing democracy it is today. How fortunate for all of us that history took a favourable turn.

In 1966, I was still working under cover as the *Izvestia* correspondent in Rome. One autumn day, I had a noon appointment with 'West', one of my oldest and most reliable Italian informers, a socialist from the generation that had fought in the resistance against Mussolini. He always brought his reports closely written on tiny pieces of paper and, according to the classical canons of spying, handed them over to me only at the end of our meetings so that if the police intervened while we were talking, I would not be caught red-handed and declared persona non grata. But sadly his health was failing. For this reason, we met infrequently on via Nomentana, a short drive from the centre for him in his old Alfa Romeo.

That day I found him waiting for me on a park bench with a copy of the newspaper *Avanti* in his hands. From the way his shoulders slumped, I could tell something was wrong. He embraced me like a father. 'Has something happened?' I asked. 'Yes, my young friend, I'm afraid so. The doctors have diagnosed liver cancer. I only have a few month left to live.'

I felt shocked and sorry for the old man, whom I had come to love. Back in spy school we had been taught to take good care of our agents. 'Sacrifice yourself but save your agent,' was the rule. 'Perhaps it's all a mistake,' I said, taking West's thin, cold hand in mine. 'No, I fear not. I've suspected it for some time. This is just the clinical confirmation. I must be philosophical. Now listen to me carefully, Leonid.

'When I was a young man, I used to go to Spain quite often and there I made a friend called Francisco. He was a bit older than me but we were both interested in socialism and that is what brought us together. Then I left and the Spanish Civil War started and Francisco became the dictator Franco. Today I think of him as a traitor, the enemy of the Spanish people and my personal enemy too. But he does not know that. If I were to turn up in Madrid, I'm sure he would still welcome me as a friend. I could write to him first, saying I was coming on a business trip. After all, I do have my own firm now. And then I could kill him. But I would need a weapon. Do you think your boys could make me a shooting pen like James Bond uses?'

My jaw fell open in surprise. 'Are you serious?' I asked. 'Oh yes, absolutely. Then my death will have a purpose, don't you see? Franco is blocking democracy in Spain. Hitler, Mussolini, even the Japanese war criminals, they were all punished. Why should Franco be the only one to go unscathed? I hope you don't consider him a friend of the Soviet Union?' 'No, of course not, but we have to think about this carefully, we need more time ...' 'Yes, but don't delay too long, my strength is failing with each day. When shall we meet again?' 'Same time next week, here on this bench,' I said and hurried off to report to my boss.

'My dear boy,' said the KGB *rezident*, 'are you sure the old fellow has not gone off his head?' 'I don't know, he seemed calm enough, quite determined.' 'We'll have to inform Moscow Centre. When have you arranged the next meeting?' 'Next week, same place.' 'OK, except you should have changed the venue. But that's not the main worry now. We must word the telegram carefully so it does not commit us to anything.' The *rezident* was not really keen on the plan and neither was I. Still we could not just turn down West's offer to remove a Fascist dictator and enemy of Communism.

Four days later, a reply arrived from Moscow Centre. The *rezident* summoned me to his safe room at the Soviet embassy, which was kept swept of bugs by our technical staff. I could not read code so the *rezident* summarised the telegram for me. I should give West the impression I had taken his offer seriously. I should not say the KGB was interested, but let him think I was acting on my own initiative. I should offer to pay his expenses and promise financial compensation for his family. At the same time I should keep an eye on his health, especially the state of his nerves. A 007-style pen would be no problem. I should keep the *rezident* informed about West, whose new codename would be 'Quill'. In other words, the bosses found the offer too tempting to refuse, but would not take any responsibility themselves and were passing the buck to me.

The next time I went to the park bench, I found West already there, pacing excitedly. 'Good news, Leonid. I've managed to get through to Franco on the phone. He remembered me and he's invited me to visit him in Madrid.' '****!' I thought. Matters were taking a really serious turn now. But I forced a delighted expression onto my face. 'Well done,' I said, 'that's brilliant. I'm going to help you with the operation. I'll pay your expenses and see your family are taken care of.' 'My dear Leonid, I don't need money, I'm not a poor man,' he protested. 'All I need is that pen and a little training and perhaps ... do you think you could come with me to Madrid and be there to meet me after I have done the job?' This time I nearly had a heart attack.

I reported to the *rezident*, who in turn sought fresh advice from Moscow Centre. The telegram came back saying the bosses had no objection in principle to me flying to Madrid. I could make it appear that I was on a reporting assignment. I could stay in the same hotel as West and wait for him. 'I'm fond of you, Leonid, but the Motherland calls,' said the *rezident*.

My meetings with West became more frequent. He was visibly wilting with each passing day but a passion burned feverishly in his eyes. He spoke a lot about Franco, remembering the good old days. I began to feel he retained a certain sympathy for his former friend.

One night I was tossing and turning in bed when I suddenly sat bolt upright. With absolute clarity, I saw the following scene: West goes into Franco's office and the dictator embraces him. Suddenly a wave of nostalgia hits my agent and he breaks down, crying: 'Francisco, my old friend, forgive me, I was coming to kill you but I cannot do it. Go to the Hotel Victoria and you will find the KGB agent who put me up to this. Here, by the way, take this pen for old time's sake.'

As soon as it was daylight, I rushed to the *rezident*. 'Lost your nerve,

Leonid?' he said. 'No, it's not that, but imagine the international scandal if my scenario proves correct. I might as well go to Franco myself with a black ball with "bomb" written on it.' 'I'll ask Moscow Centre,' said the boss. The usually mealy-mouthed reply came back. Everything was left to my discretion.

But then West did not make the next rendezvous. The phone rang in my office and a sad female voice said: 'Your friend died of a heart attack. The funeral will be at the Testaccio cemetery.' As I bade farewell to my agent at his graveside, I pondered the human impulses and intuitions that determine history. Franco himself was at this time staring death in the face and preparing to hand over peacefully to a new generation of Spanish leaders. And I was lucky enough to observe the results of this process when, four years later, I did indeed make my first trip to Spain.

'Get Yourself off to Spain'

I left Italy in 1969 and went back to Moscow to work on the desk at *Izvestia*. The new editor Lev Tolkunov, who had replaced Khrushchev's son-in-law Alexei Adzhubei when Brezhnev came to power, liked my writing and wanted me to be a straight journalist. A part of me would have enjoyed this too since, following my car accident near Rome, I did not really feel physically fit enough to play the secret agent any more. But the KGB does not easily release those who have been privy to its secrets. While I edited texts at the newspaper on Gorky Street, I used to get regular telephone calls from the 'office' up the road at Lubyanka Square. Not for one moment was I allowed to forget who my real masters were.

One day Tolkunov called me into his office and said: 'Lyonya, how's your French?' 'A bit rusty but it was my main foreign language at college.' 'I expect it's still good enough for you to accompany me to Geneva. I've been invited to an international press symposium there.' 'With pleasure.'

I will not bore you with the details of the symposium but tell you instead about the conversation I had with my editor afterwards as we walked, free from the walls with ears, by the shores of Lake Geneva. 'Lyonya,' he said, 'aren't you tired of being bothered all the time by the "office"?' 'Perhaps, but I know there are only two ways to leave the KGB – in handcuffs or feet first in a box.' 'There could be a third way ...' began Tolkunov. 'Yes, but you see the problem is that I also love adventure,' I interrupted him. 'Oh well, if you love adventure, you had better get yourself off to Spain then.'

Tolkunov explained that the Central Committee of the Soviet Communist Party was looking for a journalist who could get a Spanish visa. This may sound a simple matter, but in fact it was very difficult as the Soviet Union and Spain had no diplomatic relations at this time. Russians had fought in the International Brigades alongside the Republicans during the Spanish Civil War and when Franco came to power, many of his Spanish opponents had sought asylum in Moscow. Because of this, our two countries were still not on speaking terms. (Of course, if the KGB had thought more carefully about it at the time, they would not have toyed with the idea of me going with West to kill Franco because they would have known I could not get a visa.)

'What does the Central Committee want the journalist to do in Madrid?' I asked. 'Well, they see that Franco is leaving the political arena,' replied Tolkunov. 'The democratic movement is growing but it is not clear who will come to power next. The Committee wants someone there who can give an objective assessment of the situation. Do you think you could do that?' 'I'm sure I could,' I said, 'but first I need to fly to Rome.'

I had been on good terms with the Spanish vice-consul in the Italian capital. I knew he was a spy for the Servicio de Inteligencia, Franco's secret service, but he liked vodka and anti-Soviet jokes and I liked sherry and Spanish songs, which was a sufficient basis for a friendly relationship. There was a chance he might give me a visa. 'When can you go?' asked my editor. 'Tomorrow if you give me some money.' And so the next day I flew from Geneva to Rome.

'Amigo, what's new?' said the vice-consul when I walked into his office. 'I need you to give me a visa for Spain,' I replied. I told him that Moscow was floating the idea of restoring diplomatic relations. I needed to talk to people in Spain and write some upbeat articles in *Izvestia*. Lunch helped to soften up the vice-consul. 'OK, Leon, I will trust you,' he said. 'Come tomorrow with six passport photographs, fill out the forms, I'll see what I can do. It's true the Caudilio (leader) has been showing signs of weakness lately.' Nine months later I got a telegram from Paris, inviting me to go to the Spanish consulate there and pick up a visa valid for a one-month reporting trip to Spain.

I had barely finished reading it when Tolkunov rushed into my office. 'OK Lyonya, drop everything, I free you from all your work at the paper and you don't need to worry about the "office" either. We are going to see Boris Nikolayevich.' He meant Boris Nikolayevich Ponomaryov, the head of the International Department of the Central Committee.

I should explain here that the Central Committee was a very important organisation, more powerful than either the Foreign Ministry or the KGB. It was only one step down in the hierarchy from the Politburo, which was immediately under the Communist Party General Secretary, Leonid Brezhnev. The three organisations were, of course, bitter rivals under the façade of cooperation for the sake of our Soviet Motherland.

'Your task,' said Ponomaryov drily, 'will be to assess the state of Franco's physical and political health, find out who the new people are around him and give us a clue as to who might come to power in the future.' I was to be diplomatic and avoid compromising situations.

'There's one delicate matter ...' coughed Tolkunov, 'you see Leonid Sergeyevich is in a rather specific situation ...' 'I know Comrade Kolosov works for the KGB,' snapped Ponomaryov. 'There is no need for him to inform his chiefs about this mission.'

Nevertheless, whether from habit or loyalty I don't know, I went over to the Lubyanka and told my boss, Alexander Sakharovsky, what I was up to. 'Very good Leonid,' he said. 'Take care of yourself. You will be surrounded by Spanish counter-intelligence people. Don't get your backside bitten. And slip us a copy of your report to Ponomaryov.' He also commissioned me to do a special job for the KGB, which was to find out as much as I could about the secret Catholic organisation, Opus Dei.

Before I set off, I had one more briefing – with Anatoly Kovalyov, the head of the Foreign Ministry's First European Department. He knew little more about Spain than could be learned from reading the newspapers. But he did say one interesting thing: that wherever I went I should lead Spaniards to believe that the Soviet Union knew nothing about Madrid's gold reserves. This was a lie, of course. The Republicans had given Moscow large amounts of their country's gold during the Civil War. There was no chance of Madrid getting it back, however, because we had spent it all, mostly on weapons for the fight against Franco.

Armed with information and advice, I was ready to leave. I packed a suitcase and another bag with various trinkets including the famous Russian *Matrioshka* dolls which make, in my experience, very useful little gifts to smooth relations with the natives. Then I took an Aeroflot flight to Paris to pick up my Spanish visa. My travelling companion on this first leg of the trip was the prima ballerina of the Bolshoi, Maya Plisetskaya. I must say for a dying swan, she kept up well with this raddled old KGB agent when it came to knocking back the complimentary cognac.

The Soviet Explorer

Seen from the air by night, Madrid with its yellow neon lights looked like a glinting amber brooch. 'In the yellow tower the bell tolls,' I quoted to myself from the poet Lorca. I had read up as much as I could before coming to this country which was a closed book to Homo Sovieticus. The puzzled expression on the face of the immigration officer when I showed my green Soviet diplomatic passport also underlined what a rarity I was for the Spaniards.

I was not the only Russian in Spain, however. The KGB had an illegal agent here called Vladimir Largin. Passing himself off as a Frenchman, he ran a perfume shop as a cover for his secret activities, which mainly involved keeping up links with underground Spanish Communists. Obviously, because of the delicacy of my mission, I could not risk being seen meeting him. Instead, I was greeted at the airport by the representative of the Black Sea Shipping Line, the only Soviet official in Spain.

He was not a KGB agent but the son of a diplomat. He dealt exclusively with shipping matters but, perhaps because of his background, he was seen in Moscow as a possible future diplomat to Spain, should ties ever be restored. He was a nervous young man. 'Leonid Sergeyevich, Leonid Sergeyevich,' he whispered, 'you cannot imagine how difficult it is for me here. They follow me all the time. I'm without any support, you know.' Of course for me being followed was just an occupational hazard; indeed I sometimes felt lonely if I did not have a tail.

I checked into the Hotel Victoria, the place where West had had in mind to stay when he was planning his trip to assassinate Franco. Back in Moscow, the Central Committee had advised me to get in touch with a Spanish businessman called Jesus Santiveri Capdevila, the chairman of a firm called 'Waimer' which had once sold shirts to the Soviet Union. He would help to arrange meetings for me in Madrid and organise a fact-finding tour of the provinces. But I was not seeing him until the next morning. For the moment, I was free.

I opened a bottle of vodka and a tin of caviar from the stock I had brought with me and considered how best to enjoy myself. When I first went to Rome for *Izvestia*, I had been assigned to write an article about prostitutes who stroll around the Coliseum. This time I fancied doing a little private research with a call girl and I reckoned if I was careful, nobody need find out about it. I walked the narrow streets around the hotel until I was sure I was not under surveillance and then from the range of Madrid beauties, some favouring the mini fashion, others preferring maxiskirts, I chose a cute girl to take back to my room.

'Are you Italian?' she asked. 'On my father's side,' I said. 'My mother is a Yugoslav.' I had my fun and paid her and was thinking of giving her one of the Russian *Matrioshka* dolls as a little bonus when I suddenly realised this would be the quickest way to reveal who I really was and land myself in hot water both with the Spanish authorities and my own bosses back in Moscow. Instead I just said: 'Ciao.' 'Ciao,' she answered, 'don't worry, I'll find my own way out.'

Although I had had a late night, I woke at first light and took another walk. Both for KGB agents and tourists I would say the best time to study a city is early in the morning, before the crowds and the traffic begin jamming up the streets. In Madrid, the early morning is a particularly blessed hour because the car fumes which, even more than the neon lights, make this city yellow have not yet had time to build up.

Then the chauffeur from Waimer came to pick me up and took me to meet Señor Santiveri. I explained that I wanted to see both the capital and other cities and meet Spaniards in all walks of life before I wrote a series of articles for *Izvestia*. 'No problem,' said my host, 'we are open, you can even visit our military base at Palomares if you want. Do you have transport?' 'I'd like to hire a car,' I said, specifying the Citroën DC-24 which I used to drive in Italy as my preferred model. 'No problem,' he said again. 'One of my staff will accompany you on your travels.'

We were silent for a moment, then Señor Santiveri caught my eye, got up from behind his desk, walked over to the window and whispered to me: 'Señor Kolosov, I should warn you that this member of staff only joined our firm yesterday.' 'Thank you,' I said, 'I'll bear that in mind.'

I was due to set off touring with this 'guide' in two days' time. Meanwhile there was time to enjoy the programme of entertainment in Madrid laid on by the accommodating Señor Santiveri. I saw the statue to Christopher Columbus, with whom I felt some fellow feeling as I was in my own small way an explorer, relearning a country which had been lost to Russians for decades. I also went to see a bull-fight, which I found surprisingly exhilarating, ate paella, and looked at the Goyas in the Prado in the company of Carlos Velasquez, a distant relative of the great Spanish painter Velasquez and a fine artist in his own right. He took me to his studio and showed me his wonderful, glowing portraits. As well as likenesses of his wife, a woman to whom God had given great beauty but denied the gift of speech, there were numerous pictures of Count Leo Tolstoy, whom the painter had idolised since reading *War and Peace* in childhood. 'Spain is missing Russia,' he sighed.

I found I felt the same when I went walking later and came across the statue to Cervantes, the author of *Don Quixote*, a work of literature loved by Russians. Yes, Russia was missing Spain too.

The Minder

A pale green Citroën was waiting for me when I went back to Waimer to see Señor Santiveri again before setting out on my tour. 'She's all yours,' said my host, beaming. 'And allow me to introduce you to my colleague, Francisco Castiella Perez, who will be your companion on the road. He speaks Italian, French, English, maybe he will even pick up a little Russian on the way.'

I looked at the thin, ferret-faced man standing next to Señor Santiveri. We secret agents can weigh up a new acquaintance faster than ordinary people. This ability to make a lightning character assessment is absolutely essential in our job. My minder from Spanish counter-intelligence aroused in me no strong negative feelings, which was a good enough start to our working relationship.

'I suggest we take it in turns to drive,' said Francisco. 'That's fine by me. In any case it will be hard for me to find my way out of Madrid as I do not know the city. And I suggest we go Dutch on all our meals.' 'No, no, Señor Kolosov,' interrupted Señor Santiveri, 'you are our guest.' 'This is a business trip, I insist.' 'We'll share the costs,' said Francisco.

The logistical details settled, we set off on our trip, which was to last a fortnight. We covered some two thousand kilometres, visiting Valencia, Bilbao, Barcelona and Seville. In Toledo, famous for its metal crafts, I bought a hunting knife. In Grenada, I watched flamenco dancing and surprised the locals with a little Russian folk dancing and singing of my own. It was a treat for me to see the Spanish landscape, darker and more raw than the pretty scenery in Italy and matching the national character which seemed to me more solid than the frothy Italian stereotype. But back in Moscow, Comrade Ponomaryov was expecting me to come up with something deeper than these tourist impressions.

It was not easy. I found myself as frustrated as many foreign correspondents became when visiting the Soviet Union. Chaperoned everywhere by 'guides' who reported to the KGB and showed only what the authorities wanted them to see, they had somehow to build up a picture of what real Russian life was like. Now the boot was on the other foot and it was an odd feeling.

For the first few days of our enforced companionship, Francisco and I sniffed each other like two dogs. He praised Franco and all he had done for Spain and I praised Brezhnev and his commitment to world peace. But my minder did not try to provoke me in any crude way and once we had agreed to differ, we established a certain mutual respect and were able to relax with each other. I even had some interesting political discussions with my 'guide'.

'Francisco,' I said as we were bowling along some country road, 'what would happen if, God forbid, your Caudilio were to die? After all, he's quite old and I gather his health is not so good now.' 'And what would happen if, God forbid, your Brezhnev were to die, for we hear his health is also failing?' 'In the Soviet Union nothing would happen. A new General Secretary would come to power and the comrades would go on building Communism.' 'With us things would be a bit different. I do not think there would be another Caudilio. Probably we would get a king as a guarantor of the constitution and a parliament which would rule. Yes, evidently it would be a parliament.'

'And what about the Church? In Italy, where I worked for many years, the Vatican plays an important role. What about you Spaniards? You're also Catholics. I heard there was this funny organisation Opus Dei ...' Francisco braked and looked at me. 'Why funny, Leonid? It's a respected organisation. Are you interested in it?' 'Well yes, actually,' I said, remembering the special task the KGB had given me. 'When we get back to Madrid, I'll put you in touch with someone,' said Francisco with a helpfulness I had not expected.

To give him due credit, he did his best wherever we went to enable me to do my job. He facilitated meetings with all the Spaniards I wanted to see, from simple peasants to politicians and economists, and as far as I could tell the people spoke quite freely to me, not censuring themselves because of his presence. This was because Spain was already a relatively free country. True, in the early days of Franco's dictatorship, Communists had been executed and imprisoned and the people went in fear. But the dictatorship was loosening now. In 1970, Spain was a far less totalitarian society than my own dear country. The people I interviewed generally confirmed Francisco's view that after Franco, Spain would become a constitutional monarchy. They were also very excited to meet a real, live Russian.

The end of my trip was crowned, as Señor Santiveri had promised, with a visit to the Mediterranean port of Palomares, where Nato had a base. By allowing me access to this place – the equivalent in the Soviet Union would certainly have been closed to foreigners – the Spaniards gave the strongest evidence of a kind of glasnost in their country, preceding the openness which Mikhail Gorbachev was to bring to Soviet society by some twenty years.

The glittering blue sea was irresistible to a Russian, for whom the autumn temperature was not the deterrent it seemed to be for the black-clad locals. Stripping down to my birthday suit, I plunged into the water. 'Mind you don't turn into a polar bear,' joked Francisco, who photographed me while I swam. When I came staggering up the beach, my teeth chattering despite my bravado, he handed me a warming cup of the local Fundador cognac.

I thought nothing more of the incident and we made our way back to Madrid.

The KGB was used to using people. For me, it was a novel experience to find myself being exploited by my Spanish hosts, although in the nicest possible way. 'Look at the press coverage of your tour,' said Señor Santiveri when I checked in again at the Waimer office. '*El Pais*, headline "Russia and Spain miss each other" and a huge photograph of you. Usually only the Caudilio gets such a big picture. And here's another one.' He handed me a paper with a cartoon of my face and the following text: 'A Russian is wandering through Spain. He's a delightful chap, this journalist. You can't tell whether he is a peace envoy or a spy. But he is always smiling, like a Spaniard who has won the lottery.'

A third newspaper ran Francisco's photograph of me swimming. Here, if the Spaniards had wanted to, they could have compromised me badly, for nude bathing was of course an offence under Franco's puritanical regime. But instead they made me out to be a brave soul, open to all experiences in Spain. (I had not realised that the inviting-looking water in which I had frolicked was polluted with radiation after the Americans had had an accident with a nuclear device in the bay at Palomares.)

In short, the Spaniards launched a propaganda campaign in exactly the same way the Soviet Union used to muster and direct the media when it wanted something. Restoring diplomatic relations with Spain had been Moscow's idea in the first place. We wanted to achieve this goal for two reasons. First, we did not want a new, democratic Spain to fall exclusively under American influence. Second, we wanted the benefits of trade with Spain. But now it seemed Madrid was singing the same song.

As a result of all the publicity, I was bombarded with invitations to meet more people in Madrid. I was even invited to meet Franco himself at a cocktail party but I had to turn down this opportunity. Why? Because if I had been seen shaking hands with the Caudilio, I would have given the impression Moscow was officially endorsing his rule, one of the situations comrade Ponomaryov had in mind when he warned me not to compromise myself. Getting into bed with the wrong political leader is just as dangerous for a KGB officer as other forms of bedroom antics.

The newspaper articles also promoted a visit to my hotel by a famous and highly eccentric Spaniard, Salvador Dali. Apparently, he wanted to look at a Russian in the flesh. We had the following conversation:

'Señor Kolosov, have you seen any of my paintings?' 'Um, of course, um, I regard you more highly than Picasso.' 'Oh really, and what paintings did you particularly admire?' 'Um, the one with the giraffe, um ...' 'Do you know my wife is Russian?' 'That's good.' 'Indeed? Why do you think so?' 'Because Russian women are the most beautiful, the warmest-hearted and the most mysterious in the world.' 'Yes? Strange, I'm not so sure myself. I call her Gala, you know. Her real name is Yelena Dyakonova.'

And with that, he turned on his heel and walked out, flourishing his cane and twirling his moustache.

Secret Meetings

After we had returned to Madrid, Francisco was as good as his word and arranged for me to interview a representative of Opus Dei, the Catholic organisation in which the Lubyanka had expressed a special interest. Ordinary Russians were kept in such ignorance about religion by the atheist Soviet state that many did not even know Catholicism was a branch of Christianity just like Orthodoxy. But the KGB kept abreast of theology and trained its officers to be specialists in comparative religion so we could know our ideological foes. 'Was Opus Dei a monastic order or some kind of mafia?' my bosses wanted me to find out.

Señor Santiveri's limousine took me to a small villa, where I was to meet Xavier Aiesta, the head of public relations at Opus Dei. I was kept waiting in a cold reception room, hung with dark paintings. Eventually steps echoed down the corridor and a neat man in his 30s, dressed in a black suit, brilliant white shirt and bright tie, introduced himself as Aiesta.

'Should I call you Father or Señor?' I asked. 'Señor,' he said, 'I am an architect and am not planning to give up my profession.'

My host said Opus Dei, founded by Escriva de Balager, was neither a monastic order nor a mafia but an organisation of lay Catholics from all walks of life dedicated to doing God's work in society. I understood it was a kind of masonic lodge, where Spanish businessmen helped each other under the cover of evangelism.

Opus Dei did not interfere in politics, Señor Aiesta said. 'If the Communists come to power in Spain, we will not go against the will of God but develop a constructive working relationship with them.'

But Spaniards told me Opus Dei, which grouped all the powerful capitalists in the country, had quite another agenda – to keep the reds from power and ensure Spain became a monarchy after Franco. Although Señor Aiesta was friendly – he sent me Christmas cards for years after our meeting – I saw only the tip of the iceberg. In fact Opus Dei was an incredibly powerful organisation which infiltrated its members into ministerial positions in the government around the dying Franco and ensured that its favoured candidate, Juan Carlos de Bourbon, was named the heir to the throne.

All of this I would report back to the KGB, without letting the Central Committee know I had been doing a little work on the side for my bosses at the Lubyanka. But the meeting that followed would have to be kept secret even from them. It was a strictly private adventure, like my little fling with the prostitute.

I was sitting in my hotel room when the reception called to say that Otto Scorzeni was waiting in the lobby to see me. An Austrian who had worked alongside Hitler, he was a notorious war criminal who would have faced trial for the murder of civilians in Czechoslovakia had he not managed to escape to Franco's Spain. Under no circumstances should I, an officer of the Soviet Committee for State Security, meet such a pariah. But you see, my trouble was I was curious. I was a journalist at heart.

I invited him up and we drank a bottle of whisky together. He told me how he had been parachuted into the mountains of northern Italy to rescue Mussolini when he was captured by the Italian resistance in 1943. Freed by Scorzeni, Il Duce went to Germany, from where he was able to return to his country and set up the Reppublica Salo together with Nazi help in the north of Italy. Thus the war was prolonged. Mussolini got his just deserts in the end, of course. He was captured again in 1945, shot in Milan and hung up by the legs for all to see.

'I was not a war criminal,' Scorzeni told me, 'I was just a professional secret agent, doing my job.'

I found myself sympathising with him to some extent. 'If you had not been a Fascist, you might have been a Hero of the Soviet Union,' I said. I promised I would write about him some day. 'But not now,' I said. 'You must understand that we still live in a very complicated world. And you must not breathe a word to anyone that you have met me.'

I let him down. I wrote nothing, for I did not wish to appear to be trying to rehabilitate him. You, dear reader, are the first to know that I met Scorzeni. He betrayed me too, of course. He blabbed later to my friend Julian Semyonov, the Soviet thriller writer, that he had already met me.

'Hey Lyonya, you old rascal, you dark horse,' said Julian, ringing me up in Moscow, 'I hear that when you were in Madrid, you met Scorzeni.' 'Julian, listen to me carefully,' I said. 'It's true Scorzeni contacted me but I refused to see him, categorically refused.' 'But Scorzeni told me ...' 'Comrade Semyonov,' I said icily, 'it never happened, do you understand?'

A New Era

After just over a month in Madrid, I returned to Moscow and wrote my report for the Central Committee. I still have a copy of it.

'In Spain, the idea is gaining ground that trade and diplomatic relations with the Soviet Union should be restored. This possibility is openly spoken of not only in business circles, which would naturally be interested in the Soviet market, but also by senior officials in the present government, not to mention the Spanish Foreign Minister Lopez Bravo, seen as the main advocate of the 'dialogue with the East'. What are the reasons for this turn towards the Soviet Union? We have to look at the economic and political factors. Spain in recent years has achieved tangible progress in industrial development. There is growth in metallurgy, machine-building, car-manufacturing . . .'

That was the sort of turgid prose I had to turn out for Comrade Ponomaryov. In short, my assessment was that Spain was moving towards democracy and I recommended we lay the ground for diplomatic relations by developing bilateral trade. Then I returned to *Izvestia* and wrote something a bit racier for my paper.

'Well done,' said my editor, Lev Tolkunov, when he saw me back at work. 'Now listen, Lyonya, are you still interested in becoming a straight journalist?' 'I told you,' I said, 'it doesn't happen, there are only two ways to leave the KGB, in handcuffs or a box.'

At this, he picked up the special phone to the Kremlin. 'Yuri Vladimirovich, good morning,' he said. I realised he was speaking to Andropov, the head of the KGB. 'You remember I asked you about Kolosov? Are you going to stifle the talents of this gifted journalist or are you going to let me have him? Yes, yes, of course I'll find you someone to replace him. You can have one of my young reporters in exchange, two if you like.'

And that was it. Andropov was the most humane leader the KGB had seen. He found me a third exit from the Lubyanka.

In March 1971, I returned to Rome for another stint as *Izvestia* correspondent. I remained a reserve officer in the KGB but I was no longer active for them. Pure journalism filled my days and I was happy. I had a clean start. As far as I know, neither the Italians nor the Spaniards ever knew about my KGB past until I decided to come out of the closet by writing my memoirs.

As for Spain, the political process I had witnessed gained pace. Unlike Hitler and Mussolini, Franco was a wise dictator who brought young ministers into his government, gradually widened the powers of the Cortes, or parliament, and chose the king who would succeed him. When he died in 1975, everything was in place for a painless transition to democracy. Diplomatic relations with the Soviet Union were established six years after my visit. Soviet diplomats went out to our new embassy in Madrid and among them, I have no doubt, were those who reported to the KGB.

PARIS

Name	Kolosov Leonid Sergeyevich
Born	25 August 1926
Education	Higher, Masters degree in economics
Special Subject	Foreign Trade
Languages	Italian, French, some Serbian
Military Rank	Lieutenant-Colonel
Worked in	Italy, Spain, France
Marital Status	Married
Sports	Karate
Hobbies	Collecting old locks
Favourite Tipple	'Moskovskaya' vodka
Brand of Cigarettes	Camel

See Paris and Die

'See Paris and die,' the popular saying goes. In 1966 I was forty (terribly old, it seemed to me then) and, although French had been my first and best foreign language when I was a student, I had still not managed to see Paris.

'Of every thousand who are born, a thousand die ... so hurry up and commit your sins.' We KGB agents studied not only Marx and Lenin but also the wisdom of the Emperor Nero. That summer I felt an urgent desire to make up for lost time and wangled myself an expenses-paid trip to Paris.

I actually had a rail ticket to Rome in my pocket. I had been on one of my regular home leaves and Bronislava, the mountainous, good-hearted office manager at *Izvestia*, for which I was the correspondent beyond the Apennines, had secured me a first class berth back on the Moscow–Rome express. I was drinking a glass of cognac for the road with a few colleagues from the foreign desk when the telephone rang and the editor, Lev Tolkunov, asked to see me in his office.

'Leonid, instead of taking the train, would you mind flying back to Rome via Paris?' he asked.

'Not at all,' I said, 'the plane will be quicker. But I don't have to change in Paris. There's a direct flight to Rome.'

'Well, the thing is you see,' said the editor, a little embarrassed, 'I have a letter which I would like you to deliver to Volodin. Then you can go on to Rome.'

He meant Lev Volodin, the *Izvestia* correspondent in Paris. The reason why he could not simply post the letter was that it was personal and he did not want the petty KGB censors at the Soviet post office to read it. He knew that I worked for the KGB as well but trusted me not to pry.

'Glad to help,' I said, also agreeing to carry a parcel for Volodin – supplies of black bread, vodka and caviar I think – in addition to my own luggage.

'That's fine, then. Off you go.'

'Er, um, Lev Nikolayevich,' I stuttered. Now it was my turn to be a little coy. 'Do you think I could stay on in Paris for a week? I've never actually seen Paris ... You know how I love all those singers ... Maurice Chevalier, Charles Aznevour, Edit Piaf, Mireille Mathieu ... and, well there are a couple of jobs I ought to do there for the "office".'

Maurice Chevalier and Edit Piaf cut no ice with Tolkunov but he respected my obligations to my second employer and took the hint.

'Oh, well, if the KGB needs you there ... no problem at all.'

Now I had to square the trip with my boss up at 'Children's World', which was how we jokingly referred to the Lubyanka because of its proximity to the famous Moscow toy emporium.

'*Izvestia* needs me in Paris for a week to help out the permanent correspondent,' I lied.

'Oh, well, if *Izvestia* needs you ...' the boss said. 'Perhaps you could do something for us too while you're there?'

And so I won my holiday in Paris, which was marred only by the fact that I had to waste some valuable wine-drinking and oyster-eating time by investigating a new anti-Soviet Russian émigré organisation on behalf of the KGB. And also by the fact that the boss had asked me to observe Lev Volodin and find out why this 'clean' or bona fide correspondent was not keen to cooperate with the KGB. Some might call this an abuse of Lev's hospitality. Certainly he was a generous host to me, his visiting colleague from the newspaper.

With his wife away, Lev would not hear of me going to a hotel but invited me to stay with him in his flat. The first place to which he took me after I had dumped my case was the Moulin Rouge. In the 1960s striptease was a novelty, at least for someone coming from the puritanical Soviet Union. We ate oysters with white wine, then, against all the rules of good taste, tournedos washed down with Napoleon brandy while we watched a floor show which was quite artistically done, not just a vulgar display of tits and bums.

Eager to show me a good time, Lev suggested we hire a lady of the night. 'We can have one between two,' he enthused. 'They do that here in Paris.' But I cried off, telling him about my miserable experience being dressed down by a Communist Party morals committee after some KGB lackey informed the bosses in Moscow that I had had a jaunt with two Russian fashion models who came on a visit to Italy.

'Does the KGB ever bother you, Lev?' I continued, using the chance to probe my colleague a little.

'Yeah, those bastards from the embassy are always trying to get me to tell tales about my friends in the Soviet community. But I refuse. I think it's disgusting.'

'Quite right,' I said. 'There's no need to inform on your friends. But you ought to help the Motherland, you know. The French can be quite hostile to America even though they're part of the West. If you come across some pro-Soviet Frenchman who might make a good recruit for the KGB, you should let them know. They'll be grateful to you and see you right.'

'Do you reckon?'

'Yes, I've had some experience myself.'

'OK, I'll think about it,' he said, giving me a penetrating look. Perhaps he was beginning to guess that I worked for two masters. I thought it better to lighten the conversation again. 'More brandy?' I offered.

Late the following morning, we both woke with massive hangovers. Lev relied on hair of the dog while I found two cups of strong tea and a Roquefort sandwich helpful. Tentatively we began discussing plans for my further entertainment. Naïve though this sounds, I would have been quite happy to see the Eiffel Tower and the Arc de Triomphe but Lev was scornful of such a banal tourist itinerary.

'Remember Hodzha Nasreddin, the wise and jolly traveller from the East,' he said. 'Hodzha started with the bazaar and checked that the food was plentiful. Then he went to the cemetery and made sure that the locals remembered their ancestors. Only when he was satisfied on both counts did he honour the town by occupying it.'

Working on this Oriental principle, we set out in the evening in Lev's Peugeot-403 to inspect the market. But not any old market, rather Les Halles, the enormous wholesale market that was to Paris what Covent

Garden used to be in London. The French called it 'Le Ventre du Paris' or 'The Belly of Paris'.

While traders prepared for a long night, supplying retailers with the next day's produce, and *clochards*, or tramps, earnt a few francs by loading vegetables, elegant Parisians came from theatres and restaurants to finish off the evening in little market-side cafés. They had quaint names like Le Chien qui Fume, or The Dog that Smokes. In one of these, Lev and I sampled the onion soup, which was a speciality at Les Halles. How glad I am that I saw this great Paris tradition before the wholesale traders were packed off to a soulless modern complex in the suburbs, Les Halles were demolished and the ugly Pompidou Centre was built in their stead.

'Well, we've done the bazaar,' I said to Lev when we got back home in the small hours of the morning. 'We'll do the cemetery later. I've got a job to do tomorrow.'

Fellow Countrymen in the Other Camp

The next day, Lev dropped me off at the Soviet embassy.

'Do you want to come in with me?' I asked.

'No, I'm not in the mood for seeing diplomats.'

I went alone to see Alexei Krokhin, who worked for the KGB under the cover of embassy counsellor. He gave me instructions to call on a Russian émigré couple called Anita and Nikolai Rutchenko, who were involved with a new organisation for spreading anti-Soviet literature called the International Literature Association. 'Sniff the atmosphere there. Perhaps you'll be able to expose them in *Izvestia*,' Krokhin said.

I decided to use the opportunity to say a word about Lev.

'Volodin and I are mates,' I began. 'He's been complaining that your boys keep putting pressure on him to inform on his friends. You're alienating him and it's counterproductive because he might be willing to work for you as a "talent scout".' I meant, of course, that he might point out potential French recruits.

'Thank you, we'll bear that in mind,' said Krokhin.

When I went off later to track down the Rutchenkos, I took Lev with me. I needed him to give me respectability. He would introduce me as a visiting colleague from *Izvestia* and the émigrés would be less suspicious. As it turned out, I could not have found the way without him either. We drove for about forty minutes through heavy rain into the suburbs.

'That must be it over there,' Lev said at last. 'House 8 Bis.'

We entered a building with a gloomy vestibule, went up the stairs and by some sixth sense guessed what door we needed down the dark corridor on the second floor, for there was no number or plaque. Lev knocked.

'Can we see Anita or Nikolai Rutchenko?' he asked in Russian.

'Do you have an appointment?' replied a frumpy woman.

'Well no, we're Soviet journalists. My colleague here is over on a very short visit. We didn't have time to ring in advance.'

'Nikolai's out. Anita's on the phone. You can wait in the corridor if you like.'

While we waited among the piles of books in the corridor, we heard snatches of conversation from inside the office: 'We need to order some more copies of the journal *Sintaxis* ...' 'Yes Your Excellency, we have that edition ...' Anita must have had a Russian aristocrat in there with her. Finally she was free to talk to us.

Mrs Rutchenko was quite friendly and showed us the range of books the association offered. She even gave me a couple, a slim volume of poems by Nikolai Gumilyov, shot under Lenin and not rehabilitated until the Gorbachev era, and some ribald pre-1917 folktales, collected by Alexander Afanasiev and condemned both by the Orthodox Church and the Soviet authorities because of their filthy language.

'We're not allowed to sell the books,' Anita said. 'We act as an exchange for book lovers.'

Indeed.

But I knew, for Krokhin had already briefed me, that the association was just a new front for the CIA's 'department of special projects' which hid under the wing of Radio Liberty in Munich. The Rutchenkos ran the association's Paris branch. The 'department of special projects' had had to change its name because there had been too many articles in the international press about the way it used tourists to smuggle anti-Soviet literature into the Soviet Union.

I also knew a thing or two about Nikolai Rutchenko, who presently walked into the office and joined our little gathering.

Anita was a second-generation Russian who had been born in France and never seen the land of her fathers but Nikolai, originally from the Moldavian capital of Kishinyov, had grown up in the Soviet Union. During the war, he found himself in the Leningrad region where, in 1941, he gave himself up to the invading Nazis. In a prisoner of war camp near the former Russian imperial palace at Gatchino, he began his traitorous career, informing on his fellow prisoners. Soon he was off for intelligence training by the Fascists and by 1943 he was back on Soviet territory, shooting his own people and helping to interrogate Russian prisoners. In 1944, he joined Heinrich Himmler's 'Werewolf' brigade, which fought with the viciousness of desperation, as the Germans began to understand they were losing the war.

After 1945, Rutchenko turned up in Vienna, working for the Austrian branch of the People's Labour Union, an anti-Soviet organisation originally founded by white generals who fled to Yugoslavia after they lost the Russian Civil War. Later he went on to Paris and the KGB believed he worked for the CIA, trying to persuade Soviet citizens who visited France to defect to the West.

While Lev continued to look at the books with Anita, I got into separate conversation with Nikolai. We talked a little about the complicated politics in the community of Russian émigrés, who were always at each other's throats. In particular, Rutchenko ranted against the new waves of Jewish emigrants coming out of the Soviet Union. I understood that they represented competition for him as they had fresher information about the USSR, which the Americans might want to buy.

By nod and wink, I gave Rutchenko to understand that I did not only represent *Izvestia*. The Motherland might be ready to forgive his sins and even pay him well if he cared to become our agent and spill the beans about the activities of the CIA in Paris. But he told me in obscene terms where to go. It was the reaction I expected but there's never any harm in trying.

Now it was time for Lev and me to make a quick exit. We drove back to his flat through the rain and, when we arrived, opened a bottle of cognac.

My holiday in Paris was passing at an alarming speed. Risking Lev's contempt, I did after all go and see the Eiffel Tower and the Arc de Triomphe. And then only one day was left to honour the dead as Hodzha Nasreddin recommended. Instead of showing me the tomb of Napoleon, Lev chose to take me to the Russian cemetery at St Geneviève de Bois, where I discovered that not all émigrés were traitors like Nikolai Rutchenko.

Can there be any more melancholy place than a cemetery? You cross the border dividing the living from those who were once just as alive as you and everything seems to change. The birds sing with restraint and the leaves only dare to rustle cautiously.

The cemetery was deserted. On the door of the little white Orthodox chapel a sign said 'Come in, pray, shelter from the weather', but the door itself was firmly locked and when we looked through the window it was clear the interior was being renovated. Very Russian. Instead, we walked among the graves.

One obelisk bore an epitaph that was a modest understatement: 'Vika Obolenskaya, born Vera Makarova, Lieutenant F. F. C., 24/6/1911–4/8/1944, killed by the Nazis in Berlin.' In fact she was Princess Vera Apollonovna Obolenskaya, a white Russian émigré who played a heroic role in the resistance in occupied France. Her anti-Fascist fervour became all the greater when she learnt that the Germans had also invaded her homeland. The Nazis captured and beheaded her but not before torturing her for months in a Berlin prison. They called her 'Princess I don't know anything' because she would not give them the slightest information.

Nearby was the grave of General Anton Denikin, who fought against the Bolsheviks in the Russian Civil War. It was piled high with fresh wreaths from the French-Soviet Friendship Association, an organisation that promoted understanding between France and the Soviet Union.

'I don't understand,' said Lev. 'Why are they paying respects to a white émigré?'

'Because,' I explained, 'although Denikin hated the Communists, he remained loyal to his country.' It was true. During the Second World War, the traitorous General Vlasov, who fought on the side of the Nazis in the Ukraine, tried to draw Denikin into his army but he refused to fight against his Motherland. Stalin executed white officers captured in Europe in Moscow's Lefortovo Prison but he gave instructions not to touch Denikin who was, ideology aside, a true Russian patriot.

On the way out, we passed a group of noisy French schoolchildren being conducted round the cemetery by an elderly Russian woman. 'And this is the grave of the famous writer Ivan Bunin,' she said in heavily accented French. I felt a rush of love towards this woman who was teaching the French about our literature and greeted her in Russian.

'You are from Moscow?' she asked incredulously. 'How is my dear Moscow?'

She too rejoiced in the passing contact with us. After all, we were fellow countrymen, although fate and history had placed us in different camps.

So ended my first trip to Paris. I returned to Rome with some small achievements for the KGB. I had not managed to recruit the Rutchenkos but I had gathered plenty of material to write an éxposé of them in *Izvestia*. I portrayed them as pathetic creatures, channelling what was essentially their homesickness into endless petty intrigues. They were living proof that one should never betray one's homeland.

In addition, I had succeeded in convincing Lev of the importance of cooperating with our intelligence service. He never became an agent like me but from time to time gave the benefit of his insights on French politics to the KGB, which came to realise that this was far more valuable than gossip about who was sleeping with whom in the Soviet community. I had told him that the KGB would look after him in return and they did, although in a way that would hardly have seemed like a selling point to Lev had he known about it. When he collapsed and died in Paris, the

KGB paid to have his body transported home to Moscow. Usually Soviet personnel who died abroad were cremated because this was cheaper but the Orthodox Church says believers should be buried and generally Russians prefer to sleep eternally in Mother Earth.

Outlet to Europe

I did not realise it at the time but it turned out that my short excursion to Paris in 1966 was like a prelude to another trip I made there eleven years later, when all the themes from the first visit were developed as in a musical suite.

The first time I had just been hungry to see Paris. The second time I was desperate to break out of the confines of the Soviet Union, which had become like a prison to me. I could hardly believe it but I, a loyal KGB officer, had become *neviyezdnoi* (unfit for the privilege of travel) like a Jewish scientist with rocket secrets or some filthy dissident.

It all happened very suddenly. In 1971, I was working for *Izvestia* again in Rome, a 'clean' journalist now since Andropov, in recognition of my diplomacy in Spain, had granted my request and released me from the foreign intelligence service, just leaving me as a reserve KGB officer. I had more or less forgotten about the Lubyanka, so excited was I by the practice of straight journalism for which I think I was really cut out.

Then out of the blue, Oleg Lyalin, a KGB agent in London, decided to defect. He was a catch for MI5 because at one point in his career he had worked in the KGB's 'B' department, which carried out 'wet operations'. KGB jargon had much in common with criminal slang and 'wet operations' meant those in which blood flowed, in other words killings. The British would be very interested to debrief Lyalin about this.

But that was not all. In addition to whatever he revealed about 'B' department, Lyalin also exposed a whole network of our agents in Britain and beyond. As a result, the government of Edward Heath expelled ninety Soviet diplomats and other staff from London and other European countries began to look suspiciously at their Soviet communities.

I was affected because I had been in the same class as Lyalin at KGB school and even acted together with him in an amateur dramatics society that we used to have at the college. Looking over this distant history, the bosses at the Lubyanka became convinced that Lyalin must have named me among the other agents he betrayed. When I went back to Moscow on home leave, *Izvestia* at the prompting of the KGB told me my posting to Rome was being cut short. The Italians might make a public scandal if returned to Rome. I was not even allowed to go back and pick up my belongings. 'For my own safety', they said, it would be better if I did not leave the Soviet Union again.

This was a heavy blow to me. The door to the outside world had slammed shut. For the first time I knew the meaning of the Iron Curtain, which was a fact of life for most ordinary Soviet citizens. 'A chicken is not a bird, Poland is not abroad,' KGB colleagues used to say dismissively when they were posted to socialist rather than Western countries. But I would have been grateful even for a chance to get out to a Warsaw Pact member state.

Instead I was stuck in a desk job at *Nedelya*, the weekly supplement to *Izvestia*. It was a senior position but that was no consolation to me, who loved to be in the field. I fell into a pit of depression. I drank. I became so unbearable that my wife Eva asked me politely to leave the family for the sake of our two growing daughters.

It all seemed such a waste. (A decade later, I was to discover precisely what an absurd waste it had been when I asked Yuri Andropov himself to look into my case. He discovered that in fact Lyalin had never named me, either because he remembered me fondly from student days or because he had simply forgotten me. After this clarification, I was allowed out again in the 1980s to work for *Izvestia* in Yugoslavia.)

But back in the 1970s, I could see no light at the end of the tunnel. I was turning into an alcoholic. I was going to pieces, until I met my saviour Natalia, who in 1976 became my second wife and a year later gave me my third daughter.

After Natalia rescued me, feeding me solids instead of vodka that had become my diet and giving meaning to my life, by brain functions started to revive. I hatched a plan to get abroad again, if only for a short trip. I am convinced that the reason my career went into a cul-de-sac was that petty pen pushers in the KGB's First Main Directorate, who envied me because of the good times I had had in Italy, deliberately failed to get to the bottom of my case. It suited them to hold me back, parroting that I must stay at home 'for my own safety'. My escape plan involved circumventing these hostile colleagues.

And so I approached officers in a rival KGB directorate, the fifth or 'Poo' as we called it because of its Russian acronym. It was responsible for the ideological struggle against dissidents, many of whom relied on support from émigrés. I had done odd jobs for the 'Poo' before as inevitably my work as a journalist led me into contact with propagandists. This time, inspired by memories of my first trip to Paris, I put to them the proposal that I should go under journalistic cover to Germany and France to snoop at the centres of anti-Soviet propaganda there. They leapt at the idea.

Indeed, their enthusiasm exceeded my expectations. Soon I was sitting in the office of General Philip Bobkov, head of 'Poo', being told that my plan had been endorsed at the 'highest level'. That meant Andropov. I soon learnt why.

The KGB chairman had reason to believe that the popular bard Alexander Galich and the famous writer Viktor Nekrasov, both of whom had gone into exile in Paris for lack of creative freedom in the USSR, were suffering from the Russian disease of nostalgia and would like to come home if the terms were right. Andropov could see an enormous potential advantage in the ideological war with the West if the two came back to Moscow. But more than that, he genuinely loved literature and was saddened that Russian talent was draining away to foreign countries.

My mission was to attempt to bring Galich and Nekrasov home. I was authorised to assure them that their Soviet citizenship would be restored and they would be allowed to work without hindrance. In addition, I was asked to try and lure back two poisonously anti-Soviet Russian émigrés, creatures of a far lower order than the artists, but the terms for reconciliation with the Motherland would in their case be very different.

Naturally, when I had the backing of Andropov, the envious lackeys in the First Main Directorate were impotent to stop me. In no time, I had an external passport in my pocket again and was leaving on a train heading west. I went first to Munich and Frankfurt where, posing as a recent Russian émigré seeking work, I managed to have a look round Radio Liberty and the publishing houses Posev and Grani. Then I continued my journey on to Paris.

Mysterious Death of a Bard

Minstrels more or less disappeared from Western Europe in the Middle Ages but in Russia they are popular to this day, the most famous among them having the following of rock stars. They set their own poetry to music and accompany themselves, the only concession to the twentieth century being that they strum on the guitar rather than the lute.

In Soviet times, lesser bards belonging to an unofficial group called KSP or the Club of Amateur Singers used to meet and make music in the forests. Better-known bards appeared in concert halls as the authorities tolerated them. Not dissidents as such, they sang about life as it was really lived rather than the glowing life that the Communist Party tried to persuade Soviet people they enjoyed. Bulat Okudzhava and Vladimir Vysotsky performed in this genre. So did Alexander or 'Sasha' Galich.

Born Alexander Ginzburg, Galich came from a privileged background.

A student of Konstantin Stanislavsky, the theatre director who advocated that an actor should get inside the skin of the character he was playing, Galich served in the Soviet army theatre at the front during the war, after which he went on to write award-winning plays and film scripts. However, in the early 1960s he turned his back on the glittering world of the theatre and chose the simpler life of a bard.

The human rights activist Lev Kopelev said of Galich that he loved awards ceremonies and banquets, fashionable clothes and beautiful possessions, but far more than other members of the Soviet cultural elite he also felt the contradiction between his own affluent life and the poverty around him. His conscience pricked him when he remembered comrades who had died at the front or, returning from the war, suddenly and inexplicably found themselves labelled enemies by Stalin and sent off to cut coal in the Arctic or timber in Siberia.

'He sang about workers, prisoners, soldiers, alcoholics, petty bureaucrats and heroes of Communist labour,' Kopelev wrote in his memoirs. Galich also drank like a real Russian, for which ordinary people respected him even more.

I, too, was a fan of the bard. Even after he became more overtly critical of Soviet rule. Or perhaps it was that the authorities became less liberal. In the cultural crackdown that coincided with the crushing of the 1968 Prague Spring, the powers that be expelled him from the Writers' Union, thereby depriving him of all opportunities to perform officially. He went underground and millions of Russians listened to his ballads on illegally produced tapes passed from hand to hand. I was no exception and that despite the fact that I was a KGB officer.

With the rest of the nation I also mourned when, in 1974, Galich gave up the struggle with petty officialdom, sold his library, accepted an exit visa to emigrate as a Jew and went not to Israel but to Norway. Later, he moved on to Munich and Paris in his search of creative freedom. 'Airports are like crematoria,' wrote Kopelev again, remembering how he waved Galich off from Sheremetyevo airport, knowing he was probably seeing him for the last time.

If Galich's friends in Moscow missed him, over time and despite the freedom he found in the West, the bard came to suffer even greater nostalgia for his homeland. He wrote in exile:

> When I return ...
> Do not laugh at me, when I return,
> When I run, feet barely touching the ground
> On the February snow
> And hear the nightingales sing in February

That old song, from way back, long forgotten,
And I fall,
Defeated by own victory,
And lay my head in the haven of your lap,
When I return …

In December 1977, it seemed I was in a position to make possible that longed-for homecoming that would bring relief to Galich, delight Russians, suit the KGB and help my own career. Imagine, then, the bitter disappointment I felt when I arrived at the station in Paris to be told by KGB colleagues: 'You're too late. Galich is dead. It's in all the papers.'

The newspapers differed slightly on the details – some said it was a television antenna, others that it was a tape recorder and player – but all agreed on the main point: Galich had died from an electric shock after plugging in a newly acquired piece of electrical equipment. His body had been found curled on the floor of his flat on Avenue Hugo, his hand singed from the current.

The Russian community naturally buzzed with speculation. Some people who had known Galich said he had been useless with technical things and could easily have had such a stupid accident. But others thought it odd that a man who had at one point worked for Radio Liberty could not put a plug in properly. Soon it was being suggested that someone had deliberately sent Galich a piece of fault equipment, that he had been murdered, that the KGB had murdered him.

The late atomic physicist and human rights campaigner, Dr Andrei Sakharov, saw something suspicious in the death of Galich. 'And yet,' he wrote in his memoirs, 'I am not one hundred per cent sure that it was an accident and not murder. Eleven and a half months before his death, Sasha's mother received a strange New Year greeting through the post. The envelope contained a page from a calendar on which was typed: "A decision has been taken to kill your son Alexander." '

I put my hand on my heart and tell you that if he was murdered, it was not by the KGB. What sense would there have been in that when Andropov saw advantages for everybody in bringing Galich home to Russia and had sent me on a mission to do precisely that? The Americans had more reason to wish the bard dead as, not long before, he had successfully sued his former employers, Radio Liberty, for broadcasting his latest songs without permission. Or Galich might have given up hope of seeing Russia again and committed suicide. Or he might just have had an accident. Any of these things were possible, but not that the KGB killed him. However, at the time I was not able say this openly as my mission was secret, indeed I am telling this story for the first time only now, and the CIA continued to spread disinformation that Moscow was behind the bard's untimely death.

I had missed seeing Galich by a matter of only a few days. How often have I tortured myself since with the thought that if I had gone straight to Paris instead of wasting time in Germany, I might have reached him when he was still alive and the whole tragedy might have been avoided. Now all I could do was go and see his widow, Angelina Nikolayevna, and his best friend, the writer Viktor Nekrasov. Perhaps I could salvage something and encourage Nekrasov to join me on the return journey to Moscow.

Our meeting was arranged through the Soviet embassy, with which Galich and his wife as well as Nekrasov had had some contact, they being not wholly anti-Soviet like other Russian émigrés. We met at the café 'Au Drapeau' near the Bastille. The grieving pair were accompanied by an elderly émigré called Alexei Shuvalov, who seemed to be looking after them. I naturally kept quiet about my KGB connections and introduced myself as a correspondent from *Izvestia*.

Fighting back her tears, Angelina told me how on the morning of 15 December her husband had returned tired and unwell from a festival in Avignon. ' "Have we got anything to drink, dear?" he asked me. We had a bottle but no food in the fridge, as I was on a diet. So I popped out to the shops. When I returned fifteen minutes later, I saw him lying dead on the floor. I screamed like a madwoman. I ran to the neighbours. One of them noticed that the lead from the antenna was for some reason coming not out of the radio but out of the socket. Sasha's legs were up against the radiator, as if he was creating a circuit with his own body.'

'Some people are suggesting that agents from Moscow ...' I began.

'That's complete nonsense,' she interrupted. 'Sasha loved Russia and was preparing to return. "I'll crawl on my knees over the broken glass of all the bottles I've drunk," he said. "I'll kneel down in the church and ask forgiveness ..." By the way, did you know he recently converted to Russian Orthodoxy?'

While Angelina talked, Nekrasov maintained a respectful silence. Then when she had finished, he began reminiscing about Galich. 'People say bards are not real artists but how can that be? Everyone knew Sasha. In all of Russia, there cannot be a mine, or a fishing trawler, or a geological research station or a prison camp where people did not know and love Sasha.' I noticed that Nekrasov was quite drunk, from grief perhaps or maybe it was his usual state.

'Do you remember me Viktor?' I asked.

'No,' he said blankly.

Nekrasov went into exile before Galich. It was the same story. He was expelled from the Writers' Union and therefore no Soviet publishing house would accept his work, so he asked for political asylum while on a visit to Paris, even though he was not really anti-Soviet. He had annoyed the authorities with a book called *In the Trenches of Stalingrad*, a realistic rather than romanticised account of the famous battle in which he had fought as a young man. He was also the author of a play called *Dangerous Path* in which I had played the hero, a wounded and disillusioned officer returning from the front, in the student theatre at the Institute of Foreign Trade.

'Well, blow me,' said Nekrasov, suddenly remembering. And that gave me the confidence to broach the subject of his possible return home.

'You are a wonderful writer,' I said. 'Russia needs you. Why don't you come back? No strings attached. Everything will be all right.'

'But what guarantee do I have?' he asked, evidently imagining that he would be arrested the moment he set foot on Soviet soil.

'I give you my word of honour. The "competent organs" promise you will be free to work, you will get all your medals back,' I said, not revealing that I was with the KGB myself but making clear that the message came from them.

Nekrasov, who had continued drinking throughout the conversation, suddenly showed very visibly the effects of the alcohol.

'That's it, I've decided, I'm coming home, help me Leonid!' he cried.

'That's a most interesting proposal,' interjected the elderly émigré Shuvalov, speaking for the first time. 'Viktor and I will discuss it seriously. He's an old friend of mine, you understand. Here is my telephone number. Ring in three days and we will meet again. But now we really must be going. Goodbye.'

While I waited for the three days to pass, I busied myself with the other work the KGB had given me. It involved me going back among the anti-Soviet émigrés whom I had visited on my first trip to Paris in 1966. The Lubyanka was interested in two of them in particular: Kiril Yelchaninov, a descendant of white Russians who lectured at the Sorbonne and was involved in a smuggling seditious literature into the Soviet Union, and Oleg Krasovsky, like Nikolai Rutchenko another wartime Fascist collaborator who worked in Radio Liberty's Paris bureau.

I called on Yelchaninov at his home, a filthy tip with kids running all over the place. I offered him the chance to take his family back to Russia on condition he wrote a series of articles for the Soviet press exposing the activities of the book smugglers who were, we were sure, financed by the CIA. He threw me out, which was no more than I had expected.

Krasovsky, whom I met near the entrance to the Catacombs, was tempted by my offer of a ticket back to the USSR in exchange for grassing on his American bosses, for he was desperately homesick. I put pressure on him by producing a letter the KGB had obtained from his elderly mother in Moscow and he cried when he saw her spidery handwriting. But although I gave him my 'word of honour' that he would not be punished, provided he cooperated fully with the KGB on his return, he was too afraid to trust me.

That left only Viktor Nekrasov. Would he be taking the train back to Russia with me? In his case, I felt confident. The writer had nothing to fear and I knew he wanted to go.

However, when I rang Shuvalov, this is what he said: 'I'm sorry Leonid Sergeyevich but Viktor has been on a drinking binge. For the last three days, he has not risen from the divan and he has drunk so much vodka that he can't even remember his own name. We will bear your proposal in mind. When he sobers up, we will contact the embassy. But please don't delay your departure for our sake. Have a good trip back to Moscow.'

In fact, Nekrasov never sobered up. Two months later he died of cirrhosis of the liver.

And so my mission failed. It was just one of those things. I knew the KGB would not reprimand me; on the contrary they would praise me for having tried. But still I was disappointed.

Before I left Paris, I decided to visit the grave of Galich. I sat by the freshly dug mound, which was still only marked by a temporary wooden cross, and communed with his spirit for a while. I asked a passer-by to take my photograph for me. Then sadly I made my way to the station.

Strange really, that both my first and my second visits to Paris ended in the same place: the Russian Orthodox cemetery of St Geneviève de Bois.